THE CONQUEST OF THE SAHARA

THE·CONQUEST·OF·THE
S·A·H·A·R·A
by · DOUGLAS · PORCH

ALFRED A. KNOPF

NEW YORK

1984

◆

THIS IS A BORZOI BOOK
PUBLISHED BY ALFRED A. KNOPF, INC.

Library of Congress Cataloging in Publication Data

Porch, Douglas. The conquest of the Sahara.

Bibliography: p.
Includes index.
1. Algeria—History—1830–1962.   2. Tuareg—Algeria
—History.   I. Title.
DT294.5.P67   1984   965'.03   84-47525
ISBN 0-394-53086-1

Manufactured in the United States of America
First Edition

for my father

CONTENTS

Contents

INTRODUCTION

This is the story of the Sahara during a fraction of its history, of the people who lived in it, of a railroad that was supposed to run through it, and of the men who explored and conquered it in the nineteenth and early twentieth centuries. I believe that it is a story worth telling. In the first place, it is an interesting and compelling one, which combines intrigue, heroism and treachery in almost equal measure. It is a story which has been told only in a fragmentary and incomplete way. I have tried to draw together the various strands of the history of early exploration of the Sahara, anthropological studies of the desert tribes, and the diplomatic and military events of the conquest. In the process, I have attempted to strip away the layers of mythology which the story of the conquest has acquired at the hands of French officers who participated in it and of the procolonialist, or often simply naive, historians who chronicled some of those events. The story loses nothing thereby. On the contrary, it gains in interest.

Stories in novels may have well-defined beginnings and conclusions. However, history is, according to that tired cliché, a seamless robe, and nowhere are the seams less visible than in the story of the Sahara. Therefore, in the interest of brevity, I have been forced to impose upon myself two limitations, one chronological and the other geographical. Historians like E. W. Bovill have taught us that Europe did not suddenly become aware of the Sahara in the nineteenth century, but that there was a lengthy history of fascination and even of exploration long before the first "precursors of imperialism" set off singly or in small groups from Tripoli to report on the Sahara and the riches of the lands beyond in central Africa. What has happened to the desert since the submission of the Ahaggar Tuareg to the French in 1905—which ended effective resistance—is a subject which has already filled several books. I shall leave to other authors the task of writing those that remain to be written.

The second limitation which I have imposed upon myself, the geographical one, is as artificial and as necessary as the limitations of chronology. The Sahara is a big place. Many different peoples live in it, each with their own history. Several northern powers attempted to conquer different parts of it at different times. Obviously, events which took place on the upper Nile, in Tripolitania and the Fezzan, in the Tuareg lands of the western central Sahara, or in Mauritania had repercussions throughout the desert, and beyond. This book concentrates on the conquest of the Tuareg of the Ahaggar by French soldiers and their African auxiliaries. It is a story which spills over the borders of what today is Algeria to include Timbuktu, Lake Chad, Tripoli—and Paris. The Sahara is not a self-contained entity. It never was. To readers disappointed to find only fleeting references to Gordon, Kitchener and the Madhi, to the Sanusi wars or to the blue men of Mauritania, I offer my apologies in advance.

Books on Africa traditionally fall into one of two categories. The first lionizes the explorers and conquerors as larger-than-life heroes who braved impossible odds to bring civilization to the heart of darkness. Today, this approach has fallen from fashion, to be replaced by another which, following Liddell Hart's dictum that it is important to know what is happening "on the other side of the hill," sees colonialism as an episode in African history. However, I am convinced that the possibilities of a study of empire from the viewpoint of the imperialists, especially those on the peripheries of empire, of their methods and peculiar forms of madness, have yet to be exhausted.

Two years ago, in a book I called *The Conquest of Morocco,* I examined the predicament of General Hubert Lyautey in bringing about a colonial conquest against the wishes of the government and people of France. I discovered that he succeeded largely because he was able to deceive politicians and journalists (and subsequently historians!) about the true nature of French military methods abroad. It occurred to me that the conquest of the Sahara offered another, perhaps the best, case of a clash between the romanticism and the realities of imperialism. That this might be so is due in great measure to the men who took part. The exploration and conquest of the Sahara offer perhaps the last example of a time when Europeans could make their way in the world through a muscular heroism of the sort which received its last rites in the trenches of the Great War.

The explorers and conquerors of the Sahara comprised a bizarre collection of humanity. Not surprisingly, they left behind a bizarre collection of stories. In telling their tales, I have attempted to answer some basic questions: Why did Frenchmen want to conquer the Sahara? How did they manage to dominate a land mass "as large as two Frances" with barely two hundred men? How successful were the Saharians—the camel corps founded by the French—as a military force? While attempting to answer these and other questions, I have not forgotten France's enemies, the Tuareg. While they appear largely as shadowy figures in French reports, that many of them were also remarkable and resourceful characters cannot be in doubt.

Finally, the story of the conquest cannot be separated from its setting. For centuries the Sahara has exercised for Europeans a fascination bordering on mesmerization. Anyone who has been there cannot help being seduced by its bleak and grandiose beauty. Perhaps it is in part because the desert dwarfs the people who move over it, that the history of the conquest has received such scant attention. If the players sometimes appear to be small-bore, it is only because the scale of the stage upon which they act is so heroic.

I should like to thank some of the people who have given so much help and encouragement over the past two years, among them my agents, Gill Coleridge and Michael Congdon, for their faith, enthusiasm and valuable advice. The fellows and staff of the National Humanities Center, Research Triangle Park, North Carolina, provided the leisure which permitted this book to be written, and the good company which helped to make it a relatively painless undertaking. Chuck Elliott and his marvelous staff at Knopf have transformed a rough manuscript into a readable book. I claim the traditional author's privilege of absolving them of all responsibility for its defects and shortcomings. Lastly, I should like to thank my father, to whom this book is dedicated, for the encouragement to write it, and for so many other things.

THE CONQUEST OF THE SAHARA

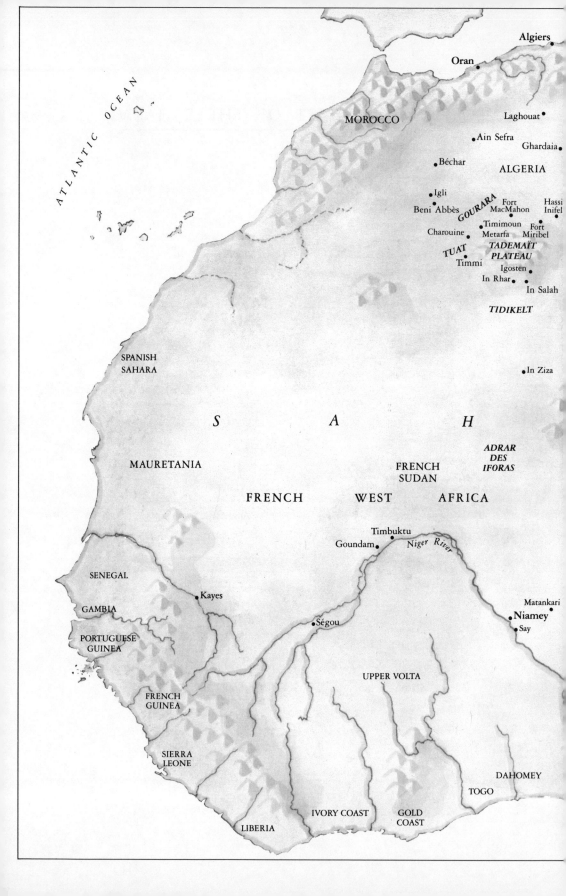

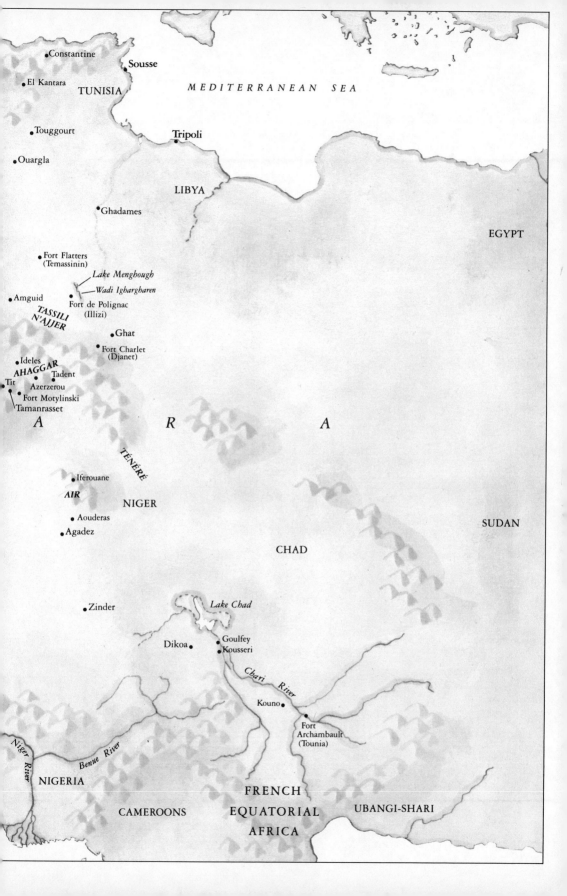

Constantine

Sousse

MEDITERRANEAN SEA

El Kantara

TUNISIA

Touggourt

Tripoli

Ouargla

LIBYA

EGYPT

Ghadames

Fort Flatters
(Temassinin)

Lake Menghough

Wadi Ighargharen

Amguid

Fort de Polignac
(Illizi)

TASSILI
N'AJJER

Ghat

Fort Charlet
(Djanet)

Ideles

AHAGGAR

Tadent

Tit

Azerzerou

Fort Motylinski

Tamanrasset

A   R   A

TÉNÉRÉ

Iferouane

AIR

NIGER

Aouderas

Agadez

SUDAN

CHAD

Zinder

Lake Chad

Dikoa

Goulfey

Kousseri

Chari River

Kouno

Fort
Archambault
(Tounia)

Niger River

Benue River

NIGERIA

CAMEROONS

FRENCH
EQUATORIAL

UBANGI-SHARI

AFRICA

I

THE
MIRAGE

In the center of an earth which cartographers like to depict in blues and greens lies a substantial area of khaki that stares like an eye out of the globe. Even here in this semifanciful, semiidealized world, this patch appears desolate and uninviting. The lighter brown of plain and dune swirls and twists among the darker ribs of ridge, plateau and mountain. Across this chaos of light and shade is written in large black lettering: *Sahara Desert.*

The geographical position of the Sahara has given it an enormously important role to play in history. The Sahara separates two continents— Europe and Asia—from the more populous and richer areas of Africa. Its vastness is almost inconceivable: 3,500 miles divide Cap Blanc on the Atlantic from Port Sudan on the Red Sea. These, of course, are 3,500 miles as the crow flies. But crows do not often fly across the Sahara. If you want to cross the desert from west to east on foot, or on a camel, or even in a Land Rover, the distance is considerably increased. The English writer Geoffrey Moorhouse attempted such a trip in the last decade, but gave up after several months at Tamanrasset in the Ahaggar massif of Algeria. While this is hardly an inconsiderable achievement, he had covered barely one-third of the distance he had originally set himself. Had he set out from London to accomplish successfully the same journey at a more northerly latitude, his camel would have taken him across the Urals and into Outer Mongolia.

It is easier to cross the desert from north to south. For one thing, the distances are far shorter. From the oasis of Biskra on the southern slopes of the Saharian Atlas where, as the tourist brochures proclaim, "the desert begins," to the fabled and decrepit town of Timbuktu, within spitting distance of the broad, sluggish Niger River, where in theory the desert should end (it obstinately refuses to do so), is around 1,350 miles. If you set out in a westerly direction from Manhattan Island, you might arrive in a small town on the south fork of the River Platte in western Nebraska with the Arab-sounding name of Ogallala before you had exhausted the distance. But again, these are crow-flying measurements. The true mileage might put you closer to Montana's Little Bighorn—in more ways than one.

The map resolutely proclaims that two roads cross the Sahara from north to south through the pie-shaped wedge of Algeria. This is partially true. The more popular eastern route is a surfaced road which will take you as far as the unattractive red mud town of Tamanrasset. From there, however, you are on your own, free to follow the confusion of faint tracks which head off in all directions, race across bone-hard plateaus, sink up to your axles in sand or simply to lose your way in a blinding sandstorm. With luck, and a good vehicle, you might arrive in Timbuktu.

During this long, hot, dusty journey, travelers with a sense of history have the leisure to reflect, indeed, to wonder, why in the nineteenth and twentieth centuries the French coveted this wilderness. The variety of the Saharian landscapes is obscured by the vast distances; hour passes upon monotonous hour: "The plains of sand give way to the dunes, and the dunes to the plains," wrote Frédéric Bernard, who accompanied the first Flatters expedition in 1880. "Nothing but sand. . . ." Even the normally ebullient English tourist W. J. Harding-King, who journeyed southward from Biskra at the turn of the century, complained that "There was always the same sandy soil, the same small bushes, the same level horizon, the same desert larks, the same hawks and ravens, the same little lizards scuttling about the sand. It was very monotonous."

Nineteenth-century travelers assumed that the Sahara had once been covered by ocean. Although this theory has since been rejected by geologists, it is a charming and, on the face of it, an altogether plausible notion. Today, if one flies over the Sahara, it looks like a land deserted by the sea. The plains, wadis (water courses) and dunes might well have been sloshed and rippled by tides and currents of a past geological age. If one walks or rides across the Sahara, the conclusion is irresistible that mammals could not find this a hospitable land. The few lizards and snakes that pad and twist over the sand are like refugees from an undersea world; the empty silence is more reminiscent of a place where water, not air, is the principal medium.

Yet, amazingly, men have adapted to this blasted land. The limestone plateaus that stretch southward from the Saharian Atlas, the last sentinels of the Maghreb, contain numerous depressions which are well watered and densely populated. In these oases, sometimes running for hundreds of miles, a mixture of Arabs, Berbers and blacks coax a few melons and tomatoes from the thin soil, raise scrawny chickens and goats, boil up locusts when a "plague" descends upon them, and rely mainly on the date palms for both shade and sustenance. Without the date, men could not live in the desert.

Beyond these pockets of cultivation, men manage to survive, but only just. In the north-central Sahara, Chaamba Arabs drift with their flocks of camels and sheep, seeking out pasture in the broad, shallow valleys where, from time to time, a freak shower of rain or rare collection of moisture causes low vegetation to appear, more gray than green.

The true desert men, however, are the Tuareg (singular, "Targui"). While the Chaamba seldom stray too far from the oases which, though poor, are essential to life in the desert, the Tuareg occupy the heart of the Sahara. As geographers are at great pains to point out, the image of the desert as an endless succession of dunes—an immense beach in search of its ocean—is quite inaccurate. The topography of the Sahara is extremely varied. Dunes there are aplenty—seemingly illimitable wrinkles of sand hills called *ergs.* But there are also plains, flat, waterless and dreaded *tanezrouft* upon which the sun's rays beat as upon an anvil. Low, flat-topped hills called *gour* (singular *gara*) sometimes dot the horizon like aircraft carriers whose flights have deserted them. *Wadis,* or watercourses, usually dry, carved out by long-forgotten storms, slice through the *hammada,* or high plateau. There are hills of respectable size, all brown, boulder-strewn and denuded of vegetation. Occasionally a ridge breaks the monotony of the plateaus—those which tower over the oasis of Djanet in the Tassili n'Ajjer rise to 2,500 feet. But by far the most impressive feature of the Sahara is the great *massifs*—the Adrar des Iforas, the Air, the Tassili and, above all, the Ahaggar whose tallest peak, Tahat, rises to 9,573 feet. These stand out like islands in a parched sea, relatively well watered and virtually inaccessible. These are the redoubts in which the Tuareg make their homes.

The Tuareg are a Berber people who occupy the central Sahara from the Tuat oases in the north to the Hausa country of northern Nigeria; from Lake Chad and the Libyan desert in the east to what is now modern Mauritania in the west. For centuries, this tall warrior people made the desert their inviolate sanctuary, accessible only to the caravans which were willing to pay the price of passage. Even the Arabs, who conquered so much of Asia, Africa and even Europe, were unable to impose their language or, in any serious form, their religion on these fiercely independent nomads. This was why they called them the "Tuareg"—the "abandoned of God."

Despite its bleakness, the Sahara is a land of great beauty, as any traveler to the desert will readily admit: "It was the awful scale of the thing, the suggestion of virginity, the fusion of pure elements from the heavens above and the earth beneath which were untrammelled and untouched by anything contrived by man." This, for Geoffrey Moorhouse, was the attraction of the Sahara. Others found beauty in the startling contrasts of the desert's varied landscapes: the "chaos of peaks and needles" of the Ahaggar massif which the sun transforms from funereal black into mountains that seem to burn with "an interior fire." The 700-mile-long Tassili ridge whose crags appeared to men camped beneath to be medieval fortresses; the oases with their date palms of deep green nestled among powder gold dunes.

But the scenic attractions of the Sahara, great as they are, hardly justified its inclusion, at great expense, in the French colonial empire. Why did the French want to occupy it? The short answer is that they did not; or, more accurately, the government had no designs on the desert, no plans to garrison and colonize it. If you had asked a French politician in, say, 1880, or even in 1900, if he wished for his country to conquer the desert, he would most probably have given you an emphatic no! If he was a sensible chap and had not been drawn into the "Colonial Party" in the French Chamber of Deputies—a hundred strong at the turn of the century, organized and directed by Eugène Etienne, the deputy for Oran in Algeria—he would have told you that colonies do not pay.

The budget for Algeria, France's most populous colony (in terms of European population), was in deficit by 93 million francs in 1910. Paris poured 3 million francs each year into the Saharian territories of Algeria, which returned to it 300,000 francs in taxes annually. Attempts by zealous government officials to increase the tax burden on the native population provoked howls of protest from officers of the Armée d'Afrique who garrisoned Algeria and administered the "tribal areas" of the Sahara. They realized—as the boffins of the Ministère des Finances, oblivious to everything but the bottom lines of their ledgers, did not—that Arabs, especially desert Arabs, equated taxation with slavery: "Taxes degrade peoples." The surest way to push an Arab beyond the bounds of tolerance was to transfer a portion of his meager wealth to Paris. When, in the 1890s, the French attempted to tax the Chaamba of Ouargla, the Arabs simply moved 500 miles further south to In Salah; beyond the reach of French officialdom, and of the French army, they took up their old profession as raiders, making life intolerable for the French-held oases further north. "Perhaps tomorrow man will be able to influence the climate and the rain, he will utilize solar heat industrially, by ways impossible to foresee he will modify the present situation of the desert," the Saharian specialist E. F. Gautier forecast in 1910. "But today, to those who have seen the Sahara, and even those who have loved it, it is impossible to pretend that it has a value in itself."

Gautier was not alone in his opinion. Even many of the men on the spot thought the idea of conquering the Sahara an absurd one: "When one has never visited and lived in these regions, one cannot imagine their desolation," wrote Major Jean Deleuze, dispatched in 1901 to report on the feasibility, and the wisdom, of establishing a permanent garrison in the newly conquered oasis complex of the Tuat. "The words: infertility—desert—void—do not do justice to the place. I am in agreement with Monsieur Foureau to employ the expression 'waste,' the 'Saharian waste.' The expression is not too strong." The desert populations were "small, miserable, wandering across the immense deserted regions and jealous of their independence." Some saw the conquest of the Sahara as vital to link the French empire in Chad and the Western Sudan with Algeria: "But what is the utility of that?" Deleuze asked. Lake Chad was just a bog surrounded by more desert. Anyone who thought that the Sahara could ever be made to pay its way was following a "mirage d'illusions" and simply digging yet another "hole into which we shall pour millions."

Deleuze was no fool. He knew exactly where to place the blame for all of this mad talk about the conquest of the desert. A few hotheads like Captain Théodore Pein could, by taking unscheduled local initiatives, put the army in embarrassing situations, provoke fights and oblige Algiers to dispatch punitive expeditions. But the real culprits were the armchair colonialists in Paris who supported them, covered for them, excused their indiscipline. "Colonial expansion has become a sport, and a very fashionable sport, which is practiced mainly in Paris" by politicians, soldiers and intellectuals, Deleuze wrote with remarkable acerbity. "Their *action coloniale* is limited to writing articles in newspapers or haranguing explorers who depart or return, posing as partisans of '*la plus grande France.'* " If they ever troubled to study more closely the places which they urged Frenchmen to explore and acquire, if they ever bothered to venture south of the Place de la Concorde, they might realize that *la plus grande France* was a charade, a papier-mâché world, large, exotic, but worthless, a poor joke played on the French people.

Deleuze certainly had his point of view, and it was one shared by the majority of Frenchmen. As an economic proposition, the colonies were almost everywhere a write-off. Few Frenchmen wanted to emigrate there. Few capitalists wanted to invest in them. (In the decade before the Great War, Russian railway bonds offered a far more tempting—and ultimately an equally disastrous—investment.) When the Compagnie de l'Oued Rirh tried to exploit commercially the date palms of the southern Algerian oases, they reckoned to make a profit of only 3 francs 50 per palm tree. Many French patriots saw the colonies as a gaping maw which devoured men and matériel desperately needed to bolster the vulnerable eastern and northern frontiers with Germany.

Why did France, then, conquer the Sahara? The question is probably best answered in terms of what a diplomat or strategist would call a power vacuum. Power vacuums always tempted neighboring states to intervene. Most of the wars in eighteenth- and nineteenth-century Europe were fought over those places where states were weak or fragmented —Poland, the German states, Italy, the Balkans. "Some damned foolish thing in the Balkans" would probably start the next war, Bismarck had predicted before his retirement. But the Balkans apart, Europe had largely resolved the problems of power vacuums by 1875. In a real sense, the Franco-Prussian War of 1870–71 can be seen as one of the last European wars fought over a power vacuum. When Bismarck provoked a confrontation with Emperor Napoleon III of France ostensibly over the succession to the Spanish throne, in reality both men had their ambitions firmly set on the four kingdoms, five grand duchies, six duchies, seven principalities, three free cities, and the French provinces of Alsace and Lorraine which made up "Germany." With Europe distracted by the war in the north, Italian Prime Minister Cavour seized the opportunity to tidy up his borders by eliminating the Papal States which cut the peninsula in half.

With the question of power vacuums largely settled on the Continent, European states began to look outward, to search out new fields of conquest. Their motives were varied. But it is certain that economic ones were less important than, until a few years ago, historians once thought. While politicians paid lip service to trade and industry, things like prestige, national honor or whatever tag one likes to apply to the wave of national fervor which swept European countries before 1914, were the raw material of ringing editorials. rousing speeches and electoral victories. Unless one understands this, then the "steeplechase to the unknown"—as French Prime Minister Jules Ferry labeled the mad rush for African lands which began in the 1880s—becomes inexplicable. Colonialism was not, as Lenin claimed, "the highest stage of capitalism." Rather, it was the highest stage of nationalism.

National tensions resulted in the expansion of the armed forces of Europe, and these, in turn, contributed their own impetus to the cause of imperial expansion: all those men, guns and ships lying idle in an age when nationalism flowed toward its spring tide. It was like a number of football sides searching for a field upon which they might compete, and no country fielded keener competitors than did France. In this way, European nationalism gave birth to imperialism, and imperialism acquired its own rationale beyond those of economics. But within these great historical currents which swept Europe in the fifty or so years before the Great War, there was plenty of room for individual initiative. Of no place was this more true than of the Sahara.

II

SHORES OF TRIPOLI

A glance at a map of the Mediterranean will confirm that it forms, in fact, two seas divided by the boot of Italy and the triangular wedge of Sicily. The finger of land called Cap Bon on the northeastern tip of Tunisia lies barely fifty miles across the Sicilian Channel from the town of Marsala. It is even said that until well into the nineteenth century, lookouts were regularly stationed on the heights behind Marsala to give warning of pirate boats sailing out of the Gulf of Tunis.

This division of the Mediterranean is important because the African shores of the western and eastern seas are so different. To the west, the mountains of the Maghreb rise up like a wall from the azure waters. These are the Atlas Mountains, which form a series of high ridges running west to east from Tangier to Tunis. Close to the Mediterranean shore, these mountains are covered with trees of pine and carob. In the broad valleys and plains which separate them, European settlers in the nineteenth and twentieth centuries managed with success to cultivate wheat and grapes. As one moves south from the coast, through the city of Constantine which sits on a pinnacle of rock, past the clear lakes of Tinsilt and Mzouri, the mountains become sharper, more barren, like jagged pieces of glass made pink by the rising sun. Across the plain of Ain Touta, the clouds clinging to the mountains, one begins to feel the first hints of the savage immensity of the Sahara. A thread of palm trees follows a wadi of limpid water through the folds of the Kantara Gorge, called "the mouth of the desert" by the Arabs. As one descends to the oasis of Biskra, the hazy line of the Aurès Mountains, bathed in mellow sunlight, stretches away to the northeast. To the south, across the salt-flecked Chott Melrhir, the Sahara runs—flat, speckled like the hide of a panther—until it disappears in a blue line on the horizon.

The southern shore of the eastern Mediterranean is very different. Here there are no mountains to keep the desert at bay, or to provide a thick strip of habitable coastline. In the east, the Sahara creeps, sandy and hot, to the sea. Despite the uninviting appearance of this coast, it was here in what is today Libya that European explorers usually caught their first glimpse of Africa. The reason for this is quite simple—Tripoli served as the major *entrepôt* of trade between the African interior and Europe until well into the nineteenth century. Caravans regularly brought cargos of gold, ivory, ostrich feathers, leather goods, pepper, kola nuts, live parrots and, especially, slaves from the bowels of Africa to be sold in Tripoli. They then returned south carrying cloth, rugs, copper kettles, iron and steel tools, needles, swords, rifles and shot, Venetian glassware and, according to Captain George Lyon of the Royal Navy, who traveled south from Tripoli in 1819, "handsome girls from Abyssinia educated in Mecca or Egypt."

Most explorers chose Tripoli as a starting point because a well-established trade route into the interior already existed. By joining a caravan bound for Lake Chad or Timbuktu, one would—barring accident—be whisked into the African heartland. Alternative routes from the west coast of Africa were also tried. But the absence of established avenues of trade and the prevalence of tropical diseases which turned the swampy coasts of West Africa into a "white man's grave" meant that connoisseurs of African travel preferred Tripoli as a point of entry.

But this tells us little about why explorers wanted to go to Africa in the first place. And why to the Sahara? There is no ready answer to this question. The lure of wealth was minimal. True, there were stories about the fabled riches of Timbuktu. But any hardheaded businessman examining the wares that caravans brought to the coast must have been skeptical even before the French explorer René Caillié visited the place in 1829 and declared it a dump. Far easier fortunes waited to be made in Asia and the Americas.

Nor can strategic necessity count as a prime mover of African exploration. The great age of imperialism awaited its dawn. In the first half of the nineteenth century, European powers had neither the resources nor the motivation to occupy vast tracts of the unexplored world. A third, more plausible explanation is provided by the desire to discourage the slave trade. In the years after Waterloo, reformers in England especially became very concerned about the question of slavery. Several of the early Saharian explorers wore out their initially friendly welcome and, incidentally, created difficulties for subsequent European visitors, by lecturing their hosts on the evils of slavery. As black women provided the main article of commerce between Lake Chad and Tripoli, the explorers' affirmations that, as soon as England established a presence in Africa the slave trade would be outlawed, received a frosty reception from black and Arab potentates and traders. It was like lecturing a used-car salesman on the evils of automobile pollution and threatening to outlaw cars. When the Europeans did succeed in discouraging slavery, the caravan trade across the Sahara diminished to a shadow of its former importance.

Specific reasons for the growth in interest about the world beyond Europe which began around 1750 are difficult to pinpoint. Perhaps it was a feeling that for too long Europe had been obsessed with its own internal quarrels and religious disputes. Wealth had increased in the eighteenth century, and so had leisure. The publishing industry boomed. Travel books became second in popularity only to books on theology. The end of the Seven Years War in 1763, like Waterloo some fifty-two years later, released a flood of men onto the job market who had developed a taste for adventure, some of whom were unwilling to content themselves with a country vicarage in Shropshire or a family shop in Hamburg. The African Association was founded in 1788 to channel their energies and finance their dreams. Quite simply, Europe wanted to know, and men like Lyon, Richardson, Denham, Clapperton, Laing, Caillié and others were prepared to satisfy popular curiosity about the source of the Nile, the glories of Timbuktu and the course of the Niger.

Personal motivations must also have played a considerable role: Exploration offered a means to fame and wealth. Captain James Cook had been feted on his return from his first two voyages to the south seas, and others dreamed of duplicating his feats in Africa. Few did. In almost every case, exploration proved a terminal occupation. Even those who survived found that they faced a host of hostile and skeptical critics on their return home, and endured experiences every bit as unpleasant as those suffered at the hands of "uncivilized" Africans. René Caillié, who accomplished a fantastic journey from Saint-Louis de Sénégal to Tangier via Timbuktu and the Sahara in 1828–29, never succeeded in convincing many eminent armchair travelers that he had not invented the whole story. Others complained that his diary was useless because it was not suitably scientific. Perhaps, but even today it makes enthralling reading. In any case, Caillié was one of the few lucky ones, not only because he survived, but also because he was able to finance a comfortable retirement from the various prizes and royalties he collected. A few others were able to translate a hazardous voyage into an academic post. Some were ignored or simply disbelieved, treated as if deranged. But the list of African explorers reads more like a necrology than a success story, and the odds on success decreased as the century progressed.

Tripoli, the "gateway to Africa," perches precariously on the edge of the continent. To those who approached it from the sea, the low and level shore around the town seemed at first to host luxuriant plantations of date palms and well-tended gardens. As the ship drew nearer, however, the trees and gardens took on a more straggly appearance. Even from this distance, the atmosphere seemed to be on fire as the sun's rays ricocheted between the sand and the squat, white houses.

Set in this narrow belt of palms and gardens which ran for ten miles along the shore but barely three miles inland, the crenellated town walls, the cupolas of the bathhouses, the minarets of the mosques and the numerous trees of Indian fig, mulberry, olive and date gave Tripoli a verdant and exotic appearance. The flags of eight European countries snapped at the ends of long poles above their consulates. But as the ship bumped against the quay, the town's air of gentle decay became obvious. At the northeast corner of the semicircular bay, the bashaw's palace squatted behind crumbling walls, "an irregular Jail looking pile," said Gordon Laing, who saw it in 1825. Here the representative of the Sublime Porte, with the exalted rank of three tails, equivalent to that of the governors of the greatest of Turkey's provinces—Cairo, Baghdad and Budapest—watched over this distant outpost of empire for his master the Sultan. Visitors to Tripoli reckoned that were the town to come under serious attack, either from the sea or from the Berbers in the hinterland, he would have been hard-pressed to do his duty; the town walls were in such bad repair that attempts to fire cannon from the parapets usually caused them to collapse. In Laing's view, a determined foe armed with crowbars could easily take the place. But this, as will be seen, was hardly true.

The arrival of a ship and the departure of a caravan were the two events that shook this town of 25,000 souls out of its lethargy. People "of uncouth appearance" crowded onto the quay to examine the new arrivals. There was also a sprinkling of the bashaw's officials, "their long flowing robes of satin, velvet and costly furs" contrasting markedly with the rags worn by the rest: "The size of the turban increases with the importance of the wearer," Miss Tully, the sister of the British Consul, Richard Tully, noted in 1783. Wealthy young Arabs also chose this moment to display their finery: "They had red cloth caps, round which they rolled two or three times a coloured shawl twisted, with one end brought round the neck, and the other flung over the left shoulder. A young Moor thinks himself quite irresistible with his shawl worn in this manner." Lyon, however, thought them disgusting: "They had a peculiar way of blowing their noses in the ends of their turbans," he recorded. Nor did their disagreeable public habits stop there. Expectoration, while common in Europe, had in Tripoli been raised to the level of a performing art, "from the Bashaw to the poorest camel driver. . . . Great men go through this ceremony with great solemnity and dignity altogether imposing, stroking their beards and thanking God for the great relief they have obtained."

Once, the curious onlookers gathered on the quayside would have had something to gawk at—Tripoli had been a major pirate haunt in the seventeenth and eighteenth centuries. Enterprising captains, most of them Anatolian Greeks, Neapolitans or Spanish renegades, had once sailed forth in great numbers to plunder the shipping and raid the islands and coastal settlements of the Mediterranean. The captives whom they brought back, especially the female ones, would fetch good prices in the market reserved for white slaves behind the great Karamanli Mosque. (A second one traded in blacks brought by caravan from the Sudan.) The most attractive might be snapped up for the great harems of Alexandria, Cairo or even Istanbul itself.

Consuls from Christian countries were kept in Tripoli primarily to deal with just such arrivals. European countries found that the best way to deal with these Barbary pirate states was simply to buy them off. Periodic bombardments of known pirate dens seldom produced more than a temporary suspension of their plundering. The most cost-effective method of managing the problem of corsairs was to pay a yearly caution to the bashaws of Tripoli and Tunis, the dey of Algiers and the sultan of Morocco. In this way, European states secured agreements exempting their ships and nationals from capture. They had little choice. Their navies were seldom large enough, or skillful enough, to catch the elusive pirates. Indeed, many of the pirates had learned their seafaring skills in the navies of Spain or Venice, or even of England and Holland, before opening their own accounts on the southern shore of the Mediterranean.

With their intimate knowledge of the inlets and islands, of the trade routes of ships that tramped from port to port along the coasts of Italy, Spain or France, and of the counter-tactics of the captains set to catch them, they were almost impossible to eradicate.

When a cannon fired from the harbor wall announced the return of a corsair, the European consuls, dressed in their best clothes, surrounded by an impressive retinue of secretaries and guards, marched down to the harbor to reclaim any of their nationals who had been caught up in the pirate nets. One wonders, however, how many illegally caught captives were quietly landed down the coast to avoid the consuls' reclaiming them. The captain might then square things with an official or even with the bashaw himself before putting the captives up for auction.

In the opening years of the nineteenth century, one country's consul was conspicuous by his absence at these proceedings—that of the young American republic. In 1801, the bashaw, annoyed no doubt by President Jefferson's refusal to pay his protection money like everyone else, declared war on the United States. One might well imagine the surprise of this Oriental potentate when he glanced over the crumbling battlements of his palace one August morning of that year, to see four American men-of-war standing off Tripoli harbor. He promptly ordered his flagship, the *Tripoli,* to punish the Americans for their impertinence.

The corsair ships found at Tripoli were small, square-rigged vessels equipped with oars that the numerous crew were expected to take up in a calm, or in the heat of pursuit. They were ideally suited for preying on the unarmed merchantmen that made up the bulk of the coastal traffic. In confrontation with a man-of-war, however, the only prudent tactic was to flee. Instead, the captain of the *Tripoli,* aware of the bashaw's gaze upon him, sailed resolutely up to one of the American ships, the sloop *Enterprise,* and attempted to board her. The result for the Africans was a disaster: Shot from the *Enterprise* splintered the gunwales of the *Tripoli,* filling the air with lethal fragments of wood, while well-aimed musketry from American marines hanging off the rigging turned her crowded decks into a charnel house. The *Tripoli* lost two-thirds of her crew. That of the *Enterprise* received an extra month's pay as a bonus.

After this scrap, the Arabs became more cautious, adopting a defensive posture, running the porous American blockade but refusing to challenge the ships that manned it. In June 1803, the Americans caught a convoy of grain ships outside the harbor, fought their way on board and.burned them. But disaster struck in October, when the frigate *Philadelphia* ran aground off Tripoli. The 409-man crew disappeared into the bashaw's prisons. A reasonable man, the bashaw offered to sell the American sailors back to the U.S. government. But the Americans' blood was up—Jefferson dispatched a strong naval force under Commodore Edward Preble. Arriving off the town in July 1804, Preble immediately dispatched a raiding party commanded by the fiery young Lieutenant Stephen ("Our country right or wrong") Decatur, which burned the captured *Philadelphia* under the very guns of the bashaw's fort. For the next three months, Preble's men were constantly raiding, boarding and burning.

Meanwhile, a far more ambitious plan against the bashaw was being hatched on the Nile. William H. Eaton, a former sergeant in the Continental Army, consul in Tunis and a fluent Arabic speaker, convinced Jefferson that revolution rather than direct attack was the way to overthrow the bashaw. Eaton found a willing ally in the exiled elder brother of the bashaw, Hamet Karamanli. Eaton's plan called for a force of a thousand U.S. Marines to be landed on the North African coast, where they would join forces with Hamet's army financed by $20,000 of Washington's money. Eaton's plan was accepted, but was so cut down in scale that in its final form it became not only impractical but virtually suicidal. Eaton was given a thousand dollars, and, together with Hamet Karamanli and a detachment of eight marines led by a high-spirited Virginian named Lieutenant Presley N. O'Bannon—a man noted principally for his womanizing and fiddle-playing—sailed south up the Nile. There they recruited an army: around a hundred Mediterranean mercenaries, a bodyguard for Hamet of seventy men, two Bedouin bands and some Arab cameleers. On March 6, 1805, Eaton led this motley force of 400 men into the Libyan desert. On April 15, they heaved up on the Gulf of Bomba, where they were met by the American brig *Argus*. That this force arrived at all was due largely to O'Bannon and his marines, who kept the mutinous and ill-disciplined force together at gunpoint.

Refreshed and revictualed, Eaton's troops stormed Derna on the Cyrenaican coast, supported by gunfire from three American frigates and by the discordant and heartrending music of the two Bedouin bands. Incredibly, their assault succeeded. On April 27, 1805, the American flag fluttered triumphantly over this Tripolitan outpost. In the United States, the press waxed rhapsodic over the victory, and John Greenleaf Whittier even wrote a poem about it. But Derna was still 750 miles from Tripoli. What was more, Eaton, O'Bannon and Hamet were now besieged in Derna by a substantial Tripolitan force. For two months, they conducted a brilliant defense, only to learn that Tripoli and Washington had signed a peace treaty even before Derna had been stormed in April. The Derna garrison was taken off by boat. The war with Tripoli had proved inconclusive, but it provided an interesting, if not strictly accurate, line for the *Marine Hymn*.

Though exotic, Tripoli was not a pleasant town to live in—the place had the appearance of a slum. One left the quayside and plunged into streets of indescribable filth, past large hills of rubbish that were constantly churned and sifted by packs of stray dogs and near-naked children. Camels and donkeys thrust through the crowded, narrow streets raising a choking dust. Occasionally, a camel would pass bearing a wealthy woman secreted behind the linen screen of an enclosed palanquin, surrounded by a large retinue of female slaves and guards: "They carry with them a great number of lights, and a vast quantity of burning perfume, which is carried in silver fillagree [sic] vases, and also large silver ewers of rose and orange-flower water, to damp the burning perfume, which, during their walk, produces a thick cloud around them, composed of the finest aromatic odours." But this could do little to keep the stench of the streets at bay. Even in the covered bazaar, a powerful smell of musk, a substance used in the manufacture of perfumes and medicines, made a shopping trip an unpleasant experience. The streets were lined with shops hardly larger than booths, from which merchants sold cloth, shoes and other leather goods, but also "pearls, gold, gems and precious drugs." Arab gentlemen sat cross-legged on marble benches covered with rugs outside the coffeehouses conversing or pulling lazily on their water pipes, while black servants thrust cups of coffee scented with cloves, cinnamon and nutmeg into their hands. Confined behind the intricate latticework covering the upper-story windows of the peeling houses which leaned precariously over the streets, the women surveyed this spectacle unseen.

In this cauldron of dust and filth, Arab, Turk, black, Jew and Christian—"the scum of Malta," according to Laing—jostled and scraped for a living. "Drunkenness is more common in Tripoli than even in most towns in England," Lyon declared in a statement which, if true, must have meant that at least half the population perished from cirrhosis of the liver. Prostitution seemed to be a staple industry. Outside the walls, nomadic Berbers pitched their low, black, camel's-hair tents. In the evenings, men from the town would wander through their camps to negotiate the purchase of a sheep, a rug or some household implement. Or, perhaps, they would simply linger by the camel-dung fires listening to a storyteller, or a vigorous song sung by hand-clapping groups of women, the choruses punctuated by their high-pitched ululations. On a clear evening, the low outline of the Gharyan Mountains might be visible to the south. But usually the flat, sandy plain called the *pianura* stretched away unhindered toward the Gefara Desert until it vanished in a haze of heat.

Europeans loathed Tripoli. To walk in the streets was an ordeal. On Moslem holy days, when religious feeling might drift above the danger mark, it was positively perilous. European consuls seldom ventured forth unless surrounded by stoutly armed bodyguards, lest madmen—held in religious awe—attack them. "They have a profound respect for idiots," Lyon noted, "whom they consider as people beloved of heaven and totally unable to think of things of this world." This respect for insanity and other forms of mental disorder was not confined to Tripoli. The English traveler Harding-King noted of one holy man whom he met in Algeria that "his holiness consisted of the fact that he was, if not half-witted, at all events silly."

In common with other North African cities, Tripoli contained a sizable Jewish community, around 5,000 souls. According to European travelers, the Jews suffered the humiliating tyranny of the Arab majority: Forbidden to go on horseback, they had to remove their slippers each time they passed a mosque, walking barefoot through the muck and debris of the streets. They were regularly assaulted, or impressed to act —inexpertly—as executioners each time the bashaw ordered a decapitation. The bodies of the executed were then suspended from gibbets in the street until they reached an advanced state of putrefaction, after, that is, a minor official had extracted money from a number of merchants and householders on the promise to display the corpse in another part of town. The heads, salted by Jews, decorated the city gates. If a Jew were convicted of a serious misdemeanor, he might be burned alive or his body smeared with honey, his hands nailed to the synagogue door, and he left to die of sun and flies.

Bad as this was, the Jews had in fact traditionally fared much better at the hands of the Arabs than among Europeans. The occasional explosions of hostility against Jews in North Africa more often sprang from protests by the most wretched sections of the Moslem population against social and political conditions, rather than from religious fanaticism. Jews, after all, were regarded as one of the "Peoples of the Book." They sprang, moreover, from the same racial and cultural roots as their Moslem neighbors. Anti-Semitism increased markedly in North Africa with the advent of colonialism, for some Jews made common cause with the European invaders, thus bringing the resentment and wrath of the Arabs down on the entire community. But historically, religious friction in North Africa was tempered by common traditions and a shared way of life.

Tripoli exuded a distinctly medieval atmosphere. Ignorance bred superstition among the townspeople. An eclipse of the sun—such as that witnessed on June 3, 1788, by Miss Tully, sister of the British consul in Tripoli—threw them into a frenzy:

> When the eclipse was at its height, they ran about distracted in companies, firing volleys of muskets at the sun, to frighten away the monster or dragon, as they called it, which they supposed was devouring it. At that moment, the Moorish song of death and *wulliah-woo,* or the howl they make for their dead . . . resounded. . . . The women brought into the street all the brass pans, kettles, iron utensils they could collect and, striking them with all their force, screaming at the same time, occasioned a horrid noise that could be heard for miles. Many of these women, owing to their exertions and fears, fell into fits and fainted.

Far worse, however, were the plagues that periodically ravaged the city, usually imported by ships infected in Egypt or Istanbul. Despite the best efforts of the authorities to banish them beyond the breakwater, some of the crew inevitably swam to shore and contaminated the town. As the disease took hold, Tripoli would be transformed into a scene that might have been lifted from one of the lower circles of Dante's *Inferno.* Houses were fumigated with a mixture of bran, camphine, myrrh and aloes salted with gunpowder. Fires were lit in the entrance halls of houses each time anyone called, the flame kept between the host, or his servant, and the caller. If a rich man were obliged to go out, he kept servants in front and behind him to make certain that no one approached. Soon, however, the streets were occupied only by the very courageous, or the very foolish.

The most somber spectacle of a plague season occurred each day at noon, when a gruesome procession bore the bodies beyond the walls to the cemetery. "Five or six corpses were bound together, all of them fastened together and hurried away to the grave," Miss Tully recorded.

> The expense and the danger of burying the dead has become so great, and the boards to make the coffins so very scarce, that the body is brought out of the house by friends to the door, and the first man they prevail on carries it over his shoulder, or in his arms, to the grave, endeavouring to keep pace with the large range of coffins that go to the burying ground at noon, to take advantage of the great mass.

People deranged by disease or by grief wandered the streets, while the lamentations of the women issued from every house: "Women, whose persons have hitherto been veiled, are wandering about complete images of despair, with their hair loose and their barcans open, crying, wringing their hands and following their families." Nor was it uncommon, Miss Tully claimed, for people to be buried alive, once the household had deemed them beyond hope, or simply because they were anxious to get rid of the infected person.

It was reckoned that fully two-fifths of the Arab population perished in this plague of 1788, while one-half of the Jews died. The higher Jewish death rate was attributed to the fact that many buried their dead in shallow graves in the courtyards of their homes to escape a heavy burial tax of 20 pataques (around £ 5 or $25) imposed on them by the bashaw. Once the disease had subsided, the town wore a desolate appearance:

> In some of the houses were found the last victims that had perished in them, who having died alone, unpitied and unassisted, lay in a state too bad to be removed from the spot, and were obliged to be buried where they lay, while in others, children were wandering about deserted, without a friend be-

longing to them. The town was almost entirely depopulated
and rarely two people walked together.

For women, Tripoli was a virtual prison. Rich women seldom left their
houses, and then never on foot or unaccompanied by guards and servants. Women of more modest means ventured out several times weekly
to visit the market, their parents or the cemetery, but always heavily
wrapped, only one eye visible beneath the folds of blanket, and accompanied by at least one female relative or servant. Only the Bedouin
women camped beneath the walls were visible—gracefully dressed in
black robes, they went about unveiled, weighted down with jewelry, their
hair plaited in small tresses cut evenly just above the eye. Miss Tully
found the effect admirable, spoiled only by the tattoos which decorated
the faces of these women: "The [Bedouin] women do not seem to be of
the same opinion as some ladies in Tripoli, who think that if they are not
too fat to move without help, they cannot be strictly handsome, and to
arrive at this, they actually force themselves, after a plentiful meal, to eat
a small wheaten loaf soaked in cold water."

Women spent by far the greatest part of their lives confined to their
houses. For virtually all of them, the house consisted of an entrance hall
with benches on each wall, beyond which was a central courtyard surrounded by pillars which was paved and ornamented according to the
wealth of the owner. During feasts and on other special occasions, the
courtyard might be decorated with carpets and cushions and filled with
guests. Behind the intricate latticework which screened the upper-floor
gallery were located the living apartments, which were both dark and
airless. The apartments on the street side of the house might contain
windows. But the only place the women could go for air was to the roof.
This was a popular meeting place, especially in the evenings when groups
of robed and chattering women climbed to the rooftops to gaze out over
the sea and catch the hint of a breeze. They shared their vantage point
with mounds of figs, raisins, dates and the washing, all of which were left
to dry there.

However severely restricted the lives of women in Tripoli must have
seemed in Western eyes, the attitude of the women themselves is more
difficult to gauge. Most probably welcomed the security of a closed house
with its encapsulated female society. Few could have entertained ambitions to compete in the man's world outside. Although life within the

household must have been extremely tedious overall, the women might break the monotony by singing, gossiping or weekly visits to the baths. What is also certain is that a man's existence was hardly less humdrum. True, he was free to roam the streets, but in Tripoli this seems to have been a dubious advantage. In the end, his life was not all that different from that of his wife. It came down essentially to long hours spent in gossip, or simply to squatting in front of his house with one or two friends, making an occasional comment on the state of the weather or the possibility of a business deal. Westerners who observed this languid and seemingly aimless pace of life condemned it as simple laziness and lack of ambition in the Arabs. This was unfair. The Arabs, like Europeans until a more recent era, simply held a different notion of time. Life was not to be rushed, but slowly savored. "Accomplishment," "success," "progress" were not ideas to which they would have subscribed. Man forgets his birth and suffers in death. He must not neglect the life in between.

To visitors, the bashaw's harem offered the most flagrant example of the low status to which Islam consigned its women. In the rambling castle that served the bashaw as residence and seat of government, the women of his harem lived out their lives in a perpetual gloom—even the courtyard was roofed with a grate of heavy iron bars. In the harem, the richly dressed women, most of whom had been introduced as mere children at the age of puberty, or purchased from a returning corsair, lounged about on cushions, mattresses or sofas covered with velvet and embroidered with gold and silver thread, eating sherbet and drinking pomegranate juice, attended by eunuchs and black female servants so numerous that it was difficult to move from room to room. "Moorish ladies seem conscious of their confinement when they see Christians, and express regret at their want of liberty," reported Miss Tully. "Not that they find the day too long on their hands, for . . . their intrigues, jealousies and fears fully employ all their hours, and which we may easily conceive when we consider that the failure of their plots would often cost them their lives."

Though Miss Tully does not tell us much on this point, the bashaw's harem was probably far less of a jumble sale of females arranged for the ruler's gratification than she imagined. Like other provincial and imperial harems of the Turkish empire, it copied in its essential features that of the Sublime Porte. In atmosphere the harem was more like a barracks than a house of pleasure, for it was organized according to a strict pyra-midal hierarchy by the senior female, either the bashaw's mother or his first wife. At the base of the pyramid were the *sagrideler,* or novices. The most talented or beautiful of the novices might be promoted after a suitable apprenticeship to the status of *gedikliler,* or "privileged one." It was only at this stage that a girl might share the ruler's bed, and one thus honored was known as *gozde,* "in favor." Those "in favor" on a regular basis were promoted to the rank of *ikbal,* "fortunate."

Miss Tully believed the occupation of bashaw's concubine to be one of the more dangerous professions which a woman might follow in Trip-oli. In this, she reflects common Western notions of harem life. At times, some women of the harem might become influential, if kept informed of events at court by the chief eunuch, their sons, or by the bashaw himself. No doubt they used all their influence to have their sons well placed. Some might even have been executed if they became involved in one of the "somber melodramas" which characterized the history of the Kara-manli dynasty. But a concubine was far more likely to die of boredom than under the executioner's axe.

European travelers complained of Tripoli's filth, but many of their own cities were hardly less squalid. Paris and London in the eighteenth and early nineteenth centuries accommodated an uprooted and largely destitute peasantry who lived principally by crime, prostitution and the meager generosity of the pawn shop in the noisome slums of the Fau-bourg Saint-Antoine and the East End. Until our own century, the pop-ular joke maintained that Naples remained the only Oriental city without a resident European quarter. Nevertheless, Tripoli, despite its squalor, was virtually the only place on the coast of North Africa where explorers were assured of a cordial welcome. Morocco was closed to them—the sultan had established Mogador on the Atlantic coast as an outlet for the caravan trade from Timbuktu, but he did not encourage Europeans to visit the interior of his country, except as captives or renegades employed to service his army's antiquated artillery. Once the French invaded Al-giers in 1830, that portion of the Maghreb remained in a perpetual state of war for the next twenty years. This, combined with the French occu-pation, disrupted the established trading routes and the caravan trade which had once gone to Algiers was now redirected into Morocco and Tripoli.

Yusuf Karamanli, the Bashaw of Tripoli for the first quarter of the nineteenth century, was perfectly at home with his town's European consuls, especially with Colonel Hamner Warrington, who became Britain's consul in Tripoli in 1814. With his own people, Karamanli was a cruel and unprincipled tyrant. His janissaries and *cologhlis,* or mercenaries, commanded by his eldest son, kept order, while he executed his enemies and extorted money from his people. Nepotism was entrenched as a system to the point where virtually no important civil or military post passed outside of the family. Gordon Laing (Warrington's son-in-law) found Karamanli to be an aloof man, and though he seemed outwardly friendly, Laing suspected that he might prove untrustworthy. Through Warrington, explorers thought they might acquire the proper letters of protection from the bashaw which, they believed, would see them safely through the desert. In fact, Warrington was a garrulous old fool who overestimated both the bashaw's influence (which ran barely fifty miles south of Tripoli) and the ease of travel in the Sahara. By needlessly sending young men, including Laing, to their deaths, Warrington probably did more to retard the cause of African exploration than any other official whose job it was to encourage and counsel. Nevertheless, if Europeans intended to enter the interior of Africa from the Mediterranean coast, then it was in Tripoli that they must start. And start they did.

III

DESERT

The Sahara was not a barrier between the Mediterranean and the Sudan. Rather, it was a veil. No maps existed of the Sahara, it is true, but the inhabitants needed no maps; they knew where they were going. Caravans regularly left Tripoli for the south. The most direct route into the interior ran through the oases of Murzuk and Bilma to Lake Chad and Bornu. A more westerly road threaded through Ghadames and Ghat to Agadez at the foot of the mountains of Air, then to Kano and Sokoto. This was also the best way to reach Timbuktu. A less-frequented route, and the one followed by the unfortunate Gordon Laing, traveled west from Ghadames to In Salah in the broad Tuat oasis, and from there south through the shadow of the Ahaggar to Timbuktu. But the fierce reputation of the Ahaggar Tuareg meant that few traveled that way, as Laing himself was well aware: "Few will attempt to travel between Tripoli and Gadamis solus, none will try it between Tuat and Gadamis, and twenty men are not safe between Tuat and Tombuctoo," he wrote. He decided to chance his luck: "I hear such accounts of [the Ahaggar Tuareg] that I shall consider myself as fortunate if I get through their territories with the loss of half my baggage. . . . I well recall the words of the Bashaw: 'If you want to go that road, you must open the door with a silver key,' and I find them too true."

Travel in the Sahara, especially for a European, could be—quite literally—a murderous business. The distances are vast, the terrain brutal and the weather pitiless. Heat is the major enemy in a land where 100 degrees Fahrenheit counts as a cool winter's day. In summer, temperatures of 150 degrees and above are not unknown. In such a ferocious heat, nature is not so much paralyzed as comatose: Caravans halted, the Arabs covered themselves with a cloth and tossed about on the burning sands like fish in a skillet, unable to sleep, barely able to breathe. However, the sandy soil of the Sahara quickly loses its heat after sunset. It has struck more than one traveler as ironic that, even in the hottest months, cold can cause great discomfort. The mercury plunges and rises like a

salmon on the end of a line, and a dawn frost will give way to temperatures hovering well above 100 degrees by mid-morning. "The heat is
almost intolerable since I left you, the thermometer at noon standing not
infrequently at 120° of Fahrenheit," Laing wrote, "which was all the
more severely felt in consequence of the cold which often prevails in the
evenings, the thermometer indicating a temperature of 75°–68°—and
once or twice as low as 62°!" The winter temperatures in the higher
altitudes of the Ahaggar often drop to below freezing. Nor is snow
unknown there.

To the discomfort caused by the extremes of temperature is often
added the ordeal of a sandstorm. This might be announced by a lurid
yellow light on the horizon or a sound like dull thunder. The dry air
crackles with electricity—any attempt to touch the canvas of a tent or a
sleeping bag produces "a real fireworks display that pops like the logs
on a winter fire." Suddenly, the wind rasps the caravan, driving the small
particles of sand before it like birdshot: "The noise is horrible, the cries
of the men and the bellowing of the camels make a lugubrious concert
which can be heard above the howling of the tempest and the peal of the
thunder," wrote Frédéric Bernard. "The next day at sunrise, the camp is
in a very sad state, everyone digging in the sand to find lost objects. After
an hour of searching, one simply gives up any hope of finding the few
tools or instruments which are still missing." " 'Bright sunshine with
some sandstorms later,' would always, judging by our experience, be a
safe weather forecast" in the desert, Harding-King remarked.

The worst thing about a sandstorm is that the scorching scirocco
simply intensifies the torturing thirst: "My throat was on fire and my
tongue clove to the roof of my mouth," Caillié remembered of his agony
brought on by the burning winds. "I thought only of water—rivers,
streams, rivulets were the only ideas that presented themselves to my
mind during this fever." The availability of water dictated all life in the
desert. In summer, a man needs to drink two gallons of water daily. A
certain amount can be carried on the backs of camels in goatskin bags
called *guerbas*. However, drinking water from these requires a strong
stomach: The water is tinged red from the leather of the *guerba*, probably
muddy, full of foreign matter including goat hairs from the inside of the
water bag, tepid and usually tasting strongly of sulfur or magnesium.
Some Europeans found that, at first, they were unable to swallow it. But
thirst soon made them less squeamish. When wells were few, water had

to be carefully rationed, distributed only when the caravan stopped for the evening: "It is difficult to describe with what impatience we longed for this moment," wrote Caillié. "To enhance the pleasure which I expected from my portion, I thrust my head into the vessel, and sucked up the water in long draughts. When I had drunk, I had an unpleasant sensation all over me, which was quickly succeeded by fresh thirst." Soon, everyone was showing the signs of thirst: lips cracked and swollen, sunken eyes, hollow cheeks and a vacant stare. One could not buy water from other members of the caravan at any price, even when begging it, rosary in hand, "for the love of God." Some were reduced to drinking their own urine.

It can rain in the desert. Sometimes five to seven years may elapse between showers. When these occur, they are usually little more than light drizzles, but they are welcomed nonetheless: "The men shouted for joy and the camels licked their blistered lips," wrote Major Charlet of the first drops of rain which he had seen in the Tassili n'Ajjer. However, their joy soon turned to alarm: "Within five minutes, it was raining cats and dogs," he continued.

> Superb waterfalls of red water full of sand splashed from rock to rock onto our heads: the wadi begins to run, then to rise. The situation was poignant with interest. We are on the left bank of the wadi, around twelve feet from the lowest point. The water comes faster and faster up a branch which runs along the right bank, separated from us by a dune covered with Tamarisk trees. The rain only stops at six in the morning, but the spectacle remains the same: the waterfalls fall, and the wadi carries its muddy water with a sound of violent wind. . . . There we spent a delicious night dreaming of boats, of naval battles and of pasture for our camels.

Because water was scarce, caravans zigzagged across the desert searching out wells and waterholes where they might rest, refill their *guerbas,* and continue on to the next oasis. As these wells were often no more than holes in the ground, sometimes covered over by sand or even camouflaged by the desert men themselves, they might easily be missed even if the caravan passed to within a half-mile—or less! "While gathering wood, one of my men brought me the rusty barrel of a rifle and a leather sack gnawed by insects," Lieutenant Guy Dervil recorded in his diary.

> It contained a yellow paper on which I could make out the words: Ouargla Bureau, native affairs, permit for Mohammed ben Ali to go to El Goléa. Date and signature illegible. Hardly had I pronounced these words than Meddhah approaches: 'Mohammed ben Ali was my father-in-law. He disappeared more than fifteen years ago!' By digging in the soil, we discovered a skull, some bones, the stock of a rifle holed by worms, a pewter teapot, two cups and, bizarre thing, a shoulder (probably of a gazelle) literally mummified. Yet another drama of thirst! The poor man died next to the wells. One hundred yards more, and he was saved!

Yet in the vastness of the Sahara, finding a well required both great skill and a fair measure of luck. Whole caravans had simply vanished because their calculations were off by a mere fraction.

Once wells were located, the real work began, as they were invariably covered over with sand. Sergeant Charles Guilleux, who crossed the Sahara with the Foureau-Lamy expedition of 1898, recalled that the worst moments were those spent digging out the wells, an operation which could take up to three days: "Suffer[ing] from thirst beside a well, that is just one more of the miseries encountered by a traveller in the Sahara." Even after hours spent in excavation, the well might be dry, or contain barely a few inches of muddy water, hardly enough for the men, much less for the animals. The hole might be a deep one with no bucket and rope to draw the water, or, if provided, the water was so full of chemicals as to be virtually undrinkable.

At the sight of a well, the caravan usually dissolved into a stampeding mob: ". . . Beasts and men ran toward [the well] and I was presented with a hallucinatory vision," wrote Lieutenant Léon Lehuraux, who watched one parched caravan rush toward a waterhole in 1916. "Children crushed in the stampede let out heartrending cries, camels, donkeys, zebus rushed with their heads lowered into the mob to get closer to the precious liquid; the women called for water with agonized cries; a terrifying spectacle, a Dantesque vision." Caillié witnessed a similar incident at the wells of Telig, where he thrust his head among those of the camels to drink.

It was usually just as well that people were too thirsty to examine closely the water they were drinking, especially if it came from a waterhole. Waterholes were small pools often idyllically set among golden dunes and shaded with date palms, "peeping from amidst the hills of sand, like a few evergreens amidst the snows of December." However, a closer inspection revealed that the water was covered with a thick green scum, was liberally peppered with animal droppings, and inevitably contained the bodies of dead camels which had fallen in and drowned when the sand banks collapsed. The wisest travelers dug wells beside these oases. Those who drank the polluted and sulfuric water were plagued by stomach disorders, and might even suffer kidney failure. But even polluted water was still a precious commodity—on the arrival at wells, quarrels invariably broke out over the distribution of "this sewer-like water."

Hunger—persistent, gnawing, demoralizing—rivaled thirst as the traveler's principal enemy. As a rule, Europeans did not find Arab cuisine to be particularly sustaining, nor particularly appetizing: "It is a point of great politeness with the Arabs to tear the meat for a stranger, as well as to squeeze up the bazeen with the sauce for him," Lyon wrote. "And as this is sometimes done with unsavoury fingers, hunger becomes an absolute requisite to induce a novice to touch an Arab meal."

The appetite of a Saharian Arab, like that of his camel, was elastic. In the desert, he might live for days, even weeks, on little more than a few dried dates, a handful of ground millet mixed with water and a little rancid fat for flavoring, which might be patted into small cakes, and salt. The young Lieutenant François Lamy, one of the pioneers of the Saharians, became virtually anorexic trying to cut his food consumption down to that of his men: "I will only be truly happy when I can survive without eating or drinking," he wrote to his parents in 1891. "At present, I am training myself for this type of existence, but I have only achieved mediocre results. I am still obliged to eat more than six dates at every meal. It's depressing." Food was in such short supply in the Sahara that a plague of locusts, regarded as a disaster in the agricultural regions to the north, was welcomed as God-sent in the desert by men who gathered them up by the sackful. They could be either boiled, fried with red peppers, salted or preserved in oil.

For hungry men, the appearance of food, no matter how revoltingly prepared, vanquished any squeamishness: Each day, Caillié watched his caravan chief, Sidi Ali, mix the millet with water, "thrusting his arms up to the elbows, a sight which would have disgusted anyone less hungry than ourselves, for water was so precious that Ali's hands had not been washed for many days. Though the beverage was warm, and very dirty, we drank heartily of it, and with the greatest delight." Those who had no food at all could only dream of it: "When a comrade came up, you knew in advance what he was going to say," Sergeant Guilleux wrote. " 'Oh!' he said, 'When I get back to France, I am going to spend all day at the table. I'll stay there for hours on end, eating good soup, good bread, good meat, everything we lack here!' " Everyone marched with their heads down, silent: "Before our eyes was always a bowl of steaming soup." The German Heinrich Barth found that, more than anything else, the lack of sufficient food taxed his strength: "It is, indeed, very remarkable how quickly the strength of a European is broken in these climes, if for a single day he is prevented from taking his usual food," he wrote.

Yet at home, the appetites of these normally abstemious Arabs could be voracious. Europeans were amazed, even appalled, at how their shrunken stomachs could contain the mountains of couscous, chickens, sheep and eggs that might be offered them several times daily in the tents of friends or relatives. As it was considered extremely impolite to refuse these invitations, or even to eat with anything less than total gluttony, Europeans found that they might suffer as much from too much food as from too little. But that was just another of the Sahara's ironies: You might drown in the world's most arid region, freeze in the earth's furnace and overeat in a land which could hardly produce a bean or lettuce leaf.

The physical conditions of desert travel were, in sum, extremely demanding, as Caillié discovered: "I have since been told that my eyes were hollow, that I panted for breath, and that my tongue hung out of my mouth," he wrote. "For my own part, I recollect that at every halt, I fell to the ground from weakness and had not even the courage to eat." But perhaps even more taxing than the physical effort of desert travel was the psychological pressure. It required mental toughness and determination of an extraordinary order to march day after grueling day over this naked and hostile land. Nothing stimulated the senses, nothing broke the horrible monotony of the voyage except the occasional oasis. And there, precisely because he was surrounded by greenery, water and relative plenty, the traveler became even more intimidated by the void that surrounded him—by the vast distances that remained to be traversed, the heat, thirst, hunger and discomfort yet to be endured. It required a herculean effort of the will to load up the camels and strike out again. Men retained their sanity by sinking into a dream world. The imagination takes over when the senses are deprived of stimulation, substituting fields and forests where only baked hammada exists, preparing gargantuan meals to take the pain out of hunger, sending clear, cool streams to slake a tormenting thirst. Like many, Laing grew sick of

> these desert, forlorn, black looking plains, these *Libya deserta*.
> The eye of the traveller roams in vain over the wide, unvaried
> superficies, in search of some object to rest upon, till at length
> wearied by a repetition of the bleak and tedious sameness, he
> is willing to pull one of the folds of his turban over his eyes,
> and to shroud his head in his Burnoosa, allowing his mind,
> which refuses to expand upon the exsiccated objects around
> him, to shrink within itself, and to anticipate in imaginative
> hope, more genial and enlivening scenes.

To the physical stamina and mental toughness required of a traveler to the Sahara, one must add a third, extremely important, quality—courage. Europeans must be prepared to encounter the often violent hostility of the population. Europeans claimed that this hostility stemmed from religious prejudice. Certainly, Christians must expect to endure many vexatious and tedious questions about religion from unschooled and ignorant men: "Do not the Christians say that God has a son?" James Richardson was asked. "That is making God like a bullock?" Small children regularly followed him about spitting and shouting, "Kafer! Kafer!" (unbeliever). But the charge that Europeans were resisted and mistreated because of religious prejudice is an exaggerated one.

Despite the fact that Islam's harsh tenets and uncompromising moral code were forged in a desert, the religion had scant appeal in the Sahara. The desert people were only lukewarm Moslems. "Many of them do not know the first prayers of the Koran," Caillié recounted. The Sahara lacked the religious infrastructure of "saints," *ulama* or religious doctors, and *zaouia,* or monastic orders, which flourished nearer to the coast. Their attitudes to religion bordered on the blasphemous: "Whom do you love more, God or me?" a Targui warrior might ask the girl he was courting. The nomadic desert tribes were condescending toward the Moslem holy men, or *marabouts,* because they were outsiders, usually city men, not "children of the tents." They respected their piety, kissed their hands and addressed them as *Sidi,* or "Lord." But reading, daily ablutions and prayer were things that did not come naturally to nomads. Their religious negligence was one way that Bedouin and Targui affirmed their independence vis-à-vis the sedentary, more devout Arab. The young Henri Duveryier recognized that the seeming religious prejudice of the desert was superficial: "Ghat attempted to appear toward me, a Christian, as a Moslem town, fanatical in its religion," he wrote of his visit in 1858. "It is nothing of the sort. Religion is simply a mask. Personal interest is what motivates this conduct."

Ironically, it was the arrival of the Christian which helped to spread Islam into the desert. Under the pressure of invasion from Italy and France in the late nineteenth and early twentieth centuries, the Sanusi order, formed in the nineteenth century to restore the purity of Islam, became firmly implanted in the Libyan desert as a force that could rally the diverse tribes and peoples of the central Sahara into a coherent resistance movement. The final conquest of the Tuareg by the French after 1905 allowed both Arabs and Islam to implant themselves in a desert where before they had met hostility and indifference.

Certainly, desert people looked down on Europeans as uncouth foreigners, believing, according to Richardson,

> That (pig's milk) forms their chief subsistence, that we have horses, cows and sheep is not at all credited by them; and that our country should be destitute of dates excites their greatest commiseration. They cannot at all conceive how we avoid falling off our islands and rolling into the sea, or how, being surrounded by water, we have sufficient room for animals to graze.

Inhabitants of any country traditionally disdain those who live beyond their borders, whose language, habits and customs are strange and poorly understood. The pride of desert people, combined with their extraordinary ignorance of the outside world, made them particularly xenophobic. If Christians were unclean because they ate disgusting things like pigs, the way they treated their women made them, in Arab eyes, unmanly: "As I sat in our tent, writing a letter, some Arabs came in, and seemed to find much amusement in seeing me write from left to right," Lyon recounted. "But, when I told them my letter was addressed to a Female, their astonishment knew no bounds, and they laughed heartily at the idea that it was possible for a woman to be capable of reading. . . . When I told him that Englishwomen were allowed to have money in their own power, and that some of them had immense fortunes, he seemed hardly to credit me." Englishmen might expect a certain amount of deference in the early nineteenth century because they had defeated Napoleon, the only European most Arabs had heard of: "Buonaparte, or as the Arabs call him, Bono barto, is in great estimation amongst them, not on account of his military achievements, but because they have heard that he has 200,000 dollars an hour and he sits on a golden throne," Lyon reported. However, much of the esteem Englishmen enjoyed in Arab eyes was forfeited later in the century when it became known that England was ruled by a woman: "I explained to them that Spain and Portugal were ruled by two other queens, but that, in France, a queen never reigns," Richardson wrote. "At the mention of this latter fact, there was a general murmur of approbation, 'El-Francees andhom oked. (The French have wisdom).' " Much of what Europeans told them of the world north of the Mediterranean was scarcely credited. Richardson's stories about the North Pole were treated as the fantasies of a demented, or devious, foreigner, which they quickly saw through: "They asked me if any Mussulmans were there and how they could fast when the sun did not set?"

Certainly, nineteenth-century explorers put down the hostility they met to the religious fanaticism of the desert. Caillié recommended an ostentatious performance of Moslem religious duties as the only way to avoid suspicion. He also fabricated an elaborate cover story according to which he had been taken by Frenchmen in Egypt and released by his master in Senegal, from where he was making his way home. But even a hurried reading of Caillié's adventures reveals that his disguise was transparent and his story found little credence. He was treated badly, not because he was a Christian, but because he was poor, regarded as little better than a beggar, friendless and an object to be disdained and reviled by the men and women of the caravan, who were themselves seldom the flower of humanity: "A poor stranger like myself, unacquainted with their language, was, in their eyes, an object of contempt," Caillié confessed. "I expected to suffer much in crossing the desert." And he was not wrong. Other explorers—Laing, Lyon, Richardson, for instance—made no secret of the fact that they were Christians, indeed, extremely devout ones. Laing even insisted on adopting European dress on Sunday and reading from the Scriptures to his servants in full view of the assembled caravan.

If religion had a part to play in the hostility which Europeans met in the desert, it was because many explorers saw it as their Christian duty to end the slave trade. Those desert chiefs who first thought that the arrival of the Christians might open up new business possibilities, quickly grasped that they intended to undermine the principal basis of their wealth. Hostility to Europeans sprang directly from this realization, and not from religious fanaticism. As exploration shaded off into colonialism, with the French pushing into the desert from the north and expanding up the Niger basin from Senegal, and the Italians and Turks squabbling over Libya, explorers came to be seen—quite rightly—as spies, outriders of a conquering people who, even under the civilized terms of the Geneva Convention, deserved death. And death is what many of them got.

A further difficulty about travel in the Sahara, and one which could not be ignored, was the sheer cost of the enterprise. This may at first seem strange, given the fact that the Sahara is one of the earth's poorest regions. It was, of course, possible to travel on the cheap. Caillié did so by passing himself off as a penniless beggar too poor to rob or murder. But he had to depend for his survival on the charity of men who had little enough for themselves and the tolerance of those who were suspicious and disdainful of outsiders, especially those who traveled without patrons or protectors. He might easily have perished of hunger or thirst. (As it was, he nearly died of scurvy.)

Most explorers preferred to travel in more comfort and safety, and with more dignity, than did Caillié. This was desirable, but it was not cheap. Three camels and two servants were considered the absolute minimum, of which some or all might need to be replaced en route. Those who hired only one servant usually discovered that he appeared on the day of departure with a cousin, "to keep me company." In many respects, the servants took more getting used to than the camels, especially for those, and there were some, who wished to travel in European style: "He would pick up the different articles of my clothing when he thought that I was not looking and examine them minutely, with a mixture of awe, amusement and curiosity which it was very ludicrous to see," Harding-King wrote of his servant, El Haj.

> He could not understand me at all. Why a man should eat with a knife and fork instead of his fingers, why he should comb his hair instead of shaving it off, why he should be so particular about having his boots and shoes brushed, and why in the name of Allah, Mohammed and all the saints in the Moslem calendar he should want to go to the trouble of *washing,* unless he were going to say his prayers, he could not in the least understand. . . . El Haj's idea of washing cutlery and plates was to break them, or wipe them with any piece of rag or the corner of his *haik,* or saddlebag, or with mud from the yard of the caravanserai.

El Haj was finally relieved of his duties when he dried the dishes with the gun cloth.

Equipment—harnesses, saddles, *guerbas,* etc.—and the provisions required for a desert crossing had to be purchased. It was prudent to have letters of introduction from the bashaw to see one safely through from Tripoli to Ghadames. These were not cheap: "At the moment the Bashaw was professing such disinterested conduct, a glance of his eye and the rubbing together of his thumb and finger gave strong indications that he expected something more substantial between them," the egregious Hamner Warrington wrote of his negotiations for Laing's letters of introduction. It might also be wise to pay someone in the caravan— a substantial merchant or the caravan leader himself—to see that one came to no mischief at the hands of fellow travelers. More important, each caravan had to purchase a safe-conduct—called *debiha* or *anaïa* in southern Morocco, *ghefara* in the central Sahara—from the tribes through whose territory one had to pass. As these tribes seldom had the cohesion to allow one leader to impose his will, this almost always involved paying protection to several people to cross the same patch of ground. Also, free-lance brigands might attach themselves to the caravan, single out the Europeans, and demand protection money: "There is only one way to get through without difficulty," the Frenchman Henri

Schirmer wrote, "and that is to buy in advance the protection of the strongest." "But," he cautioned, "everything is permitted against the foreigner," including the charging of exorbitant prices: "If you are not one of them, you pay for everything."

The most costly item for any desert traveler without a doubt was the traditional hospitality for which the desert was famous. On the face of it, this might seem a contradiction: Travelers were usually greeted in the camps of the nomads by women who immediately spread mats for them and placed bowls of *zrig,* curdled camel's milk, in their hands. In the oases, important travelers might expect an invitation to dinner from the Turkish governor, if there was one, or an important caid. But desert hospitality had its costs. Nomads expected cigarettes, sugar and tea in return for their meager meal. "What goes by this name [hospitality] in the desert is most often disguised begging," Schirmer wrote. "The Saharian feeds his guest as a good Moslem should, but he expects a present which will exceed in value that which he has offered." Lyon complained that hospitality was offered only to those "who can repay them tenfold for their pretended disinterestedness. Their religion enjoins that should a stranger enter while they are at their meals, he must be invited to partake. But they generally contrive to evade this injunction by eating within closed doors." "Arab hospitality is all ostentation and calculation," Schirmer concluded.

A meal might also be used to put a European in his place, as a mild insult and reminder that they regarded the *roumi* (a pejorative term for European) as an inferior. Duveyrier's servants prevailed upon their master to return a meal which had been sent by a Tuat sheik, as insufficiently copious and not in keeping with the standards that someone of his status might expect. (The food did not survive the return journey, however, as his servants "spilled it" in the streets.) Harding-King's servants were also horrified to hear of the insulting hospitality which their employer received.

Two mugs and three large horn spoons, or rather ladles, were provided among the four of us. I immediately seized one of the mugs and the nearest spoon and successfully eluded every attempt which was made to share them with me. A bowl of sour camel's milk and another of a horribly *murgerous*-looking soup [*murger* was a type of Arab soup] were brought in, the *sheykh* muttered grace—Bismillah—and the feast began.

The milk was first handed round. The *sheykh* just sipped it as a guarantee that it was not poisoned and then handed it on to me. I took a sip, as in duty bound, and passed it on; the soup followed in the same manner, but as no one took more than a sip the lid of the *couscous* dish was removed and the bowl emptied over the pile.

Each person's share of the dish was divided off from that of his neighbour by a hard-boiled egg embedded in the pyramid of *couscous*. I didn't like the look of those eggs at all. They belonged to that class which has been described as being suitable "for electioneering purposes." I left them severely alone.

That *couscous* was as full of surprises as those "bran pies" which are given to children to dive into at Christmas time for presents. I never knew what was going to turn up next. Now it was a half raw potato, now it was a carrot, sometimes it was a goat chop; these last we ate with our fingers, and then flung the bones under the table or anywhere else which came handy.

One particularly tough bit of goat which the *sheykh* dug out of the pile and handed to me as a special favour was quite beyond my powers of mastication. I was obliged to seize an opportunity when my host was not looking to get rid of it by dropping it under my chair. I did not, however, succeed in doing this unobserved, for one of the servants who were attending upon us, noticing my action, picked up the half-eaten piece and, retiring to a corner, finished it himself.

As soon as we had satisfied our hunger upon the *couscous* it and the greasiest cloth were removed, and some dates, some excellent coffee, and a packet of rasping Algerian cigarettes were produced. Then came tea—green tea, brewed strong—and after that, at about ten o'clock, the party broke up.

The Arabs did not always feel the need to offer hospitality as an excuse to relieve the European of his possessions. Everyone in the desert from the bashaw through the guides and servants to the meanest Haratin (sometimes called "black Berbers," who provided much of the agricultural labor in the oases) seemed part of a silent but transparent conspiracy against the *roumi*. Every oasis contained a "crowd of loafers" who were eager to help load the camels, and who "were anxious to inspect, and if possible to appropriate, some of my belongings." A good guide would keep these crowds off "with curses and blows from a thick stick." But too often they seemed to be in league with these "street Arabs," making jokes with them at the *roumi*'s expense, insisting that someone be paid to perform some dubious service like guarding equipment, fetching leaves down from the trees for the camels or running some inconsequential errand.

The guide's position in this system of wealth distribution is easy enough to understand. The arrival of a European offered a golden opportunity not only to grow moderately wealthy by desert standards, but also to increase his status among his own people. He became the intermediary between the wealthy European and the population, the man able to make the bounty flow. How often were travelers told by their guides, as was Geoffrey Moorhouse: "The man is the son of a famous marabout. He is a great chief. All the *nasrani* [Christians] who meet him give him something. He wishes you to give him tea and sugar." Feeling alone and unsure of himself in an alien land, completely at the mercy of those whom he has hired to steer him through his travels, the foreigner reluctantly doled out yet more of his precious possessions, things impossible to replace in the desert. But it was not so much the goods as the "face" which the traveler resented losing. He knew that he was being cheated and thereby humiliated by men whose language and customs he could understand only imperfectly. This increased his sense of isolation, frustration and, ultimately, anger. This is the principal reason why travelers' accounts assume such intolerant tones.

By the general standards of travelogues, Laing was relatively restrained when he reported that "the Arabs, both high and low, are as if by nature constituted beggars." He blamed the rapaciousness of their governments and the jealousies of their neighbors for this fact, for it discouraged the accumulation of wealth:

> The majority of the population will be satisfied in having their present wants supplied, and leaving the morrow to shift for itself; but as these cannot always be furnished at pleasure, they are of course compelled to resort to begging. . . . From an Englishman, whose liberality they have often experienced, they will scarcely beg, asking for a supply of whatever they desire as a matter of right, and with about the same expectation as is evinced by a horse neighing for the corn which he sees ap-

proaching him in the hands of a well-known groom. A refusal from an Englishman is beheld with astonishment and even compliance . . . is accepted with a thankless appearance of dissatisfaction and discontent.

No products were more in demand than medicines. No matter how great the contempt for Europeans in Africa generally, white men were universally recognized there as the greatest practitioners of the medical arts. In consequence, the despised *roumi* was everywhere badgered for medicines and medical advice, in the mistaken belief that all of them were experienced doctors. In North Africa, travelers had to make a little medical knowledge go a long way. Medicine as practiced in the desert was quite primitive. At best, it consisted of first aid too vigorously applied. A scorpion bite, for instance, was rubbed with garlic or cauterized with a hot iron. This drew out the poison, but was extremely painful and left a nasty scar. A tourniquet was applied to the limb of one bitten by a poisonous snake, but as inevitably it was left on for too long, the muscles atrophied from lack of blood. Applying hot irons to the point of pain was the most favored remedy, followed closely by charms and amulets, scraps of paper upon which snippets of Koranic verse were scribbled, and which were then worn around the neck or pinned to the clothing.

There were also various folk remedies: For instance, when Caillié complained of colic, the treatment was to spit on his stomach. Attempts at internal medicine were always misunderstood: "Many of the women required a great deal of explanation, as to how things taken in the stomach could relieve a headache," Lyon reported. However, another of his cases was more worthy of pity: "Her case was hopeless, for, according to her husband's and her own account, she had been three years with child. Such mistakes are frequent here, as many women take this method of deceiving their husbands to avoid being divorced for sterility. The lady left the house very much irritated at my giving her no remedy for the complaint."

Arab medicine offered a range of treatments which ran from the harmlessly ineffective to the ultimate cure: "It is thought that one-fourth die of the disorder, and three of the remedies made use of," Miss Tully opined. A cough might be treated with a mixture made up by boiling fat with coffee grounds. "If a dying person be in too much pain (perhaps a fit), they put a spoonful of honey in his mouth which in general puts him out of his misery (that is to say, he is literally choaked)." Laing complained that he had to deal with a great deal of hypochondria:

> But there were others of a more melancholy stamp, whose relief it was far beyond the reach of man to minister to: of the former cast, was a healthy, robust young man, who desired some medicine to make him stronger, a short man who wished something to make him grow bigger, and a thin one who thought some medicine might make him fatter. Of the latter was a poor feeble aged woman within a few days of eternity, to whom I could administer nothing that might in the least benefit her, but gave her a portion of Magnesia by way of satisfying her. I pitied her in my heart, but great indeed was my surprise when she enquired in a dying and tremulous tone if the medicine wou'd *help her to bear children!*

While Europeans could be scathing about the hypochondria and medical ignorance of the desert dwellers, they were forced to admit that the Sahara was a remarkably healthy place, at least when compared to many areas of sub-Saharan Africa, where a colonial posting might be tantamount to a death sentence. "The Moors are not subject to severe illnesses, an exemption which they probably owe to their temperance," Caillié wrote. Headaches were the most common complaint, as were stomach disorders caused by bad water. Ophthalmia was widespread, as was rheumatism. Cases of syphilis were frequent among caravan men, and, according to Father Charles de Foucauld, among the Tuareg, whose sexual promiscuity contrasted sharply with the relative abstemiousness of the Arabs. A poor diet had its effects: Men on long desert trips occasionally suffered from scurvy, and European doctors were led to conclude that desert people suffered from malnutrition. Certainly, by Western standards they were remarkably thin. The worst disease in the desert, malaria, was to be found principally in Murzuk. It spread to the east, however, when the conquering French replaced the primitive wells and foggaras—lateral shafts dug into the sides of limestone hills—of the Algerian oases with artesian wells; these wells flooded the oases, creating lakes in which mosquitoes could breed. Duveyrier reported that every Turkish governor of Murzuk save one had died in his insalubrious posting. But a diet which consisted essentially of dates, milk and cheese was a healthy one, and the spare frames of the desert people helped them to lose heat more easily. " 'Unless a man is killed,' the Arabs say, 'he lives forever in the desert.' " The Tuareg, especially, were renowned for their longevity, and ages of eighty and above were not uncommon, although it must be stressed that there is a definite correlation between areas of great longevity and those of few statistics. Wounds heal quickly in the dry heat, and many insects do not survive. "The only endemic disease is madness."

The constant demands made on the traveler for presents, food and medicines made desert travel an extremely costly business, a fact seldom recognized in Europe. Laing was told by London "explorers" that "expenses might be as simply calculated as the price of a seat on the Mail or passage in a steam vessel." As a consequence, the list of projected expenses prepared for him by his father-in-law, Hamner Warrington, was rejected as over-costed by half:

A rough Calculation of Expences
to convey Major Laing & Party
to Tombuctoo & the termination of the Niger.

To His Highness before leaving Tripoli . . . . $ 2000
To have untouched on your arrival at
     Tombuctoo . . . . "   3000
A present to Hateeta to conduct
     you to Twat . . . . $ 500
Do. to the Sheikh sent by the
     Bashaw . . . . " 500   "   1500
Hateeta's Friend at Twat to
     take you to Tombuctoo . . . . <u>" 500</u>

The Moor recommended by Messrs
     Denham & Clapperton . . . . " 150
Governor of Godames Ghadames . . . . . . " 250   "   700
Small expences unforeseen say . . . . <u>" 300</u>

To Purchase Camels, Horses,
     Mules, to arm & clothe
     camel Drivers, say . . . . "1000

Expences from Tripoli to   "   2000
       Tombuctoo, say .... "1000

on departure from   "   9200
       Godames,   to the Bashaw .... "2000
from Twat   "   " .... "2000   "   8000
from Tombuctoo   "   " .... "4000

                                           $17,200

N.B. These sums are certainly large but are in my opinion necessary to ensure success to the Mission as well as your
personal safety, and every One of the Africans will expect
to make a sort of Harvest of your liberality, & by thus
purchase their fidelity, it will leave a lasting Impression of
a generous & disinterested Conduct evinced by the English Nation.

                         H[amner] W[arrington]

In fact, Warrington's calculations, like those of so many of his contemporaries, fell far short of the mark. They counted the presents and
payments for the bashaw, other minor officials and sheiks but neglected
to include those for the small army of men and boys who would inevitably coagulate around their caravans and insist on payment for performing
petty duties. They packed provisions for themselves, their guides and
servants, little realizing that they would be expected to feed half the
desert population as well. Even the largest and best-planned expeditions,
like the Flatters expeditions of 1880–81, inevitably ran short of food in
the face of a population of beggars and pilferers. It was difficult to refuse
them without incurring their hostility.

One of the most expensive items in the budget of any traveler was
his camels. The first meeting between a European and a camel is always
memorable. Four thin legs support a large, shaggy body surmounted by,
of all things, a hump. At the end of a long neck is fixed a small, elongated
head which is wildly out of proportion with the rest of the animal. The
globulous and heavily lidded eyes together with a large mouth whose
jaws are constantly sliding backwards and forwards in the act of chewing
a cud, compose an expression of contented stupidity. The whole effect is
ludicrous in the extreme. "To a remarkable ugliness, this beast joins a

ridiculous timidity," wrote Bernard. "If you load her, she protests; you unload her, she does the same thing. Give her a handful of grain or forage, she might take it, but she will give out heart-rending sounds. In short, it is difficult to find a being more denuded of intelligence. . . . The Arab horse is well aware of his superiority." The Arabs disagreed. To them, the camel's seeming arrogance suggested intelligence: "The Prophet has one hundred names," they said. "Man knows only ninety-nine. The camel knows the hundredth." "Nature, after creating the desert, repaired its mistake by creating the camel," runs an Arab proverb.

However absurd its appearance, the camel is ideally suited to the Sahara. The hump, which is a store of fat, permits it to go for long periods—though not too long—without eating. Concentrated in one place, the fat does not spread over the body, where it would prevent loss of heat. By feeling the hump, an experienced cameleer can tell how many miles of travel are left in his beast. The camel also stores water in the tissues of its three stomachs, a more efficient system in hot, waterless climates than that of storing it in the plasma of the blood, as do human beings. Cameleers, when faced with death by thirst, might kill the camel and tap the stomach tissues, which emit a greenish, nauseating liquid. Without the camel, the desert could not be crossed, much less inhabited.

And yet, despite its marvelous adaptation, the camel is a fragile animal. Its endurance is phenomenal, but it is also limited. The animal's eating habits are flexible, but it prefers to eat almost constantly; if kept too long without food, it will lose its appetite and die. Caravans were, therefore, required to meander to find pasture rather than move in a straight line between oases or wells. Officers of the French camel corps discovered that for every ten days a camel spent on patrol, it required between fifteen days and a month in pasture to recuperate.

The quantities of water that a camel can absorb are impressive: "As soon as the pool comes into view, these beasts run toward it," Lamy wrote. "They dive in, sometimes even lie down in it, and at the same time satisfy the call of nature in the very water which they are sucking up in long draughts. One sees their stomachs inflate little by little until they become as large as one of those boats that one pulls onto the beach, the keel in the air, in front of the bandstand at Cannes." But a caravan of thirsty camels, sometimes numbering 1,500, often found that an oasis or waterhole simply did not contain enough water. In these cases, the attrition rate among them might be high indeed. By prodding and kicking it, a cameleer might squeeze a few more miles out of his beast until, at last, it simply knelt down. Unable to move, it would be abandoned, and die a few hours or days later.

One can do many things with a camel. One can even hunt with them: Arabs, with the aid of a long stick, would gently guide a camel from behind toward a grazing antelope or gazelle. The game would take no notice of the camel, until the hunter was close enough to step out from behind his mount and fire. One can even eat camel. This, however, was done only as a last resort, as they were far too valuable as beasts of burden. Still, if a camel was obviously on its last legs, it might be dismembered and thrust into the cooking pot. As the meat was difficult to preserve, as much as possible was eaten on the first day, the entrails and stomachs being considered special delicacies. The results of such a feast on the stomachs of men who had marched for days on short rations can well be imagined. The highest act of love for a courting Targui was to kill a camel (taking care, of course, that it was an old one), and offer a piece of raw meat to his paramour: "I cut out a steak from the most tender part and stuck it on the end of my lance," the *amenoukal* (chief) of the Ahaggar Tuareg remembered of his youth. "To offer a very red steak, still steaming with life, to the woman one adores . . . what a beautiful expression of love." Harding-King was not so sure. Tiring of interminable meals of goat stew, he ordered his cook to diversify the menu: "I thought I told you not to buy goat for me," he barked when the result was put before him. "It's beef," the Arab replied. As the nearest cow was at least three hundred miles away, Harding-King expressed skepticism. "Not cow's beef—camel's beef," came the answer.

As a beast of burden, the camel requires more delicate handling than does a horse or a mule. Pack camels carry triangular saddles made up of two pairs of two short, slightly curved sticks lashed together at the top with strips of palm rope or rawhide. Crossbars are then added, and the saddle is tied with a girth. Loading or unloading a camel is accomplished only after much confusion and many invocations to Allah. First, the camel must be made to kneel: "El Haj caught hold of the beast by the long hair of his neck and cleared his throat at him in as loud and revolting a manner as possible, and at the same time dragging his neck downwards, and hit him violently on the shins with his stick," Harding-King reported. "The camel dropped down to his knees with a grunt." The loading could then proceed. "These [kneeling] animals move their necks from left to right to chase away [the cameleer], and open a large, stinking maw bawling in the most ferocious manner," wrote Dr. Robert Hérison. "The movement of their neck resembles that of an erect snake moving its head, sticking out its forked tongue. . . . The mehari drools, vomits up the grass it has been chewing, curls its split upper lip. It seems a very dangerous animal, and its molars are impressive." Two men, stripped to the waist, lash the packages and sacks of dates in striped bags called *kerratas* to the frame with ropes made of palm fiber. Then the camel is released. If luck is with him, he will shed his load in the process of getting to his feet. Then the whole operation recommences, the men sometimes shivering in the cold dawn air, sometimes perspiring in a heat which would immobilize a European, but always swearing.

Mounting a riding camel requires both athletic ability and courage in fair measure. Like pack saddles, riding saddles are also triangular in shape, but have seats, backrests and pommels which vary in design and decoration according to the region and people. These are placed across the forward slope of the hump and leveled by a cushion formed of several blankets. The saddle is extremely comfortable. The problem is how to get to it: "When one contemplates the armchair perched so high up, one asks how to climb up," wrote Major Paul Duclos of his first encounter with a camel. "One looks for the ladder. But there is none." The solution is provided by making the camel kneel. One grasps the pommel and springs up, making a half-turn and landing with both legs astride the pommel. The camel then rises, throwing the rider backwards, forwards and backwards again. "The beast is up. One has a splendid view, but finds that the saddle needs some banisters."

As soon as one has acquired a head for heights, however, camel-riding is a relatively easy business. French officers who joined the Saharians found it a snap after the rigors of horseback training at the cavalry school at Saumur. The rider sits in the saddle, guiding his mount by applying pressure on the neck with his bare feet. A camel moves at a leisurely pace: a thick, shaggy pack camel at two miles per hour, while a more streamlined mehari moves at four miles per hour. The beast can be got up to a trot, and even a gallop, by the warm use of the riding whip, or sometimes by the prodding of a cut in the shoulder maintained for this purpose. But the effect of the legs flying about in all directions seemingly without coordination is comic, and the camel cannot sustain it for long, unless doped.

The idea that camel-riding causes seasickness is a myth, although one that dies hard: When, in 1843, a French officer, Colonel Carbuccia, formed the first experimental camel corps in Algeria, he selected his men from among those who had been least affected by seasickness on the crossing from France. When the camel begins to walk, "the vertebral column comes alive with a surprising serpentine movement." The ride may be bouncy, but it is never rolling. It is like rocking backwards and forwards on an unstable plate. Six feet off the ground, the rider feels like "the lord of creation."

When all the camels are loaded and the head ropes attached, the caravan stands waiting. Then can be heard the call of the caravan leader: *"Nemchou Iallah!"*—"Depart, by the grace of God!"

IV

OASIS

The departure of a caravan can be compared to that of a ship on a long ocean voyage. The sadness of leavetaking mingles with the sense of impending adventure, even danger. The immensity of the distances to be crossed, the grandeur of the enterprise about to be undertaken, calls up feelings of nobility tinged with anxiety. "In the midst of these vast deserts, the wells of Mourat, surrounded by 1,400 camels and 400 men of our caravan who were crowded around them, presented a moving picture of a popular town," wrote Caillié, whose sentiments must have been similar to those of other explorers.

> It was a perfect tumult of men and beasts. On one side were camels laden with ivory, gum, bales of goods of all sorts; on the other, camels carrying on their backs Negros, men, women and children, who were on their way to be sold at the Morocco market; and further on, men prostrate on the ground, invoking the Prophet. This spectacle touched and excited my feelings. . . . I imagined . . . that I should be the first European who had set out from the south of Africa to cross this ocean of sand, and the second in this undertaking. The thought electrified me; and while a gloom hung on all other faces, mine was radiant with hope and joy. Full of these sentiments, I hesitated to mount my camel and to penetrate fearlessly into the deserts. . . . I felt as if I was mounting the breach of an impregnable fort and that it was incumbent upon me to sustain the honor of my nation by divesting myself of every kind of fear and braving the new peril. A boundless horizon was already expanding before us, and we could distinguish nothing but an immense plain of shining sand and over it a burning sky. At this sight, the camels uttered long moans, the slaves became sullen and silent, and, with their eyes turned toward heaven, they appeared to be tortured with regret for the loss of their

country, and with the recollections of the verdant plains from which avarice and cruelty had snatched them.

In fact, the departure was a long and tedious affair to organize. Those coming from the north might wait weeks for an audience with the bashaw to obtain the necessary letters of introduction and safe conduct, as Laing discovered: "It was not until the thirteenth day after my arrival that His Highness the Bashaw condescended to honour me with an audience," he wrote.

> Various are the rumors which were in circulation with regard to the cause of the Bashaw's coolness: one day it was said that His Highness never received anyone during Rhamadan, which at the time of my arrival was twenty days old; the next, it was rumored that His Highness had received a douceur from another Government [a reference to the French] to throw obstacles in the way of my accomplishing that object which they were desirous of effecting from another quarter; a third day the rebellion which had arisen in the Garian Mountains was assigned as the cause of the delay, and with every morning's sun fresh conjectures were formed. . . .

Such delays, while annoying, gave explorers time to buy camels and supplies and, if wise, to pitch camp several miles from Tripoli "to get the loads arranged." Together with the delays of officialdom, the leisurely pace of preparation tried the patience of Europeans anxious to be on their way. They would inquire about the departure date, only to be told "soon." When James Richardson complained, he was told: " 'You don't understand, you see, we have a day for buying oil, another day for barley, another for skins, another for doing nothing, etc.' It seemed to me a bungling way of doing business." But, what was the hurry? These men lived by no clocks. They had no deadlines to meet. "Deliberation comes from God," they said, "haste from Satan."

Besides, there was much to do before one set out. Few would venture on a long and hazardous journey without first consulting a fortune-teller. The tools of a fortune-teller's trade were few: A book upon whose pages were written a series of "dot and dash like markings," and a handkerchief full of sand. With these, he could chart the ups and downs of the coming trip by throwing the sand onto the page and studying how it fell over the markings. Others hired scribes who sat behind tables in the streets to send last instructions to a wife or cousin, while a gaggle of men stood over the letter-writer and his client debating the choice of words among themselves. And there always remained a last game of draughts to be played. Besides, the atmosphere which surrounded a departing caravan was electric with activity, and men must have been reluctant to abandon it for the empty silence of the desert. Vendors circulated among the crowds selling boiled locusts, sour milk or kabobs with cries which European ears found grating and unpleasant. "Arabic is not a pretty language," wrote Harding-King. "As a rule when an Arab speaks, he gargles the words in his throat, swears like a cat on the 'ain, coughs on the Hs, clears his throat on the Gs, and spits on the Ds and Ts," although he admitted that when the desert Arabs spoke "with their soft melodious voices and sing-song intonation," Arabic lost its harshness and became "quite a pretty and musical language."

And then, one morning, more as if by magic than as the result of any prearranged plan, the caravan would depart.

There was something uncomfortably disorienting, almost unnerving, about the abrupt transition from the noisy bustle of Tripoli to the limitless horizons and muffled silence of the desert. The Arabs sang to themselves, almost as if to prolong the illusion that civilization and human presence as represented by the town might be carried with them. But there was no satisfactory way to shut out the savage immensity of the Sahara. Suddenly, one felt minute and extremely vulnerable. Nature itself seemed threatening, and even the dullest imagination began to conjure up attacking nomads about to spring out screaming from behind every dune.

Europeans found themselves wishing out loud that the dispersed caravan would draw together for safety: "We marched in the most glorious disorder," Richardson wrote. "Some went before, some behind, straggling along, others far to the right, others far to the left, a mile or two apart. We had the appearance of an immense line moving to invest the Mountains *en masse,* for there seemed to be no common point to which we were advancing in such a tumultuous array." The caravan spread out in this way so that the camels might graze on the sparse vegetation. But this did little to lessen fears that this made the caravan especially open to attack. In the initial stages of the march from Tripoli, this danger was somewhat lessened by an escort of the bashaw's troops. But their appearance hardly inspired confidence. "They are poor, miserable devils to look at, hungry, lank, lean, and burned to blackness," Richardson said of his escort.

> Armed with matchlocks, which continually misfire, and covered with rags, or mostly having only a single blanket to cover their dirty and emaciated bodies. Some are without shoes, and others have a piece of camel's skin cut in the shape of a sole of the foot, and tied around their ankles: some have a skull-cap, white or red, and others are bare-headed.

The land behind Tripoli is not all "dreary desert." Turning its back to the Mediterranean, the caravan would pass through a band of dunes which opened onto a plain covered with long speargrass and wild thyme. Flocks of sheep dotted the landscape or crowded around wells where shepherds emptied endless buckets of water into wooden troughs. The cameleers stretched out over a broad front would sing to their animals, or curse them, while Arabs on horseback bolted over the plain, shooting off their muskets at nothing in particular: "They would let go their bridles, start off at full speed, take aim, fire and wheel with an adroitness and dexterity truly admirable," wrote Laing.

If the Mediterranean wind at their backs brought a few drops of rain, then "every heart beamed with gladness." If, however, a hot scirocco puffed up from the south, then men and animals fought for breath as they inched their way across increasingly stony ground toward the Gharyan Mountains—a set of low, bare hills populated by peasants who lived in mean stone houses implanted in the hillsides. Here, the caravan usually rested and purchased its last provisions before plunging into the Sahara; here, too, it lost its military escort, which returned to Tripoli. Laing found these mountains fairly prosperous, covered with flocks of sheep, herds of camels and horses. However, Richardson witnessed the rapacity of the bashaw's administration there. Tax gatherers backed up by soldiers went from house to house seizing animals: "One or two men, who were imagined to have something, though they had nothing, were held by the throat until they nearly suffocated."

A guide was essential for a trip through the desert. Mounds of dirt and branches marked some of the routes in southern Algeria, but elsewhere the caravan seemed to strike out across virgin and unexplored country. Traces of previous caravans might have been blown away by the wind. In any case, it was dangerous to rely on camel tracks as route markers, as they might be those of grazing camels. Europeans marveled at the ability of desert guides to find their way through this blank terrain. Some reported that they steered by celestial navigation. Others disagreed, pointing out that though they knew the names of the constellations and told stories about them, they did not steer by them. Caillié argued that the fine eye for detail which the desert men possessed allowed them to guide themselves on terrain features: "A sand-hill, a rock, a difference in colour in the sand, a few tufts of herbage, are infallible marks which enable them to recognize their situation," he wrote.

> Though without a compass, or any instrument for observation, they possess so completely the habit of noticing the most intimate things, that they never go astray, though they have no path traced out for them, and though the wind in an instant completely covers with sand and obliterates the tracks of the camels.

It was all very well noting details. But what if there were no details to notice? Guy Dervil followed his guide over two hundred miles of flat, featureless *tanezrouft* in southern Algeria, often marching at night, to emerge exactly at the wells of In Azaoua. The feat was especially impressive as the wells were full of sand and therefore invisible, unless one knew exactly where to look: "This old man must have swallowed a compass," he concluded. Moorhouse believed that there was nothing mysterious about these desert guides—they simply knew the way. This probably constitutes most of the truth. But there was more to it than that. Like Mark Twain's Mississippi River pilots, guides exchanged information and acquired experience, so that gradually maps of the desert, even places which they had never seen, became etched on their brains. This—combined with a fine eye for detail, a good sense of direction and a feeling for the desert that no European could acquire—made them seem endowed with a sixth, supernatural sense, a misconception on the part of outsiders which the guides themselves were in no hurry to correct.

Caravan routes were like rivers, lines of commerce and communication in the Sahara. The speed with which news traveled in the Sahara always surprised Westerners. Despite the vast distances, the relatively small but highly mobile population circulating incessantly between the Sudan and the Maghreb gave the desert the atmosphere of a small village. Caravans marching south might overtake the *smalas,* the extended families, servants and other hangers-on, of wealthy sheiks on the move, the men engaged in falconing, the women hidden from view inside *basoors,* substantial tentlike structures of richly colored cloth that swayed precariously on the backs of the camels. Caravans coming in the opposite direction would be stopped and asked for news, or even food—bargaining might start with the two parties bawling at 200 yards, so that by the time they came together, the deal was concluded.

Then the formal greetings would begin: "May God give you many greetings," the men would say, kissing their own hands and touching their foreheads. The stranger was always addressed in the plural, the theory being, according to Captain Corneille Trumelet, that one was also addressing the guardian angel. "His peace be with you."/ "Peace be to you."; "No evil."/ "No evil."; "How are you?"/ "No evil, thank God."/ "May you and yours be safe."/ "No evil, thank God." These salutations could continue for some minutes while the men sized each other up. Those who did not know each other might touch right hands and then kiss the tips of their own fingers, or, if nodding acquaintances, they would kiss each other's hands before kissing their own: "How have you been?"/ "On you, only light burdens."/ "May only good happen to you."/ "No evil." "The most effusive greeting takes place when two relatives or great friends meet," Harding-King wrote.

> It is a curious sight to see two brawny, bearded camel-drivers suddenly relax their habitual *morgue,* fall upon each other's neck in a public place, kiss each other repeatedly, first on one shoulder and then on the other, finally winding up with a resounding smack of a kiss on the cheek or forehead, and then walk off hand in hand smiling with a childlike expression of delight on their faces.

But even if the men were not so intimately acquainted, it was assumed that everyone had at least heard of everyone else: "Unfortunately, the etiquette of the desert forbids you to ask the identity of any traveller whom you may meet," Harding-King continued.

You may ask him where he is coming from, where he is going to, or questions of a similar nature, but you must on no account ask him who he *is*. There is a polite fiction to the effect that every man you meet, even if he is the commonest camel-driver, is such a well-known personage that any inquiries concerning his identity are unnecessary.

Whichever route a caravan followed, it inevitably led to one of the oases. The oases are the keys to the desert. They are like islands in a trackless ocean, harbors where travelers can rest, resupply and, above all, drink. The principal oases of Tripolitania and the Fezzan—Ghadames, Murzuk and Ghat—are small in comparison with the Tuat complex of oases which curves for almost 300 miles around the Tademaït Plateau in central Algeria or that of the Tafilalet in southeastern Morocco. A flurry of palm trees set in narrow depressions in the desert floor, they appeared to travelers "like a thick streak of black on the pale circle of the horizon." The arrival of a caravan was a major event in these places: "Crowds of well dressed people came out to bid us welcome as we approached, and our reception was truly cordial, decent and respectable," Laing reported. The caravan was then swallowed up by the inviting greenery. The sensation was delicious: "Carrots, parsnips, watermelons, gourds, and other vegetables covered the ground in luxuriant profusion," Harding-King wrote of Touggourt.

Above grew quinine-trees, apricots, lemons, fig trees, and oranges, while over all spread the leafy canopy of the palm tops, protecting the lower growths from the scorching rays of the sun. The sunlight filtered through their interlacing fronds fell in great splotches of gold upon the tangled greenery below. Gorgeous dragon-flies darted hither and thither in all directions. The air was filled with the musical hum of bees and the myriads of tiny insects. Close by the water babbled through its narrow bed in a *segia* [an irrigation channel], and overhead the doves of the oasis buffeted and cooed with their soft melodious notes in the tops of the palms. The air was warm and heavy with the perfume of orange-blossom and the varied indefinable scents of a tropical garden.

Through an often dilapidated gate the traveler would enter "the dark intricate labyrinths of [the] closely built town." The streets, covered passages running beneath the houses, were of such complexity that it was impossible to negotiate them without a guide. The streets of Ghadames opened periodically onto small squares surrounded by stone benches decorated by gossiping men. In the central plaza were situated a sparely decorated mosque, the governor's residence and a number of small shops. In contrast with the streets, which contained mounds of rubbish and the bodies of dead animals, the houses were, though spartan, clean and comfortable: "Of square construction with terraced roofs, and only dead walls exposed to view," Laing wrote.

> The interior of the houses exhibits nevertheless a degree of comfort, and occasionally even of elegance, the walls of the house being plastered with considerable skill, divided into paneling [sic] of oblong squares, painted ornamentally, with recesses in which are fixed pier glasses [and] small earthen ornaments. . . . The rooms on the ground floor have no other light than that admitted by the doors which open into the square courtyard, but those in the upper stories have the advantage of skye light.

While the houses were generally well kept, insects could be a problem. The flea could not survive the dry climate of the Sahara, and outside of Murzuk mosquitoes were not prominent; lice, however, were a torment. But what unsettled travelers most were the scorpions—large, green creatures which infested the oases and which the hot weather seemed to bring out in droves.

Because the oases were the crossroads of Africa, they were a microcosm of the continent, real towers of Babel where Arabic, Tamahak (the Tuareg language) and various black African languages mingled in the streets: Laing was amazed to be addressed "in pure Bambarra"—a language of West Africa—in Ghadames, barely 300 miles from Tripoli. Arab and Tuareg nomads camped on the fringes of the palm groves, sometimes banging on the thick palm-wood doors of houses to demand food. Sedentary Arab merchants, or those with a few date palms and gardens "who can afford to procure slaves to do the work for them, are very idle and lethargic," Lyon wrote of the upper classes of Murzuk.

They do nothing but lounge or loll about, inquire what their neighbours have had for dinner, gossip about slaves, dates, etc.; or boast of some cunning cheat which they have practiced on a Tibboo, or Tuarick, who, though very knowing fellows, are, comparatively with the Fezzanners, fair in their dealings. Their moral character is on a par with the Tripolines though, if anything, they are rather less insincere. Falsehood is not considered as odious, unless detected, and when employed in trading, they affirm that it is allowed by the Koran for the good of merchants. However this may be amongst themselves, I must say that I could never find anyone able to point out the passage authorizing these commercial falsehoods.

Europeans denounced the desert dwellers wholesale as lazy beyond belief. The only position to which an Arab aspired in life, according to Trumelet, was the horizontal one: "Is not the Moslem the most formal denial of the proposition that man was created to work, either with his hands or his mind?" They failed to appreciate that these attitudes underpinned a social hierarchy in which "conspicuous leisure" was the highest aspiration and mark of prestige. Relatively well-off Arabs regarded manual labor as demeaning. When French officers freed the slaves in the southern Algerian oases and then tried to conscript everyone to perform manual tasks, many Arabs shifted their residence to the unpacified Tuat oases rather than suffer this indignity. Nomadic Arabs and Tuareg would willingly work with camels, but refused point-blank to do any domestic or agricultural tasks. These were left to those on the lowest rungs of the desert's social hierarchy—the Haratin and blacks.

The Haratin are sometimes called "black Berbers," being of mixed ancestry. Their skins are dark, but otherwise their features are more Berber than Negroid: "Their cheek bones are higher and more prominent, their faces fatter, and their noses less depressed and more peaked at the tip than those of the Negros," Lyon wrote.

Their eyes are generally small, and their mouths of an immense width, but their teeth are frequently good. Their hair is wooly, though not completely frizzled. . . . They are a cheerful people, fond of dancing and music, and obliging to each other. The men almost all read and write a little, but in everything else

they are dull and heavy. Their affections are cold and interested, and a kind of general indifference to the common inci-
dents of life marks all their actions; they are neither prone to
sudden anger or exertion, and are not at all revengeful.

The lack of energy noted by Lyon may have been due to malnutrition, for the Haratin earned their living by tending the gardens and palm
groves as sharecroppers in return for one-fifth of the crop they produced,
plus whatever else they could conceal. As the crop was seldom large
enough to feed the oasis, they must have existed on short rations indeed.
Most lived in small two- or three-room mud houses in the corners of the
gardens, or in round huts constructed of branches called *zeribas*. They
usually spoke Arabic, keen to distance themselves from their black relatives who retained Central and West African languages. In common with
most oasis dwellers, they lived a life of general torpor, stirring themselves
into activity only to pollinate the date palms or perform other agricultural
tasks. Otherwise, they slept through the hottest part of the day and spent
much of the night lying in the cool sand of the street and exchanging
gossip with neighbors. The monotony of life was occasionally broken by
celebrations during which great quantities of *lackbi,* a beer made from
fermented millet, were consumed. Palm wine—"frothy, sharp, agreeable
to drink, fizzy," wrote Robert Hérison; "it goes to the head"—could
also be bought, but was more expensive than *lackbi,* because cutting the
bark of the palm to take the sap from which the wine was made usually
killed the tree. A clear alcohol could also be distilled from palm sap:
"His Negresses kept the still on the fire night and day, and much mystery
was observed on the occasion," Lyon wrote of one Murzuk sheik who
even allowed the *roumi* to transgress the sanctuary of his harem to ob-
serve it. In any case, he noted that the men of Murzuk were "very good
humoured drunkards."

At the bottom of the social hierarchy of the oases, one degree below
the Haratin, were the black slaves. Most had been brought up from the
Sudan in slave caravans which early explorers—many of whom were
dedicated abolitionists—described in vivid terms. Blacks rounded up in
slave raids or taken in tribal wars in the Sudan were sold to Arab slavers
who transported them across the Sahara. In their eighteenth-century
heyday, caravans brought as many as 5,000 slaves annually from the
Sudan to Tripoli. Many of these blacks failed to arrive. A desert crossing

was a hazardous business for everyone, but blacks suffered most both from the brutality of the slavers, seldom the most tenderhearted of men, and from being at the extreme end of the supply chain—when water or food ran short, it was the blacks who went without. Men were usually chained together by the neck for the duration of the journey, while women and children were allowed to roam freely. As many of the women carried young children, the burden sometimes became too great. Caillié noted that the slaves suffered especially from thirst, and if they faltered and fell, they were savagely beaten by the slavers. When Lyon attempted to prevent an Arab from beating his slave, he discovered that "my inter-ference was greeted with no very polite expressions, and my endeavour-ing to prove that the poor black was a human creature as well as his master, exposed me to much laughter and contempt." When he allowed an ailing black woman to ride on his horse, "[She] was abused every five minutes by her master for feigning sickness."

Despite the horrible ordeal they were forced to endure, the slaves were usually the jolliest company to be had on a journey. Even Heinrich Barth, self-described as a zealous advocate of the abolition of the slave trade, remarked that the slave caravan which he saw in the Air "looked rather merry than sad—the poor blacks gladdened doubtless by the picturesque landscape, and keeping up a lively song in their native mel-ody." Apart from the occasional beatings suffered by the black slaves in his caravan, Lyon recorded that the children chased about while the women "walked together and sang in chorus, nearly the whole day, which enlivened them and beguiled the way. There was a merry boy too, who frequently kept the Kofflé in a roar of laughter by mimicking the auctioneer who had sold him . . . at the Morzouk market a few weeks before."

When a slave caravan arrived in one of the oases, the slaves were sometimes sold to oasis dwellers, or bought by others who would rest and fatten them for the Tripoli market. "[The seller] runs from side to side of the street, crying in a shrill voice the price of the last bidder," Lyon wrote of Murzuk, "and standing on tiptoes . . . the poor creature follows him at a trot, like a dog, to the different groups of merchants who are sitting on the sand." Prospective buyers examined the slave's mouth and felt his muscles. Attractive girls might be subject to a more thorough examination. Sometimes the buyer might spit in the palm of the slave's hand. If the black wiped off the spittle in disgust, he was believed to be willful and rebellious. If he did nothing, or politely wiped it off on his loincloth, he was thought sufficiently docile. Women fetched far higher prices than men. Young and pretty girls might expect to become the concubines of the wealthier merchants, while the older, less attractive women would serve out their lives as domestic menials. Men were less useful because there were few tasks that could not be performed as well by a Haratin or by the son of an Arab and his black mistress. In fact, they might get up to great mischief if left to idle about the house, so that some could actually be murdered if they found no buyer.

About their living conditions once they found a home, one can only speculate. According to Laing, the slaves of Ghadames "are treated with so much kindness and have so many privileges" that their situation was far superior to that of blacks in the West Indies. They were allowed to earn money and might purchase their freedom, he claimed, for a mere fifty dollars, which "affords a powerful incentive to industry." Unfortunately, they were given "at certain periods to indulge in the wild extravagant amusements peculiar to the country from which they have been transported," in particular that celebrating the date harvest, at which time "the giddy and thoughtless will sometimes squander away" their savings in this "season of pleasure."

James Riley, who was taken prisoner by desert nomads after his ship ran aground on the African coast, agreed that slaves were well treated, and freed after several years of service: "The Negros are seldom punished with stripes," he wrote. "They are extremely cunning, and will steal anything they can get at to eat or drink, from their masters, or indeed anyone else. If they are caught in the act of stealing, they are only threatened, and promised a flogging next time." In any case, the blacks were no worse treated by the Moor than were his own wife and daughters, who "are considered as mere slaves." The Arabs often quipped that the definition of a slave was he who martyred his master. A Targui who mistreated his slave was badly thought of, and any slave who was discontented with his master merely had to cut the ear of the camel of the man whose slave he wished to become. As the master was responsible for his slave's action, he had to give the slave in compensation for the damaged camel, and in the process lost face. Still, though this might have worked well enough for black men, women fared less well. One of the favorite amusements of desert men was to send a girl to collect wood or perform some other errand. Once she was well away from the camp, they would follow and rape her. The Tuareg were especially known for their quick tempers, and might stab a slave in a moment of anger.

The attitude of the slaves to their condition is less easy to learn. Some might have found the life of a concubine, domestic menial or agricultural laborer a definite improvement over their life in the Sudan, with its tribal wars, slave raids and diseases. Others, those with cruel and overbearing masters, might have been less happy. But life everywhere in Africa was insecure. It was all *Inch Allah*—the will of God. In certain black groups long subject to slavery, a slave mentality had taken hold: "Though I know that I am free in Timbuctu, I also know that I still belong to my master," the Englishman Robin Maugham was told by an African as late as the 1940s. "For how can I really be free? I know that when the French leave the country, my master will take me again. As soon as the French go, the Belen will be taken as slaves again. That is why I still feel myself a slave."

In the early stages of the conquest, the French attitude to slavery was at best ambivalent, at worst inconsistent. Some officers freed slaves in their districts, only to find that no one was left to do the work. Others actually obliged slaves to remain with their masters in an attempt to kill the traffic in slaves. Still others devised systems whereby a slave could buy his freedom after so many hours of work. But because there were so few French and they were more concerned with policing the unruly nomads than with the affairs of the oases, slavery was allowed to continue long into the twentieth century. Some officers actually adapted to the system so well that they bought slaves themselves.

As a consequence of the mingling of blacks, Haratin, Arabs and nomads—Chaamba, Tuareg, Tibbu and Berber—these minute pockets of greenery, virtually lost in the khaki wastes of the Sahara, were extremely cosmopolitan places. However, to these divisions based upon wealth, race or labor was added yet another—that of the *sofs*. In the Arab world, the *sof* is the method by which a town or tribe formalizes its internal divisions. In theory, the parties represent progressive and traditionalist factions within a community, although their positions on any particular issue may change with dizzying rapidity. Arabs contend that their differences are essentially theological ones, while Western authors tend to see them as splits over economic interests. They also probably contain a strong element of family tradition, local or village rivalry and sheer bloody-mindedness. Whatever the basis of the divisions between Arabs, their quarrels might split the oasis down to lower orders of Haratin and slaves. Henri Schirmer found that Ghat, for instance, was divided between the Turkish and Tuareg parties. Even in the camps of nomadic Chaamba Arabs, tents of the *Cheraga* (easterners) were carefully segregated from those of the *Gharba* (westerners). The two factions refused to socialize with each other, prayed at separate mosques and even occupied separate streets in the town. Richardson compared the Ben-Wezeet and the Ben-Weleed of Ghadames to the Whigs and Tories of England. But they were in fact more like the Montagues and the Capulets. The oases were crisscrossed with invisible boundaries delimiting the "no-go areas" for the respective members of opposing *sofs*. Richardson's caravan made enormous detours to avoid sections of Ghadames occupied by the rival *sof*. "The idea of a common interest," Schirmer concluded, "does not exist."

It was virtually impossible to govern this mélange of races and *sofs,* and the Turks, wisely, did not try. They gradually extended their control southward from Tripoli in the nineteenth century, but this was hardly more than a flag-showing exercise to discourage the French from moving into Libya from neighboring Algeria. The Ottomans did not have the strength to govern the desert, and they knew it. Consequently, Oriental inefficiency was not accompanied by Oriental despotism. In those areas beyond even the nominal control of the sultan's governors, complete anarchy ruled: "Ghat, like all the Touraick countries, is a republic," Richardson was told by the Turkish governor of Ghadames. "All the people govern."

When "all the people govern," quarrels over the sparse resources of the desert became inevitable. The major resource in dispute was, inevitably, water.

Water came principally from wells, often deep ones, which penetrated to the bedrock. Well diggers (called *rhetassa*) their ears covered with grease, and working in groups of three, slowly deepened the hole, taking turns to go down at the end of a rope and bring up dirt and rock in palm-leaf buckets. When the bedrock was struck, the well diggers would climb out and hurl iron bars at the limestone until it cracked and the water rushed out. A second type of well called a foggara was found principally in the Tuat. A foggara is essentially a horizontal shaft which runs into the hillside and serves as an aqueduct. The difficulty of the foggara is that it requires constant attention lest it silt up or even cave in. The principal job of the slaves in the Tuat was to maintain them. When the French abolished slavery, the foggara gradually deteriorated, and most have since been replaced by artesian wells. Water was vital for those who owned the date palms and for those who cultivated the gardens beneath them. Unfortunately, because of an extremely complicated system of inheritance, these might not be the same person. It was not at all unusual to own a tree but not the ground on which it stood. This might not have caused problems were it not for the fact that the date palms and the melons and other products of the desert gardens have radically different water requirements.

If the camel allows man to move in the desert, the date palm allows him to survive. The date is to the desert dweller what rice is to Chinese —the staple food. But it is far more than that. The trunk of the date palm provides timber for roofs and fence posts, and fiber for sacks and ropes. The central part of the leaf can be woven into baskets, bags, brooms, mats and sandals. The stone of the date can even be ground to make date coffee. The date is so important to the desert that, if you inquire about the size of an oasis, the answer will be enumerated in date palms, not in human beings. Consequently, the date palm must be carefully nurtured: The female palms must be artificially pollinated and the trees watered—but not too much. The Arabs say that the date palm "has its head in the fire and its feet in the water." In fact, overwatering can kill a tree, and was often a source of disputes in the oases.

In theory, the distribution of water was rigorously managed. Haratin or slaves drew water from wells and poured it into a network of *seguia,* or channels, which funneled it to the gardens. Each palm grove and garden was entitled to a certain number of *sa'as*—or hours—of water per week. This was measured by a curious water clock kept in the mosque. The one which Harding-King saw in southern Algeria was no more than a tin cup with a small hole punched in the bottom. This was placed in a basin of water. When the water seeped through, causing the cup to sink, the watchman would climb the minaret and announce the change of hour. The Haratin would then close off certain *seguia* and open others, thereby directing the water to other gardens.

In practice, however, the distribution of water reads more like a description of a siege during the War of the Austrian Succession than of a primitive but smoothly functioning system: "One of the parties will dig a ditch to divert the water from its course," wrote Schirmer. "The other will retaliate with a subterranean channel; fights, ambushes, explosion of mines, construction of a fort bristling with rifles and blunderbusses, nothing is neglected in the war around a well."

The oases, then, were the way-stations, the junctions, of the paths of the Sahara. However inviting their appearance, they also reflected both the scarcity and the violence of the desert. Still, there was far more danger to be met outside the oases than within. The dangers of desert travel were provided less by the lack of water than by the inhabitants of the desert wastes—the Tuareg.

V

THE
PEOPLE OF
THE VEIL

There was probably no people who excited the curiosity of nineteenth-century Europeans more than the inhabitants of the central Sahara—the Tuareg. Their appearance was in great part responsible for this fascination: tall, dressed in flowing black robes, armed with a spear, broadsword and shield, the head of each Targui warrior swathed in a *litham* recalling the visored helmets of medieval knights, from which only their eyes were visible. They disdained firearms as "the arms of treachery," more, one suspects, because they had so few of them rather than out of any moral commitment to the *armes blanches.* Perched on their camels, these men looked still more impressive. Their quasi-medieval appearance, together with the fact that their saddles, swords and shields made of gazelle hide were decorated with the cross, led some to conclude that the Tuareg were Christians who had been driven into the desert by the Arab invasions of the seventh and eleventh centuries. As if to give substance to this view, the Arabs themselves sometimes called them "the Christians of the desert," and *Tuareg* (as noted earlier) is an Arabic word meaning the abandoned of God, a reference to the fact that for many years this Berber race rejected Islam and finally adopted it in only a halfhearted fashion. The Tuareg referred to themselves as the "Kel Tagelmoust"—"The People of the Veil."

The romantic fantasy that the Tuareg were Christian infidels was soon dispelled by the evidently total absence of Christian sentiments among them. Travelers soon discovered that the Tuareg were ruthless brigands. "The scorpion and the Tuareg are the only enemies you meet in the desert," the Arabs were fond of saying. "Pillage is our work," they told outsiders. "With the Tuareg," wrote Henri Schirmer, "the idea that man is free and a brigand is so inseparable that the same verb (Iohagh) means 'he is free' and 'he pillages.'" "It is useless to appeal to their hearts," the German traveler Nachtigal declared. "They would not understand you."

The Tuareg's cold-blooded behavior was sometimes put down to an existence that hovered between mere poverty and actual starvation. Scattered across several million square miles of the world's least hospitable terrain, they were caught up in a constant and all-consuming struggle to survive. Their food consisted almost exclusively of the milk of sheep and camels and any roots they might grub up in the desert: Lieutenant Guy Dervil even saw a family of Tuareg dig up anthills to retrieve the reserves of grain and seeds. "The Tuareg live very simply and take so little trouble about their food that for Europeans it is almost uneatable," wrote the British anthropologist F. R. Rodd.

There were, however, some things that the Tuareg would not eat. One afternoon, Dervil caught a *waran,* or Egyptian monitor, a large desert lizard sometimes five feet long, which resembles a small crocodile. Short of provisions, he gutted it and tossed it into the cooking pot. Just as he was about to eat, his Chaamba guide came into camp and was invited to join in the meal: "A waran!" the Arab exclaimed, glancing at the steaming piece of meat on his plate, and then looking cautiously over his shoulder. "Do you realize that the Tuareg believe the waran to be their grandfather? If they saw us . . ." The men poured the mess onto the ground. "Roumis eating the ancestor of the veiled men!" Dervil wrote. ". . . What repercussions in the Ahaggar! I still tremble when I think of it."

For a people scattered as they were over such a vast area, and living on the very margins of survival, the Tuareg had a surprisingly complex social organization, one that reflected their primary activity—raiding. For the nobles within each "drum group," raiding was indeed their only function. A drum group was so called after the large, hemispherical drum set outside the tents of all major chiefs, the sound of which called all warriors to battle. The nobles were fed by serfs who tended their goats and camels (nobles called their vassals the Kel Ulli—"People of the Goats"), while manual tasks were performed by slaves, most of them blacks captured in the Sudan. Though there was often much competition between drum groups, relations within each group, despite the rigid class divisions, were generally harmonious. This was largely because the social system was not exploitative but based on give-and-take: the nobles offered protection to their vassals, and when they were off raiding, left behind their camels not only to be tended but to be used, if the vassals wished, for trade or domestic purposes. Another subgroup, the *ineden,* or "blacksmiths," thought by historians to be possibly of Jewish origin, served the Tuareg as armorers, jewelers, woodworkers and general handymen. They were also respected as healers and herbalists, and feared as magicians. Because they fell outside the drum group and spoke a language of their own called Ténet, the *ineden* were held in low esteem by the Tuareg. Europeans routinely referred to them as the untouchables of the desert.

At the summit of a loose federation of drum groups reigned a chieftain, or *amenoukal,* the most powerful being the amenoukal of the Kel Ahaggar, the "People of the Ahaggar." He was elected by the assembled chiefs of the drum groups, and his office therefore had no divine sanction, as did, for instance, that of the Sultan of Morocco. Although many Europeans saw him as a kind of desert potentate, his role was in fact more like that of a lord chief justice, an adjudicator of disputes among the people of the drum groups—with the minor difference that disappointed litigants might simply ignore his judgment. The Tuareg were far too independent to allow themselves to be ruled; the amenoukal's authority, as the French were to discover to their cost, was only nominal.

Noble Tuareg, sometimes accompanied by their serfs to whom they often rented arms for money or a share of any prizes which might be seized, swaggered through the oases, threatening people or entering houses and demanding to be fed. They might also raid the flocks of the Chaamba in the north, or even of other Tuareg. Their favorite targets, however, were the caravans that plied the desert. Large caravans might depend on their size to barge through, while small ones might try to sneak by unnoticed. But most caravans took the precaution of purchasing a *ghefara,* or "pardon," from the Tuareg before passing through the desert. This was a complicated and often dangerous business, as, inevitably, a number of Tuareg would all demand money for safe passage through the same particular stretch of desert. An Arab merchant might be forced to pay several protectors. But such was the treachery of the Tuareg that the merchant might be robbed by his protectors as soon as he passed out of their territory and into that of another. "The greatest misfortune about traveling through the country of the Touaricks is their chiefs have not sufficient power to control the people, for whose actions they will not always be held responsible," wrote James Richardson. "One day you may meet with the best of men among the Touaricks, the next day with a band of robbers, such is the uncertainty and the insecurity of the desert."

In the event, caravans, even large ones, became particularly easy
prey for the Tuareg. The vulnerability arose from their very organization.
Despite the contentions of some writers, a caravan was not a disciplined
unit under the iron leadership of one man whose authority "is as absolute
as [that of] the captain of a ship." Rather, it was a loosely affiliated and
mobile confederacy of merchants over which the caravan chief had little
authority: "It is exceedingly difficult to keep these various groups of
merchants together," Richardson recounted.

> Each group is its own sovereign master and will have its own
> way. The commandant is constantly swearing at each party to
> get all to march together; now and then he draws his sword
> and shakes it over their heads: "You are dogs," he says to one;
> "You are worse than the Christian Kafers among us," (myself)
> he bawls to another. . . . One would think the merchants, for
> their own sakes, would keep together, but no, it's all *maktoub*
> (God's will) with them. If they are to be robbed and murdered,
> they must be robbed and murdered, and the Bashaw and all
> his troops cannot prevent it.

In 1926, the British anthropologist F. R. Rodd recorded a conversation between two Tuareg in the Air reminiscing about a raid on an
Arab caravan between Murzuk and Bornu:

> Then we had news of a caravan of Arabs coming down
> the road from Murzuk, but my men were afraid, for all the
> Arabs were supposed to have rifles—they were only old stone
> guns [flint-locks]—and horses to pursue us. We took counsel,
> and I agreed to go in and stampede the horses, when my men
> would rush the caravan, which was camped in the open under
> a dune. The dune had a little grass on it. [He then drew a
> rough map of the battle-field on the sand.] So we hid for the
> night behind another dune, and I crept in on the sleeping
> caravan and lay still till dawn, behaving like a Tebu. In the cold
> before dawn my men came up, but the Arabs saw them a little
> too soon and the alarm spread. My men rushed the caravan all

right, but one Arab got away on his horse, bareback, with a rifle, and nearly created a panic among my men when he sat down to shoot at us from a hill. He only fired two shots and they did no harm, but my men ran away till I showed them that we had picked up the only other two guns of the caravan. Then my men regained courage. We took two hundred laden camels with 'malti' [cotton stuff], tea and sugar, and we emptied even our waterskins to fill them with sugar, and still so had to leave much on the ground."

SELF [RODD]. "What happened to the Arabs?"

AHODU. "A few were able to run away—the rest died."

ALI. "Was that the caravan of Rufai el Ghati?"

AHODU. "Yes; why?"

ALI. "I knew the man: he was my friend: and were Muhammad el Seghir and El Tunsi and Sheikh el Latif there?"

AHODU. "Yes, I killed them myself, but there was a child . . ."

ALI. ". . . who was not killed but was found with his head all covered with blood. He was sitting on the ground playing when someone found him."

AHODU. "Yes, it is so."

ALI. "I was in Bornu then, waiting for that caravan. Ai! There was dismay in Ghat when the news came there. It was you who did that! I did not know till now. The boy was my sister's son. His father was her husband."

AHODU. "Yes [relapsing into silence]; and we also got another caravan that time."

SELF. "Will you come on a raid with me one day?"

AHODU (quite seriously). "Wallahi, anywhere; and my people will come too, and many more, if you want."

SELF. "But where shall we go?—there are no caravans now."

AHODU. "Never mind, there are some fine female camels in Tibesti."

In fact, Rodd's account gives a false impression of Tuareg tactics, for seldom did they emerge screaming like Apaches from behind a dune to fall upon an unsuspecting and unprepared caravan. Their methods were far more subtle: Operating in small groups of from three to twenty men, they first attached themselves to the caravan, protesting their friendliness, making themselves useful, all the while seeking out the most vulnerable members—the small merchant and, especially, the *kafir* or unbeliever—men who might be concealing wealth, men whom no one would protect. For, despite its size, a caravan's normal method of self-protection was not unlike that adopted by the enormous herds of zebra or antelope of the African savannas when attacked by a lion—flight. Each man calculated the odds, reasoning that were the Tuareg allowed to cut out one of their members, murder him and make off with his camels, then the rest could leave in peace, as Heinrich Barth discovered:

> When a party of Tuareg appeared, one of the men shouted "Lords! Lords! Our enemy has come." Everyone reached for their rifles and prepared to offer a stiff defence. A warlike spirit seemed to have taken possession of the whole caravan; and I am persuaded that, had we been attacked at this moment, all would have fought valiantly. But such is not the custom of the freebooting parties: They will cling artfully to a caravan, and first introduce themselves in a tranquil and peaceable way, till they have succeeded in disturbing the little unity which exists in such a troop, composed as it is of the most different elements; then they gradually throw off the mask, and in general obtain their object.

When the "mask" came off, which was usually in the dead of night, the results could be devastating, as Laing discovered. "Five days before twenty Tuaric on Mahreis [camels] joined the Kofflé [caravan] and continued with them," Laing's camel driver Mohammed reported to Warrington.

> At the time mentioned, they surrounded Laing's Tents and Baggage and without saying a word fired into them, one ball striking Laing when asleep in the side but with little Injury, they then rushed on the Tents cutting the canvas and cords, on which I raised myself, I received a sabre wound on my Head,

which brought me to the ground. They entered Laing's Tent, and before he could arm himself He was cut down by a sword on the Thigh, He again jumped up and received one cut on the Cheek and Ear, and the other on the right arm above the wrist which broke the arm, he then fell on the Ground where he received seven cuts the last being on his neck.

Nor were the servants spared, being cut down and killed as they attempted to flee. No one in the numerous caravan came to Laing's defense. On the contrary, they hurriedly loaded and fled south, leaving the badly wounded Laing and his remaining servants to catch up as best they could.

The Tuareg evoked wildly diverse reactions in the Europeans who encountered them. Those of a more romantic outlook saw them as the last of the noble savages, albeit indescribably filthy ones. For the Tuareg seldom washed. When Lyon—impressed by the filth of one Targui which, even by the normally unhygienic standards of the Sahara, contained a touch of the grandiose—inquired why he did not wash, he was told: "God never intended that man should injure his health, if he could avoid it: water having been given to man to drink and cook with, it does not agree with the skin of a Targui who always falls ill after much washing." French Captain Maurice Benhazera wrote that although the Tuareg claimed that washing was unhealthy, "it's above all because they badly feel the cold." When they prayed, if, that is, they bothered to pray, they used sand rather than water to carry out the traditional ablutions required by Islam. In fairness to the Tuareg, it must be remembered that Europeans themselves refused to recognize the benefits of bathing until well into the nineteenth century. Before then, even the splendor of European royalty was somewhat diminished by the pungency of the unwashed regal person. The combination of dirt and the dark blue dye from their clothing made the skins of the Tuareg extremely dark: "It gives one a shock to remember that the Tuareg consider themselves a white race," wrote Robin Maugham after listening to two Tuareg speak disparagingly of blacks.

In contrast to their personal filth, the camps of the Tuareg were remarkably clean and well ordered. The flat camel-hair tents were each divided into a man's and a woman's half—the one containing saddlery and weapons, the other cooking utensils as well as rugs, cushions, sacks

71

of clothes and provisions, lamps, mirrors, "a sort of violin," and low wooden-frame beds which were placed outside the tent at night. The tents of the slaves were pitched at a respectful distance of fifty yards or so, and were less well appointed: "The furniture of the tents was extremely scanty, consisting only of a few cushions, some very dirty rags, and one or two cooking utensils obviously of European manufacture," Harding-King wrote.

Many Europeans found the Tuareg to be an extremely dignified people: "Of all their characteristics, the one I have most vividly in mind is grace of carriage," wrote Rodd. "The men are born to walk and move as kings. They stride along swiftly and easily, like Princes of the Earth, fearing no man, cringing before none and consciously superior to other people." The noble Tuareg were especially impressive: "You can dress a serf as well as you like," the Tuareg said, "But he will always lack something." Benhazera agreed:

The allure, the walk, the carriage, the features (when the veil is drawn over the forehead), a *je ne sais quoi* which one cannot explain, everything tells you rightly that the Targui before you is a noble." With a serf, even a well-dressed one like those who became moderately wealthy toward the end of the nineteenth century by moving into the caravan trade, "their features are less fine, their movements less graceful, their look less assured, and one says to oneself: he is an *amrid* [serf].

In Africa, where so much was strange to Europeans, the Tuareg's "Caucasian type of face" offered them a deceptively reassuring link with their own continent. The "large forehead, black eyes, small nose, prominent cheekbones, delicate lips, white and beautiful teeth," of the women made them especially attractive: "Their features resemble more those of European than of Arab women." The dignity and physical attractiveness of the Tuareg were increased by their tall, thin frames, upon which their dark robes hung gracefully: "The torso of both the men and the women is well developed," Duveryier wrote. "The arms and legs, elongated, muscular, end in small and well formed hands and in feet which would also be beautiful were it not for the big toe, which has an ugly protrusion caused by the sandals they wear." Duveryier also found the men "strong, robust, tireless." Robust and tireless they may have been. Strong they were not. The Tuareg believed that the stone or metal bands which they wore around their biceps gave them strength. But the French doctor Robert Hérison never once lost to a Targui at arm wrestling. When he attempted to demonstrate the virtues of gymnastics in building strength, they thought that he was saying his prayers.

Some commentators have recently pointed out that the commonly accepted image of the tall Tuareg is a false one, for the average height is only five feet eight inches, and the tallest Targui ever seen only measured six foot six inches, just enough to begin to interest an American basket-ball coach. But in the nineteenth century, and especially in the Sahara, five foot eight inches was a very respectable height. Although no figures exist, the Arabs must have been considerably smaller in this period: When the Frenchmen (who, as a nation, are seldom thought of as large) of the Flatters expedition prepared to go off into the desert, they found that they had to have all their clothes and sandals specially made because those available in the shops of the Algerian oases were too small.

Of all the European travelers, Henri Duveryier was the most im-pressed by the Tuareg. His description of the virtues of this noble race read like a cross between Sir Walter Scott and the Boy Scout Handbook: brave, hospitable, faithful, patient, tolerant of the defects of others, in-dustrious, charitable, magnanimous, haters of oppression, and so on. The list is virtually inexhaustible. It was almost too good to be true. It *was* too good to be true.

Europeans praised the virtues of the Tuareg for a variety of reasons. Some, like Duveryier, were young and naïve (he was only eighteen years old when he made his famous trip into the Sahara in 1857), or otherwise eager to seek out virtue in a society which they believed to be less corrupted than their own by avarice and ambition. Or, like some modern anthropologists, they may have been genuinely struck by a people who, if vindictive toward their Arab enemies, were full of spontaneous benev-olence and affection for their families and other members of their own group. Believing the Tuareg to be misunderstood, they became their advocates in the outside world, and in this way too often gave a biased and incomplete picture of desert society.

No doubt there were good and bad people among the Tuareg as within any other group. However, it is equally certain that, before the French conquest, the value system of the warrior elite which dominated

Tuareg society meant that raiding and plunder were held in high esteem. Among the Tuareg, status was measured in camels and fine clothes, especially if these were acquired in combat. The fact that the authority of their chiefs was only nominal made lawlessness a way of life, and rendered it unlikely that the murder of outsiders would be punished. To this must be added the Tuareg contempt for and feeling of racial superiority over other groups in the desert—including Europeans. The French advance into the Sahara only stimulated their natural defensive instincts. It is therefore hardly surprising that the Tuareg should elicit such diverse reactions from visitors. Duveryier's unsophisticated comments on their generous character were blamed by many for the misunderstandings which led the Flatters mission to disaster twenty years later. The eleventh-century Arab traveler Ibn Battuta might be accused of prejudice when he described the Tuareg as "a rascally lot," but his opinion was shared by many, including the English traveler Harding-King, who wrote of the first Targui warrior he met that "he was without exception the most shifty looking customer that I have ever seen."

If the Tuareg had one defect, even in the eyes of their most devoted admirers, it was that of pride: "As haughty as a Hoggar" was a common Arab expression. Despite their great poverty, or perhaps because of it, the Tuareg were obsessed with appearances: "The Tuareg are extremely coquettish." Beautiful clothes, jewelry and a litham knotted in a fashionable way reflected a man's dignity and station. When Robert Hérison dressed up as a Targui, he was told that the way he had knotted his litham was "vulgar. . . . Elegant people make a bow on the neck, which allows you to draw it over the mouth when you wish, or to loosen it, and this allows it to fall gracefully over the shoulders."

In common with the Victorians, who regarded several layers of clothing as healthy even in the hottest weather, the Tuareg maintained that clothes must be not only beautiful but many. In mid-summer with the temperature hovering around 130° in the shade, Benhazera once saw a Targui add a thick burnous to his attire, which already included blousy trousers, a shirt and a *gandoura,* a white woolen cloak or gown with wide sleeves. Over this might be knotted several silk cords, and as many as twenty amulets pinned on the chest to ward off evil. If a burnous was thought particularly fine, it might be worn inside out to show off its silk lining.

Clothes were such an important part of a Targui's dignity, that when, in 1903, Amma ag Doua wanted to prevent the chief of the Ahaggar Tuareg, Moussa ag Amastane, from submitting to the French, he raided his camp and made off with his best clothes. As it would have been unthinkable to appear at an important parley in traveling clothes, the French were obliged to wait for over a year until Moussa could build up a wardrobe sufficiently splendid to undertake talks. French officers found that to be treated with respect by the Tuareg, they had always to appear before them in full dress uniform, except, of course, that they remained barefoot, as their camels were guided by the feet. This was much appreciated by the Tuareg: "Tuareg and French officers are the best-dressed people in the world," they announced confidently.

After clothes, camels were the Tuareg's most important status symbol: "To own camels, and yet more camels, is the ultimate ambition of every Targui," wrote Rodd. "A man may be rich in donkeys, goats or sheep, or he may have houses, gardens and slaves, but camels are the coveted possessions." Whenever they spoke of someone, the first question asked was "How many camels does he own?" Many Europeans found this constant gossiping about "the quality of their clothes, the value of their camels, their elegance," extremely tedious. And, of course, camels formed the main object of plunder on raids, not merely, as some have written, because they were easily transportable, but because their acquisition raised the status of the owner.

The Tuareg had other, less endearing traits, quite apart from a disagreeable inclination to murder travelers. Begging, while widespread in the desert, was taken to extreme lengths by the Tuareg: they did not ask for something, they demanded it. If refused, they were likely to throw back their sleeve, uncovering the arm to the shoulder in a threatening gesture. This was because, in their arrogance, they considered everyone else, even the French officers who were eventually to defeat and govern them, as inferiors who were obliged to give them what they wanted as *mouna,* or tribute. Tuareg women were slightly more subtle: They would squat on their heels with their backs turned literally inches from the nose of the person of whom they intended to ask something. As it was undignified to speak directly to a man, the request was relayed through a black slave. The first word of Tamahak which outsiders learned was inevitably *attini,* "give me." The Tuareg were forever devising ingenious excuses for relieving visitors of their possessions. When members of the Dag-Rali tribe at Tamanrasset discovered that Dervil had a half-Targui "wife" at

In Salah, he was immediately besieged by "cousins" who, after congratulating him, suggested that a little tobacco, tea, sugar or flour would be most welcomed by his new in-laws: "My toilet soap has disappeared; no more matches, my pocket mirror has gone. If I listened to everyone, I would be naked."

Sometimes, however, Targui pride would assume surprising manifestations: "One day while I was sitting beneath a tamarisk tree, before a bowl of camel milk, a wheat cake and several 'Tikomarin' [small dried goat cheeses], a young and elegant warrior emerged from behind a bush, greeted me, and squatted down," wrote Dervil.

> His look burned with covetousness, so I offered to share my meal. He threw himself on the food and gobbled it up in an instant, after which he confessed that he had not eaten in four days! Come to ask for the hand of a young woman of the tribe camped close by, he dared ask for nothing, and his food exhausted, he lived on air and hope! This gallantry impressed me. I offered him a little rice and several pounds of dried dates. A year later, to my profound surprise, he sent me a pair of embroidered sandals and an arm dagger: a rare example of thanks among those people who prefer to receive rather than to give.

Such was the avariciousness of the Tuareg that serfs would sometimes be driven to shifting camp when they could no longer endure the demands of the nobles whom they were expected to support in return for protection from raids.

To their arrogance, the Tuareg added superstition. This was understandable. There is something about the wilderness of the Sahara that stimulates the imagination: its emptiness, its silence broken only by "the weird unaccountable droning to be heard on a still night," the mirages, everything which encourages men of simple science to believe that their land is inhabited by *djenoun,* "the people of empty places" or "people of the night," who might even nestle in an empty food bowl if it is not turned upside down. In this stillness it is quite possible to believe that mountains move, that they converse and even marry, that an enchanted oasis "planted with the most splendid palm and fruit trees in creation," remains hidden in the folds of sand. Indeed, Harding-King was told that many men had visited this oasis:

In its midst, surrounded by magnificent gardens, where fountains play in marble basins, gorgeous singing birds warble all day long, and trees bearing precious stones instead of fruit grow by the side of babbling streams, a splendid palace is planted. Its walls are of alabaster, porphyry, jasper, and jade; the windows are set in diamonds, rubies, and pearls; delicate arabesques cover the roofs; domes and minarets of gold flash and sparkle in the sun. . . . Many men have visited that palace, but none have yet been able to enter its doors. Beautiful damsels appear upon its roof and beckon to them from its windows to approach; but when, in answer to their invitations, they attempt to enter its walls, that palace always recedes before them, and no mortal yet has ever been able to set foot upon its threshold. Men, captivated by the loveliness of these sirens of the desert, have followed that palace about the oasis until they fell and died before its walls of exhaustion and fatigue, while those beautiful damsels still stood above them on the roof and lured them on to destruction.

But the *djenoun* are not the only beings to be feared. Men may cast spells: Hérison found that his guide, an Ahaggar Tuareg named Ag Othman, refused to walk barefoot at Djanet, an oasis dominated by the Ajjer Tuareg, for fear that someone would make a sign over his prints, which would cause him to die within a year. The Tuareg covered themselves with amulets to ward off the evil eye and refused to discuss their flocks or camels lest someone cast a spell on them. Dervil found that one of his Tuareg Saharians refused to leave his quarters at Biskra, a tourist resort on the edge of the desert, because an Englishwoman who had obviously taken a fancy to him "keeps looking at me in an evil way." Dervil also discovered that a box of simple magic tricks sent to him in In Salah by a Paris friend was enough to ruin his "marriage": "Khatty fled to a corner and stared at me with a black look stamped with terror," he wrote.

Realizing that I had gone too far, I wanted to reassure her and took her in my arms laughing. She resisted and escaped, at the same time murmuring an invocation which protects against Satan and his demons! Never, subsequently, was I able to tame her and I remained for her, if not the Devil himself, at least his most faithful lieutenant.

The combination of superstition and arrogance made the Tuareg difficult to subdue. Even in defeat, they would continue to consider themselves superior to their conquerors. When the French attempted to demonstrate the advances of civilization, the Tuareg merely attributed their technical superiority to sorcery. An airplane was a "tent that flies;" a car, a box in which *djenoun* had been imprisoned—the starter was the beating which made them go. Even when a record of women singing was played for them, they believed that the women had been imprisoned in the phonograph: "You are lucky," they told French officers, "you can always have your women with you," and they asked to look "in the singer." But whatever inventions the French could conjure up, they still remained at the Tuareg's mercy in the desert because they depended on them as guides. Ironically, the Tuareg found Europeans "credulous."

Many people (as noted earlier) excused the Tuareg's murderous behavior by claiming that their brigandage was necessary for their survival: "The struggle for life, the effort made by everyone to reach the same object, food, has hardened their hearts as it has strengthened their bodies," wrote Schirmer. They murdered outsiders to live, but seldom murdered each other, practicing within the group "honesty, faithfulness, openness." But in fact, the Tuareg seldom raided for food or for the necessities of life. They were only interested in luxury items—slaves and, above all, camels—which would bring prestige, not subsistence. Food they begged (or demanded) from the serfs who provided it for them, or took in the oases. In any case, they needed little of it. But a man who raided for camels, even if he murdered to get them, especially if he murdered to get them, was held in great esteem. In this rivalry among Tuareg nobles, the travelers inevitably suffered.

The Tuareg were also remarkable because, in at least two respects, they seemed to stand the customs of Islamic North Africa on their head. In the desert, it was the men, rather than the women, who wore the veil. For the Tuareg, nothing more symbolized their separateness, and their independence, than the litham. The litham is a veil made up of individual pieces of Sudanese cloth which, when sewn together, measure about four yards long. The significance of the litham is a subject which has greatly agitated anthropologists. Some link it to the superstitious fear that evil spirits may enter the body through the mouth. Others have argued that it is a purely practical piece of clothing designed to protect against the sun and sand, and to ease the headaches from which the Tuareg frequently suffer. In settling this debate, the Tuareg themselves are most unhelpful—when asked why they wear a veil, they reply simply, "because I am a Targui." Their blood enemies, the Arabs, offer another explanation: They use the litham to mask their ugliness.

Probably the most remarkable aspect of Tuareg society was the position occupied by women. Especially in comparison with Arab women, who were only thought beautiful if they had "such a degree of obesity as will render [them] unable to walk without two assistants," the tall, elegant figures and delicate features of Tuareg women were much appreciated by Europeans. Harding-King especially noticed their delicate hands and wrists which allowed them to wear bracelets which no Englishwoman could wear, while Sergeant Guilleux saw a noble woman whose "poor rags badly hid from view a superb body which would have inspired a sculptor." Noble women especially were conscious of their dignity: "They are never familiar like negro or negroid women," wrote Rodd. "They are gay but not infantile." Even the old women "looked typical aristocrats and conscious of their breeding." Apparently, their character matched their appearance: Tuareg women were considered extremely independent, even overbearing, and would leave their husbands and return to their parents on the slightest pretext. For this reason, many men preferred to delay marriage until their mid-twenties, contenting themselves with black concubines. And divorce was frequent.

Tuareg women were proud because they were powerful. Among the nobles, Tuareg custom determined that inheritance passed through the female line: "The stomach holds the child," the Tuareg said. Unlike Arab women, Tuareg women could divorce their husbands at their request. They went unveiled, like women in other Berber societies. While Arab women were almost always illiterate, Tuareg women were better educated than their menfolk. It was the job of the mother to teach the writing of the language—Tamahak—to her children. This was no easy task: "The writing 'Tidinar' goes indifferently from left to right, or vice versa: up and down, or down and up, poor in vowels, is difficult to translate and re-read even for him who wrote it," wrote Dervil. "Their function is to council and to charm," wrote Rodd of Tuareg women. "They make poetry and have their own way." As all domestic chores were left to slaves, the noblewoman's days were devoted to embroidery and leather work. Tuareg women were held in such respect by their men that they were not even molested during raids among Tuareg: French officers found that when they attacked a Tuareg camp, the men would flee, leaving the women defenseless. At first they thought this cowardice, until they realized that the Tuareg considered women to be immune from attack, and expected them to be accorded the noncombatant status conferred on Red Cross workers on Western battlefields.

The other intriguing thing about Tuareg women, and yet another aspect of their society which differed so radically from that of their Arab neighbors, was their attitude toward sex. It was quite common for Europeans (and Arab men too, for that matter) to claim that Arab women were promiscuous and locked up in the houses and harems for their own good. But this view reflects a prejudice that was seldom, if ever, tested. In Tuareg society, the relationship between the sexes was far less constricted. "Men and women toward each other are for the eyes and for the heart, and not only for the bed [as among Arabs]," the Tuareg said. Even after marriage, a Targui woman was expected to keep a number of male friends who were encouraged to visit her tent even when her husband was away. How far these relationships were allowed to develop has been hotly debated. The English writer Lloyd Briggs has compared the relationship between men and women to that of courtly love in medieval European society: The Tuareg woman is to be admired, not touched. "The fact that these ladies can allow a very considerable degree of sexual intimacy and still avoid actual intercourse without resorting to violence seems to be due essentially to the simple fact that they are held in great respect by their menfolk," Briggs writes.

Others were not so sure. Father Charles de Foucauld, who lived for fifteen years among the Tuareg and composed the first dictionary of their language, claimed that there was no word for "virgin" in Tamahak. He warned Robert Hérison not to go to an *ahal*, a Tuareg celebration, because the women all had syphilis. It may have been as Kipling wrote, that "in the imputation of things evil, and in putting the worst construction on things innocent, a certain type of good person may be trusted to surpass all others." But Briggs' comparisons with courtly love strike one as being all too intellectual: An icy maiden would have few suitors, whether she lived at the court of Eleanor of Aquitaine or in the Ahaggar. "In fact, the women are more or less easy, certain among them sleeping with anyone, others only giving their favors to a small group of friends," wrote the French anthropologist Henri Lhote. "But to sleep with only one man would be judged in very bad taste and a sign of perversion."

Certainly, the *ahal* was a celebration unmatched in other Islamic lands. The young, unmarried women, heavily painted in lurid shades of yellow, white and red and virtually bulletproof in their heavy metal jewelry, gathered in front of a tent where an older woman played tunes in a persistent minor key on an *imzad,* a one-string violin. Gradually, the men arrived, sometimes after journeys of a hundred miles, but always careful to change into their best clothes before appearing. When the crowd was sufficiently large, the women began to wail their high-pitched songs. Sometimes the men replied by improvising songs about battle or the charms of a particular girl. They might then elect a "sultan" and a "sultana" who would put embarrassing questions to everyone and impose penalties for unsatisfactory answers.

"The pot is about to boil over! Your donkey has got loose! Your camel has run away! Your wife is crying for help! What do you do?" the women might ask the men. "I would pull the pot from the fire, tie up the donkey, run after my camel and when everything is in order, then I would look after my wife!" would be the inevitable light-hearted reply.

Later at night, when the music and banter begin to subside, the women wandered off separately, each followed by two or three admirers, to a secluded spot while "the neighbors seem to take no notice." There, she allows herself to be courted by the men who take turns whispering in her ear or transmit messages by tracing designs with their fingers in the palm of her hand—drawing a circle and then touching the center of it, meaning that he wants to be alone with her. If she replies by drawing a line from wrist to fingers in his hand, he has been refused, but if she traces this line and then retraces it in the opposite direction, then he must leave with the others and return alone later. When the young couple are at last alone, they begin by rubbing noses. "The kiss is excluded, because it is unknown." "From here on things proceed naturally, sometimes going very far indeed," writes Briggs, "but rarely as far as imaginative writers would have us believe."

Perhaps, but Captain Benhazera, who lived with the Tuareg for six months, wondered "What must happen to the virtue of young girls with these sort of customs?" Whatever went on in the final stages of the *ahal,* the Tuareg were very much attached to this social event: When the Ahaggar Tuareg at last submitted to the French, their greatest fear was that their conquerors would outlaw the *ahal.* Illegitimate children were rare, and to have one was a great disgrace. However, Lhote claimed that they practiced birth control (withdrawal or, as the Dutch peasantry used to say, "leaving the Church before the singing") or abortion, or simply went away to have their child. Briggs hints darkly that infanticide was not unknown and perhaps even widely practiced, not merely among the Tuareg but throughout the Sudan. Benhazera attributed the high divorce rate among the Tuareg to quarrels over infidelity—Tuareg men claimed that they would not hesitate to kill their wives caught *en flagrant délit,* but in practice they simply ordered them back to their parents.

This, then, was the people who held the key to the Sahara, the enemy which any potential conqueror had to master—a tough people, inured to the hardships of the desert, scattered in small pockets over a vast and virtually inaccessible land. But wherever the conquerors might come from, it would certainly not be from Tripoli. In 1830, the French captured Algiers and began to extend their conquest into the Algerian hinterland. By 1870, they had reached the fringes of the desert, and men of vision, inspired by the American example, began to dream of a railway which would link the Mediterranean with central Africa. In this way, the Transsaharian project was born, and the stage was set for the first episode in the history of the conquest—the Flatters mission.

VI

TRANSSAHARIAN

The Transsaharian railway was not the brainchild of Charles de Freycinet, but he was responsible for nudging it one more step closer to reality. Freycinet had three passions in life: railways, colonies and politics. The first he came to naturally. He was an engineer and graduate of Paris' prestigious Ecole polytechnique. He shared with many of his generation an abiding faith in the value of railways as a force for modernization and national unification. France had lagged very much behind other European countries in railway building in the 1860s and 70s, and now that he was minister of public works he intended to rectify that.

His second passion—colonial expansion—was a direct outgrowth of his patriotism. Like many Frenchmen, perhaps more than most, he felt deeply the humiliation of 1870. He had been among the first to argue that French greatness in Europe must be reconquered on the shores of Africa. A colonial empire would restore French pride and allow her to be looked upon as an equal by her European rivals. Unfortunately for Freycinet, his was not a view widely shared in France.

Politics he came to almost by accident. On September 4, 1870, when news reached Paris that the Sedan garrison had surrendered with its Emperor Napoleon III, republicans immediately flocked to the Hôtel de Ville to proclaim the Third Republic. It was an inauspicious beginning: France was invaded, and her capital soon invested. The other main French army, besieged at Metz, surrendered in October. At Tours, Léon Gambetta, son of an immigrant Italian grocer, attempted to organize a defense by calling up a *levée en masse* of all able-bodied French males. The task of organizing these new armies fell to Freycinet. He made a mess of it, but it was not altogether his fault. Republican mythology taught that the Great Revolution had been saved from defeat in 1792–93 by the national guard. Frenchmen were Europe's natural soldiers, patriotic, warlike, able at the drop of a decree to take up "the gun behind the cabin door" with a minimum of military training. Even Napoleon took little trouble to train his troops, simply mixing in the new levies with his veteran *grognards*. A man could learn to fire his rifle while marching to the sound of guns. The rest was *élan* and *furia francese.*

Had Freycinet taken the trouble to consult the archives, he would have discovered that the national guard of 1792–93 was in fact composed in great part of deserters from the regular army. In any case, he and Gambetta, who as fiery young radicals had consistently opposed the expansion of the regular army under Napoleon III, now had the chance to put their theories into practice. Their conclusion, inevitably, was that there was something to be said for military expertise after all. With only a handful of regular soldiers who had been stranded in Algeria or who had managed to slip through the Prussian nets thrown around Sedan, Metz and Paris, they attempted to turn out the invader. It proved a hopeless task. After a few futile and bloody attacks, the French lost heart. Without officers and NCOs to stiffen their lines, discipline crumbled. General Ducrot's Army of the Loire lost more than 70,000 men through desertion, virtually the equivalent of the entire German force facing them. Early in 1871, the French capitulated.

Despite their lack of military success, Gambetta and Freycinet came well out of the war. They had earned the respect of many, even on the Right, who before had denounced republicans of their ilk as dangerous revolutionaries. Furthermore, the experience of war had matured them, tamed them. They had acquired a taste for power, and with it an enhanced sense of the responsibility. When, after a period in the political wilderness, the republicans returned to the front benches of the Chamber of Deputies in 1879, it was inevitable that these two men would be among the leaders. Gambetta's premature death in 1882 cut short the role he would play. But Freycinet would remain a premier force in French politics for half a century.

In 1879, however, only a gambler with a highly developed sense of risk would have put his money on Freycinet. His appearance was decidedly inconspicuous: small, neat, his hair only beginning to show the flecks of gray which would help to justify his nickname—"the White Mouse." But this unassuming man would become one of the power brokers of the Third Republic. Indeed, he already was. It was because of a small number of people like Freycinet that the Third Republic could continue to function at all. Bitter rivalries between left and right meant that governments could count themselves lucky if they survived for nine months. The Third Republic would have collapsed into total chaos were it not for a handful of men like Freycinet, men who occupied safe seats in a turbulent parliamentary world, who were able through discreet diplomacy to hammer out the compromises which allowed the Republic to survive another year. They could not make the Third Republic stable, but they could at least provide the experience, and the continuity, to keep the regime from choking to death on its own rhetoric and drowning in its own contradictions.

Freycinet's quiet talent must have been apparent as he presided over the opening sessions of the Transsaharian Committee in the summer of 1879. A less homogeneous assortment of people would be difficult to imagine: soldiers with some experience of the Sahara; geographers supposedly expert on the desert (but who had never actually been there), many of them from left-wing university circles and hostile to the *Africains* —soldiers whose primary service was in Algeria; engineers long on technical knowledge but extremely naïve about desert conditions; a sprinkling of chamber-of-commerce types with Algerian interests; and politicians with their own axes to grind and constituencies to defend.

The actual transcripts of the committee's meetings have vanished, although fragmentary reports survive. From these reports, we can piece together a fairly complete picture of what happened during those days in July 1879: After a few introductory words by Freycinet, the floor was given to Monsieur Adolphe Duponchel, an engineer from Montpellier, whose book, *The Transsaharian Railway,* was largely responsible for the railway fever sweeping, if not the country, at least important sections of Parisian opinion. Duponchel outlined for the benefit of his audience the arguments which he had already made in his book published the previous year. The Americans had set a great example, he told them, when in 1869 they "drove the golden spike" which tied together two oceans and united the country in an indissoluble union. Railways were precursors of civilization. Wherever the steel tracks were laid, towns and villages sprang up, communication increased, men were ripped from their isolation and exposed to the influences of a wider world. This had worked for America and Europe. It was now the duty of civilization to bestow its benefits upon Africa:

> The great humanitarian crusade upon which Europe seems resolved to bring the African continent into the currrent of general civilization, can never succeed until we arrive in the

heart of the country, no longer as beggars disguising their nationality, like Mungo Park or Caillié; nor as ambassadors without prestige, as other English explorers travelling under the protection of a Moslem caravan, with a safe conduct from a pacha of Fez or Tripoli, but with all of the material resources at our disposal, with all the prestige of irresistible power, which alone can impress the spirit of these barbarous peoples, used only to respect force and to submit to its yoke.

The image of Africans cringing before the irresistible power of the steam engine is, of course, absurd. Nevertheless it is a forceful one, and we may imagine that, if Duponchel's oratorical talents were up to much, and the committee had indulged in a good lunch beforehand, he might even have brought his audience to their feet. This passage set the tone. He then came down to the technical details. One must not underestimate the difficulties of building a railway through the desert, but neither must one exaggerate them. The Sahara would offer a far easier passage for a railway than did the western United States. Water, of course, was the main problem. But by establishing a series of artesian wells and reservoirs every fifty kilometers, joined by pipes and pumps to carry water over high ground, this difficulty might be overcome. The problem of shifting dunes could be tamed simply by planting crops on them to fix the sand (what marvelous crops these were to be, Duponchel never says). Nor was the hostility of the desert tribes a serious factor. Those who lived in the oases were "pusillanimous and unwarlike." As for the Tuareg, they were far less fearsome than Apaches. "By making one or two examples we will quickly tame the most incorrigible raiders of the desert." Besides, as soon as they realize the advantages which the railway will bring to them, they will welcome it. The benefits to France were obvious—the railway will open up "the riches of the Sudan" to French exploitation (what those "riches" are, is never spelled out). The final question—who, in the absence of the large numbers of Irish and Chinese who had built the transcontinental railway, would be foolish enough to volunteer to build this monstrosity through the desiccated, unpacified Sahara—had a simple answer: "our idle youth." The Sahara would become a dumping ground for France's social undesirables.

"The tropics only six days from Paris!" In 1879, this seemed almost inconceivable. But it fired the imagination. We have no way of knowing if anyone publicly challenged the assertion that the Transsaharian would open up the Sudan where "one hundred million consumers offered an immense opening for our products." If anyone seemed concerned by the difficulties of selling the major French exports—lace, gloves, perfume and Bordeaux—on Lake Chad, we have no record of it. The question of how one laid track through land which France did not control also seems to have received little attention. It all went to prove that the desert was not the only place where men might be led astray by mirages.

But already the diverse interests which this project had brought together, and the frailty of the Third Republic which attempted to cater to them all, threatened to bring about a general collapse. The immediate question which preoccupied the committee was, where should the railway begin? Every town in Algeria believed itself the natural railhead and sent its mayors and deputies to say so. Inevitably, they clashed not only with each other, but also with the geographers and engineers who held their own ideas based upon entirely different criteria. When it became obvious that the committee could not agree, Freycinet attempted to hasten a decision by dividing it into two subcommittees. Even this failed to produce results. To keep the Transsaharian idea from losing momentum, Freycinet suggested that two surveying parties be dispatched, one given the relatively easy task of reporting on the pacified area between Laghouat and El Goléa, and the other assigned the far more difficult job of exploring the unconquered terrain south of Ouargla. Command of the latter expedition fell to a scholarly lieutenant colonel named Paul Flatters.

On the face of it, Flatters seemed an excellent choice to lead what was to be the first large-scale reconnaissance into the Sahara. He issued from what might be termed a military family, insofar as such families had been able to establish themselves in this period. His father had traveled from Westphalia to study sculpture in Paris, only to be swept up in the last phase of the Napoleonic wars. Indeed, the Flatters family was already demonstrating a precocious talent for throwing themselves into lost causes—it was as the allied armies closed in for the kill in 1814 that Jean-Jacques Flatters joined the French army. Napoleon had been forced to scrape the bottom of the barrel to stay in power, even to enlist (and commission!) artists, and German artists at that. J.-J. Flatters was only briefly a soldier, from February to July 1814. He then took up his hammer and chisel once again and continued, more or less, to earn his living.

As far as art can be made to pay, Jean-Jacques made it pay, modestly, by doing busts of the famous—Goethe, Byron, General Foy, the hero of the French left in the Bourbon Restoration, to name but a few—for sale to museums or private collectors. He even set up a workshop to increase his production, only to lose his profits eventually to a confidence man.

The family of Paul Flatters's mother had served the Revolution and Empire as soldiers. In 1792, Simon Lebon had joined the National Guard to defend the French Revolution from invasion. He spent the next twenty-three years tramping Europe in the vanguard of Napoleon's army until, a colonel, he was finally retired on half pay in December 1815. Napoleon's defeat was also a personal tragedy for Colonel Lebon. While stationed in Naples in 1807, he had married into one of the first families of the Neapolitan aristocracy. When he returned there at the conclusion of the Napoleonic Wars, however, he discovered that all doors, even those of his wife's family, were closed against those who had served "The Corsican Ogre." Lebon returned to Paris, where he died barely three years later, leaving a wife, a young daughter and a small pension.

In 1830, the daughter of Colonel Lebon, Emilie-Dircée, married Jean-Jacques Flatters. Two years later, in 1832, Paul was born. His childhood, one imagines, was not a happy one. The family was neither rich nor healthy. In 1845, Jean-Jacques Flatters died, when his son was barely thirteen years old. One of his clients and patron of the Association des artistes, Baron Taylor, undertook to pay for Paul's education, but in Laval, not in Paris. In 1850, when his mother died, Paul Flatters was left an orphan, and a very impoverished one at that.

The combination of Paul Flatters' poverty and his background probably dictated his choice of career. In October 1853, Flatters left the French military academy of St.-Cyr, ranked sixty-fifth of 230 students. Algeria presented the best options for a fairly ambitious young man with neither the cash nor connections to secure the choice assignments in France. Since 1815, the French army at home had dozed in a tedious routine of garrison life broken only by periodic revolutions in 1830 and 1848. Ambitious men, exciting men, went to Algeria as lieutenants and captains and returned generals—Cavaignac, Lamouricière, Saint-Arnaud, Maurey-Monge, to name but a few. Life there must have seemed exotic to a fresh second lieutenant as he embarked at Marseilles to take up his first posting with the Third Zouaves. He could not have known that his choice of regiment would virtually remove him from the scene of the main battles which would be fought over the next twenty years in the Crimea, Italy, Mexico and ultimately in France. Algeria became a military backwater once the Maghreb had been conquered and the French had pushed to the edge of the Sahara. They could go no further: They possessed neither the means nor the desire to do so.

Service with the Zouaves was picturesque, but monotonous. The Zouaves had been founded after the 1830 invasion of Algeria to accommodate the Turkish mercenaries who served the Dey of Algiers, but the stock of North African soldiers had quickly dried up. Although they retained the balloon trousers, short jackets and turbans of the old Bachi-Bouzouks, the Zouaves were all French. Paul Flatters grew bored. In 1856 he requested a transfer to the Arab Bureau, and that request was granted.

Life in the Arab Bureau was far different from regimental service. The Arab Bureau had been created by the conqueror of Algeria, Marshal Thomas-Robert Bugeaud, to administer the North African population. Even after 1871, when civilians took over administrative duties in the newly created departments of Constantine, Algiers and Oran from the soldiers, the tribal areas away from the coast continued to be directed by Arab Bureau officers. For a man like Flatters, Arab Bureau service in 1856 must have seemed a God-sent escape. The French army of the Second Empire was resting very much on its laurels, as the Franco-Prussian War was to prove.

As the army lost its reputation as the torchbearer of the Revolution and increasingly came to be seen as a police force in the service of reaction, young men of liberal ideals shunned a military career. The economic development of France, although slower than that of Britain and Germany, offered alternative careers to young men of good family. Increasingly, the officer corps was recruited among sergeants promoted through the ranks. In the Second Empire, two-thirds of French officers were ex-rankers, many of modest backgrounds—so modest, in fact, that not a few among them were illiterate. Indeed, the Prussian crown prince was shocked in 1870 when presented to a captured captain of Zouaves unable to write his own name. The French officer corps which Paul Flatters joined in 1853 was of very uneven quality. A few officers were of high caliber, and with these men Flatters must have felt at home. But most hardly offered stimulating company, preferring as they did to frequent low bars, often in the company of prostitutes, and transporting the rough humor of the sergeants' mess into the *cercle des officiers.* In Algeria, especially, the army had acquired a very rough-and-ready character. Officers with connections avoided the place, using their contacts to secure plum jobs near Paris, or even in the Imperial household. Flatters had no connections. His escape had to be the Arab Bureau.

By now, it had become apparent that Flatters was far more at home in a bureau than a bivouac. He mastered Arabic, both literary and colloquial, and began to take an interest in the history and customs of the people he had been sent to administer. In 1863, Flatters wrote *Histoire ancienne du Nord de l'Afrique avant le conquête des Arabes.* This book, directed at educated Moslems, was very much slanted toward the view that the Arabs and Islam were alien importations into this essentially Berber land. The governor general liked it so much that he ordered the book distributed among all the Berber tribes of the Kabylia. To be fair to Flatters, the *Histoire ancienne* was not completely devoid of scholarship. It was based at least in part on the "excavations" carried out in Constantine as developers, after having devastated old Algiers, transformed this significant site on a rocky plateau surrounded by a deep gorge into another dreary European township.

Two years later he dressed up his research for a European audience under the title *Histoire de la géographie et géologie de le province de Constantine* and finally, in 1879, a long article entitled "Etude sur l'Afrique septentrionale des origines à l'invasion arabe" in the academically prestigious *Revue historique.* None of these shows Flatters to be a particularly gifted scholar. But in an age before universities developed the techniques (and the jargon) which allowed them to corner the market on scholarship, local geographical societies welcomed the diligent amateur, especially one who had traveled and had firsthand experience of his subject. Much of the original ethnographic research in North Africa was carried out by Arab Bureau men, and some of it, though very much of the pioneering variety, is very good indeed.

But there was another, less attractive face of the Arab Bureau, and one which led it to be much criticized. Together with scholarly types like Paul Flatters (who had faced prejudice in an army which, like most, prided itself on its battle honors rather than its publications) sat officers who possessed fewer scruples and had joined the Arab Bureau for what they could get out of it. And that might be quite a lot. Some bureau officers squeezed, if not modest fortunes, at least comfortable livings from their positions. It was easy enough to do. They made the law in these remote villages away from the European settlements near the coast and the larger French garrisons. Therefore, they were courted and bribed. The Arab Bureau officer always possessed a beautiful house. He might own other houses and a few pieces of land and even a mistress furnished by an influential member of the community. If he was really unscrupulous, he could grow rich by conniving with the local caid to strip the richest men of their property. Most were only modestly crooked, and contented themselves with the generous trickle of *baksheesh,* rather than risk scandal by becoming too rapacious. But around the Arab Bureau, a whiff of corruption mingled with the musty odor of scholarship.

It must have been difficult for young officers to resist the temptations laid before them in Algeria. Napoleon III did not pay his officers well—on the contrary, they were among the worst paid in Europe. Not for them the brilliant messes of the English army, with its regimental silver and champagne ostentatiously called for by rich subalterns. In France, officers spent their lives in the modest hotel rooms of dreary garrison towns, a pair of crossed swords above the mantelpiece the only decoration, negotiating with the hotelkeeper for a group-rate bed and board. A campaign—and Napoleon III laid on several—represented a financial disaster for men who had to buy their own uniforms, pay for their own food and provide their own horses. Consequently, a campaign had to be made to pay for itself. How else could the men pay off their debts contracted on mobilization and defray the expenses of a campaign, except by plunder? (In 1830, not a few officers had made substantial fortunes by stripping Algiers of its wealth, including even the mosaics in the mosques, which were shipped back to Paris for sale.) The remedy, of course, was to pay officers a salary large enough to make such practices unnecessary. It was hardly their fault that France had a nineteenth-century moral code while retaining, from this point of view at least, a military organization that dated from the eighteenth century.

Given their relative poverty, it must have been quite easy for French officers in the Arab Bureau to slip into the easy give-and-take of Oriental corruption. Seldom were cases in North Africa decided on their own merits. The man with the largest pocket won.

Young officers possessed an imperfect understanding of the societies they administered. They most often learned Arabic rather than the Berber dialect, which meant that they had to communicate through one or two interpreters. New to the village, they seldom had an inkling of the complexity, or the antiquity, of many of the feuds they were called on to arbitrate. Morning after tedious morning, they sat in their offices listening to a parade of problems, arcane disputes over a goat, the diversion of a stream, or the hacking down of an apricot tree, "stories which would put you to sleep standing up" wrote Major François Lamy, who commanded the Arab Bureau at El Goléa in 1891. He gives an example:

A young bedouin, obviously poor, comes in to tell me a typical story about a woman. He was married. His wife left him and went home. The husband did nothing and she remained in her father's home for a year. When the idol of his soul failed to return the young husband took a second wife, but his first father-in-law accused him of giving to his second wife the property belonging to his first, and threatened to take him to court. Now, the plaintiff declares that he has kept nothing from his first wife, not even a good memory, and he has given nothing to the second but his hand and his heart, which are his only property. How do you make a decision in a case like this? To extract me from my embarrassment, my madhoui [interpreter] sitting in his chair, and who wants to gain a reputation as my intimate counselor, says that it is all camel blather and that I have better things to do than to listen to this nonsense.

Consequently, Lamy dispatched him to the *cadhi,* or religious judge

who would be happy to judge a case which my previous studies do not qualify me to pronounce upon. Would Solomon have said it better? The man left laughing, and I am rid of him for a few days. But my subjects are not always so easily mollified. I get out of it as best I can, but only after listening to them with the greatest patience. One should never rush things. I leave it to time to resolve many disputes. While they will tell you differently, the Chaamba lie a bit, steal a bit and are slightly treacherous. They are as quarrelsome as Normans. There is not one of them on good terms with his neighbor, with his brother or even with his father. They detest each other as much as they detest us, and, as soon as two of them meet they start to wrangle.

Even for an honest man, especially for an honest man, this sort of life must have been tedious. But this is how Paul Flatters spent almost twenty-five years of his life! He had missed both the Crimea and the 1859 campaign against Austria in Italy. In 1870, he had been shipped off to a comfortable POW existence in Germany before he had a chance to distinguish himself in the field. Almost the only shots he had heard fired in anger were against his own countrymen during the repression of the Paris Commune of April–May 1871. Algeria and the Arab Bureau offered pathetically little: day after day spent in thankless tasks in primitive outposts among a people whom one could never really comprehend and who only grudgingly accepted the French presence in Algeria as *la loi du plus fort.* Gradually, the first enthusiasm waned, one lost the habit of companionship with one's own kind. Life was a constant adversarial relationship—you had to be tough with Arabs. If they suspected weakness, they would exploit it mercilessly.

Paul Flatters did not even have the consolation of family life, though he did find a wife. In January 1863, he returned to Paris on three months' leave. There he paid a visit to his old school friend from Laval, Max Le Gros, where he discovered that his friend's sister, Sara-Marie, whom he remembered as a child, was now an attractive woman of nineteen. The thirty-two-year-old captain asked for her hand, and was given it, along with the dowry required of all officers' wives to ensure that the household could survive (which they certainly could not do on a French captain's pay). But for Sara-Marie to follow him to Africa was out of the question: Algiers was considered too primitive for a woman of breeding, and the *bled,* the rough hinterland behind Algiers, was certainly no place for a lady. So she remained in Paris, where for the next fifteen years they saw each other intermittently, during his leaves or for the relatively brief periods when he was given a regimental assignment in France.

These long years of exile seem to have taken their toll on Paul Flatters's health, and on his character. Algeria in these years was a terribly unhealthy place. Disease—typhus, cholera, smallpox—regularly ravaged the population and the French army as well. Far more French soldiers perished of disease than from Arab bullets. Flatters seems to have avoided the most lethal epidemics, but the heat, the filth and the poor food undoubtedly sapped his strength, as it did that of so many *bledards.* His prolonged banishment also seems to have undermined his ability to command. In Algeria he was both policeman and judge, a man whose job it was to mollify, to cajole, to adjudicate, to see that his community ran smoothly. These years seem to have dulled the sharp edge of command, the ability to make rapid decisions, to give orders. It had been so long since he had led French troops that he was no longer sensitive to their needs or their values. This was not a splendid *condottière,* a swashbuckling conqueror. Flatters was simply a man used up in middle age.

But neither Freycinet nor the Transsaharian Committee knew this when they recalled Flatters from his desert exile at Laghouat to testify on the feasibility of laying a track from Algiers to the Sudan. To them, he seemed the obvious expert on desert problems. In 1876 and 1877 he had written three reports for the government on the caravan trade between the Sudan and the Mediterranean. Rereading these reports today, one certainly does not gain the impression of a particularly strong intellect. Couched in a flat, bureaucratic prose, they spell out the prejudices of the day: If the Transsahara caravans no longer came to Algiers (and they had not since 1830), it was because of the malevolent influence of the "fanatical" Sanusiya religious sect. Flatters also blamed the deaths of the three "White Fathers" assassinated near In Salah in January 1876 on the Sanusiya (the fact that there were no Sanusiya in In Salah was conveniently overlooked).

The reports are nevertheless of great interest, for they tell us three things. First, and most obvious, Flatters was well aware of the turbulent state of the desert and of the fact that any European unable to protect himself there would almost certainly be assassinated. In 1869, the Dutch explorer Miss Tinne was killed near Murzuk by her Tuareg guide. In 1870, two Frenchmen—Dournaux-Dupéré, a native of Guadaloupe, and Ernest Joubert—who had set out to cross the desert were murdered between Ghadames and Ghat by six Chaamba Arabs whom they trusted because they belonged to a tribe which had "submitted" to the French. In January 1876, three Catholic missionaries, Fathers Paulmier, Ménorel and Bouchand, were killed south of In Salah. In that same year, naval Lieutenant Louis Say and Gaston Lemay were assassinated in the shadow of the Ahaggar. The following year, the German explorer Erwin du Bary, who had traveled extensively in the desert, sat down to dinner with the

Turkish governor of Ghat; it proved to be the last meal he ever ate. The governor, had he ever been brought to book, would no doubt have testified that poor du Bary choked on a date stone. The accepted opinion, however, was that he had been poisoned. To these names, one can add several others of men who had been chased out of the desert, barely escaping with their lives.

The second conclusion Flatters drew, and one that follows from these deaths, is that neither the merchants of Tripoli, Ghadames, Ghat and Murzuk, nor their Turkish overlords, would look favorably on any railway which took trade away from them and redirected it to Algeria. One must take note, he wrote, of "the suspicious attitude of independent natives and of the neighboring Moslem governments [meaning the Turks] who naturally want to keep for themselves the profit of the commerce with the interior of Africa." The fear of French penetration was very real, so much so that the Tuat oasis "has officially affirmed its allegiance to the Sultan of Morocco," while the Turks had taken over Ghadames and Ghat "in a transparent attempt to put obstacles in the path of direct relations which we might establish with these oases." The Arabs also knew that the French would outlaw the slave trade, which was the lifeblood of the caravans. (The antislavery attitudes of the French, he suggested, might be played down.) Nor could it have been news to Flatters, although he does not mention it in his reports, that the deaths of the explorers were not merely the work of homicidal maniacs, but had received the blessing, if not the financial backing, of the Turks and the merchants of the Fezzan, keen to discourage French competition. His conclusion, written into his second report, of October 18, 1876, was that only by force could the French carve out a zone of influence in the Sahara, otherwise "it is evident that the direct route from the Sudan to Ouargla must be considered definitely lost." In his third report, of April 1877, he argues that expeditions of isolated explorers would only add to the carnage. France should launch a reconnaissance in force of 250 to 300 well-armed men as "the only practiced means" both to discover the lay of the land between Southern Algeria and the Sudan and to establish the preponderance of French force in the central Sahara.

Flatters's third point is in many ways the most interesting one, for it tells us much about the nature of French colonialism. After comparing prices of several items of European manufacture, he notes that in most cases the British products in particular are far cheaper than those of the

French. He implies, although he does not state categorically, that the enormous effort required to open a trade route to the Sudan will benefit, not the French, but the British. The obvious question to ask is, "Why go to the trouble and expense of opening a trade route which will simply line the pockets of Manchester and Birmingham merchants?" But Flatters did not ask that question. He simply wrote that "it is up to businessmen to decide according to technical calculations which they alone are competent to carry out." The essential question of whether or not the enterprise could be made to pay for itself was forgotten in the debate over how the expedition into the Sahara was to be constituted.

At least these reports demonstrate that Paul Flatters was very much in touch with the questions of the day, even though, in 1879, it would have been difficult to find a more remote garrison in the French empire than Laghouat. He spent his days listening to the endless litigations of his Arabs, hunting with their chiefs, and collecting animals for the menagerie he had established outside his headquarters—jackals, foxes and various sorts of birds and reptiles. And then, one day, the letter arrived ordering him to appear before the Transsaharian Committee in Paris. What a relief it must have been to break the dreary monotony of his desert existence. What was more, it was a chance to see his wife and young son. He hastened to pack his bags and take the track north.

VII

FIRST EXPEDITION

The Parliamentary world which Paul Flatters encountered for the first time in October 1879 must have dampened his enthusiasm for exploration, if only slightly. To the divisions in the Transsaharian Committee, over where the railway was to begin, was added that of how the expedition was to be organized. Already demonstrating a precocious mastery of the subcommittee, Freycinet convened yet a third one on October 27, 1879, to discuss this very question. But it too was at loggerheads. Common sense might have dictated that this decision be left to Flatters. His presence, however, served only to entrench their differences. Corpulent, with a high forehead, chiseled features, thick brows above sky-blue eyes and a neatly trimmed moustache, Flatters looked far more like a banker than a grizzled veteran of more than twenty years of Algerian service. Only his tanned face betrayed him as an *Africain*. Periodic bouts of sciatica caused him excruciating pain, while his personality was not rendered more attractive by a violent temper and fits of depression. If not actually too old, at 48, to endure the punishment of a long desert journey, he certainly no longer exhibited the resilience of youth. This must have been apparent to the members of the committee as they listened to Flatters outline his plans.

As we have seen, Flatters was aware of the dangers of desert travel. He proposed to surround himself with a strong escort—200 *tirailleurs* (riflemen) recruited in the Algerian Tell, the mountainous region near the Mediterranean coast, and armed with bolt-action chassepot rifles. However, most of the committee objected that a strongly armed column would either intimidate the Tuareg or inspire them to retaliate against what they must see as an invasion of their territory. Diplomacy, not force, was the way to proceed in the desert. A few realists spoke against this view: "You may say that you want to be peace-loving," the ex-commander of Ouargla, General Arnaudeau, told them. "You can be as peace-loving as you like. But what is the good of having yourself assassinated peacefully?" The general's warnings were brushed aside. The subcommittee was foundering, split between soldiers and civilians. Freycinet had a quiet word with the lieutenant colonel: "Must modify your plans . . . whole thing will collapse . . . just a few minor rearrangements to satisfy opinion." Flatters allowed himself to be persuaded, so that Freycinet could announce that "Monsieur le Colonel Flatters has now modified his plan, and the new expedition which he proposed to undertake will be organized upon a completely different basis." That "basis" was spelled out in a subsequent letter to Flatters from Freycinet dated November 7, 1879: a "native escort" with which he was to "establish contact with the Tuareg chiefs and try to obtain their support." He ended by encouraging Flatters "to hasten your preparations for departure."

This was gratuitous advice. No one knew better than Flatters that winter is the best time to travel in the desert. But as a result of the delays and debates of the Transsaharian Committee, the desert crossing could not begin before spring. The debates had also attracted a good deal of public attention, which meant that there was no shortage of applicants eager to join the mission. Flatters selected his European collaborators; thirty-four-year-old Captain Pierre Masson, regarded as one of the army's most promising officers, would act as his chief of staff. Two civilian engineers, Emile Beringer and Jules Roche—together with two employees of the Ponts et Chaussées, the department of bridges and highways, Cabaillot and Rabourdin—would help to survey the route. Major Robert Guiard, an army doctor, artillery Captain Frédéric Bernard, sub-lieutenants Frédéric Le Châtelier and Henri Brosselard, and several batmen rounded out the European contingent. They spent the rest of November and December in Paris organizing the departure. In early January, these men gathered at the Gare de Lyon with a few members of their families who had come to see them off. The atmosphere was subdued rather than gay as they boarded the train for Marseilles.

Algiers in 1880 was just beginning to take on the look of a civilized town: the Boulevard du Front de Mer, supported by vaulted arches, connected the harbor with the Place du Gouvernement on the bluff above. From there, one could look out over the almost perfect semicircle of the Bay of Algiers filled with the small wooden boats of the Maltese and Neapolitan fishermen bobbing in the breeze, the larger steamers and "that happy little boat that goes to France." (Everyone dreamed of boarding it for the crossing home, sooner rather than later). Behind the seafront a multitude of terraces, minarets and houses of startling whiteness climbed the hill until they disappeared into the "somber greenery" of pine, carob and olive trees which clothed the summit. In the narrow, twisting streets of the Arab quarter, merchants sat before pyramids of oranges, sacks of herbs and spices, pieces of raw, dripping meat or fires over which brochettes of lamb were gently smoking. The air was permeated with the soft, indefinable odor of an Arab *souk,* or marketplace. The outline of the Kabylia Mountains, some snowcapped, stood like sentinels above the town. The air seemed to vibrate with sunlight.

And yet, despite its splendid situation, Algiers was not a beautiful town. When the French had invaded it in 1830, they had destroyed much of the old center, replacing the well-adapted Moorish houses with ones of European design, many of which were so poorly built that they collapsed. Napoleon III had ordered the construction of the Place du Gouvernement to give the jumble of buildings a touch of civic dignity: Its arcades contained shops and cafés where one could sip coffee and admire the white crenellated walls, cupolas and domes and high square minaret of the Djena-el-Djedid mosque, one of the few Moorish buildings to have survived French redevelopment. Through this square passed the cosmopolitan life of Algiers—mountaineers from the Kabylia, their heads swathed in turbans, Arab peasants wrapped in their cloaks of red wool, Neapolitan fishermen in blue trousers, the inevitable pipe clenched between their teeth, Spaniards and Italians who worked in the town's many building sites until they could save up enough money to purchase a small farm in the bled. The army was everywhere in evidence, the resplendent uniforms of the Armée d'Afrique adding a splash of martial color to what was already a splendidly barbarous parade. The schizophrenia of Algiers society was most apparent in the dress of the Jewish men: They wore traditional embroidered waistcoats and black balloon trousers, but their shoes and hats were European. "They have their feet and heads in civilization," wrote Trumelet, "the rest in Barbary."

Beyond its color and social diversity, however, Algeria was a deeply unhappy country. Impoverished peasants and the uprooted members of the urban proletariat from the Mediterranean littoral, only half of whom were French in 1880, had flocked to Algeria in the thousands. The Spaniards usually brought their families and most often settled small homesteads in the west, toward Morocco, so much so that Oran became very much a Spanish town. Because the Spaniards put down roots, they tended to make good citizens. Not so the Frenchmen and Italians, who came without their families to seek their fortunes and who usually ended up competing with Arabs for menial jobs, living in hot, overcrowded slums where most of the cooking was done in the stairwells, drinking, getting into fights where the principal weapon was the head (and the loser always drew a knife) and into debt with Jews who loaned money at fifty percent interest. Indeed, Algiers acquired a reputation for high crime and low morals—men spent their time in the town's low bars and cafés, in the Arab brothels in the Casbah (or, if feeling flush, with Spanish girls in the European *maisons d'aisances* lower down the hill) or simply taking up with women whom they seldom troubled to marry. So many children were regularly abandoned on the steps of the cathedral that the Bishop of Algiers, Monseigneur Dupuch, had to establish an orphanage at Ben Aknoun to take care of them.

Economically, Algeria lived in a permanent depression. For decades farming was a gamble, because of the insecurity of the countryside, the aridity of the soil and the difficulty of getting crops to market. After the phylloxera epidemic wiped out the vineyards of metropolitan France in the 1870s, Algeria enjoyed a brief period of relative prosperity as a wine-growing area. But with the reestablishment of the French vineyards, the viticole economy in Algeria remained a depressed one. Virtually the only way to make money in Algiers was on government contracts.

Algerian society was as politically volatile as it was socially diverse. Algeria had been run as a military colony until the Third Republic handed the job to the civil administration following the Franco-Prussian War, and in the process allowed the various divisions and animosities in Algerian society to assume a political form. Deputies carved out constituencies among Italians, French and Spaniards, appealed to the lowest instincts and racism of the European population, to their fear that one day they might be cast out by the subdued but sullen mass of Moslems. To D. F. Sarmiento, a future president of Argentina, who visited Algeria in 1845, "The colonists seemed to feel as if they were living in the crater of an inextinguishable volcano." When all else failed, the politicians could play the anti-Semitic card: "In Algeria, anti-Semitism is the best form of class struggle," declared the Algerian socialist René Viviani, who would become French Prime Minister in 1914. Riots against Jews—nasty, distasteful, but fortunately seldom very bloody—not infrequently broke out, stimulated by the frustrations of a socially and economically insecure white population, a frustration typified by their adaptation of the words of the *Marseillaise* into an anti-Semitic anthem.

His official reception in Algiers was cordial, but to Flatters's surprise, the Algiers press was hostile, denouncing the expedition as a waste of money. At Constantine, the party put up for eight days at the Hôtel d'Orient, which was soon assaulted by merchants eager to sell horses, presents to be distributed en route, and other goods which could not be purchased in France. The hotel soon resembled a warehouse, the rooms piled high with packages. The keenness of the merchants to close a deal was such that Flatters's batman, Corporal Bâcle, pitched one persistent Arab down the stairs. On January 25, 1880, they left Constantine, moving south under a leaden sky. A fine winter drizzle turned to slushy snow toward nightfall. The road soon became a quagmire. The horses slipped and fell in the mud, and even the carriage carrying Flatters and the four engineers overturned at midnight in "a detestable cesspool," obliging them to walk ten miles in the black of early morning. The miseries of the Frenchmen were only partially mitigated by the joy of the inhabitants, who had not seen rain in four years. At the Kantara Gorge, the weather changed as if by magic. To the north of this gray wall, the late winter weather of the Tell remained cold and wet. One passed through "the mouth of the desert" into summer. The deep green sprawl of Biskra lay at their feet, bathed in a warm sun.

South of Biskra, the track continued over a "lugubrious" clay plain, the route marked by small mounds of mud and sticks. At intervals of a day's march, caravanserai had been established by the French—spartan blocks of gray mud built beside a well with rooms for officers and a dormitory for everyone else. Here, a solitary traveler could always purchase a bowl of *murger* from the Arab custodian, a soup made of brackish water into which one added "several onions, a quantity of garlic, a handful or two of Arab pepper and any kitchen refuse which may be handy." The small caravan followed the Wadi Righ, through dunes and past small promontories capped with the forts called *ksars,* until it arrived at Touggourt.

Approached from the north, Touggourt appeared an "immense forest" of 400,000 date palms set in a small depression surrounded by dunes. The town was a maze of tunnels, the streets having been roofed over to keep out the sun. From time to time, a space allowed light and air to enter, and people to congregate on "raised seats of earth blackened and polished by continual use." These tunnels teemed with humanity:

Men sat upon the seats at the side, knitting socks, sewing burnouses, plaiting fans from slips of palm leaves, smoking, talking, or cobbling their shoes. Others stretched themselves out
at full length, drew the hoods of their burnouses over their
heads, and, with their shoes for a pillow, sleep the sleep of the
lazy and the unemployed. Children swarmed everywhere. Little
girls of five, clad in dark blue, staggered along, carrying on
their backs smaller children clad in—well, very little at all.
Children sprawled upon the seats and round the knees of their
fathers and big brothers. Boys on stilts formed from the mid-
rib of a palm leaf, with a block of wood tied on to it almost a
foot from the ground, ran along, crying out imperiously "Treg!
Treg!" [way], to clear the road. Gaunt, hungry-looking dogs
on the lookout for garbage slunk by, and goats of the black,
hornless breed of Touggourt hurried bleating past, to disap-
pear suddenly through an open door into an Arab house beyond. Now and then a dyer from the market pushed his donkey
laden with blue and bright red cloths through the throng.
Arabs, bringing home their dinner of charred sheeps' heads
and trotters, mixed with the crowd. Wild-looking specimens of
humanity from the desert came along with donkey-loads of
firewood, and women swathed entirely in dark-blue cotton,
showing not even an eye, carrying water in quaintly shaped
earthenware jars to their houses from the wells, hurried fur-
tively by, their anklets clinking with every step they took. Sometimes a *sheykh* in his scarlet burnous rode by on a mule, or
an Arab trooper from a spahi regiment, ducking his head to
avoid the palm-trunk rafters of the lower parts of the road,
emerged from one of the darker tunnels, and unceremoniously
scattered the crowd in all directions as he trotted through
them.

Caravans like Flatters's camped outside the walls, where "the smell
of camels, the Arabs' cooking, and the smoke of their fires hung heavily
in the warm, still air. The hum of the old city behind mingled with the
low gurglings and grunts of the camels, the crackling of the fires, and the
quiet, guttural speech of the men."

Flatters did not retain a pleasant memory of Touggourt; "The Jews,
who are many in this town, bought up everything, so they could sell at a

higher price," he wrote. "Therefore, we shall buy nothing." This was not quite true. He did buy eight camels. And other members of the expedition appreciated the stores of the Jewish merchants, stocked with everything from glassware to good wines: "The most varied and the best known," Captain Bernard wrote, "which we discovered with stupefaction showing off their distinguished labels between a piece of calico and a pair of boots." Touggourt offered other pleasures, such as, for instance, the gardens of the Agha, with their immense number of quail and doves: "The new wheat forms a lawn of deep green between magnificent alleys of gigantic palm trees. . . . The gardens are well maintained and bisected in every direction by little brooks of clear water which flow freely."

Some no doubt took the opportunity to visit the Arab café, where the men played *damwah,* a sort of Arab draughts, while two girls, Oulad Nails from the mountains to the north who, it was said, worked as dancers and prostitutes until they could collect enough money for a dowry, danced over the floor of trampled earth accompanied by "a deafening banging and sweeking" from a small band. From time to time, the dancers would stop and put their scarves over the shoulder of a man, a sign that they wanted money. He would lick a franc piece and stick it to the forehead of one of them. But the officers and civilians of the mission had a better look at Arab dancing during a dinner given for them by the Agha: "The Nailiat girls, dressed in their best clothes, the latest Saharian fashion, began to walk, slide rather, in cadence to the strange rhythm of Arab music, so monotonous yet so attractive," Bernard recorded. "It is a sort of quadrille in which the figures possess a most attractive originality and character. The dancers cross, turn slowly, put out their bare arms covered with gold bracelets with gestures of a nobility and fullness which have nothing in common with the jumping about of our modern dances." The men watched this entertainment "lazily resting their elbows on a pile of cushions while drinking their coffee and smoking their kef."

At Touggourt, the chief of the *zaouia* (monastery) of Temasin, which loomed over the town like a medieval fortress, offered Flatters a *muqaddam*—one of his senior administrators—to accompany the mission. This offer touched off a brief argument between Flatters and Lieutenant Le Châtelier, who feared that the religious prestige of the *muqaddam* might undermine the authority of the commander, especially with the Chaamba cameleers, who were not subject to military discipline. Perhaps Flatters interpreted this as an expression of lack of confidence, for he exploded with rage, telling Le Châtelier that he would prefer to leave all of the Europeans behind rather than dispense with the services of the *muqaddam*. There the argument ended. But it suggests that many of the officers doubted Flatters's abilities as a commander, and possibly doubted the wisdom of launching an expedition composed of such diverse and potentially undisciplined elements into dangerous territory. This was the first display of an open rift in the expedition.

Ouargla, where the expedition would truly begin, was reached on February 25, 1880. "What a magic spectacle," Bernard wrote. "It is an immense plain of white sand, dazzling beneath the rays of a fiery sun. A chain of strangely jagged cliffs close it in on all sides, forming a reddish backdrop for a grandiose half-circle of 800,000 palm trees of the oasis . . . the somber greenery of an immense forest." The entry into the oasis matched the magnificence of the view: Flatters was met by the Agha of Ouargla, Abd-el-Kader ben Amar, dressed in a white burnous, his horse carrying saddlebags made of panther hide. The simplicity of the Agha's dress contrasted sharply with the red burnouses and highly decorated saddlery of his entourage. Horsemen galloped about firing their rifles into the air, while a small band added to the din with their "awful instruments." The Frenchmen made their way slowly into the oasis in the middle of a swarm of people, "men and children ran between the legs of our horses who whinnied and grew nervous," Bernard remembered. "In front of the Casbah, the Arabs carried out one last fantasia, and it was in a swirl of dust and smoke that we dismounted and entered the building," while the ululations of the women echoed over the rooftops.

Ouargla lacked the architectural dignity of Touggourt. "Everything is in ruins in Ouargla," Duveryier had written, "habitations, inhabitants, even morals." Most of the houses were one-story affairs built of sun-dried brick called *tob*. Small, triangular windows punctured the white-washed walls seemingly at random, as did low doors which were almost as wide as they were tall, and which were surmounted by crude mud latticework. These doors also bore huge wooden locks which were opened with keys the size of a policeman's truncheon. In the middle of a tortuous labyrinth of streets sat the *ksar*. Behind its high walls, square towers and moat full of stagnant water, an animated market opened each morning at dawn and continued until it became too hot to trade, which was around ten o'clock. Merchants sat cross-legged beside baskets full of vegetables, dates, charcoal or *guerbas* full of stinking, rancid butter which was pockmarked with the traces of sampling fingers. The market was organized in the medieval fashion, each product occupying a section of the dusty square. The butchers' corner was the least agreeable: The decapitated carcasses of sheep dangled by their hind legs next to the hind-quarters of camels. Flies coagulated on the raw dripping meat. The place reeked of pestilence. Perhaps it was to cover these odors that many oasis dwellers stuffed scented things in one nostril: "The effect is ludicrous in the extreme," Harding-King wrote. "To see a negro, for instance, walking about with some bright coloured flower or piece of orange peel, or, as I once saw, a small onion sticking from one of his expansive nostrils and showing in startling contrast to the shiny blackness of his face is sufficient to provoke a smile from even the most wooden-faced individual in existence."

In small shops measuring barely a few yards square which burrowed beneath the arcades that surrounded the square, traders from the Mzab, a string of oases set in a deep valley around the town of Ghardaia, sold candles, matches and soap, as well as products of Arab manufacture—knives, slippers, rope, *haiks* and sandals. Mzabites formed a dissident religious sect, sometimes called the Puritans of Islam, which had sought peace by occupying a remote oasis. Ghardaia became the Salt Lake City of the Sahara. In other essential ways, however, the Mzabites were more like Jews than Mormons: Industrious, shrewd bargainers, their close-knit family groups drawn even tighter by a sense of religious difference, the Mzabites had managed virtually to monopolize trade in the Saharian oases. (Jews seldom wandered this far south, although one or two had followed the French flag there: "The Jew and the flea are two pests which one does not meet in the desert," the Saharian Arabs said.) The Mzabites now demonstrated their business acumen: One of the conditions set by the Transsaharian Committee was that the Flatters party must travel *en civile.* But in Ouargla, when the Frenchmen tried to buy Arab clothes, those in the shops were far too small for them. The Mzabites produced complete wardrobes for twenty-five Frenchmen in two days.

It was here that Flatters got down to the more serious, and tedious, business of recruiting his guides and cameleers. He rejected the services of a "tribe" of Chaamba Arabs who "presented themselves, their caid at their head, to carry me they said on their shoulders, an Arab expression which means one can count on them." He wrote that he wanted to avoid appearing in Tuareg country with an invasion force of Arabs. Perhaps also, this old Arab Bureau man preferred to recruit his force from more disparate elements so that they could not as easily act in concert to undermine his authority.

Whatever his reasons, by March 5, 1880, when the Flatters mission left Ouargla for the south, it numbered twenty-five Frenchmen, eight of whom were soldiers from the *Bats d'Af*, a penal battalion; two spahis from the Arab Bureau; two Arab cooks; twelve guides, two mounted on horseback and the rest on camels; seventy Chaamba cameleers; and the *muqaddam* from the *zaouia* at Touggourt. By all accounts, it was a pretty motley crew. Bernard, for one, had no faith in the Chaamba, and noted that they "would probably run at the first Tuareg attack." Flatters would easily have found good men for a raiding party; but to ask proud Chaamba to appear before the Tuareg as little more than hired hands was too much. Most probably preferred to stay at home. Those who volunteered were not the flower of Ouargla, and served only for the daily pay of 4 francs given to guides and 2 francs for cameleers. The Frenchmen who were in charge of them had no knowledge of camels, of Arabs or of the desert. Conflict, therefore, was inevitable. Flatters had attempted to hedge his bets by ordering twelve soldiers at Biskra to follow him. But at Ouargla he was commanded to send them back north.

The departure from Ouargla was subdued: "Silence reigned among us, each one buried in his reflections," Bernard wrote. The Agha accompanied them for the first day as the party filed out into the "land of fear," following a low line of *gour*, their stark cliffs supporting horizontal plateaus. The nakedness of the land only deepened the pessimism of the French. Flatters fretted over his dwindling reserves of cash—only 67,000 francs remained of his original allocation of 233,496 francs and 25 centîmes (a round bureaucratic figure). The constant delays had meant that the year was much too advanced. It could not, in fact, be worse. March is a killer month in the Sahara—temperatures rise and fall with such rapidity that the body has difficulty adjusting. Furthermore, the Chaamba had seized the opportunity to unload their sick and decrepit camels on the inexperienced French. Nor was the morale of the Europeans improved by the stories which the cameleers told with relish about the atrocities of which the Tuareg were capable. But they continued south through a corridor between two *ergs* of dunes which undulated to the horizon, the monotony of the journey broken only by short detours to hunt gazelle and antelope, and by a greyhound, the dog of one of the cameleers, which raced over the dunes in pursuit of game while everyone shouted encouragement. The water became increasingly undrinkable, and the cooking of the Arab chefs increasingly inedible.

On March 20, at the wells of Ain Taiba, the first dispute between the Chaamba and the French occurred. Many of the cameleers had replaced their worn-out *guerbas* by the simple expedient of appropriating the newer ones of the French. Indeed, petty thieving seemed endemic in the expedition. When Lieutenant Le Châtelier, who was in charge of the cameleers, attempted to reclaim the stolen property, the Chaamba took up their guns and grouped around a dune. The French did likewise, and it looked for a moment as if the Flatters expedition was about to commit suicide. Flatters defused the situation by relieving Le Châtelier of his command. It was a bad decision, for it demonstrated that the lieutenant colonel was no longer in control of his expedition. Resentment against Flatters among the Europeans was great. To them, he seemed capable of performing any sacrifice to mollify the Arabs, while he spoke to them in the most brusque manner each time they ventured away from the caravan to hunt. The Arabs were left in no doubt that it was they who were in control, and they wasted little time in capitalizing on it.

Flatters marched southward through the Gassi El-Adham—"the *gassi* (firm ground) of bones." Here, in 1849, over 500 camels taken in a raid by Ajjer Tuareg had perished from exhaustion and thirst. The men also had to take care to keep the camels away from the *efelebleh,* an extremely poisonous plant which looks like lettuce. Here, the cameleers announced that they would move no closer to the Ahaggar. They would continue only if Flatters turned east, toward Ghat. The growing realization that command had slithered from his grasp had unsettled the colonel. He grew irritable, silent, and wandered off from the camp at night alone. In the end, he gave in, and ordered his company to march southeast.

The reasons for this extraordinary decision can only be guessed at. It was pointless to go to Ghat. The Fezzan was already well explored. If geographically Ghat provided the best route for the Transsaharian railway, that route had been rejected because it passed through territory claimed by the sultan of Turkey. Flatters's brief was to go into the Ahaggar. One can only suppose that given the choice between Ghat and retreat to Ouargla, Flatters chose the former.

In any case, the decision would not take him far. The expedition moved out of the dunes across a hammada of boulders and arrived at the small oasis of Temassinin, later to be named Fort Flatters by the French. Despite its small, white-domed marabout which housed the tomb of a saint in the middle of a small oasis of palm trees, Temassinin appeared desolate under a copper sky, the palms whipped by a burning scirocco. "The interior [of the marabout] is covered with colorful handkerchiefs, with several silk cloths, and embroidered Muslin," Flatters wrote in his diary. "There is a crowd of small vases containing wheat or barley," and, the Arabs claimed, precious stones. "They firmly believe that whoever touches one of these objects will die immediately."

At Temassinin, Flatters sent out some of his guides with letters in an attempt to make contact with the Tuareg, who so far had studiously —some thought ominously—avoided him. He did not have long to wait. On April 2, 1880 the expedition moved out of the oasis toward Khafousa, or black mountain, already visible on the horizon. It took three days to arrive at its base, having endured yet another sandstorm which lowered the temperature to the freezing point. From there, they moved along the valley of the Wadi Ighargharen, over low dunes, when, suddenly, on April 6, two Tuareg appeared out of nowhere, their camels at the trot, coming toward the expedition. Suddenly, about one hundred yards away, they reined up abruptly, leapt to the ground with great agility, and stood, their legs slightly apart and their lances planted in the ground. Flatters approached them. They were extremely well armed—lance, sword, shield, rifle and revolver stuck in their belts. The only thing they lacked was bullets. The lieutenant colonel addressed them in Arabic. They said they were looking for camels, but the Europeans suspected that they had come to spy out the expedition.

The two Tuareg accompanied the expedition as it continued through narrow valleys filled with low gum trees. At night, the camp was assailed by swarms of insects so thick that, with a sizzle, they extinguished the candles. Finally, on April 8, when the Tuareg departed, Flatters showered them with presents. This proved to be another mistake, for it excited the acquisitiveness of the Chaamba, who now began to ask for presents for themselves. Flatters distributed a few gifts to their leaders, hoping to buy peace, but this simply served to make the rest more jealous—they invaded the colonel's tent and demanded their gifts. Flatters became furious and shouted at them. But it was no use. They

simply laughed at him. The cameleers were now divided into two *sofs*—
those who had received gifts and those who had not. They constantly
quarreled with each other and refused to obey orders. "The colonel is
almost in despair, he does nothing and no one dares do anything," wrote
Captain Bernard. "In any case, it is too late now—we make those work
who are still willing, and think of other things." For five days the caravan
remained immobilized—the guides refused to go any further south, and
Flatters walked about "feverishly" outside the camp, fleeing at the approach of his subordinates.

On April 11, they again set out toward the east, following the dry
bed of the Wadi Ighargharen. To the south loomed the peaks of the
Tassili "like so many somber phantoms of a fantastic dimension." The
next day, two Tuareg with a woman ventured into the camp. They offered some dried antelope meat, "a horrible preparation which the Colonel buys for a fantastic price." At five o'clock in the evening, as the
French were about to eat, someone shouted that a group of Tuareg were
approaching. The Tuareg stopped behind a dune to change into their
best clothes. Flatters and his Chaamba did the same. The two groups
met; the thirty or so Tuareg, dressed in their robes of dark blue, advanced in a long line. Flatters delivered a speech to each in Arabic, a
language which at least some of the Tuareg would understand. They then
settled down to a dinner of camel meat. The Chaamba, acting on the
Arab principle of "kiss the hand you cannot cut off," began animated
conversation with the Tuareg, and it was probably here that the Tuareg
learned of the dissensions within the expedition.

The Tuareg rode with Flatters as he followed the valley until, on
April 16, they arrived at Lake Menghough, a body of water about 500
yards long. The French bathed, swam and even caught five fish, the
largest of which measured two feet. But the idyllic spot soon swarmed
with Tuareg who emerged from the rocks and hills, demanding to be
fed, to see a doctor, wandering into the tents taking whatever struck their
fancy. The children especially were "horrible little beggars, with a prim-
itiveness and at the same time an audacity which was unbelievable."
What was more, the Tuareg refused to allow Flatters to proceed to Ghat
until Ikhenoukhen, the amenoukal of the Ajjer Tuareg, had sent his
permission. On April 20, Flatters ordered his expedition to move toward
Ghat. They had shifted barely 400 yards when they found the route
barred by a party of between sixty and eighty Tuareg. Flatters called his

officers together. Some were for shooting their way through. Flatters refused: This would have violated his instructions. Besides, his Chaamba were unreliable. The Tuareg assured him that the permission to continue would arrive soon, and was only delayed while their chief negotiated with the Turks. But Flatters probably realized that they were disputing who would get the protection money, or, worse, they were plotting to strip him of his wealth before falling on the demoralized caravan and butchering them.

That night, Flatters ordered the sentries doubled. At six o'clock on the morning of April 21, 1880, the French began a retreat toward the north. Flatters placed the rear guard under the command of Captain Masson and commanded him to "die to the last man if need be so the convoy can get away." That was not necessary. Only a few Tuareg followed, and they were quickly discouraged by a few well-aimed shots. The dangerously diminished stocks of supplies were strictly rationed.

The return journey was unremarkable except for the fact that Captain Masson convinced Flatters that the only way to save the expedition, and perhaps their careers as well, was to dispatch a letter to the amenoukal of the Ahaggar Tuareg promising to visit him during the following winter: this would commit the French government to finance the "second phase" of the expedition, as Flatters called it to avoid putting the label of failure on the first one. On April 27 Flatters did so. Bernard believed that Flatters acted "against his better judgment." Perhaps, but he forged ahead of his slower caravan to reach Paris and begin the delicate process of prying more money from the Ministry of Public Works. Whatever doubts he may have entertained, Flatters exhibited nothing but optimism in his letters: "We need money," he wrote to Lieutenant Colonel Belin, his successor at Laghouat. "The Tuareg can be bought, but they know the price of things."

Others, however, harbored no illusions. When Captain Bernard arrived at Ouargla, he went immediately to the mess to drink wine and eat a mutton stew with potatoes served on a real plate. He for one had had his fill of desert travel, especially under the command of Flatters.

VIII

MASSACRE

Paul Flatters returned to Paris with almost indecent haste from the desert in May 1880 to face the unenviable task of explaining to the committee why he had abandoned his mission. Even before he left Algeria, he had begun his campaign with a letter designed to convince Charles de Freycinet, his principal sponsor, that this had not been a setback, simply a "pause." (Freycinet lost his portfolio before the letter arrived.) Flatters tried to put a brave face on his failure, but the real reason for his retreat was almost certainly that he had lost control of his men. The simple fact was that he was unfit for command, especially command of such a hybrid expedition. To be fair to him, even a more energetic officer might have had difficulty under the conditions imposed by the Transsaharian Committee. But the real question is: why did Flatters insist on leading a second expedition into the desert when he could no longer have harbored any illusions about the difficulties involved?

About this we can only speculate. His official diaries and letters fairly froth with optimism, which could only have been for show. Flatters was a deeply troubled and probably a pessimistic man. Duty and patriotism must have played a part, as did ambition, the dream of expanding the footnote which he had already earned in the history of the Sahara into several chapters. The first European to push an expedition across the Sahara to Timbuktu, the trailblazer who would make possible the first railway which brought "civilization" into the heart of darkness, was bound to be a celebrated man, remembered with the greatest of African explorers. After thirty years of obscurity, Flatters was desperate not to lose his only opportunity to salvage an indifferent career.

Flatters sought to convince his Paris sponsors that his retreat had been simply a question of *reculer pour mieux sauter*. He had been made "perfectly welcome" by the Ajjer Tuareg, he told them. Not only had he not met "the slightest hostile opposition," but also his expedition had seen "the crowning act of friendliness and of good neighborliness between Algerian Chaamba and Tuareg."

When the Transsaharian Committee met on June 16, 1880, Flatters was upbeat in person, stressing the positive accomplishments of his first expedition: He had surveyed the route south of Ouargla and gathered geological, hydrological, botanical and zoological data of interest to scholars. He had turned back when only six days from Ghat, he told them, because to have proceeded without first obtaining permission from Turk and Tuareg "might perhaps have raised a diplomatic issue." He had been unable to linger at Lake Menghough as the Tuareg were rapidly devouring his provisions. "The second phase of the operation is relatively simple," he told them, and would consist of taking a more westerly route to the Ahaggar massif and south to the Sudan, "which would appear even more brilliant in the eyes of the public." His words were greeted with enthusiasm: Henri Varroy, who had replaced Freycinet as minister of public works, congratulated him warmly and urged his colleague in the War Ministry to promote Flatters to the rank of colonel. (The ministry replied, stolidly, that Flatters would not have the necessary seniority for another year.) Varroy had more luck with the Minister of Education, who pinned the decoration of *officier d'instruction publique* on Flatters' military tunic during the following Bastille Day celebrations.

When the Transsaharian Committee met for a second time on June 28, 1880, however, the atmosphere was less ebullient, more thoughtful. A. Duponchel, the civil engineer from Montpellier, could not attend. But even he sent a cautionary letter, casting doubt on the ability of an expedition to cross the desert in the face of Tuareg hostility. Flatters brushed aside these fears. With a slight rearrangement of his caravan—namely the replacement of his Chaamba cameleers with forty-seven tirailleurs of the Armée d'Afrique—his force would be more disciplined and better able to defend itself. At the same time, Flatters was careful to reassure the committee, and the not insubstantial number of antimilitarists among them, that this would not alter "our essentially peaceful character in the eyes of the Tuareg because our better disciplined escort will inspire less distrust, while at the same time guaranteeing better security."

If the committee was not swayed by this argument, then he had another, more decisive one: He had written the amenoukal of the Ahaggar Tuareg that he would return in the winter. The "Honor of France" had been engaged. There could be no turning back.

This may sound a trifle farfetched today. But the France of the 1870s and 1880s was still smarting from her stinging defeat at the hands of

Bismarck in the Franco-Prussian War of 1870–71. The pretensions of the premier power in Europe for 200 years had been shattered in the course of a few weeks. The epochs of Louis XIV and Napoleon I were now only faint memories. If France, with new and powerful rivals on the Continent, was to reconquer her position in the world and her self-respect, she must look abroad, south of the Mediterranean, to Africa. Flatters's promise must therefore be honored. What he neglected to tell the members of the Transsaharian Committee, what they could not know until it was too late, was that the amenoukal of the Ahaggar Tuareg had replied to Flatters's letter in no uncertain terms. Flatters was unwelcome: "We have received your letter, we have read and understood it; you tell us to open the road to you; we will not open it." With less enthusiasm than the year before, the committee voted Flatters the funds necessary for a second trip into the Sahara.

This time, Flatters had decided, he would go well armed, prepared to meet trouble. To this end, he exchanged many of his cameleers for more disciplined tirailleurs. But there was still one thing Flatters' expedition lacked—a forceful leader. He had spent too much of his career mediating the arcane disputes of the Arabs of Laghouat to be able, now, to command. But the committee could not know this. They listened to his optimistic speeches, accepted his excuses, and coughed up more funds.

Captain Bernard and lieutenants Le Châtelier, Brosselard and Rabourdin knew better, and requested other assignments. To replace them, Flatters found five men, only one of whom—thirty-six-year-old Lieutenant Joseph de Dianous—was an officer. Two others were French sergeants, a man named Dennery and a twenty-eight-year-old Breton, Joseph Pobéguin. In all, this "second phase" involved eleven Frenchmen, forty-seven tirailleurs, thirty-one Chaamba cameleers, seven Chaamba guides and a new *muqaddam,* Si Abdelladir ben Hammden, for a total of ninety-seven men and 280 camels. The huge and cumbersome command tents had been replaced by small, round two-man tents, *en bonnets de police,* for the Europeans, each one equipped with folding tables and beds. As an extra precaution, Flatters ordered that the expedition camp each night in a square, the mess tent and the smaller tents of the Europeans in the center, and the soldiers, cameleers and baggage occupying the perimeter. Arab dress had been abandoned in favor of "flannel shirts, large cloaks with hoods and laced hunting boots ...

warm blankets, broad flannel belts, light slippers for riding camels or walking on sand," and broad-brimmed hats made in Paris.

Flatters's second appearance before the Transsaharian Committee had served only to deepen his pessimism. His expedition was now more solidly, and more realistically, organized. But the confusion that ruled the Transsaharian Committee had only increased, if that were possible, over the summer: Various Algerian towns continued to dispute which was to become the railhead, businessmen formed "more or less imaginary [companies] for the exploitation of the Sahara," even though the Tell remained undeveloped. "It has become more difficult to travel to Laghouat in a carriage than to go by camel from Laghouat to the Sudan," he wrote to his wife. Nor was Flatters a well man. His sciatica had flared up again, requiring up to four shots of morphine each day as well as "cauterizations with a hot iron." He could not walk for more than thirty minutes and was comfortable only in a reclining position. Had the committee realized this, they surely would not have renewed his command. But there were other reasons for scrubbing the expedition: Féraud, the French Consul at Tripoli, had warned that the amenoukal of the Ahaggar Tuareg might not be entirely welcoming, and that he expected "trouble among the Tuareg." Flatters believed that it was too late to bow out. By December 18, 1880 he was 380 miles south of Ouargla, complaining by letter to his wife that this was "terrible country . . . when we arrive at the wells, one must uncover them and work for hours to water man and beast."

Flatters was also faced with that difficulty which afflicts all Europeans who travel in the Sahara—he did not know whom to trust. Rather than increase his confidence in his own experience and ability, the first expedition had further undermined it. Now, he refused to believe anyone. Féraud's warnings were brushed aside. Flatters's distrust of his Chaamba guides had deepened into contempt. In common with so many Saharian explorers, the initial dreams of adventure and glory curdled into a sense of helplessness and isolation which affected his judgment, for he now began to make a series of decisions that would have been simply silly were their consequences not to prove so tragic.

The first of these was to announce that he planned to lead his expedition to In Salah in the oasis complex of the Tuat, long known as a hotbed of resistance to the slow, methodical French advance into the desert. In fact, Flatters had no intention of going anywhere near In Salah.

His reason for this deliberate piece of deception, he wrote to his wife, was so that the Tuat will prepare to resist him "and we will more easily go about our own business" elsewhere. As In Salah was very much under the thumb of the Ahaggar Tuareg (indeed, at that very moment the amenoukal was said to be there on business), this announcement must simply have reinforced the determination among the Tuareg to resist Flatters. On this point, however, Flatters seems to have been taken in by his own deception. "I want to carry out a pacifistic exploration," he wrote to Lieutenant Colonel Eugène Belin at Laghouat. "But one must not forget that we represent France. The people of In Salah come to us when they wish. It is only fair that we can go to them. The Tuareg have given their word to let me pass. And the devil take me if I do not do so proudly and with a will, as do people who have confidence in their undertaking." But Flatters was bereft of confidence. He behaved bravely enough on paper—indeed, writing seems to have provided some kind of therapy, a way of building up his self-assurance. But as soon as he was confronted with the flesh-and-blood problems of command, as soon as he had to issue an order or make a decision, that confidence which had been inflated at the writing table sputtered away like air rushing out of a balloon. He slunk away from camp to walk in the solitude of the desert, or, if unable to escape, flew into a fit of rage against anyone who asked him for a ruling, who required him to decide.

Any man with a sense of self-preservation would have executed an about-face and returned home. The situation in Paris was so confused as to make it now extremely unlikely that anything substantial could be salvaged from the mess which masqueraded as the Transsaharian Committee. In a long letter to his wife written on Christmas Day 1880, Flatters poured out his contempt for the amateur explorers who "do not speak a word of Arabic," the geographers, the politicians and functionaries who debate the route of the railroad, bombard him with advice, place obstacles in his path, but who "know nothing." The situation in the desert must have made him more nervous, for it contained a distinct hint of menace: Numerous camel tracks suggested that an inordinate amount of activity preceded the expedition, perhaps even a mobilization against it. His guides smelled treachery. Was it not strange, they asked, that Aitarel, the amenoukal of the Ahaggar Tuareg, had not come to meet the expedition when it passed to within three days' ride from In Salah? "I don't want it to be like last year when the Chaamba made me miss my goal," he told them. "Believe me, if you want to be my friend, do not try to prevent me from going to the Hoggar." He even threatened to shoot anyone who opposed him. This did little to calm the nerves of the mission. When, on December 26, one of the sentinels fired at a jackal, pandemonium broke out in the camp as soldiers and cameleers stampeded toward the ammunition cases.

The expedition continued its march "through a desert of rock and sand." Quite a few camels perished from exhaustion. On January 9, they encountered a small caravan at the wells of El Hadjadj, who informed them that Aitarel was hostile to the mission. Flatters' guides attempted once again to convince him to turn back. But the lieutenant colonel was adamant that they continue.

On January 18, 1881, the expedition reached the Amguid Gorge. Wedged between a long chain of dunes to the west and the "confused" ledges of the Tassili escarpment—"a twist of rocks of all shapes"—to the east, Flatters found the Amguid sinister: "We are at this moment at the foot of a mountain of enormous rocks," he wrote to his wife, "cut by a gorge at the bottom of which runs a stream: The first running water which we have met in the Sahara! There are fish in the water, but it seems a bad sign: There were also fish in the lake where we ended our last voyage. . . . Will the fish inadvertently bring us bad luck?" His guides informed him that the land beyond the Amguid was unknown to them. Flatters made camp, and together with his guides, struck out southward on a reconnaissance.

During the five days spent at Amguid, one of Flatters's guides, Cheik-ben Bou Djemaa, who had been dispatched to In Salah to track down Aitarel, returned in the company of a Targui named Mohammed, bearing a letter from the amenoukal. The content of the letter was straightforward enough, but its tone depends on which translation one accepts. Flatters was informed by Aitarel that he was welcome to pass through the Ahaggar, but he was not encouraged to tarry: "Take the most direct road," it read, "for we do not care to see you come into our *douars* [camps]." Bou Djemaa recounted that when he had arrived at In Salah, Aitarel had already departed with a large number of men and 500 camels. He tracked Aitarel for five days before he caught up with him at Wadi Menyet. There, he remained for over a week, until Aitarel finally decided to send his "Uncle Chikkat [in fact, it was his brother-in-law], a good man, who is as myself, and will guide you."

Flatters's pessimism evaporated, as did that of many of his men. Here, at last, was the breakthrough they had been waiting for.

On January 25, Chikkat ben Hanfou rode into camp. "He was a very tall, thin old man with dark skin, a space between his teeth, and a short white beard," Private Messaoud ben Djerma remembered. "He wore a Tunisian skull cap held in place by a black scarf, from which dangled an enormous silk tassel which fell over his shoulder." Flatters pronounced him "a brave old man," although he believed that Chikkat's task was to speed them through the Ahaggar as quickly as possible.

Morale was high as they broke camp on January 26, and moved down a deep ravine that snaked between cliffs 2,100 feet high. The dark foothills of the Ahaggar were visible to the south, and the weird shapes of the Tassili loomed to the northeast. On January 29, Flatters wrote his last letter: "When you receive this," he told his wife, "we shall be in the Sudan," followed by a grandiose sketch of his plans to march to the mouth of the Niger and return the following year via Ghat. This was tourism on a grand scale. On January 30, he dispatched his journal to Ouargla.

For what happened to the Flatters expedition after January 29, 1881, we must depend upon the testimony of the surviving tirailleurs and Chaamba. Though the country was difficult, the Tuareg guides were very friendly with the Arabs and extremely interested in their Gras rifles. The prophets of doom seemed to have been proven stunningly wrong. Nevertheless, Flatters must still have experienced a twinge of uncertainty. There were all those tracks that crossed and recrossed their line of march. And the guides? Chikkat seemed solid enough, but he was an unknown introduced by Cheik-ben Bou Djemaa, a man recruited in passing at Ouargla, who had for the moment returned to his *douar* laden with a suspicious number of presents given to him by the Tuareg. The mission was entirely in the hands of two Tuareg guides. The travelers must have felt extremely vulnerable as they picked their way through a waterless land of huge boulders, some of them 900 feet high, which made dwarfs of men and camels alike. On February 2, as they emerged from these mountains onto a level plain, the two Tuareg guides informed Flatters that they could not remember the way. Flatters camped while the two men went in search of water. They returned at nightfall, and on February 4, led the mission to the next wells. Over the next days as the caravan crossed the rocky plain of Amadghor, men and animals suffering in an unseasonable heat, the guides repeated this maneuver several times—asking Flatters to make camp, going ahead to find water, then returning to lead a section of the caravan with the camels and *guerbas* to the wells.

Flatters was not completely unwary. It did occur to him as odd that the guides kept insisting that they were lost. His compass also told him that he was being led southeastward rather than to the southwest where he wanted to go. However, the most peculiar event was the reappearance of Sghir-ben Cheik, one of his Chaamba guides who had returned home at the Amguid Gorge. The manner of his reappearance was even more suspicious, for he was in the company of two Tuareg and dressed as one of them. In fact, at first Flatters did not realize who he was, until the other Chaamba recognized him despite his Tuareg disguise. On February 10, 1881, a Targui named El Alem came into camp claiming to have been sent from Aitarel to guide them to the Sudan. He demanded an outrageous sum for his services. Flatters hesitated, then gave him 1,000 francs as a sort of down payment. El Alem departed with Sghir to take this payment back to his camp.

On the following day, a deputation of thirty Ahaggar Tuareg arrived in the camp. They wandered among the baggage, demanding that they be given virtually everything in sight as presents. Their leader, Tissi, the son of Chikkat, affected great friendship for Flatters, slapping him on the back and marveling at his possessions. Flatters distributed gifts in his tent, but they simply demanded more. The lieutenant colonel grew angry and shouted that he was not afraid of them. When the Tuareg had departed, the French realized that two of their camels were missing. The tirailleur sent to retrieve the animals found them tied to a bush. But as he led them back to camp, several Tuareg attempted to seize them, and had to be frightened off with several shots from a revolver. The tirailleur also noticed a substantial party of Tuareg lurking in the distance.

On the 13th, El Alem returned to the caravan, having deposited his 1,000 francs in a safe hiding place in the company of Sghir. Cheik-ben Bou Djemaa warned Flatters to be wary of Sghir. It was good advice: On the night of the 13th, Sghir attempted to convince his fellow Chaamba to desert. Flatters spoke to them in an attempt to reassure them, and then informed Sghir that no one was leaving until they reached the Sudan.

On the 14th, the expedition entered a region of ravines and precipitous cliffs. The following day, the country became easier. Tamarisk trees began to appear among the rocks on the valley floor. On February 16,

1881, the caravan got underway at first light. Much of the water had evaporated from the *guerbas* in the excessive heat, and the situation for the camels had reached a critical stage. At ten o'clock in the morning, the guides informed the lieutenant colonel that they had missed the wells, which lay in the mountains to the southwest. Flatters exploded with rage. But he had no choice but to make camp.

What happened next varies in detail according to which source one uses, but the general line of events is easy enough to follow. Flatters, Captain Masson, the engineers Béringer and Roche, and Dr. Guiard mounted on their camels, set out toward the wells, preceded by the Tuareg guides and Sghir, who rode about fifty yards in front. They were followed by a dozen Chaamba and tirailleurs leading their camels, commanded by Sergeant Dennery. Other camels were to follow as soon as they had been unloaded at the camp. Lieutenant de Dianous, Sergeant Pobéguin, the civilian engineers Santin and Marjolet, and Private Brame remained at the camp with forty men.

The water party marched toward the mountains on a path that became increasingly difficult. The heat was suffocating as it rebounded off the slabs of stone. The camels marched single file through the rocks. Flatters called out to the guides, who signaled that the well was only a short distance away. Flatters and his party descended into a small valley formed by three ravines that cut through the black, rocky hills. At the center, in a small clearing among the tamarisk trees, the well was visible. At this moment, Bou-Djemaa, who had wandered off to hunt gazelle, whipped his mehari at full speed toward Flatters, crying "Colonel! You are betrayed! What are you doing here? Go back to the camp!"

"You and your Chaamba have bothered me since last year," Flatters shouted back. "It's not true. Leave me alone!" He dismounted and began nonchalantly to walk around the well.

"Colonel! You are betrayed!" Bou-Djemaa repeated.

Flatters looked up to see a swarm of Tuareg shouting their war cry. He began to greet them, but it was only too apparent that their intentions were hostile. He ran for his mount, as did Captain Masson. Neither made it. Some accounts say that Flatters brought down a few of his attackers with shots from his revolver before he was hacked down. The other Europeans suffered identical fates. Sergeant Dennery grouped his cameleers on a small hillock and fired until he ran out of ammunition. Then he too perished with most of his men.

The Tuareg rounded on those who straggled toward the well in small groups. Private Messaoud ben Djerma, smoking a cigarette of *chih,* a plant with a strong odor of absinthe, led his camels through a deep cut between the rocks, "when suddenly, from behind a hill, came several camels at great speed, covered with their light white shields which can stop iron, and carrying their large, double-edge sabers in bandoliers, the riders shouting and brandishing their lances which were two yards long." The tirailleurs formed a line shoulder to shoulder and opened fire: "We kept them at a distance at first, because their camels were afraid of the firing. But we had little ammunition, and as soon as they no longer feared a fusillade, the Tuareg charged and engaged us in a hand-to-hand fight in which they had all the advantages." Unable to counter the broadswords and lances of the Tuareg with their empty carbines, the tirailleurs fled. The Tuareg, preoccupied with rounding up the camels, allowed the tirailleurs to escape.

The man who now took command of the mission—Lieutenant de Dianous—also appears to have inherited Flatters's lack of resolve. When the first stragglers appeared with news of the massacre, Dianous's initial reaction (almost a reflex among Europeans in Africa) was to accuse them of lying. He then ordered the baggage to be stacked to form a square rampart and awaited the attack which he believed imminent. A moment's reflection should have told him that the Tuareg, having secured the camels and thus the overwhelming advantage, had no need to attack. Why should they risk their lives against entrenched tirailleurs? Time was very much on their side. When Dianous finally did set out for the well, it was with a pitifully small reconnaissance party of twenty men. He arrived on the heights above the well only at four o'clock in the afternoon, almost five hours after the ambush. From this vantage point, he saw that the small valley was swarming with Tuareg—more than 200 of them, and with camels. According to some reports, the appearance of the French threw the Tuareg into a momentary panic, and they stampeded for a better defensive position on the crest of a small ridge. Surely, this was the moment for Dianous to attack—a short, crisp charge that would take advantage of Tuareg confusion. Dianous could have cut out a few camels and scurried back to camp. This was his only chance—his last chance—and he bungled it. Without camels, he was a dead man anyway. Better even to die here, quickly, gloriously, than to perish by inches on the very long walk back to Ouargla.

Dianous chose discretion over valor, and hurried back to camp to await an attack rather than to charge the Tuareg, who were still milling about just over the hill. Even had he not secured camels, he might have inflicted casualties enough to discourage an effective pursuit. Instead, he ordered a retreat which was to become a death march.

After nightfall, Dianous directed his men to abandon everything they could not carry and return to Ouargla, seventy-five days' march away. At eleven o'clock they set out, resting for a few hours the following day (where three survivors of the massacre joined them), before setting out again for another night march. On the 18th, a party of Tuareg passed by, but did not attack. Wells were found at frequent intervals. Food, however, was scarce. On the 21st, they dined on four greyhounds belonging to the Chaamba cameleers which had followed them since Ouargla. They also came upon four camels, one of which they slaughtered for food.

As they marched northward, the scarcity of food and water gradually sapped the strength, as well as the morale, of the survivors, only too aware that they were being shadowed by bands of Tuareg. Their marches became shorter, and the stops more frequent. One tirailleur, driven to desperation, attempted to shoot himself. The others plodded on, chewing roots or pieces of leather to appease their thirst. On February 27th, they arrived at a well and easily chased off the few Tuareg who guarded it. They had come barely 110 miles. Ouargla was still more than 800 miles to the north, and already they were exhausted. Hunting parties returned empty-handed. Another camel was killed for food. On March 2, they left the well. The engineer Santin was unable to walk, and the load of one of the camels was distributed among the men so that he could ride. Soon, Dianous was reduced to the ultimate humiliation of buying, at exorbitant prices, two camels as well as provisions from the Tuareg who were following them. Some of these provisions were dates and dry biscuits which had been left behind by the expedition.

On March 8, several Tuareg who had asked unsuccessfully to parley with Dianous the day before, again approached the column. Dianous sent four tirailleurs to speak with them. The Tuareg claimed to have had nothing to do with the massacre, and swore upon the Koran that they sought only to help the Arabs back to their base. Dianous agreed to talk, but took the precaution of surrounding himself with five well-armed men. Two Tuareg walked out to meet the lieutenant, one of whom was Tissi, son of the treacherous guide Chikkat. Tissi claimed to be full of pity for the French party and ready to make amends. He would give them dates, sheep and camels within three days. Could Dianous send twenty men to fetch all of this bounty? This was a transparent attempt to reduce the French numbers still further. However, Dianous agreed to send five men, even though he could have had few illusions that he would ever see them again. In the meantime, while they waited for their supplies, Tissi gave Dianous a bag of crushed dates, which were distributed.

On March 9, 1881, the French party arrived at the wells of Ain el-Kerma to find them occupied by about one hundred Tuareg. Dianous ordered them to leave, which they did, but only to occupy a small hillock a short distance away. Sergeant Pobéguin proposed to Dianous that they attack, but the lieutenant refused. Tissi reappeared, to offer another bag of dates to the French party. These were eagerly accepted and immediately distributed. As soon as he put one of these dates into his mouth, Private Messaoud ben Djerma "felt devoured by an inextinguishable thirst, his throat was burning and his legs paralyzed." Within minutes, virtually every man in the French camp was foaming at the mouth and raving like a maniac. The dates had been mixed with the poisonous plant *efelehleh*. Men tore off their clothes, clawed their throats, ran about firing shots into the air, or simply ran out into the desert, never to reappear. Some of the Chaamba had feared treachery and had refused to eat the dates. They began to subdue their raving companions and restore a semblance of order. The Tuareg did not attack. They did not need to. They settled down cold-bloodedly to enjoy the final agonies of the mission.

And agonies they were. On March 10th, Dianous, now in a semi-comatose state, agreed to send six men, including the *muqaddam,* to collect several sheep in the Tuareg camp. The six were brutally and treacherously murdered. According to one witness, Pobéguin wanted to assault the camp, which was only a few thousand yards away, but was again restrained by Dianous. The pitiful band of survivors staggered toward the Amguid Gorge, only to find its water guarded by the Tuareg. At last, Dianous ordered an attack. But it was too late. The Tuareg were now armed with captured weapons and the tirailleurs were in no fit state to fight. Their attack was one of desperation in which any notion of military science seems to have been forgotten. Most of the surviving Frenchmen were killed. Santin died of exhaustion and poisoning. This left Sergeant Pobéguin in command of the remaining thirty-four tirailleurs and Chaamba.

Pobéguin, too ill to walk, mounted one of the remaining camels. Two of the wounded were also lashed to camels by the survivors. On the 11th of March, four tirailleurs deserted (and miraculously made it back to Ouargla). All the camels were killed and eaten, save one which was led away by two other deserters. The mummified remains of a camel were discovered and devoured. The party was on the verge of physical and moral collapse.

What happened next would send a ripple of horror through France when news of the massacre finally reached Europe. On March 22, one of the tirailleurs offered to go in search of the camp of one of the mission's original guides. Pobéguin agreed and the tirailleur set off. Hardly had he left camp when three other tirailleurs followed and murdered him. They soon returned to camp bearing the bloody remains of what they claimed was a mountain sheep. It probably escaped the notice of no one that the flesh was human. For three days they sat beside the wells of Hassi el-Hakjadj in a state of almost complete torpor. Finally, on March 25, Pobéguin summoned up his last reserves of energy and of authority, and ordered his men to march. Nine of them could not move. They were left behind. Pobéguin led sixteen men slowly northward. They had gone barely two miles when they heard shots coming from the direction of the wells. Private Belkacem ben-Zebla was sent to investigate. What had actually happened at the wells will never be known, but Belkacem returned with a fair quantity of human flesh which was eaten raw by the men. Three of them then made the short trip back to Hassi el-Hakjadj to eat what was left.

Sergeant Pobéguin was alive—just. Belkacem ended his misery by emptying his revolver into the unfortunate Breton, who was then eaten. The refugees eventually met a shepherd, who led them to the rescue party sent out by the Agha of Ouargla who had been alerted by the four tirailleur deserters on March 28. Finally, on April 4, almost four months after the massacre, eleven half-dead Chaamba and one tirailleur staggered into Ouargla. A handful of others also came in, claiming to have been taken prisoner or otherwise separated from the group.

On April 2, news of the disaster reached France. The initial wires based on the garbled information culled from the survivors announced that Flatters was being held prisoner in the desert. The Tuareg were roundly condemned. No one thought to blame the Turks, who almost certainly encouraged the Tuareg in their resistance. The popular press called for vengeance: "We march from insult to insult, from defiance to defiance, from humiliation to humiliation," the *Evénement* proclaimed. "The honor of our name, our legitimate influence, the security of our Algerian enterprise, the grandeur and the economy of our projects in Africa require that we exact a prompt and energetic revenge for so much bad faith, perfidiousness and ferocity." But vengeance had to be post-poned. An invasion of the Sahara by the army was out of the question. They were not equipped for it, and their bases were too distant. An armed expedition might meet with a disaster greater than that which had befallen Flatters. The Agha of Ouargla offered to lead a *razzia* (raid) to punish the Ahaggar Tuareg. This too was rejected. The diplomats argued that some countries might object strongly to such an invasion. Nor were the soldiers convinced that it would be effective.

While the French debated how Flatters might best be avenged, they were overtaken by other events—the French invasion of Tunisia, which occurred in 1881. This invasion coincided with an uprising on the Mo-roccan border led by Bou-Amama. The Armée d'Afrique had its hands full, and the Flatters disaster was buried by these more pressing matters. Buried, but not quite forgotten. Madame Flatters was voted a pension by the French parliament, which also sent money to erect a monument to her husband at Ouargla. But Flatters, and the need to avenge him, became a minor obsession among a small group of French soldiers who dreamed of one day extending French control from the Mediterranean to the Niger. Until well into the twentieth century, these Frenchmen observed the ritual of erecting a few stones in memory of Flatters in prominent places in the Ahaggar, monuments that the Tuareg usually dismantled at the earliest opportunity.

The Flatters disaster did have one bizarre postscript. Almost fifteen years after the event, a man of mixed French and Tunisian parentage, a one-time military interpreter named Djebari, claimed to have met Flatters and three other French survivors of the massacre during a trip through the Sahara: "I saw them, these four valiant survivors of the Flatters mission, who have suffered for fourteen years the effects of a cruel and dishonorable captivity," he wrote in a pamphlet entitled "The Survivors of the Flatters Mission." According to Djebari, the Frenchmen had been sitting in the middle of an assembly of Tuareg notables "discussing can-nons and fortifications with an extraordinary competence." It is testi-mony to the fantasy which the Sahara inspires that his accounts—and his offer to ransom the captives for 30,000 francs!—were taken seriously.

He was brought to Paris, introduced to Madame Flatters and taken to visit various ministries. However, it was only too apparent that Djebari was quite mad (he regularly took morphine for an abscess of the liver). Those who knew something of the Sahara pointed out that the journal of his voyage, together with many details of "The Survivors of the Flatters Mission," were sheer invention. Djebari was arrested when he threatened to kill an Arab Bureau officer, and quietly forgotten.

Flatters' memory, however, lived on. In 1899, the Foureau-Lamy mission made a special detour to visit the scene of the ambush: "No vestige of this unhappy event survives, and we could find only a few very small fragments of calcinated bone, a left humerus, rather far from the well, and which might belong to Captain Masson killed at a certain distance, and a small piece of sole, obviously of European manufacture," the explorer Fernand Foureau wrote. Inevitably, they erected a monument to Flatters on the spot.

IX

THE
SOUTHERN APPROACHES

The effect of the Flatters massacre on the French was perfectly predictable. After a brief period of incredulity, followed by calls for revenge, most of them soon forgot the tragic episode. If Flatters had been massacred by Germans or English, then that might have been something to get upset about. But serious rivalry among the big powers in Africa was still more than a decade away. True, French and Italians had gone through some ritualistic saber-rattling over Tunis in 1881. (In fact, it was here that General Boulanger, the military governor of Tunis who in 1889 was to lend his name to a movement to overthrow the Third Republic, first came to public notice.) But the majority of Frenchmen were indifferent to the world beyond Europe. They adopted the eminently sensible view that any place which did not already have a Cook's office was probably not worth acquiring in any case. The world beyond Europe was dangerous: if one ventured into it and got butchered, *tant pis*. That was precisely the position they adopted in 1885 when a column under Colonel François de Négrier was ambushed near the Vietnamese town of Lang-son and forced to retreat with serious losses. The Chamber of Deputies condemned Prime Minister Jules Ferry for being so foolish as to send troops to places like Indochina, and promptly brought down his government.

This attitude began to change with the Siam crisis of 1893, when the English and French quarreled over who was to gain the preponderant influence in that country. The dispute with Britain over control of the unclaimed world reached its apogee in 1898, when Captain Jean Baptist Marchand appeared on the upper Nile at a place called Fashoda and demanded that his country's "historic rights" in that region be recognized by England. The diplomats defused the crisis. But the small group of dedicated colonialists in France led by Eugène Etienne, deputy for Oran, realized the political dividends to be achieved by harnessing the trusted horse of French chauvinism to the colonial bandwagon. This they were able to do successfully in the conquest of Morocco; by making the

Kaiser the villain, rather than the sultan of Morocco, they were able in time of crisis to whip up the volatile nationalism of Frenchmen to support their campaign of colonial conquests.

The problem of those who wished to bring the central Sahara under the French flag was twofold. First, even among men as ingenious as these colonialists (a fair number had received a Jesuit education), it was hard to make out a plausible case for a French conquest of the desert. The rumor that just prior to the massacre, the Flatters party had come across a field of emeralds just waiting to be harvested, was played for all it was worth. But it found little credence. Presumably, if the Ahaggar had a great repository of precious stones, then the Tuareg would have been among the wealthiest peoples in Africa, rather than existing on the margins of survival. Others spoke of the great mineral wealth of the Sahara. But how did they know? Anyone who went out with a rockhammer to do a little prospecting was turned back or murdered. (In fact the only use the French ever did find for the Sahara was as a testing ground for atomic weapons.)

The second aspect of the problem was this: The desolation of the Sahara, its complete absence of economic potential, might have made little difference if someone else had wanted it. But, unfortunately for the French colonialists, no one, not even the English, was that shortsighted. On the contrary, they invited the French to dispose of the central Sahara as they pleased. The Anglo-French Convention of August 5, 1890, swapped English hegemony in Zanzibar for that of France in Madagascar. It also contained a paragraph which allocated to the French the territory running south from her Mediterranean possessions (Algeria and Tunisia) to a line running from Say on the lower Niger to Barruwa on Lake Chad. This, in theory, removed almost all of the diplomatic objections to a French takeover of the Sahara. But the problem was not there. The British minister responsible for this concession, Lord Salisbury, regarded it as a great joke and one of the triumphs of his career: "It is what a farmer would call 'very light land,' " he declared to Parliament in a statement sure to produce an outbreak of mirth among the Tory squirearchy. "We have given the Gallic cockerel an enormous amount of sand. Let him scratch it as he pleases."

Such declarations were bound to have colonialists with Saharan interests frothing with rage. Indeed, it was this sense of outrage which led French colonialists to found the Comité de l'Afrique française in the wake of the treaty, because they felt that the Quai d'Orsay was not sufficiently sensitive to French interests in Africa. Besides, Salisbury was not playing the game. The French needed an ogre, a villain, and for centuries "Perfidious Albion" had filled this need. Now the English were actually telling the French that they could do what they wanted with that dreadful place and laughing among themselves that it was like handing a comb to a bald man. It was too much.

Jules Cambon, the governor general of Algeria, took up Salisbury's challenge: "Well then, we shall scratch this sand, we shall put rails on it, plant telegraph poles, make artesian wells spring up from the soil." But very few were deceived. Even the eminent Sahara specialist Henri Schirmer declared that the French claim to the central desert "has a value only as a title of passage" to the Sudan, but as Paris had relinquished her claim to the richest areas of the Hausa country of northern Nigeria, it was hardly worth passing that way: "The country which we have been given north of the Barruwa-Say line is not worth building a railway to for the purposes of colonization. . . . Let us finish once and for all with this legend of the richness of the Niger bend, which haunts the best minds with the tenacity of old errors." The government shared his view.

However, economics do not tell the whole story—there was also a diplomatic wrinkle. The French were gradually advancing into the desert along three lines of oases. In the east from Biskra through Touggourt to Ouargla; in central Algeria from Laghouat to Ghardaia and El Goléa; and finally in the west along the Moroccan border south of Ain Sefra through Taghit and Igli to Beni Abbès. These tentacles reached toward the oasis complex of the Tuat with its principal town In Salah. The difficulty occurred because the Tuat was claimed by the sultan of Morocco. The fact that the sultan could neither garrison the Tuat nor collect taxes there did not diminish his claim in the eyes of the faithful, who accepted him as their spiritual leader and head of the Dar el-Islam, the House of Islam. If anyone ruled in In Salah, it was the Ahaggar Tuareg. But Great Britain supported the sultan's claim to the Tuat. Cambon argued in vain that the Tuareg could be brought to heel by seizing the oases where they came to reprovision: "It is sufficient to occupy the ports of this sea to be its master," he proclaimed. But for the moment he must content himself with the establishment of two "fortified caravanserai" on the desolate plain of Tademaït which he christened Fort Miribel and

Fort MacMahon. These lay across the two principal routes to the Tuat, and less pleasant places would be difficult to imagine—mud blockhouses which stood like small pimples on a plain totally devoid of water and vegetation. They might have been taken straight out of *Beau Geste,* except that even the Foreign Legion declined to garrison them. This task fell initially to tirailleurs and, later, to "Saharian" troops, which in the 1890s were principally infantry raised in large part among freed slaves in the southern oases. Miribel and MacMahon were a combination of penal colony and military disaster. The soldiers who lived there could move only as fast, and as far, as they could walk, while the camel-mounted Chaamba were able to earn a fairly comfortable living by raiding the supply columns that lumbered south from El Goléa.

In the north, therefore, the French were condemned to be frustrated, to wait, to be raided and punished. Some argued that an invasion of the Sahara would be an easy affair to organize: "Several hundred Europeans would have nothing to fear from 1,200 to 1,500 Tuareg warriors, armed with lances and with flintlocks," Schirmer declared. But the simple truth was that, in the 1890s, the French did not have the military capability to invade the desert. A heavily armed column might easily meet disaster—the Tuareg did not even have to adopt a scorched-earth policy; nature had done that for them. A *harka* (war party) of French-led Chaamba offered a second solution. But these were difficult affairs to organize and discipline. The Chaamba's instincts were to raid rather than to conquer. And even if successful, the French would need light, camel-mounted troops to make a conquest stick. In 1890, that force was not even a glimmer in the eye of its future creator, Colonel Henri Laperrine. Therefore, in the north, the conquest of the desert was stalled by the diplomatic issue of the Tuat and by the lack of a camel corps capable of a desert invasion.

This encouraged colonialists to contemplate an invasion in reverse —from the Sudan. The "Sudan" is far greater than the modern nation which bears that name. In fact, it encompasses the area immediately south of the Sahara running east to west for the entire breadth of Africa. The British eventually were to conquer the Eastern Sudan by traveling up the Nile. The French began their slow invasion of the Western Sudan from their coastal bases at Dakar and Saint-Louis de Sénégal. By the early 1890s, they had penetrated inland to what today is the western portion of Mali as far as the town of Ségou on the Niger River.

The 1890 treaty had removed all of the possible sources of diplomatic conflict with Great Britain over the Sahara save the Tuat. The treaty had also opened the possibility of a territorial union of French colonies from the Mediterranean to the Congo. The Sahara was perhaps worthless in economic terms, but it was a key piece in the African jigsaw. "Without any great effort, without any real sacrifice . . . with a single treaty, we have secured the recognition by Britain (the only power whose rivalry we need fear) that Algeria and Senegal will in the near future form a single domain," the Quai d'Orsay crowed. "Today the government can tell the nation that this vast African empire is no longer a dream, a distant ideal . . . but a reality."

It was not quite a reality. It had first to be conquered. The momentum of conquest shifted away from Algeria, where it had stalled, to the Sudan. French troops striking east from Senegal would secure the southern fringes of the desert and, it was believed, make possible the conquest of the desert from the south.

That the initiative for the conquest of the Sahara might come from the Sudan is not at all surprising, given the peculiar conjunction of circumstances that prevailed in Africa in the last decade of the nineteenth century. The first thing to be grasped is that, unlike British colonialism, which at least contained a mercantile element, French colonialism was almost exclusively military. No Cecil Rhodes existed to encourage French youth to take up the "White's Man's Burden" in Africa (and incidentally to make a fortune). French civilization "drove forward in a mortuary cart" of military expansion. The second important fact is that there was in this period a direct correlation between the ability of soldiers to conquer territory and their distance from Paris. Ouargla and the other oases of Southern Algeria occupied by the French were too close to Algiers to enjoy the luxury of being able simply to ignore inconvenient orders.

Besides, the heroic era of Algerian conquest was well and truly past. The Armée d'Afrique, which at one time in the 1830s and '40s had been the repository for the Army's bad boys—the Bugeauds, Cavaignacs, Changarniers, Saint-Aulaires, and others—had now settled down into a semirespectable, if picturesque, corps which performed garrison duty every bit as dull as that of metropolitan France. Their colorful uniforms were virtually all that remained of their imperial past. Algeria, at least the coastal part of it, now was an integral part of the *métropole,* complete with prefects, mayors and chiefs of police. The Armée d'Afrique, although it retained its name, was officially no more than the 19th Corps d'armée, complete with mobilization plans which would ferry it to Lorraine in the event of attack. Consequently, most of the bad boys, the ones in search of real adventure, had drifted with the colonial tide to the Sudan.

If the conquest of North Africa had been, and with Morocco it was to continue to be, essentially an army enterprise, Indochina and the Sudan were very much the province of the French navy. The French colonial army emerged from the marines, and was officially part of the navy until the army made a successful takeover bid in 1900. In the 1880s, marine officers, often recruited from St.-Cyr's most rebellious and least studious elements, grew bored simply guarding the French coastal enclaves in Senegal. Like Bugeaud before them, their longing for employment led them to pick quarrels with their near neighbors and even to start wars, wars which their superior firepower, together with the superior discipline of their Senegalese tirailleurs, usually allowed them to win. In the process, however, the colonial army acquired a reputation among their more sedate colleagues at home as "a collection of hooligans."

In the early 1890s, there was scarcely one of these "hooligans" who did not dream of acquiring the title of "the Conqueror of Timbuktu." Since René Caillié had visited Timbuktu in 1829, the myth of the great golden city in the center of Africa had been shattered: "On entering this mysterious city, which is an object of curiosity and research to the civilized nations of Europe, I experienced an indescribable satisfaction," he wrote.

> I never before felt a similar emotion and my transport was extreme. I was obliged, however, to restrain my feelings, and to God alone did I confide my joy. . . . I looked around and found that the sight before me did not answer my expectations. I had formed a totally different idea of the grandeur and wealth of Timbuctu. The city presented, at first view, nothing but a mass of ill-looking houses, built of earth. Nothing was to be seen in all directions but immense plains of sand of a yellowish white colour. The sky was a pale red as far as the horizon; all nature wore a dreary aspect, and the most profound silence prevailed; not even the warbling of a bird was to be heard. Still, though I cannot account for the impression, there was

something imposing in the aspect of a great city, raised in the midst of sands, and the difficulties surmounted by its founders cannot fail to excite admiration.

Caillié estimated the population of Timbuktu at around 10,000 souls, most of whom lived in one-story houses of dried brick (poorer citizens lived in straw huts). "The streets of Timbuctoo are clean and sufficiently wide to permit three horsemen to pass abreast." But everything had a "dull appearance." The people seemed indolent, and there was little commerce: "In comparison with Jenne, the market is a desert," he wrote. Heinrich Barth, who visited Timbuktu in 1855, wrote that he was "disgusted at the custom which prevails in the houses like that in which I was lodged, of using the terrace as a sort of closet."

One reason for the decline of Timbuktu was obvious—the place was terrorized by the Tuareg: "They roam about the village and behave in the most arbitrary way," Caillié wrote,

> making the inhabitants give them provisions and other property—in fact, seizing whatever they can lay their hands on. . . . The Moors entertain a profound contempt for the Tuareg, and when they would express their utmost hatred of them, they compare them to Christians, whom they suppose to be the same kind of vagabonds and depredators. . . . When the chief of the Tuareg arrives with his suite at Timbuctoo, it is a general calamity, and yet everyone overwhelms him with attentions and sends presents to him and his followers.

Although few French officers could have believed that Timbuktu was a wealthy town, it did retain both a romantic and a strategic fascination. Any officer who could lay claim to the title of its conqueror might justifiably expect a page all to himself in the *Livre d'or de l'armée coloniale.* One man who entertained such visions was Lieutenant Colonel Eugène Bonnier.

Bonnier was virtually born afloat. A native of the island of Réunion in the Indian Ocean, he joined the naval artillery while still in his teens. He had seen service in Tonkin and the Sudan. At the relatively young age of 37, he was already a lieutenant colonel and military commander of the Niger region. One might suppose that his relatively rapid promotion was due to his superior intelligence and military talents. These may have played a part, but only a small one. Every year of service in the colonies counted double for promotion, so that in the normal course of events a colonial soldier might expect a more rapid rise than a line officer in France. But if the rewards of colonial service were greater, so were the risks. The problem was not so much "nigger bullets," as soldiers in France contemptuously called them. That was almost the last thing to fear. Between 1830 and 1847, the most active years of the Algerian conquest, only 304 French officers had been killed in action. The greatest killer was not the enemy, but disease. Malaria, blackwater fever, typhus, cholera were only a few of the delights that awaited French soldiers in the Sudan. Promotion became a lottery, with the survivors drawing the winning numbers.

But survival in itself was not quite enough. For the French colonial army was not unlike a club, not a very exclusive club, but a club nonetheless. The requirements for admission were very different from those of the French army's other elite group, the general staff. The general staff was an intellectual and bureaucratic oligarchy recruited among the more bookish members of the officer corps. Patience, caution, care for detail, diplomacy and *politesse* were the things that helped staff officers up the promotion ladder. Staff officers must own a pair of white gloves, be able to flatter the generals and make small talk with the prefect's wife.

The colonial army cultivated a somewhat different ethos. Few of its officers had earned a reputation at St.-Cyr for anything but indolence and indiscipline. In many respects, this was hardly their fault. It took a special kind of personality to endure the tedium and harassment, the petty regulations and rote learning that characterized life at France's military college in the nineteenth century. Consequently, many of the men who subsequently chose a colonial career did so because they had no choice. There might be some exceptions to this general rule—if, for instance, a colonial campaign were much in the news around graduation time in the spring, then young men higher up the class list might opt for colonial service. But in general, the colonial army collected the rebellious, the misfits, the "hooligans."

The typical *officier soudanais* had three characteristics: He was extremely ambitious, headstrong and utterly disdainful of his civilian superiors, and sometimes of his military ones as well. (Metropolitan officers might have added a fourth characteristic—their colonial colleagues, in their view, lacked intelligence. But that was sheer prejudice.) This had a peculiar effect on the nature of French colonialism. The acquisition of vast lands in Africa was not the result of decisions taken within the government. Rather, it was done on the initiative of bored *officiers soudanais* looking for a fight. If England acquired an empire "in a fit of absence of mind," as was often claimed, the French empire was acquired in an orgy of military indiscipline.

Why was it so difficult for the French government to control its soldiers in Africa? There were several reasons. The first was the sheer distance which separated Paris from the Sudan. News (and orders) traveled slowly, and some news never traveled at all. By the time Paris learned what their soldiers were about to do, they had already done it. It was very difficult to withdraw from territory once conquered. Governments could easily be blackmailed with arguments about blood spilled, sacrifices made, the retribution which would be meted out to the loyal natives who had aided the French cause and, the clinching one, "the honor of the flag."

Secondly, it often was very difficult for Paris to know where their soldiers actually were. Accurate maps of Africa were very difficult to come by in France. While there is no evidence that *officiers soudanais* actually altered the names of towns to throw Paris off the scent, as General Hubert Lyautey was later to do in Morocco, the series of exotic African names must have been very confusing to ministers sitting in Paris, and most of them required some time to grasp the significance of a particular military advance.

Lastly, it became very difficult, if not impossible, for the government to discipline their headstrong soldiers in Africa. This was due to the instability of governments in the Third Republic and to the ramshackle nature of French colonial administration. With governments surviving only nine months on average, it was almost impossible to impose a firm policy in France, much less in Africa. Their preoccupation with their own survival made ministers vulnerable to pressure from colonialists in the Chamber of Deputies, who were more than willing to protect their young protégés in the Sudan from government retribution. Nor did a clear line of authority exist between Paris and the Sudan. Africa south of the Sahara was nominally the province of the colonial ministry, which after occupying various locations in Paris, eventually came to rest on the Left Bank, on the rue Oudinot. It was known familiarly as "the ashtray of ministries," and occupied the very bottom rung in the ministerial pecking order. The portfolio of the colonies was often in the possession of men who had little interest in, or little knowledge of, colonial questions. The "rue Oudinot" was staffed largely by men who had failed to find alternative employment in more prestigious ministries.

The situation in the colonies was even worse. While in Britain, colonial service was seen as a respectable calling which attracted the poorer, but nevertheless honorable, sections of the middle class, in France the colonies became a catchbag not only for the unemployed, but also for the unemployable: "A barber, a peanut vendor, a navvy with the right connections, can be named an Administrator of Native Affairs without the slightest concern for his abilities, his intelligence, his attitudes or his aptitudes," read a pamphlet published in 1911. Barely half the recruits to the colonial administration before 1914 had even a secondary education, and twenty-two percent were judged incompetent by their immediate superiors. These men obviously found it difficult to impose their authority on commanders in the field, who had minds of their own. Therefore, from top to bottom, from minister to the most minor functionary, both the quality of its personnel and the clarity of its policies were suspect.

But the confusion of colonial administration did not stop at the rue Oudinot. Africa was not the exclusive province of the colonial ministry. The Quai d'Orsay arrogated to itself questions of boundaries and relations with neighboring British colonies, and therefore had a vested interest in ensuring military discipline. Their integrity as diplomats depended upon it. The colonial army fell under the jurisdiction of the naval ministry, while army officers were also frequently seconded to Africa. With all these overlapping lines of authority, any attempt to discipline a marine for some unscheduled military initiative, for an act of brutality or even for dealing in slaves, almost always came to nothing in the interministerial rivalry that characterized government in the Third Republic. When, for instance, the new undersecretary for the colonies, Théophile Delcassé, wanted to discipline Colonel Louis Archinard, one of the *enfants terribles* of the Sudan, for refusing to obey orders from Paris, the naval ministry simply promoted the colonel to brigadier and gave him a plum assignment in Paris on the rue Royale, just across the street from Chez Maxim's.

The departure of Archinard from the Sudan is not without relevance to the story of Timbuktu. Even though he left under something of a cloud, his "disgrace" had done nothing to alter the basic principles upon which Archinard had constructed his military career. "The absence of instructions from the colonial administration may be taken as a tacit authorization to use your own judgment," he told his close friend Eugène Bonnier, who succeeded him as military commander of the Sudan. And Bonnier intended to do just that. Even before he left France to take up his new post, he had made up his mind to seize Timbuktu. He had been given no orders before boarding the ship at Bordeaux on August 5, 1893, for the voyage to Dakar. In the absence of instructions, he decided to rely on the Archinard formula, "use your own judgement."

But instructions were on the way in the form of the newly appointed governor general of the Sudan, Albert Grodet. Delcassé, frustrated in his attempts to discipline Archinard, decided that at least he could prevent a repetition of similar misdemeanors with the appointment of Sudan's first civilian governor. Grodet had already served as governor of Martinique and French Guiana, where he had acquired the reputation as a tough boss who tolerated no nonsense from his subordinates, which is certainly why Delcassé chose him for the Sudan. He was also famous for his poor judgment and mismanagement, but then competence was not an essential requirement for French colonial postings. Grodet's orders were clear: He must hold French expansion in check. Delcassé wanted no more African territory. He had too much as it was.

Bonnier was very much aware of what was at stake. If his dream was to be realized, he had to launch his expedition before Grodet arrived. On December 26, 1893, the day Grodet appeared at Kayes on the Senegal River, Bonnier set out from Ségou, 350 miles to the east. Bonnier concluded, not without reason, that Timbuktu would prove extremely easy to take. It was neither surrounded by a wall, nor guarded by a militia. He would be able to pluck it like an overripe plum. The only problem might come from the bands of marauding Tuareg, who for years had made life miserable for the inhabitants of Timbuktu. But with a force of 204 Senegalese tirailleurs, commanded by 9 European NCOs and 13 officers, all very well armed, plus two 80-millimeter cannon, small tubes which could be easily dismantled for transport, he would have nothing to fear from a few ragged, ill-armed desert tribesmen. With this force, preceded by two slender river-gunboats under the command of naval Lieutenant H. G. M. Boiteux, he set sail in a flotilla of pirogues, small dugout canoes of the type used by blacks on the Niger. A second column, under Major Joseph Joffre, the future commander-in-chief of the French army, set off overland with vital supplies which would eventually be needed at Timbuktu by Bonnier's tirailleurs.

Barely had Bonnier left Ségou than a message arrived from Grodet informing Bonnier that he had assumed command. On December 27, 1893, Bonnier replied that he was merely on an inspection tour of the northern frontier. The lieutenant colonel knew full well that by the time his letter reached Kayes, he would be well on the way to Timbuktu. In four days, the lazy current of the Niger had taken Bonnier the 150 miles from Ségou to Mopi, a busy market town on the right bank of the Niger where it meets the Bani River. At eleven o'clock on the morning of January 1, 1894, Bonnier launched his pirogues once again in the direction of Timbuktu, 200 miles to the northeast. About 50 miles north of Mopi, the Niger enters a region of marsh. The channel of the river sometimes becomes difficult to define, and the current becomes so sluggish that the tirailleurs were forced to paddle their overladen canoes. The inexperienced infantrymen's attempts to maneuver the heavy pirogues, most showing only two or three inches of freeboard above the water, caused several of the boats to sink, including one carrying one of the artillery pieces.

To add to Bonnier's troubles, Lieutenant Boiteux had left Mopi against Bonnier's orders and raced ahead to Kabara, Timbuktu's port on the river about ten miles from the town. Bonnier was furious with Boiteux. The young lieutenant had a reputation as a reckless and intractable officer, but then this description could fit at least seventy-five percent of French officers serving in the Sudan. Certainly, Boiteux's two gunboats, small as they were, were at least steam-powered and would prove useful to the inexpert mariners who struggled upstream, shipping more water than they paddled. There was also the question of close reconnaissance and support from Boiteux's guns, should Bonnier's foundering fleet run into trouble. But that was unlikely.

These marshes contained a few sizable villages inhabited mainly by black fishermen, and which also served as ports for the raft and pirogue trade on the Niger. Bonnier felt there was nothing to fear from them. The Tuareg's natural aversion to water should keep them well away from these marshes. The real reason, one suspects, that the lieutenant colonel was furious with his young naval subordinate was that Boiteux had jumped the gun on him and arrived first at Timbuktu.

In fact, Bonnier had reason to thank his lieutenant. As the tirailleurs splashed northward from Mopi, a message arrived from Grodet ordering Bonnier back to Ségou. However, Boiteux's undisciplined rush for Timbuktu had provided his commander with the perfect excuse to forge ahead: Bonnier replied to Grodet that Boiteux's gunboats had run into trouble at Kabara, and he had to paddle to their rescue. Besides, he informed Grodet, Timbuktu had "seriously offered" its submission and requested a French garrison. Boiteux had arrived at Kabara on December 28, 1893. He had docked, and, with four Europeans and a few black sailors, had walked into Timbuktu, unmolested. But while he was in the town, the Tuareg attacked his boats, killing seventeen of the men on board. Grodet, having now learned that Bonnier had been planning this expedition since November, was furious, and sent out letters on January 5 relieving both Bonnier and Joffre of their commands. But these orders arrived too late.

On January 10, 1894, Bonnier's flotilla glided into Kabara. The lieutenant colonel left one company of tirailleurs at Kabara, and with the other marched to Timbuktu for a stormy confrontation with Boiteux. The lieutenant was unrepentant and even began to swear at his commander. Bonnier ordered him confined to quarters for thirty days. This seems light punishment for a man who, as commander of an escort, ran off and left his convoy unprotected and unsupported in the presence of the enemy to indulge in his own adventure, and one that needlessly cost the lives of seventeen of his men, and then swore at his superior when he was finally brought to book. Military custom should have dictated that, at the very least, Boiteux have his buttons cut off and his sword broken, and be drummed down the gangway for gross insubordination and dereliction of duty. But one must remember that this was Africa in the heyday of colonial expansion, not Europe. For the French officers who took part, the Sudan had been transformed into a military Klondike, where every one of them was prospecting for promotion, decorations and glory. The case of Boiteux was not exceptional; and thirty days' confinement was the normal punishment.

In retrospect, Boiteux appears to have escaped lightly. Bonnier was to pay a far heavier penalty, indeed, the ultimate one, for his indiscipline and for the contempt in which he held the Tuareg. At eight o'clock on the morning of January 12, 1894, Bonnier left Timbuktu to a garrison of fifty tirailleurs and marched southwest toward Goundam to rendezvous with the support column under Joffre—who was also having problems with insubordination in his ranks.

Major Joffre had not been cut from the same piece of cloth as most of his Sudanese colleagues. The Franco-Prussian War had interrupted his studies at the Ecole polytechnique, and like other cadets he had abandoned his books to fight. After the war, he completed the course, took up a commission in the sappers, and settled down with his young wife to enjoy the comfortable, if uneventful, life of a garrison soldier in France. Joffre was far too attached to his creature comforts, especially *les plaisirs de table,* to go hiding off to a corner of the world where people ate, well, God knows what!

With his wife's unexpected death in 1884, however, Joffre's perspective changed completely. Grief-stricken, he sought an escape in colonial service. It was to prove a turning point in his career, for in Indochina, the Sudan and Madagascar he earned the rapid promotion that he certainly would not have received at home. Nonetheless, Joffre was a very cautious, deliberate, rather stolid man, very different from most of the young officers who surrounded him. Joffre simply pretended not to notice, and carried on designing his fortifications, planning barracks and river ports—until the day Bonnier needed a man to command the overland supply column to Timbuktu. Joffre was the senior man, after Bonnier, in the region. So Joffre took on the unaccustomed duty as convoy commander.

He left Ségou on December 28, 1893, with 400 troops—two companies of tirailleurs, a squadron of spahis and a battery of 80-millimeter mountain guns, 700 native porters and 200 horses and mules, marching in three files. At night, he formed a square, almost always placing at least one side against a body of water, and personally set out sentinels and patrols. His caution probably explains why he survived and Bonnier did not. He was plodding toward Timbuktu when, like Bonnier, he received Grodet's orders to return. Why did he not obey? He subsequently argued, like Bonnier, that he could not leave French troops stranded without support in Timbuktu, and so he simply ignored Grodet's order to retreat. However, another story, and one that received wide credence in the army, held that Joffre was about to turn back when he was confronted by a young Lieutenant Henri Laperrine, who informed the major that if he retreated, then Laperrine would take his Sudanese spahis and march ahead without him. Given what we know about the character of both of these men—Laperrine was later to play a major role in the conquest of the Sahara—the story sounds altogether plausible.

In any case, Bonnier and Joffre were not destined to meet. January 12, 1894, the first day of Bonnier's march from Timbuktu to Goundam, a distance of fifty miles, was uneventful. Bonnier must have supposed that his force of around 150 men and his artillery would discourage any Tuareg attack. The following morning, they surprised a Tuareg camp and acquired 500 sheep and not a few camels. Any wise commander would have feasted that night on a few dozen sheep and let the rest go. But this was difficult to do in the Sudan. Booty had been the enticement that caused most of the tirailleurs to enlist in the first place. To allow sheep to wander off when they were only a few miles from the market at Goundam was simply throwing away cash. Nevertheless, these animals considerably slowed Bonnier's progress.

For most of the day of January 14, Bonnier's column skirmished with small parties of Tuareg. At six o'clock in the evening, they made camp in a small clearing in the bush that measured 100 yards wide by 200 long. The men pulled together a square stockade of prickly bushes, against which they stacked their rifles. The animals, the numbers of which had been swelled to almost a thousand by the camels, cattle and sheep captured during the day, were left outside the barrier.

At four o'clock on the morning of January 15, 1894, Bonnier's camp was assaulted by what they estimated to be one hundred Tuareg on camels and many others on foot. In the dark, it must have been impossible to tell. The tirailleurs stampeded to find their rifles. Few managed it, for the Tuareg were among them before they could organize an effective defense. Captain Nigotte, the only officer to survive, was knocked from his horse and crawled away into the bush. That he managed to escape, together with several of the NCOs and quite a few tirailleurs, was due largely to the fact that the attackers began to pillage in earnest once they realized the French were routed.

Despite the contempt in which French officers held the Tuareg, it could escape the attention of no one that, for the second time, the desert men had inflicted a crushing defeat on a French force that was superior, if not in numbers, then certainly in weaponry. How far the Tuareg tactics were "unfair" was a matter of some debate. Nigotte claimed that the

Tuareg were able to get close to Bonnier's stockade by crawling through the legs of the animals outside. But Tuareg later questioned about the attack denied this. Another version used to explain the Tuareg success held that they first stampeded the captured animals through the camp to create confusion. The animals certainly stampeded, but probably as a result of the attack rather than as a prelude to it. Besides, as most of the captured animals were sheep, they would have caused little damage to the French camp. Perhaps they added to the confusion, but they did not create it. The Tuareg were prepared to use surprise, they said, but seldom stealth. They had charged the French camp as they always charged, from a distance, on camel back, jumping to the ground before engaging the enemy. If the tirailleurs were asleep at four o'clock in the morning, and, more to the point, if they had chosen not to sleep with their rifles, this was hardly the fault of the Tuareg. The fact that Bonnier was incompetent did not diminish the Tuareg's bravery, nor the extent of their victory —eleven officers, two European NCOs, the native interpreter and sixty-eight tirailleurs killed.

The grisly task of bringing the bodies of the whites back to Timbuktu for burial fell to Joffre: "In a clearing, at the foot of a thick bush, was a mass of corpses, probably those of the tirailleurs, while in the middle and to the south, other bodies lay in various postures," Joffre, writing in 1915, remembered. "We left the place with a sense of quiet and powerless rage which is extremely trying."

In France the general consensus was that Bonnier had got what he deserved. The press led what Charles Herrisé, one of those deputies who could always be counted upon to defend the army, called an "odious campaign." He categorized Grodet's treatment of officers who had merely overstepped orders as "brutal," and demanded his recall. (Joffre had been sent home for disobeying orders but, typically, had been promoted to lieutenant colonel and reassigned to Madagascar.) But Herrisé was very much in a minority. Most newspapers, including the influential *Le Temps,* condemned the military indiscipline which had characterized the campaigns in the Sudan. The publication in March 1894 of the report on the massacre in the *Journal officiel* also deflated Bonnier's military reputation, criticizing especially his failure to patrol and to put out more than a few pickets. *La Libre Parole,* the newspaper of the despicable anti-semite Edouard Drumont, argued that Bonnier had actually been on his way back to Kayes when he was butchered, and then went on to accuse

Grodet of having close connections with Jewish financiers. But this counterattack by the extreme right had little effect. In the words of Canadian historian A.S. Kanya-Forstner, "the Goundam massacre had shattered the myth of the Sudanese military's professional brilliance and had largely discredited them in the eyes of the French public." Nevertheless, they had secured Timbuktu for France.

In the history of French politics, a veil seems now to have been drawn over the Western Sudan. The reason was simple: Massacres like those of Flatters and Bonnier, rather than kindle a spirit of revenge in the French population, put them off the whole idea of colonial conquest. More astute commanders avoided risky operations because they realized, like Lieutenant Colonel Joseph Gallieni, the future hero of the "Taxis of the Marne" in 1914, that "a new catastrophe would again sadden French public opinion and roll back our work in the Sudan." Furthermore, it was in no one's interest to reveal what was actually going on there. A fair number of young, ambitious and arrogant French officers seem to have believed that brutality was the only way to make France's name respected among the blacks. The difficulty lay with the fact that they were virtually impossible to restrain, as Grodet discovered. His military commanders continued to ignore him, despite the salutary lesson of Timbuktu. Punishments of thirty days' confinement failed to deter them. Grodet's only real option was to purge the soldiers from administrative positions and replace them with civilians. But given the turbulent state of the countryside, this was out of the question. Therefore, the conquests continued. Grodet could only shrug his shoulders in helplessness and content himself with the moral support of the government.

While officers were aware that there must be no more disasters like that of Bonnier, they also realized that they must move with haste to stake out their claims in central Africa. The problem lay with the Anglo-French Convention of August 5, 1890, which had neglected to mention what was to happen to Lake Chad and the territories lying to the east and south of it. In fact, French colonialists suspected that Germany and Britain had already marked out the choicest pieces of real estate for themselves. This fear spurred colonial soldiers, backed by colonialists in France, into new orgies of indiscipline: "We soldiers know only that there are territories in Africa which ought to belong to us and that the English and the Germans are in the process of appropriating them," Gallieni wrote in 1891. "We are trying to beat them to it." No one really knew much about central Africa. Neither London, Paris nor Berlin pretended to control it, nor were any of them sure that they wanted to. In 1894, the French took Timbuktu, but Timbuktu is still over 1,000 miles from Lake Chad. Nevertheless, it was clear that some sort of agreement on central Africa must be hammered out among the powers.

For the French colonialists, the 1890s were in many respects a golden age. Under the able guidance of Eugène Etienne, the *parti colonial* was moving toward its maximum strength of 102 deputies by the turn of the century. How many of these deputies were actually dedicated colonialists is hard to say. Certainly they were dedicated diners. Not for the colonialists the smoky back rooms of dingy political offices. They met in restaurants, good restaurants, and belched and applauded their way through speeches about the great work of empire-building, so much so that they acquired the label of *le parti où on dîne*. When one of their critics pointed out that other parties too held political banquets, they retorted that theirs was *le parti où on dîne bien.*

But quite apart from the quality of the food, the *parti colonial* was also acquiring some political muscle. The 1893 elections had returned a strongly center-right parliament. While the colonialists were a cross-party grouping, their political center of gravity was very much on the center-right. Therefore, they felt at home with the new government, or rather governments, for this was also a period of dizzying political instability. But there was nothing wrong in that. Governments preoccupied with their own survival were easily influenced, and easily fooled. They had time only for a cursory consideration of colonial issues, if they considered them at all. The Marchand expedition to the Upper Nile which in 1898 brought Britain and France to the brink of war was discussed only once by the cabinet, and then only for a few minutes. Many other expeditions were not considered at all by them. That was all right with the colonialists. They preferred to do things on the quiet.

Apart from the advantage of shaky governments, the colonialists also had two *pistons,* or friends, in the governments of these years: André Lebon and Gabriel Hanotaux, who between them shared the colonial and foreign ministries for much of the time between 1893 and 1898. Hanotaux, especially—a well-known historian who had abandoned a comfortable academic career for the rough-and-tumble of political life— allowed himself to be carried along by the colonialists into a growing rivalry with the British in central Africa. Thus, imperial rivalry, rather than any economic motive, provided the main thrust for the drive into Africa.

In 1896, a joint Anglo-French commission was at last set up to define a border between the French sphere of influence in the north, and that of the British in Nigeria to the south. They took their time about it. Working on the principle that possession is nine-tenths of the law, they dragged out negotiations, took hours over lunch and adjourned for long recesses so as to give their respective soldiers and explorers time to send out missions and stake some sort of claim to the disputed territory. The British followed their traditional practice of drawing up trade treaties with native chiefs. The French were more direct in their approach. They had nothing to trade, so they simply dispatched soldiers to occupy the land. This, it must be stressed, was not part of French government policy, although it was connived at by men in the Quai d'Orsay and the rue Oudinot. French colonial policy was made outside the government, in the banquets of the *parti colonial* and by French soldiers in the field. French soldiers followed a slash-and-burn policy in central Africa, and everyone kept quiet about it, everyone, that is, except the British. In 1897–98, several of the French expeditions wandered into the Hausa lands, which had been ceded to Britain in 1890, and burned villages. At one point, British and French troops actually exchanged shots. By March 1898, London had had enough. The *Times* demanded that French officers who had run amok in Nigeria be brought to book. George Goldie, the governor-general of Nigeria, brought in troops from the West Indies which raised British military strength in Nigeria to 250 officers and 4,000 men. Under the command of Colonel Frederick Lugard, this subsequently became the famous West African Frontier Force. Their task was to protect Nigeria, not from internal rebellion, but from the French army.

But these squabbles in central Africa were in many ways only a diversion. The real prize (if a prize it was) which the French coveted was the Nile. If, they reasoned, they could establish a presence on the upper Nile, then they could force the British to recognize their "historic claims" to Egypt. In 1896, an expedition of 300 Senegalese tirailleurs under the command of Captain Jean Baptist Marchand quietly left the mouth of the Congo River moving northeast. Their destination was to be Fashoda, 3,000 miles and two years away.

It is in this context that one must see the next episode in the history of the Sahara—the Foureau-Lamy mission of 1898. In 1897, the French military attaché in London began to send a stream of reports which indicated that the English had designs on Lake Chad. Like Timbuktu in the early years of the decade, Lake Chad now became the goal of a number of French colonial soldiers. Its seizure was also seen as part of *la politique de haut Nil* which was being pursued in a semiofficial way in Paris. The conquest of central Africa was believed essential to support the Marchand mission. Otherwise, Marchand and his tirailleurs would be isolated and easily overpowered by the English (which was precisely what was to happen).

The conquest of the Sudan and of Lake Chad was vital to the conquest of the Sahara. The 1890 Convention had invited the French in Algeria to look southward. But the conquest of the Sahara did not make sense unless the Sudan was also in French hands. The desert was the corridor through which the French hoped to run their Transsaharian railway. But the Flatters massacre had proved that one could not build a railroad through territory, or to territory, which one did not already control. "In Africa, as in Europe, the only irresistible argument is force," General Gustave Borgnis-Desbordes, the governor general of Senegal, said in 1891. "It is the only one which fanatical and warlike Muslims are capable of recognizing. . . . Today the Blacks are well aware that a peaceful expedition by a white man is only the prelude to a merciless and unceasing commercial exploitation. They take up arms in self-defence and who can blame them?"

Lake Chad replaced Timbuktu as the new El Dorado in the feverish and fertile imaginations of the colonialists. (Those who pointed out that Lake Chad was no more than a swamp were ignored.) The view that Lake Chad was an area of immense economic importance had reawakened interest in the railway. On June 14, 1898, Hanotaux and Sir Charles Monson signed a convention delimiting the frontier of northern Nigeria. The status of Lake Chad, however, was left vague. The French, therefore, dispatched three columns to secure the territory around it. One expedition under Major François Lamy and the veteran Saharian explorer Fernand Foureau were to leave Algiers, cross the desert and establish a presence in the Air, around Agadez. A second column under two young officers, Captain Paul Voulet and Lieutenant Charles Chanoine, were to strike eastward across the Sudan to reconnoiter the territory between the Niger bend and Lake Chad. (There is also some indication that they intended to join Marchand on the Nile.) A third party under Emile Gentil left Brazzaville in the Congo to secure the lands south of the lake.

French historians have written of the "race for Lake Chad" as if it formed part of a deliberate policy. On the surface, this appears plausible. The three-pronged offensive does import something of a Napoleonic flavor into African exploration. However, if in retrospect the three expeditions appear to have been coordinated from Paris, it was only by accident. In reality, they were far more *ad hoc* affairs. There was no grand design thought up in the French cabinet. Each officer lobbied the ministries separately for funds and had only the vaguest notions that there were others doing similar things. The functionaries dithered while governments collapsed and new ministers made up their minds. That the three columns would eventually converge on Lake Chad after various adventures—and misadventures—was very far from anyone's mind. The "race for Lake Chad" was more like a game of blindman's buff. Like most things the French did in Africa, it had a very improvised quality about it.

Nevertheless, the conquest of the Sudan is an essential event in the history of the Sahara. The Tuareg were numerous between the Niger bend and Lake Chad. Furthermore, it is here that the Tuareg of the Ahaggar came to trade, reprovision and raid for slaves. If the French controlled the Sudan, then this was bound to have consequences further north in the Ahaggar. It would essentially leave the Ahaggar Tuareg only the oasis of Tuat, and to a lesser extent the smaller oases in the Fezzan, to which they might go for supplies. The noose would be drawn even tighter around the desert. If the Foureau-Lamy mission managed to cross the Sahara, the first expedition to do so, then it would also mean that the initiative for the conquest of the desert would shift back from the Sudan to Algeria.

So the "race for Lake Chad" was to influence the history of the Sahara. That there was only one team in this race went unnoticed by the French. They thought, or rather they wanted to think, that the British and the Germans were close on their heels. So they ran for all they were worth.

X

MORÈS AFFAIR

Our received image of nineteenth-century explorers is one of solitary men. In many respects, however, this view is a false one. Resourcefulness and self-sufficiency they must have possessed to an astonishing degree. But they also must be men of the world, able publicists and fund-raisers with influential contacts in academic and governmental circles. Without financial backing, exploration was beyond the reach of all but gentlemen tourists. Nor did they expect the results of their travels to go unnoticed. They craved fame and publicity. They did not wish to remain anonymous.

Perhaps this was part of the reason why, in 1876, Fernand Foureau abandoned a comfortable middle-class existence in France to emigrate to Algeria, where, after a brief and unsuccessful stint as a farmer, he took up a career in exploration. To a certain degree, his new vocation was inherited—his grandfather had toured America and lived among several tribes of Indians at a time when that sort of anthropological research might have cost him his scalp. If by 1898, the French knew any more about the central Sahara than they had at the time of the Flatters disaster seventeen years earlier, it was due largely to Foureau's persistent exploration: he had made no fewer than eleven trips into the desert. The remarkable thing about Foureau, and one thing which set him apart from many other Saharian explorers, especially the later ones, was that he had survived. He had done this essentially by setting limited goals for himself. Rather than set out on blockbusting adventures like Caillié or Barth, he sought to deepen his knowledge of the area to the south and west of El Goléa—the Tademaït Plateau, the Great Eastern Erg, the northern fringes of the Tassili. In the process, he had made contacts with Ajjer Tuareg, contacts which, alas, did not open the Sahara to him. On the contrary, if some Tuareg proved to be well disposed, they had not sufficient authority to guide him safely through the territory. This was the old problem of the anarchy of the desert, of the amenoukal's lack of power. Foureau drew the obvious conclusion: If the Tuareg could not be persuaded to open the door to the Sahara, then it must be forced.

Foureau's views were important for the history of the Sahara. His many expeditions and writings had gradually established him as a recognized expert on the desert. When, in the spring of 1892, Henri Duveryier, the author, in 1864, while still in his early twenties, of *Les Touareg du nord,* walked into a wood near Paris and put a bullet into his brain, Foureau inherited the mantle of France's premier Saharian expert. For years, Duveryier had been the *doyen* of Saharian studies, consulted by every ministry and learned body, even though his information was not only long out of date, but also often inaccurate, reflecting the naiveté of the eighteen-year-old traveler. Many people decried the baleful influence of Duveryier, whose belief that the Tuareg were essentially good, simple, misunderstood folk had helped to convince ministers and committees that persuasion, rather than force, was the way to deal with them. Misunderstood the Tuareg certainly were. But the French had for years tried to use the politics of the carrot to get around them. Now, perhaps, the time had come to take up the stick. Foureau, who knew the desert better than any living Frenchman, agreed and was prepared to say so. With the French ranging themselves on the starting blocks for the great "race for Lake Chad," perhaps the time had come to send an expedition into the Sahara which was capable of blasting its way through. Foureau was placed in charge.

One would have thought that at forty-eight, Foureau might have been searching for a more comfortable position than that of leader of a large-scale invasion of the Sahara—a position in the colonial ministry, perhaps, or secretary of a geographical society. Certainly, the enterprise was more substantial by far than any other he had yet undertaken and promised to be more difficult to direct.

However, Foureau was not asked along simply because of his extensive Saharian experience. Rather, his appointment as titular chief of the expedition was meant to camouflage a mission of colonial conquest. As this was to be a military expedition in all but name, it must have a military commander. The one chosen—or rather, the man who chose himself—was Major François Lamy.

To see these two men together, one might easily have confused the soldier with the civilian. Foureau exuded the asceticism of the desert—a long head perched on a thin neck, and a tall, spare frame, made him seem as if he had been constructed for heat loss. His brown, wrinkled face had the appearance of a much-used chamois. Only a few crinkles of hair twisted up from his near-vacant scalp. There was nothing particularly decorative or handsome about Fernand Foureau. Like a camel, he appeared to have been designed for the sole purpose of survival in dry regions.

François Lamy, on the other hand, looked like a refugee from the diplomatic corps. His face was intelligent, even handsome. His beard was cropped to form a long wedge at the chin, and his moustache tickled into two points which reached out from the corners of his mouth. A pince-nez balanced precariously on the bridge of his nose completed the Quai d'Orsay effect and concealed a pair of eyes which had the softness of the myopic about them. Lamy looked far more like a man used to riding a carriage through the Bois de Boulogne than one who took camels through the desert. In fact, he had been in the army since the age of ten, when his father, who had been invalided out of the navy and retired into the hills behind Cannes, sent him to Le Prytanée de La Flèche, a military preparatory school reserved for the sons of officers. La Flèche straddles the Loir River as it meanders to meet the larger Loire several miles to the south at Angers. The white plaster walls of the houses and their red Roman tiled roofs combine with the vineyards which cover the gently rolling countryside around the town to give La Flèche just a hint of the Midi. What Lamy thought of the Prytanée is not recorded. In these years around the time of the Franco-Prussian War, the cadets led a spartan existence in vast dormitory rooms, rising before first light to splash their faces with cold water in the fountains of the school courtyard, existing on bread and the interminable *rata,* a stew made from beans and whatever other vegetables were in season. Most young men subjected to this sort of regime at a tender age are repelled by the idea of a military career. Lamy obviously was not, for he went straight from the Prytanée to St.-Cyr in 1876.

Money was probably the deciding factor. Lamy's mother hoped that her son would follow in her father's footsteps and become a solicitor. But an education in the law may have been beyond the family's means. The fact that he had been sent to the Prytanée, which originally had been set up for the sons of officers killed in battle, and which was, unlike other secondary schools in France, entirely free, indicates that the Lamy family was strapped for cash. (Later, after he was commissioned, Lamy sent a large portion of his pay to his mother.) Whether or not he possessed a military vocation, he did well at St.-Cyr, graduating in 1879 fifty-fourth in a class of 340. It was a respectable class ranking, and one which would have allowed him to select a good regiment in France. He did not.

Instead he chose the Algerian tirailleurs and was sent to Blida. On the face of it, this seems a strange decision. In 1879, young French officers were waiting expectantly for the war of revenge with Prussia. That they would have a rather long wait was not yet apparent, so much so that many refused service abroad out of fear that they might miss it. Also, the Armée d'Afrique was in the army's bad books: As most of the French generals who had performed so disastrously against the Prussians were *Africains,* it was presumed that there must be something wrong with the army in Africa. Medals and promotions must have been won too cheaply there. Serious officers, therefore, would henceforth remain in France. Why Lamy chose Algeria, and the rather lowly tirailleurs at that, is a question whose answer we can only guess. Perhaps his father's tales of travels and discoveries played a part. Lamy certainly lacked the cash and connections to stake out a brilliant career in France. Perhaps, also, talk of the Transsaharian which filled the newspapers in 1879 stimulated a taste for exotica. We know that he attempted to sign on Flatters's second mission but, fortunately, was turned down. But whatever his reasons, Lamy's decision meant that he was well placed to play a leading role in France's colonial expansion which began in the 1880s. He was with the French force which invaded Tunisia in 1881. In 1884, he went to Tonkin; in 1891 he became commander at El Goléa, where he experimented with camel-mounted troops and, he claimed, converted to Islam. He left El Goléa in 1893, when his post was incorporated into the Arab Bureau (he detested the extra paperwork), and was sent to the Congo. Life in the jungle was very different from life in the desert: "The path gets worse and worse," he wrote from the Mangi River in October 1893.

> In places one is obliged to suspend a tropical creeper and let it slide along the jagged rocks. In others, the water comes up to the belt. At last, we arrived at the banks of the Mangi. This river is more than fifty yards across and one yard deep. I send the black who knew the ford ahead of me and I wade into the black water. In this place, the bottom is muddy and when the mud gives way under the feet it is a horribly disagreeable sensation. The crossing is made without difficulty, the water comes

up only to my chest. The night rains which fell in the mountains swelled the river and we can recross it only by swimming.

Quite apart from the difficult terrain, the Congo was an eye-opener. Lamy was plagued by unreliable porters—and no wonder, as they were paid in bottles of cheap alcohol. In any case, the experience made him long for his dear Sahara, and helped to convince him that the Sahara must be conquered to form the bridge between France and her African empire. He feared that he might not be present on the day the French flag was raised over In Salah. (He would not, but for reasons which he could not know.)

However, the Sahara had to wait, for the French were up to their eyeballs in trouble in Madagascar. In 1896, the Hovas, who had at first cooperated with the French, rose in rebellion. Joseph Gallieni and his chief of staff, Hubert Lyautey, had been dispatched from Tonkin to quell the disorder. The rebellion could not have come at a worse time for the colonial army. Colonial soldiers, defying the orders of Grodet, were still running amok in the Sudan and had few troops to spare for Gallieni in Madagascar. Indochina was relatively quiet. But Indochina seldom remained quiet for long. Tonkin had just endured an extended period of upheaval, and few troops could be spared from police duties. As it would have been politically unthinkable to request conscripts from France to fight a colonial war (patriots and the left alike would have condemned denuding the northeastern frontier for the sake of a colonial adventure in the Indian Ocean), this left only one place to turn—North Africa. Captain Lamy was given the task of raising Berbers from the mountainous Kabylia region in Algeria for service in Madagascar. In the process he proved that recruiting methods change little over the centuries. Lamy promised them action, when in fact they were needed to convoy supplies. Using a fair measure of chicanery, Lamy enticed 1,500 Algerians onto the *Guadalquivir* docked in Algiers, for the long trip to Madagascar.

By the time they arrived in Majunga on June 9, 1895, these Algerians had reason to repent of their decision. The conditions of passage had been bad enough, but what they found at Majunga was far worse. The beach was piled high with putrefying supplies, while other ships stood offshore to unload still more. Their task was to move the stores inland on the backs of 6,000 mules which had been assembled on the beach. Unfortunately, few of the mules had been broken, and most took to harness "like a dog with a saucepan tied to his tail." Without shoes or medicine, badly fed, Lamy's Algerians perished by the score. But death in Madagascar respected no nationality—over eighty percent of Frenchmen serving in this campaign with the military engineers also died of disease.

Lamy, seeming to live a charmed life, did not feel the slightest shiver of malaria. He saw a bit of action around Tananarive in 1896, and the following year, aged thirty-nine, was promoted to major. It had not exactly been a meteoric rise. Lamy seems to have been regarded by his superiors as something of a workhorse, adept at organizing convoys and other support tasks. Gallieni decorated him with the Order of Radama for his geographic work in compiling forty maps of the island. But that seems to be as far as the resident general was prepared to go. Lamy was obviously not part of Gallieni's charmed inner circle, a circle that included Lyautey and a stable of other officers destined for stellar rank. So Lamy asked for an extended leave to return home via South Africa.

One might be forgiven for surmising that Lamy's firsthand experience of South Africa on the eve of the Boer War was responsible for his next assignment, and the first real break in his career—that of aide-decamp to the president of the republic, Félix Faure. How else can one explain the surprising appointment of a hardened *broussard* (bush fighter) to the coveted ranks of the *maison militaire* of the Elysée Palace? However, this appointment owed less to South Africa than to Algeria. Lamy arrived at Le Havre on June 6, 1897, and spent most of the summer drifting around Paris waiting for his orders. During this time he met Jules Cambon, then in his last weeks as governor general of Algeria before moving to Washington as French ambassador.

Cambon's enthusiasm for Saharian exploration shaded off into fanaticism. To him, the time seemed ripe to give a serious impetus to the Transsaharian project. Interest in the railroad had revived in 1888, and two years later yet another interministerial committee had been formed to study a route. Now that the French conquest of the Sudan was underway, the momentum for the Saharian conquest might again be shifted back to the north. In Lamy, Cambon must have thought that he had found his man. Of course, one can never know by which devious route Lamy arrived at the Elysée, but it seems reasonable to speculate that it was due to Cambon's influence. Lamy possessed desert experience. What he would need was a period in Paris to make contacts and gather support for an expedition. What better place to start than the Elysée? With that on his calling card, Lamy was sure to open a few doors. Félix Faure was known as a great friend of the army and would probably help Lamy in any way he could. The new governor general of Algeria, Julien Laferrière, favored an aggressive policy in the Sahara. This was a combination of circumstances which Lamy could not afford to let slip by.

But there was more to Lamy's appointment, and to his projected mission, than meets the eye. Cambon admonished the major "to avenge our compatriots and take up their unfinished work." Historians have assumed that Cambon was referring to Flatters, and he probably was. But he was also referring to the Marquis de Morès, and it was to this man, rather than to Flatters, that Lamy owed his new opportunity.

The Foureau-Lamy mission, indeed the whole chain of events which were in seven short years to bring the central Sahara under French control, began with the bizarre and virtually unknown story of this man. Antoine de Vallombrosa, the Marquis de Morès, was born in 1858, son, on his father's side, of a Spanish family which had moved to Sardinia in the fifteenth century, and through his mother related to the Duc de Cars. He was educated at St.-Cyr and the cavalry school at Saumur, but left the army after a few years to marry a New York heiress. It was not uncommon in the decades before the Great War for impoverished European aristocrats to seek out American money (and vice versa). The dandified French cavalry officer must have seemed immensely attractive to the banker's daughter from New York. She certainly acquired the fancy name she no doubt coveted, but that was about all she got. Attempts by her father to initiate his new son-in-law into the mysteries of high finance were not just unsuccessful but positively disastrous. Morès was far more interested in the *après banc,* and after several disappointing years, his father-in-law acceded to one of his whims and purchased for him a 26,000-acre ranch in the Dakotas. Morès met with no more success on the prairie than he had in the bank. He annoyed most of his neighbors by throwing strands of barbed wire everywhere, and in the Dakotas of the 1880s, annoyed neighbors had the disconcerting habit of reaching for their guns. Morès's reputation as an indefatigable duelist served him well, and he survived mainly because he was an excellent shot—indeed, he sent several cowboys to Boot Hill. But his position soon became untenable. He quarreled with everyone, including the cattle merchants and meat dealers. What was the good of having 26,000 acres full of cattle if no one would buy them? So Morès sold out and, after traveling in Tonkin and hunting tiger in India, returned to Europe in 1888.

In Paris, Morès fell in with a decadent crowd of aristocrats and hangers-on and wasted time in dueling and at the gambling tables, so much so that his family, with official complicity, took legal action to separate him from his fortune and tie him to a strict allowance. But America had given Morès more than a wife. She had also bequeathed to him a passionate hatred for capitalism, and this decadent, dandified aristocrat declared himself to be a "republican and socialist." In 1893, he traveled to Algiers and gave a lecture on "International Relations and the Monetary Question," and afterward wrote a pamphlet entitled "The Secret of Finance."

In fact, Morès knew as much about international finance as J. P. Morgan knew about camels. Like many men of poor education and simplistic views, Morès was a passionate believer in conspiracies. One of the favorite conspiracy theories of his day was that Anglo-Jewish finance gripped the world by the throat, and Morès swallowed it like a hungry schoolboy: Jews and Anglo-Saxons, the "masters of gold," were also the "corrupters of the Latin spirit." Such views naturally attracted the attention of Edouard Drumont and his anti-Semitic *Libre Parole.*

Drumont and Morès were like two superstitious men haunted by the same ghost. They became fast friends, and through Drumont, Morès became a man of influence in right-wing nationalist circles. From here, it was but a short step to an interest in colonial questions, upon which he held characteristically eccentric views. He accused the Republic of having abandoned central Africa to the English, and called for a Franco-Islamic alliance that would open the Sahara and the Sudan to trade with the Mediterranean. In 1896, after having declared that his life had been misspent and he would seek "a useful and glorious death," he traveled to Algeria to investigate the possibilities of crossing the Sahara to effect his cherished Franco-Islamic alliance against England. In southern Algeria, the French officers he met were polite but decidedly cool. They warned him that the Tuareg were dangerous, and that the Sahara was no place for an amateur explorer. In fact, they were very much worried that his prospective murder would set back the relations with the Tuareg so laboriously built up since the death of Flatters. Morès sent the Tuareg some grain, hoping to buy their goodwill. When this failed to produce any results, he returned to France.

He did not remain there long. In Paris, he learned of the Marchand mission and of colonialist plans to force a showdown with England over Egypt. His brain was now thoroughly overheated: He must cross the Sahara; if Algeria offered an unfavorable starting point, then he would try Tunisia. On March 20, 1896, he arrived in Tunis, and nine days later gave a public lecture in the Théâtre français which was attended by the commanding general of the Tunis garrison, several important officials of the Residency, and a crowd estimated at 2,000 people. They were treated to typical Morès fare, a call for a Franco-Islamic alliance to throw off the financial yoke of England and open the Sahara to France: "That day will spell the ruin of England and put an end to the universal oppression of high finance." In a steadily rising tone, he painted for them a tableau of a Moslem uprising in Egypt and India against Britain, so that from "Dunkirk to the valleys of the upper Nile officers will go off to serve to the cry of 'France and Liberty!' " Morès must have been an electrifying speaker, for the Théâtre français was by now fairly heaving with what the *Dépêche Tunisienne* described as an "enthusiasm which bordered on delirium." In this excited state the audience unanimously voted a motion of support for the Mahdi, who by that time had been dead for a decade. His followers, however, had been kept busy butchering every person— white, black or brown—they could get their hands on, and laying waste to the upper Nile. As this Islamic resistance movement was directed largely at the British and might even threaten their hold on Egypt and Suez, Morès and his followers thought it important to encourage it. Copies of the motion of support were dispatched to the president and prime minister of France, the prime minister of Great Britain, the sultan of Turkey and . . . the Marseilles Chamber of Commerce! What these grateful recipients must have thought of Morès's *ordre du jour* is not difficult to guess. Such foolishness had not been seen in print since the Italian *Risorgimento*.

Nonetheless, Morès received more than polite attention from official circles in Tunis. The reason is simple: Once the fanciful rhetoric and conspiracy theories were stripped away, Morès's sentiments were not noticeably distinguishable from those of other colonialists. All were violent Anglophobes. All wanted to beat the English to Lake Chad and to remove them from the upper Nile and possibly all of Egypt. All hoped that the Transsaharian would one day link French Africa from the Mediterranean to the Congo. Furthermore, Morès, despite his eccentric views, had important connections in nationalist circles in Paris. Certainly most colonialists found Drumont's anti-Semitic diatribes distasteful. But to the joy of the colonialists, the nationalist right had discovered the usefulness of colonial issues as a way to embarrass the government. (They were going to have a field day when, in 1898, the French government refused to go to war to support Marchand's claim to the Upper Nile and instead relinquished it to the English.) Therefore, the radical right had to be courted and colonialists had to be careful not to offend their emissary, Morès.

That Morès was not entirely sane is clear from the way in which he now shot off into the desert. It was May, a suicidal season to travel. On the eve of his departure, he still had no notion of which route he planned to follow. He gathered camels and equipment to the value of 12,000 francs, 3,000 francs worth of merchandise to trade in the Sudan and 4,000 francs in coin, all provided by "friends." The military attaché at the Residency attempted to discourage him, only to find himself denounced by Morès as an agent of Anglo-Jewish finance. Morès had a number of tracts printed which excoriated the Residency in vivid terms. He then returned to the military attaché's office, and by threatening him with a scandal, obtained the necessary visas. On May 14, 1896, at the Café de l'Oasis in Gabès, another speech much along the lines of the first one at Tunis was warmly applauded by the European residents. Before he set out, he sent a letter to the Mouvement Antisémite de Constantine telling them to seek reprisals among "the Jews of Algeria" should he come to any harm in the desert. Although the officers in the French posts along his route of march in southern Tunisia had orders not to help him, he managed to charm them into giving him much useful advice and even to mislead them about the route he planned to take—through Ghadames and Ghat. Before leaving Tunis, he had given his word that he would not venture into territory claimed by the Ottoman sultan: Any mischief he might create there would certainly complicate relations with the Sublime Porte and with the Ajjer Tuareg. He had solemnly promised to travel through southern Algeria, and it was probably the prospect of being able to pass Morès on to Algeria that induced Tunis to let him go in the first place.

When his Chaamba cameleers learned that he was to go to Ghadames, some of them became decidedly mutinous. On June 5, 1896, at the small southern Tunisian oasis of Mechiguig, he paid off his Chaamba.

They demanded more money and rifles. When Morès refused, they left shouting threats. On June 8, the Tuareg arrived as arranged, bringing with them a number of black porters and camels. On the following day, they set out toward Ghadames, and trouble began almost immediately. The camels were in poor condition and the harnesses broke constantly, requiring frequent stops. The thefts of equipment, which had begun on the previous evening, continued, and Morès had words with several of the Tuareg. Then some of the Chaamba whom he had dismissed on the previous day rejoined the caravan and, together with the Tuareg, attacked Morès. The Marquis tried to turn his camel around to flee, but at this critical moment, it refused to budge. In frustration, Morès drew his revolver and shot the beast. It was his ultimate foolish act. The camel tumbled on its side and lay, heavy and inert, on Morès's rifle which, try as he might, he was unable to extricate. Despite this, and despite having been wounded in the head, Morès gave a good account of himself with his revolver, killing three of his attackers and wounding others. He must have imposed some respect, for he was not killed outright, but died several hours later, no doubt weakened by fatigue and blood loss, from a wound in the neck. Two of his black servants escaped and brought the news of his death back to Gabès.

News of Morès's assassination sent a shudder of outrage through the nationalist press: *La Patrie,* for one, called for a "crusade against England" and demanded that Ghadames be given to France as reparations. General Louis Archinard called on his country to "kill as many Tuareg as possible." The ubiquitous Djebari managed to squeeze a little more mileage out of his contention that the Flatters survivors were still alive in the desert (Morès had apparently believed Djebari's fantasies and planned to make contact with Flatters). Drumont's *Libre parole* raised the pitch of its anti-Semitism a few notches in honor of their martyred friend. The remains of the unfortunate Morès were retrieved by three Arabs, and returned to Tunis for a funeral mass during which the Archbishop of Tunis intoned to the thousands in the congregation, "France, who in 1830 purged the Mediterranean of the Barbary pirates, must now eliminate the pirates of the desert."

The Residency came in for a good deal of scolding because of their failure to protect Morès. But this came to nothing. The Residency replied in a perfectly reasonable tone that they had repeatedly warned Morès of the dangers of desert travel, that he was ill prepared, inexperienced and naïve and had met the fate he courted. As for reprisals against Turkey, the murder had taken place on Tunisian, not Ottoman, territory. If anyone bore a share of the responsibility for Morès's death, it was the officers in southern Tunisia who had disobeyed orders and helped him on his way. But this matter was too delicate to be laundered in public. The attitude of the Residency toward Morès's adventure had been characterized by hesitation. They opposed his plans but feared his nationalist friends, and consequently failed to give very clear directives. An attempt to discipline these officers might cause embarrassment, and Tunis was anxious that *l'affaire Morès* be forgotten as quickly as possible.

However, there was one group of men eager to keep the Morès affair alive, and that group was made up of officers serving in southern Algeria. Led by Lieutenant Théodore Pein, the commander at Ouargla, they used their contacts with the Chaamba gradually to draw up a list of those guilty of Morès's murder. In October 1897, Pein dispatched a *harka* of his Arabs in pursuit of El Kheir, one of the guilty Chaamba, who was camped near Temassinin. The *harka* wounded El Kheir, but he nevertheless managed to escape by joining a party of Ajjer Tuareg. The *harka* had to be content with El Kheir's family, whom they brought back captive to Ouargla. Despite this failure, Pein's efforts to track down the murderers were given a new impetus by a bounty offered by the Marquise de Morès. The prospect of payment, combined with a desire to raise his prestige with the French, brought Mohammed Taieb ben Brahim of Ouargla into the search. By using his religious prestige as a marabout, he convinced three of the guilty Chaamba—El Kheir, Hamma ben Cheik, and Hamma ben Youssef—to give themselves up to the French authorities in Tunisia, by promising that they would receive a pardon and that El Kheir's family would be released. Two of them claimed to be innocent, but the youngest, Hamma ben Youssef, confessed in May 1898.

At this point, the *affaire Morès* acquired another layer of baroque intrigue. The Marquise de Morès, together with an ex-Boulangist deputy, Jules Delahaye, accused the Residency of having orchestrated her husband's murder. The Jews and the English inevitably were accused of having masterminded the foul deed, but as it was very difficult to bring them all into court, Delahaye and the Marquise contented themselves with singling out Lieutenant Colonel François Rebillet, who was neither Jewish nor English but the military attaché in Tunis who had quarreled violently with Morès on the eve of his departure.

Rebillet was regarded as one of the army's most brilliant officers and, had he not resigned as a result of the scandal that now broke over his head, would almost certainly have become a general. He had graduated from the Ecole polytechnique into the military engineers, and had seen action in the Franco-Prussian War. In 1877, he attended a two-year course at the Ecole de guerre which qualified him for the general staff, the closest the French army came to creating a Brahmin caste within its ranks. In 1880, he had transferred to North Africa and there discovered his vocation. Rebillet's name is on the list of unsuccessful applicants for the Flatters expedition, but he compensated himself by joining the French invasion of Tunisia in 1881. He became a fluent Arabic speaker and served in various native affairs posts until, in 1895, he had been transferred to the Residency in Tunis. One of his commanding officers described Rebillet as having "a weak appearance but very tough; tireless, well turned out and an excellent horseman; an excitable nature, energetic, impressionable and strongwilled; hard working; gifted with a superior intelligence. . . . The best officer I have in my command." High praise indeed. However, Delahaye denounced Rebillet as a sinister character, a Freemason who had maintained a corrupt caïd in place in southern Tunisia and who had money invested in the caravan trade. Morès's initiative, Delahaye's theory went, threatened to upset Rebillet's interests in southern Tunisia and the Fezzan. So, after having unsuccessfully attempted to stop Morès by legal means, he surrounded him with guides in his pay who informed the Tuareg that Tunis would not be unhappy if Morès were murdered.

After almost two years of legal maneuverings during which the Marquise and Delahaye attempted to have the case moved to Constantine, where they reckoned that Morès's anti-Semitism would elicit the sympathy of a jury of *pieds noirs,* the trial finally opened in Sousse, Tunisia, in July 1902. By this time, one of the captive Chaamba had died. Delahaye failed to prove that Rebillet had planned Morès's murder. The court sentenced the two surviving Chaamba to death, as well as three other Chaamba and fourteen Tuareg in absentia. The Marquise de Morès asked that the sentence of one of the condemned Chaamba, El Kheir, be commuted to life imprisonment, in the belief, no doubt, that he might still have more of a story to tell. Rebillet took the Marquise and Delahaye to court for defamation of character and won a 5,000-franc judgment. This did not stop Delahaye from publishing his version of *l'affaire Morès* in three volumes in which Rebillet's name is replaced by X.

The court no doubt came to the right decision. But Delahaye may have been closer to the mark than many people believed. His theories about a gigantic conspiracy of Anglo-Jewish finance of which Rebillet was the cat's-paw were, of course, sheer fantasy. But there were a number of irregular goings-on in southern Tunisia that were traceable to the Residency, which controlled them through Rebillet. Corrupt and incompetent caids were maintained in place because they served French interests, and French money had been invested in the caravan trade, not, as Delahaye claimed, to make Rebillet a rich man, but to attract private capital into the region. And as for the charge that the Residency had played a part in Morès's murder, the *Dépêche Tunisienne* probably put its finger on the true role in an April 26, 1902 article: While there was certainly no evidence that the Residency premeditated Morès's murder, they nevertheless bore a "moral" responsibility for his death. It was apparent to the Arabs close to power that Morès was regarded as a damned nuisance by the government. "Monsieur de Morès was assassinated by natives who, in very good faith, thought they were doing a favor to the governors of Tunisia." The Tuareg had murdered people far more important than Morès, and no reprisals had followed. Why should it be any different this time?

It should not have been any different. If the government had had its way, then Morès would have dropped into quasi-obscurity along with Miss Tinne, Dournaux-Dupéré, Flatters, Père Richard and any number of other explorers killed by the Tuareg. Officialdom was in no hurry to divulge the methods by which they ruled southern Tunisia. But even more, they did not want to jeopardize relations with the Tuareg, even if they were murderers. It had been the tenacity of Captain Pein that forced the issue by producing three of the guilty men. In this way, he could open the Saharian question again, bring it to public notice and break out of the confinement of Ouargla and El Goléa. By forcing a breakdown of relations with the Tuareg, *l'affaire Morès* had shattered the policy of diplomacy and commercial penetration of the desert which had been followed since the death of Flatters. Combined with the "race for Lake Chad," it meant that the way was now open for a more active policy in the Sahara. And François Lamy would be the first man to benefit.

So, thanks to Morès, Lamy, whose career until now had been touristically interesting but professionally unrewarding, was to have his chance. At the Elysée he was kept busy from seven o'clock in the morning until ten o'clock at night opening the President's mail and running errands to various ministries. It was a solitary life for a bachelor, and almost every night he dined alone in the mess. Nevertheless, his schedule of one week on, one week off, left him plenty of time to pursue his own project.

Organizing a mission of this sort required both patience and public relations. The War Ministry might release the troops for the expedition, but they would do little else. Lamy needed money, but the other ministries, and above all, the private foundations, were unlikely to back a purely military venture. While not wanting to fall into the same trap as Flatters, Lamy realized that his mission must be given a façade of scientific research. This was one reason that he sought out Fernand Foureau. The other was that Foureau had important contacts in the education ministry and with the Société de géographie de Paris. In fact, the Société de géographie had offered 300,000 francs to Foureau for an expedition which would traverse the Sahara and link Algeria with the Sudan. Lamy was like a poor suitor in search of a rich bride. The two men met in August 1897 and worked out a package of scientific research which would be carried forward at the point of a bayonet. They then took it from ministry to ministry, talking, cajoling, pleading until, little by little, they extracted commitments and cash, helped by Félix Faure and the deputy for the Loire, Charles Dorian, who also asked to be included in the party. On March 5, 1898, the *Mission saharienne* received official approval, with a budget of 500,000 francs. Best of all, their instructions were vague: "Join Algeria to Chad," if possible join with the other missions which might set out from the Sudan and the Congo, and get home any way you can.

As the departure time had been set for the autumn, Lamy only left Paris in September.* After a brief stopover to see his mother near

---

* In a way, it was a pity that he left the Elysée when he did, for he was to miss all the excitement. The following year, Félix Faure's butler was brought running to the presidential bedchamber by female screams. There he discovered the President's red-headed mistress, Madame Steinheld, in a most significant state of undress, overcome by panic—the president lay on his back, quite dead, but his fingers still clutched her hair. "Thus," wrote one Parisian daily, "the President of the Republic died on the job"; whereas the right-wing *Petit journal* published a frontispiece showing the President expiring in bed surrounded by his bereaved family.

More seriously, Félix Faure's death came at an unfortunate time. A moderate and a friend of the army with great prestige in parliamentary circles, Faure might have been able to mitigate some of the excesses of the Dreyfus years which his faceless successor, Emile Loubet, proved unable to do. Faure's funeral was seized

Cannes, he boarded the steamer at Marseilles for Algiers, the same steamer which was transporting the new governor general of Algeria, Julien Laferrière, and his family to his new posting. It was a useful acquaintance to make, and Lamy spent a few days in Algiers introducing Madame Laferrière to the scenic delights of "la ville blanche" and attempting to convince her that Algerians were not all "ogres." He also seized the opportunity to give a stern lecture to the caids who had come up to greet the new governor general, explaining that he would hold them "collectively responsible for any accident" which might overtake his mission in the northern Sahara. Whatever the outcome of his expedition, he told them, he would write a full report to the president about their behavior.

Lamy thought this menacing harangue had produced an excellent effect on his audience. Today, it reads like the speech of a bully. However, if placed in context, perhaps it seems slightly less so. For this was the very moment that the Fashoda crisis was building up a full head of steam. The Marchand expedition, having slogged clear across Africa, had raised the French flag over their Nile sandbank on July 10, 1898. Kitchener had wiped out the Mahdi's forces at Omdurman, across the Nile from Khartoum, on September 2 and then opened the envelope containing the secret orders to proceed to settle matters with Colonel Marchand upriver. War between France and England looked likely in the early autumn of 1898, and Lamy and his fellow soldiers must have been puffing themselves up to their full height. The Arab caids had merely received the benefit of the new warlike spirit which rippled through the army.

Perhaps, the threat of war also helps to explain what was, according to Lamy, an enthusiastic response to his call for recruits. This is all the more surprising given the appalling experience of many Kabyles who had signed up with Lamy several years earlier for the trip to Madagascar. Most, of course, had not returned, and that fact alone spoke volumes. Nevertheless, if Lamy is to be believed, when he traveled up the coastal

---

upon by the preposterous Deroulède as an occasion to harangue the military escort to march on the Elysée, which they wisely declined to do. Deroulède was locked away for a few years. But the episode helped to convince the new prime minister, René Waldeck-Rousseau, that the army was in a dangerous mood and capable of a *coup d'état,* and justified a series of military reforms and petty reprisals which lowered both the efficiency and the morale of the French army in the years before the Great War.

plain behind Algiers to Blida, the garrison of his old regiment the First Algerian Tirailleurs, he was fairly overwhelmed with volunteers: "The 400 men of the detachment descended on the company bureaus and all asked to sign on," Lamy wrote. "We were obliged to lock some of them in the barracks to prevent them all from volunteering, and this included the officers and all of the NCOs." He "creamed off" the companies to collect 212 tirailleurs and 13 spahis. (Lamy was also to pick up 51 Saharian tirailleurs and 29 Saharian spahis en route.) This number included 9 officers, 2 doctors and 31 French corporals and sergeants. He also packed two Hotchkiss 42-millimeter cannon, each provided with 200 shells. The Société de géographie de Paris might have been surprised to discover that their money had gone to finance a military expedition, for the "scientific" basis of the Foureau-Lamy mission was so weak as to be virtually nonexistent. Apart from Foureau, the mission counted only four civilians: Charles Dorian, the deputy for the Loire, was clearly along for the ride. The naturalist, Jacques du Passage, was considered too young and was sent back only days after the mission started. This left Noel Villatte, an astronomer, and Leroy, the official photographer, who was forced to abandon most of his plates during the trip.

Despite the fact that it was under the nominal command of Fernand Foureau, this mission had one clear goal—that of colonial conquest. Fairly bristling with ironmongery, the Lamy mission was prepared to shoot its way through the desert. A military expedition must be given a military sendoff. At 5:45 on the morning of September 20, 1898, the Blida garrison was drawn up by the train station for what was described as *"une cérémonie brève mais touchante."* The regimental band blew and banged their way through the *Marseillaise,* while the tirailleurs in their red balloon trousers, embroidered waistcoats and fezes presented arms. As the train which was to take their comrades as far as Biskra, "the gateway to the desert," groaned into motion, Colonel Ménestrel yanked two pieces of gold fringe from the regimental flag and pressed them into Lamy's hand. The major, his eyes brimming with tears, placed them in his billfold as the train disappeared behind the hill.

XI

FOUREAU-LAMY MISSION

Anyone looking at a modern-day map of the Maghreb may wonder why Algeria occupies such an outsized slice of the Sahara while her neighbors to the east and west, Tunisia and Morocco, seem to cling precariously to the continent. Perhaps Algerian nationalists do not like to admit it, but their country's possession today of a disproportionate share of the desert is due to the acquisitiveness of her colonial conquerors. We have documented the conflict between colonialists and anticolonialists over the Sahara, as well as the competition in Africa between British and French. However, what is not generally realized is that a fierce rivalry also existed between soldiers in the different French colonies. Algeria triumphed over her two neighbors because her soldiers were the more aggressive. In the 1890s, officers in both Tunisia and Algeria had plans to expand their administrations into the desert. Thanks largely to Captain Théodore Pein, the prize went to Algeria. The Foureau-Lamy expedition was a victory for the advocates of military conquest over those who favored peaceful penetration through trade and quiet diplomacy. But it was also a victory for Algeria over Tunisia, whose soldiers now had to be content with a very small slice of the Saharian cake.

On the face of it, Lamy's expedition appeared invulnerable. Certainly, the Tuareg would not be able to overwhelm it by force. While Flatters had been a commander of more than ordinary mediocrity, Lamy was hardheaded and resilient. He was most unlikely to split his force and trot down some narrow ravine where he might easily be bushwacked. He would deal with the desert men from a position of strength.

In another sense, however, this expedition combined all of the elements of a potential disaster. While Foureau had great experience of desert travel, and Lamy had spent some time at El Goléa, few of his tirailleurs had handled a camel. Lamy did not trust the Chaamba to staff his expedition. In a sense he was right, for their indiscipline and even treachery were well documented. Lamy was to content himself with forty Chaamba *sokhrar,* or cameleers. But this was hardly enough to shepherd the 1,004 camels which he had collected at Ouargla from all over the desert. His Kabyles and French NCOs would simply have to transform themselves into cameleers. The *sokhrar,* distributed two per section, would become their teachers.

But the inexperience in dealing with camels, while very serious, was only part of the problem. As the Foureau-Lamy expedition made its way south from Biskra to Touggourt and Ouargla, it grew like a snowball by acquiring tirailleurs and Chaamba cameleers until, at the jumping-off point, it numbered 381 men. To cross a hostile desert with 381 inexperienced men and 1,004 camels was like trying to maneuver a battleship in a three-acre lake with a crew composed of Sea Scouts. The basic problem was the same—there was not enough water. To be sure, sizable caravans of Arabs had crossed the desert for centuries. Most had made it. But Caillié's account demonstrates that they arrived only after great hardship and often the sacrificing of many of the "expendable"—i.e., the black—members of the caravan. The crush at the wells could be terrible. Often there was not enough water for the people, much less the camels. Tuareg and Chaamba survived in the Sahara because they traveled light, fast and in small groups. Lamy seems to have let his military training get the better of his common sense—in his desire to provide for his own defense, his expedition threatened to capsize under the weight of its own armor plate. Foureau and Lamy had opened themselves to the possibility of a lingering and thirsty death.

Any insurance company sent to expertize the Foureau-Lamy expedition as it made its final preparations at Ouargla would not have touched them, at any premium. One thousand camels was a big order in southern Algeria. After deducting those of the various caids, and of men who had paid bribes to have theirs exempted from requisition, together with the refusal of El Goléa, ironically Lamy's old command, to contribute any camels at all, the quality of those which finally arrived, some from as far away as Gérryville near the Moroccan frontier, was uneven. The quality of the saddles and harnesses was poor. It did not take an expert to realize that the pack saddles wounded many of the camels, especially if they were badly loaded. Sores became infected, and an infected camel soon died. An experienced cameleer would spend much of every evening tending the sores of his camels. An inexpert one might not notice until it was too late.

At Ouargla, Lamy's tirailleurs milled around between blinding sandstorms loading over five thousand bundles of tobacco, tea, coffee, sugar, salt, tinned meat, flour, rice, candles, dates, couscous, potatoes, oil, soap, bullets, artillery shells, scientific instruments, water barrels and *guerbas,* as well as personal effects. During the day, they were "invaded by thousands of flies which do not leave us alone for an instant," Lamy complained. "But the nights are marvelous; no mosquitoes; the sky is a deep blue, sprinkled with thousands of stars . . ." On October 23, 1898, the Foureau-Lamy mission set out from Ouargla to march to Lake Chad, a distance of 2,000 miles.

Even before they left Ouargla, Captain Emile Reibell, the officer responsible for the camels and cameleers, feared that he might not be able to keep his caravan in a suitably tight defensive group. Now he was convinced that they did not lend themselves to "militarization." The stupid beasts spread out over the plain, snatching mouthfuls of dry bush which grew in clumps every few meters, and in the process virtually throwing the rider to the ground each time they lowered their necks.

But this was only part of the problem. Before leaving Ouargla, each section carefully branded their camels with their own distinctive mark. However, each morning when they returned from the night's pasture, a few camels inevitably were missing, whether because they had been stolen by marauding Chaamba, as Sergeant Charles Guilleux believed, or because they had simply wandered off. As is usual in most armies, men attempted to make up deficiencies by borrowing from their neighbors. This inevitably led to fights, as no tirailleur relished having loads and no camel to carry them. To get around this, the men began to sneak out of the camp each night to place their section's brand on any beast they could lay their hands on. Soon, the camels were covered with so many brands that no section's claim would stand up in a court of law, so the quarrels continued: "I recognize my camel, he is marked on the tail."

"No! He's not yours, look at this mark on the neck."

The first stop was at Ain Taiba, a stinking pond about fifty yards in diameter surrounded by a few scrawny palm trees. The water was so polluted that the tirailleurs were obliged to dig holes next to the oasis, and even then the water reeked of sulfur. A second problem, that of cooking meals for so many men, was also beginning to get out of hand. The large number of cooking pots required a large number of fires, which in turn meant that a great deal of wood must be collected. Each evening, each section sent out foraging parties with camels to gather up brushwood and dig up roots, so that the camels returned with grotesque bundles of sticks strapped to their backs. This inevitably led to more nicks and cuts, which became infected, and the health of the camels deteriorated still further.

The expedition soon settled into a regular routine: Rise at dawn, gather the camels, load them (several times!), then trudge over the dunes and stony plains until late evening, when camp would be made. On November 12, they arrived at the wells of Temassinin for a prearranged meeting with Captain Pein and his Saharian spahis, who had gone ahead to establish a camp. This was the occasion for a small celebration, and Foureau broke out the phonograph which he had brought along "to seduce the natives." But this was almost the last thing they would have to celebrate for some time. Already Sergeant Guilleux was complaining that the 200 grams of flour allocated to each man per day, which was mixed with water, patted into a small cake and thrown on the coals, was hardly sufficient, especially since November 18th, when they had begun to toil through the tortuous boulders of the Tassili. Foureau had hired twenty Chaamba, one of whose primary duties was to hunt food for the expedition. "They are paid five francs per day, or a total of a hundred francs per day (for the twenty)," wrote Captain Reibell. "Since we left Ouargla twenty-three days ago, this makes an expenditure of 2,300 francs. Now, they have killed only one antelope and sixteen gazelles. That puts the cost of the gazelle at 165 francs and the antelope at 660 francs! That is a tidy sum and we have a pretty little band of scamps on our coattails!" Perhaps, but many of the men were beginning to think that cheap at the price. "We began to know what hunger is," wrote Guilleux. "Yet had we known what the future had in store for us, we would have thought ourselves very lucky." The soldiers consoled themselves by smoking. Anyone who lit one of his precious cigarettes was immediately surrounded by a dozen tirailleurs who disputed among themselves who was to have *el kemia,* the butt. They were usually disappointed, for the owner smoked until it burned his fingers. Only then did he flick the smoldering remnant at the waiting crowd of scavengers.

Food, already the major preoccupation, soon became an obsession. Lamy bought a few dates, salt and rancid Arab butter made from sheep milk from a caravan traveling in the opposite direction. He also sent some of his cameleers home as useless mouths to feed, and a number of other Arabs, no doubt sensing disaster, seized upon this opportunity to turn back northward. "Is this the flight of rats from a sinking ship?" Reibell wondered. A few Tuareg began to come into the camp selling dates at five francs for a handful. They refused to bargain. It was outrageous, but they found ready customers: "We did not count our money," Guilleux remembered. "We gave it by the handful. What did the price matter? We had to eat and we would have given our last shirt for several bad dates, quickly devoured in a corner, away from the view of our comrades." On December 8th, they bought a few sheep: "Heads, feet, intestines, everything went into the pot." Any camel which faltered was butchered and roasted.

In every desert expedition, *il y a des longeurs*. This stage of the Foureau-Lamy mission reads like an encyclopedia of tedium, and of misery. A Frenchman died of dysentery. The officers broke out their dress uniforms. The body was laid out on a stretcher, covered with a tricolor, and carried a few steps to a shallow grave. Even here, the Frenchmen retained the ability to improvise a ceremony. On they plodded, the caravan stretched out for miles, down the ravine of the Wadi Samene. Huge black boulders towered over them, as they threaded through the ash gray tamarisk trees which crowded the narrow ravines. At one point, the column was forced to blast a path through the rocks with dynamite. The nights were cold, and in the mornings the *guerbas* were covered with a thin layer of ice. "And always hunger," wrote Guilleux, who managed to spend a night next to a sack of dates, surreptitiously chew a hole in the cloth, and steal a little extra nourishment. When at last they dropped down from the mountains of Tindesset, the valley of Tikhamnar, its low dunes interspersed with tamarisk and gum trees, it seemed an Eden. But morale was beginning to slip. The tirailleurs' uniforms were stiff with filth and sweat, and the men were tormented by lice, which especially attacked the middle of the body around the belt. "Everyone speaks less and less," Guilleux wrote. "Nothing happens. It's always the same routine—the march, the interminable march, then water the camels, take them to pasture, inspect things, go search for water." The officers fared slightly better, at least on Christmas Day, when they treated themselves to couscous flecked with pieces of mountain goat, a second course composed of various tins of food mixed together, in which *tripes à la mode de Caen* and *saucisses aux choux* featured prominently, roast camel was the *plat de résistance* and there were dates for dessert, washed down with two bottles of champagne. A few corks were also popped on January 1, 1899, to see in the new year. But these celebrations could do little to lift sagging morale. The countryside was spectacular but oppressive. It was like wandering through the cemetery of a morose race of giants—black needles of rock shot skyward like obelisks or mournful church towers from which the bells had been removed. And everything was blanketed by a deathly, eerie silence. Foureau wrote that it was like being in the midst of a "dead city," which even the glare of the sun did nothing to enliven: "The countryside gives the sensation of a painful embrace and of heavy oppression," he wrote.

The guides informed Lamy that the way ahead was virtually without water or pasture. The tirailleurs were set cutting grass and gathering wood. The nights were cold, down to twenty degrees Fahrenheit, "like being in Siberia," Lamy wrote, when he could write, for the ink froze in the bottle. The nerves of the men were taut—they expected at any moment to be attacked by Tuareg. But there was nothing. Even nature seemed anesthetized, for not even a bird sang in this baked wilderness. On January 8, after a week's rest, the column again moved toward the south, skirting the eastern edge of the Ahaggar massif. On January 20, they arrived at the wells of Tadent. Again they rested while Lamy led a small reconnaissance to visit the spot where Flatters had been attacked. While he was away, a convoy of dates sent out from Ouargla arrived: "All faces are beaming with happiness," Guilleux recorded. "There will be something to eat." Too much to eat! For two days, the men gorged themselves on dates, boiling them, roasting them, baking them, eating them raw, until many were holding their stomachs in agony.

On January 24, Lamy returned to find that the state of his camels had deteriorated from poor to critical. Starved and mistreated for more than two months, most were near collapse. They were in such bad condition that even the famished soldiers who slaughtered them found their meat to be inedible. And this when one of the worst sections of the voyage lay before them—the vacant, blasted, featureless Ténéré. Although they were only going to skirt the western edge, this could require at least a seven-day forced march, as there would be no place to stop and rest. On January 27, they set out. The following day, a caravan of dates which should have arrived a week earlier caught them up with "so many dates we don't know what to do with them," Lamy wrote. The soldiers knew what to do with them—they fed them to the camels which they were in the process of beating forward across the plain. But this simply gave the animals dysentery, and they dropped even sooner. The men shouldered their loads and staggered forward: "The camp had the appearance of a slaughterhouse," wrote Guilleux on February 2. "We saw nothing but camels lying outstretched, agonizing, the neck twisted and the head between the legs." In six days, ninety-seven camels perished.

They rested for a week on the far side of the Ténéré at the wells of In Azaoua, where another convoy of supplies reached them. What they were to do with all the supplies when the camels, or rather those camels still left, were spent, posed a problem (forty-three more had died at In Azaoua). Lamy constructed a small fort, placed a great quantity of the supplies in it, and left it to a small garrison. He would return for them—when he arrived somewhere! What these men thought as they watched Lamy walk out of camp on February 11, 1899, is not difficult to imagine. Few must have believed that they would again see him, or, for that matter, anyone whom they knew. Lamy moved southward. Thirty-five camels died during the first day's march, nineteen on the second, fifteen on the third, as they wound down narrow canyons and climbed over large rocks.

Then, finally, they emerged on the plains of Air. "What joy!" Guilleux exclaimed. They were whipped by a scorching scirocco, and the camels were still dropping by the dozen. But there before them were green plants, not the ash-gray vegetation they had seen for the past months, but plants which were actually *green*. The tirailleurs sat around the campfires pensively rolling the leaves between their fingers, and listening to the unaccustomed sound of birds and crickets. They made their way to the small settlement of Iferouane which lies on a plateau at the foot of the Tamgak mountains.

There they were met by a deputation of Tuareg elders who advanced toward them in long, slow strides, poking the earth with their long lances, their swords dangling in decorated leather scabbards at their sides. Iferouane was not much of a settlement, no more than a few conical huts with leaves for a roof. But it was a settlement. Human beings lived there. Furthermore, it was an indication that the desert was behind them. Iferouane was not exactly tropical. This was, after all, the Sahel, the area of transition between the Sahara and the rain forests further south. But it was pleasant—indeed, the French were to call this area the Switzerland of the Sahara.

Lamy was not entirely taken in by its beauty, however. This was still Tuareg country, and Lamy took the precaution of establishing a square fort, constructed of rocks and baggage. He was to remain at Iferouane for three months, mainly because he could go no further. Of his original 1,004 camels, only 585 skeletal beasts remained. The Tuareg promised to bring Lamy 500 camels, so he settled down to wait. Soon the French camp resembled a village of tents and straw huts, through which black women walked, their hair matted and glowing with strongly smelling rancid butter and "their enormous breasts falling like old bags on their inflated stomachs," selling cheese and sour milk, or stopping to sing their slow regular songs, always the same five flat notes, beat out on a primitive drum or simply by clapping hands. "The odor of butter, of their sweat and their filth form an eminently toxic, asphyxiating, suffocating mixture," wrote one French soldier. Be that as it may, some of the men soon found mistresses among these market women.

At first, after a 1,800-mile walk through the Sahara, Iferouane seemed to be an "enchanted paradise." But the soldiers soon grew tired of it. Pasture for the camels was far away, and the daily treks there were fatiguing, especially as rumors that the Tuareg were planning an attack became more frequent. On March 8, a Chaambi and a tirailleur were murdered while out with the camels. The local notables offered excuses: It was that tribe, or this faction. Lamy intended to play no part in their politics. He simply prepared to defend himself for the attack which he expected would come on March 11. Sentries were reinforced and every man slept beside his rifle.

Sergeant Guilleux woke up on the morning of March 12, 1899, surprised that he had enjoyed a full night's sleep. The sun was over the horizon. Everything was quiet, so he began to go about his business when he heard the ululations of the women and "that infernal music." He looked up to see a compact mass of black-robed men emerge from a clump of palm trees, lances and knives waving above their heads. Actually, he probably saw them more clearly in his memory than he had at the time. Lamy wrote that he heard "a great rumble, some piercing cries, and an indescribable hubbub," 300 to 400 yards from the camp, but that the dust and morning mist prevented him at first from actually seeing anything. What he finally did see was extremely impressive: a dark mass of humanity rumbling forward toward his fragile breastworks, the Tuareg on camels and the blacks on foot, some actually clinging to the tails of the camels and urging them forward by thrusting knives into their haunches. Lamy stood calmly, "a sarcastic smile on his face," until they were well within range: "You see them, the brutes!" he shouted. "Well, just like at target practice." Target practice was never like this.

The French square, reinforced with their 42-millimeter cannon, threw out a wall of lead. "This caused an indescribable confusion in their ranks," Guilleux wrote. The front row tried to escape, but the press from behind was too great. On they came, for nearly a quarter of an hour, some to within fifty yards of the camp. The fire from the French square kept them beyond the range of their lances, and they possessed no more potent weapons. The ground was littered with corpses. Patrols were sent out to follow the traces of blood, which led off in all directions. They returned with fifty camels, and one prisoner upon whom was found, it was claimed, the weapons of the Chaambi murdered on March 8th. Lamy had him executed.

Lamy sent 150 men to collect the small garrison left behind at the wells of In Azaoua. As they could transport only a fraction of the supplies back to Iferouane, it was decided to consume as much as they could and burn what could not be carried. When the order was given to begin eating, "We embraced, we laughed, we cried with joy. . . . The bronzed faces radiated happiness," Guilleux said. After gorging themselves for two days, they built an enormous bonfire and burned the remaining supplies and marched away from the "sinister spectacle," many of the men in tears.

The next two months at Iferouane were frustrating ones. The men simmered in a sweltering, humid heat which reached most days into the hundreds. The camp was taking on an air of permanence: More *zeribas* had gone up, blacks pounded millet in wooden mortars, and a ditch was dug around the square. But that was part of the problem. Lamy had not come this far to settle in. He wanted to move on. But his reserve of camels was down to 200. His negotiations with the locals brought him many promises, but few camels. He contacted the sultan of Agadez, a town 200 miles to the south, only to be reproached for having invaded the Sudan. The sultan promised to send millet if he were paid, but no camels. It was, at least, an honest answer.

The news that a French expedition had left the Niger bend headed for the Air reached them on April 13. This merely increased Lamy's impatience to leave. But how? What was left of his camels were attacked by crows who lighted on their backs to pick their ticks, and in the process created more infectable sores. His herd was "melting like wax." At this point, Lamy seems to have been at the end of his tether, exasperated by the refusal of the Tuareg and the sultan of Agadez to give him camels. According to Guilleux, Lamy and Foureau talked for most of the night of April 22–23, 1899. Lamy wanted to burn most of the supplies and go on a campaign of extermination and vengeance against the Tuareg before his expedition perished ignominiously *in situ*.

Foureau disagreed. It was not simply that he was a civilian and Lamy a soldier. Above all, Foureau was a man of infinite patience. He had not survived eleven expeditions into the desert by panicking in a tight corner. But something had to be done. If the Tuareg would not sell them camels, then they must resort to the time-honored method of acquiring them in the desert—the razzia. In this they were helped by a Targui named Raiou, who offered to lead them. Lamy accepted gratefully. The first party sent out returned with a large number of camels on June 3. Lamy distributed champagne mixed with water to them. Other raids were dispatched, but they were less successful, bringing in only captives, women and old men too slow to escape, whom they would later offer to exchange for camels. He also commandeered a caravan of donkeys which had been sent up from Agadez with a load of millet.

On June 8, Lamy ordered everything possible loaded onto the captured donkeys and camels and the seventy-five original camels which still survived: He planned to march on Agadez. No one slept that night. With hatchets, they broke open the tins of condensed milk, drank all they could, and poured out the rest. The tirailleurs fashioned small cloth packs and stuffed everything they could into these. "Every head wore an enormous turban to carry the cloth which later would serve to make clothes. I never saw such a pillage." However, on the 9th, when the order to move was given, the animals were too heavily laden. Lamy ordered that they be unloaded and charged only with bullets, medicines and food. He had a large fire built and ordered the tirailleurs to throw their improvised packs on this. "This was the cruelest moment of the mission for all of us," Guilleux remembered. The men placed their packs on the pyre, "slowly, piously, with tears in their eyes." Some even threw their medals on the flames. Guilleux reckoned that it would have taken only the slightest provocation from the crowd of Tuareg who watched this spectacle, for the soldiers to have rounded on them, so angry were they with these people who refused to give them camels. But still the caravan was too laden to march. Lamy designated two men per section to burn the effects of their comrades, on the principle that one should ask one's friend to prune one's rose bushes. It worked. On the 10th, the column left Iferouane for Agadez.

The country through which they marched was mountainous and bleak, covered with black rocks and little vegetation. The guides, seven black women who had attached themselves to the mission, had only the vaguest of notions where the route lay, and repeatedly led them along the wrong paths. The tirailleurs sustained themselves on dry biscuits and coffee and cursed the day they ever volunteered for this mission. They no longer looked like an army, but more like a troop from the *commedia dell'arte* dressed in a motley of costumes. Everyone, including the officers, was now barefoot. Guilleux had fashioned a pair of trousers from an empty date sack. But at least he had trousers. It was difficult to tell who was a sergeant and who was a court jester.

It took them two days to walk the thirty miles to Aguellal, from which, on June 13, Lamy led a strong raiding party of 150 men into the low rocky hills. He returned having captured three camels and four horses, and dragging one dead man and four wounded from a Tuareg ambush. Another man died of sunstroke, and five more were also prostrated by the heat.

On June 24, after detonating a large pile of surplus ammunition, Lamy formed his men into a tight square, each face measuring a hundred yards. It was perhaps the method of march prescribed by the textbooks, but over this terrain, broken by deep ravines and steep, rocky ridges, it was madness. The tirailleurs toiled on beneath an oppressively overcast sky, frequently retracing their steps, as the black women realized—yet again—that they had taken the wrong path. On June 25, they buried ten thousand cartridges they could no longer carry. There was virtually nothing left to eat. The soldiers drank coffee, rolled cigarettes of donkey manure, and stole what they could from each other. The donkeys were mutinous, and the tirailleurs seemed to want to imitate them. A near-fatal lassitude settled over everyone. As each halt was called, they collapsed and refused to move: "The men no longer feared punishment," Guilleux wrote, "nor death." Only the knowledge that they were surrounded by Tuareg and thousands of miles from any possible help kept the expedition from melting away.

As they crept southward, however, Guilleux noted that "the country is getting better." It may have been a deceptive impression. The narrow

valleys of the Air are filled with thickets of dum palms while the moun-
tainsides, washed by the seasonal rain, are covered by low, green scrub.
They are agreeable enough to look at, but nearly all the bushes and trees
are thorned, some viciously so, with recurving barbs. Every plant seems
to be on the defensive and the effects of the burrs and sharp edges of the
spear grass on the tirailleurs' bare feet can be imagined.

On July 6, they spied the palm trees and conical huts of the village
of Aouderas across a rocky plain. From a distance, it appeared enchant-
ing. On closer inspection, it was both dilapidated and deserted. The men
rifled the houses but came up with only a few onions: "The faces are sad,
and everyone is asking himself what we are going to eat in this damned
country." It would be nice to see a human being. But it was obvious that
the inhabitants were fleeing in the face of the French advance. Lamy
attempted to raise morale by organizing a parade to celebrate Bastille
Day. The tirailleurs marched past in a quick step, their bare feet raising
a considerable quantity of dust, while a few curious blacks looked on. A
caravan of donkeys sent by the sultan of Agadez came in with a load of
sorghum, which the tirailleurs pounded with rocks and made into cakes.
But these did little to appease their hunger, and even made many of the
men ill. On the 24th, Lamy set his column in motion once again. Three
days later, the square minaret of the mosque of Agadez was visible eight
miles distant across the plateau. On the following day, they camped
beneath the town walls.

Agadez was not an old town by the standards of the Sahara, having
been founded only in the fifteenth century as a depot for the gold trade
between Gao and Tripoli. It had never prospered. It lay off the main
caravan routes, and the surrounding countryside was controlled by the
Tuareg, who also imposed a sultan on the town, black like most of the
inhabitants. By the nineteenth century, the gold trade had dried to a
trickle, and Agadez existed by manufacturing crude leather goods and
by dealing in salt. One of the sultan's traditional duties was to lead the
annual caravan—called the *taghlam*—which every autumn made the
400-mile journey across the dreaded Ténéré to Bilma to collect salt,
which was subsequently traded with the Hausa. Even as late as 1908, this
caravan numbered 20,000 camels. Such a huge caravan inevitably became
a target for Tuareg raiders. The attrition rate in camels in such desolate
country was huge, and the route between Agadez and Bilma was well
marked with the bones of dead camels.

Heinrich Barth, who had visited Agadez almost a half-century before the arrival of the Foureau-Lamy mission, declared that it "left upon me the impression of a deserted place of by-gone times; for even in the most important and central quarters of the town most of the dwelling-houses were in ruins . . . and one or two wretched conical cottages, built of reeds and grass, in the midst of them, showed anything but a regard to cleanliness." "Small hills of rubbish" littered the streets, and women washed clothes in pools of stagnant water. The walls on the east side of the town were crumbling, and people feared to venture out into the "desolate countryside beyond" because of the Tuareg. However, in the afternoon, the marketplace did a lively trade in camels, vegetables and meat, and in a covered hall constructed of palm trunks and roofed over with palm leaves, were merchants selling cloth, beads, necklaces, sandals, saddles and other goods. "Tall men with broad, coarse features, very different from any I had seen before, and with long hair hanging down upon their shoulders and over their face in a way which was an abomi-nation to the Tawarek," stood about arguing over the price of goods, until someone would run to fetch the master of the market to settle the deal for them. Horsemen armed with long lances, only one toe in the stirrup and a string of bells around their head, thrust through the crowd, "while numbers of large vultures, distinguished by their long naked neck of reddish colour and their dirty-greyish plumage, were sitting on the pinnacles of the crumbling walls, ready to pounce on any kind of offal."

On July 29, 1899, the sultan of Agadez came out to the French camp, which had been established within cannon shot of the walls. Lamy drew up his men in two hedges, had the bugle blown and a ceremonial shot fired off from one of his cannons. It was difficult to say how far the sultan was impressed. Foureau was ill with fever and, dressed in a purple cotton undershirt, was looking even more emaciated and hawk-faced than usual. Charles Dorian was in his smoking jacket with his deputy's insignia, not for reasons of ceremony but because he had nothing else to wear. A few of the officers had made hats out of palm leaves and every-one was barefoot. The sultan, a black man whose head was swathed in a white cloth so that nothing but his eyes was visible, was brought to see Foureau and Lamy, who asked for camels and food. The sultan promised both things.

For two days the French waited. On July 31, Lamy decided that he ought to jog the sultan's memory. With the bugler and the flag in front, he marched 200 men into the town. They went straight to the mosque, where the tirailleurs fell on their knees to pray while a few dozen senti-nels kept their rifles trained on the crowd of heavily armed Tuareg who gathered menacingly in the background. Lamy's show of force produced some results, for some of the blacks began to drift into the French camp to sell chickens, and the sultan sent some millet and sorghum. The French waited for another week until, on August 9, they discovered that the man with whom they had been dealing was not the sultan at all but one of his viziers. Lamy aimed his two guns at the town and threatened to bombard unless the sultan appeared immediately. He did. Foureau covered him with abuse and demanded the camels and a guide. The sultan did not have the camels, but he did produce several hundred donkeys. This would have to do. Lamy had them loaded up and on August 10, 1899, they marched out of Agadez.

The land to the east of Agadez is exceedingly bleak. The expedition set out to cross it in August, with a scirocco blowing like the breath of a blast furnace. The wells were virtually dry, and after a few days, they had run out of water. At eleven o'clock on the morning of August 18, the expedition walked back into their old camp at Agadez. Lamy was fu-rious. He claimed that the guide had deliberately misled them, and had the unfortunate man shot. Lamy was in a filthy mood, and would prob-ably have done far worse had Foureau not restrained him. What would have been the good of destroying Agadez? The inhabitants simply would have fled, and the mission would have faced starvation. With difficulty, Foureau imposed his view.

Foureau and Lamy settled down to two months of "interminable discussions" with the sultan. Food came into the camp, but not much: "The ration is always the same," Guilleux wrote. "The natives bring us just enough so that we do not die of hunger, but little enough so that we suffer." Nor did camels appear. Everyone in the expedition from Fou-reau to the lowest private assumed that this was part of a deliberate policy. But they were probably mistaken. The country simply did not have the resources to feed these extra mouths, nor the sultan the author-ity to procure the camels which Lamy demanded. After all, it was in his interest to move the French on. Presumably, if he could have laid his hands on the camels, then he would have gladly given them to the un-welcome visitors, just so they would leave. But the camels belonged mainly to the Tuareg, and they did what they pleased.

Apart from a gnawing hunger, life in the French camp was not all dreary. It soon became a refuge for a number of black slaves who seized the opportunity to escape from their masters. They naturally gravitated to the section of the camp occupied by the Saharian tirailleurs. Most of these were freed black slaves from Ouargla who spoke Hausa like the natives of Agadez. It had been Captain Pein's idea to form them into rifle companies, both because they were cheap to keep and because, as ex-slaves, there presumably was no love lost between them and the Arabs of the northern oases who had been their masters. These Saharian tirailleurs quickly acquired "wives." Their corner of the camp was always the most animated, with much music, dancing and wrestling matches between bare-breasted black women, put on for the entertainment of the men, the object being not to throw one's adversary, but to rip off her loincloth. Otherwise, the soldiers might wander down to the wells to admire the women, who were not embarrassed in the least to strip off their garments in front of them to bathe.

By late September, Lamy had grown decidedly impatient with the delays, and sought ways to put pressure on the sultan to have him deliver some camels. He marched his men around and through the town several times in a demonstration of force. He then shot some Tuareg hostages whom he had held prisoner for several months. When this still failed to produce the camels, he had his men surround the town wells and told the sultan that no one would drink until he had his animals. This, inevitably, did the trick. In desperate circumstances, the sultan must have offered the Tuareg a price for their animals too good for them to refuse. On October 17, the tirailleurs loaded their belongings on the assortment of camels, donkeys, and cows which had been collected for them, and shook the dust of Agadez from their feet. In two days, they had marched fifty miles south on the road to Zinder. It was not an easy march. At first view, the steppe "resembles a cultivated plain of France," Foureau wrote. But the greenery hid spines and nettles which made each step of the bare feet a torment. The blacks who congregated in the villages of round huts and conical roofs, were curious rather than hostile. On October 28, the last surviving camel from Ouargla collapsed and could not be moved.

On November 2, as they approached Zinder, they were met by a detachment of Senegalese tirailleurs under the command of a Frenchman, Sergeant Bouthel. Guilleux wanted to cry, and he was not alone. The Algerians, their bare feet swathed in rags, "looking," according to

Foureau, "more like a collection of bandits than a mission made up of honest men," tramped between a hedge made up of Bouthel's Senegalese on the right and a densely packed mass of brightly dressed blacks led by the Sultan of Zinder on the left. Men dashed about on richly decorated horses, raising dust and firing their rifles into the air. "There are archers on horseback, but what is most remarkable is the sultan's band made up of horsemen carrying large double bells and trumpets, but trumpets three yards long," Foureau recorded in his diary. This brightly colored crowd undulated toward Zinder, singing, beating on drums, firing rifles, raising a cloud of dust pierced by shafts of sunlight.

After the empty desolation of the Sahara, Zinder appeared an oasis of civilization. There was something reminiscent of North Africa in the square mud houses, many of which bore crude towers thirty feet high, and in the medieval-looking fortress which dominated the town from a rocky hill. This is where the French had established their headquarters. The tirailleurs dispersed among a number of small huts which had been prepared for them by Bouthel, who had also thoughtfully provided new uniforms for everyone.

The Senegalese made them feel right at home: "Bonjour. You French, you white, not Arab!" a huge black tirailleur said to Guilleux, and promptly led him off to their camp. To the Algerians, the Senegalese seemed to live in some style, complete with wives and children whom they took on campaign with them. When they departed on a mission where they might have some serious fighting to do, they left their families under a tight guard—and the women with locked chastity belts! "I had often heard them spoken of as a joke," wrote Guilleux, "but I had never seen them." The Senegalese women were really very nice, and the Algerians were beginning to feel distinctly dissatisfied with the "wives" which they had acquired in Agadez. The best thing about Zinder for the Algerians was that, for the first time in a year, they felt the absence of menace. The men could walk through the tortuous streets without their rifles, visit the market which was held under an enormous jujube tree where tattooed women squatted in the sand with butter, beans, rice, salt, onions, cloves, or limes neatly arranged on mats before them. Others offered peanuts, tobacco leaves, kola nuts or pots of strong-smelling goat's milk for sale. Vultures, their scraggly necks silhouetted against the blue sky, looked down from the walls, as the Algerians strolled about, stopping to sip *dola,* a drink made of fermented honey and millet which tasted not unlike cider, or eat highly spiced cakes fried in butter. "An odor of human flesh which would upset the strongest stomach hangs over everything." There were also plenty of *horizontales* about. Guilleux allowed himself to be led away by one. But just as he was about to get down to business, she extracted a well-chewed wad of tobacco from her mouth, and he fled in disgust. He wandered back to the marketplace, where some Tuareg, accompanied by a drum, were putting on a puppet show. The puppets were no more than sticks wrapped in rags, with a "large ball, horrible, misshapen, which was supposed to resemble a head."

The presence of Sergeant Bouthel was the first indication that the proposed link-up of the three missions which set out from various parts of Africa in the autumn of 1898 to move toward Lake Chad might actually take place. That Sergeant Bouthel had arrived in Zinder at all had required great luck. For all their adventures over the past year, Foureau and Lamy must have been amazed at the story which Bouthel told. At this point, we should turn back and trace the fortunes of the expedition to which Bouthel had belonged—the Voulet-Chanoine mission.

XII

MEN WHO
WOULD BE KINGS

The story which Sergeant Bouthel had to tell, that of the Central African Mission, is one of the most extraordinary in the history of African exploration. It also remains among the least known. Most histories of colonial conquest make only oblique references to it, if they mention it at all, for the simple reason that colonialists in the government and the army successfully suppressed it. When a quarter of a century later, one of the participants in the drama, General Octave Meynier, attempted to write of it, that portion of his book was removed under a law that forbade officers to publish without permission of the Ministry of War. Other historians subsequently discovered that many of the relevant papers in the archives of the government of the Sudan had been lost or intentionally destroyed. The official inquiry into the Central African Mission was a whitewash. However, the testimony gathered by the board of inquiry, three cartons of depositions and documents, still exists in the archives of the colonial ministry on Paris's rue Oudinot. A study of the papers allows us to reconstruct the history of this expedition, and perhaps to arrive at a verdict substantially different from the official one.

In 1897, Captain Paul Voulet and Lieutenant Charles Chanoine had led an expedition from Senegal to conquer the empire of Wagadugu, commonly known as the Mossi states, located in what is today the Upper Volta. Since the five states had been established in the eleventh century, a fierce spirit of independence combined with a high degree of organization had permitted them to repel the attacks of the powerful empires of Mali and Songhai which, in other epochs, had established hegemony over the Niger bend. However, a long and proud history proved to be no defense against the two young adventurers from France. They had left a trail of destruction which had been remarkably bloody even by the sanguinary standards of Western Sudan. Burned villages and summary executions were their preferred methods of conquest. Chanoine wrote to

his father that blacks were "barbarians and savages." Presumably, extermination was about as good as they might expect. Voulet announced to
the governor of the Sudan in 1896 that "after the destruction of several
large villages, all resistance will be finished. . . . With the Samos, one has
to punish a certain number of villages. It is this way that we end an
intolerable situation." To place these two men at the head of an expedition was like combining Attila the Hun and General "Bomber" Harris,
architect of Britain's bombing campaign in World War II, in dual command. Nor was their brutality directed exclusively at the enemy: both
officers were also famous for frequent use of the flat, and even the sharp,
of their swords on their own men. One officer described Chanoine as
impulsive, ruthless, "cruel from cold-bloodedness and out of pleasure."
"Voulet was intelligent, educated, but one found in him diversely opposite characteristics," Lieutenant Paul Joalland, one of the officers who
accompanied the Central African Mission of 1898, said of his commander. "On one hand, a true love of blood and cruelty; on the other, a
sometimes ridiculous sensitivity. Very courageous in the face of danger,
he had a great fear of sickness. . . . He had a weak character and was
dominated by two wicked people, Chanoine and his black mistress."

Even if the Frenchmen who volunteered to serve with Voulet and
Chanoine had not served under them before, the colonial army was a
small world. Their bloody reputations must have been common knowledge. We can only speculate about why these officers and NCOs offered
their services, but the answer is probably ambition. Most colonial soldiers were churned by ambition. Why else would they endure the dreadful climates, the disease and the prospects—and very real they were—of
early death? Exoticism, at least in the initial stages, probably played a
part, as did the desire to escape the straitjacket of the metropolitan army
and the stuffiness and sheer boredom of bourgeois France. But colonial
service was one of the few ways a man of modest origins and without
real connections in France might make his mark on the world. As a
consequence, the atmosphere of the colonial army was intensely competitive. Ambitious officers and NCOs would see colonial service as a promotion track which would take them more quickly to the top.

The simple fact is that, despite their reputations for brutality, reputations which were well known in the colonial army and on record in the
office of the governor general of the Sudan, Voulet and Chanoine were
regarded as young officers with a future. Paul Voulet, son of a Parisian

doctor, was only thirty-two years old in 1898. One can suppose that like so many other colonial officers, he had been rebellious and a failure at school, for despite his relatively comfortable upbringing, he had enlisted as a private in the marines at the age of nineteen. His charm and relatively good education served him well, because he was promoted to sergeant within a year, and four years later commissioned a sublieutenant. Voulet had mastered his trade in Indochina and the Sudan and in 1896–97 had been placed in charge of the Mossi expedition. Despite the horror stories that leaked out about his methods, or perhaps because of them, Voulet won the praise of his superiors and was named to lead the Central African Mission in 1898. The sad fact was that as far as the French colonial army was concerned, the ends justified the means. To borrow a Napoleonic metaphor, Voulet might have cracked a few eggs, but he made the omelette, and that was what counted.

Charles Paul Jules Chanoine had arrived by a slightly smoother path. His father was a general, and even served briefly (ever so briefly— from September 17 to October 25, 1898) as French war minister. It will come as no surprise that this did not exactly hurt young Chanoine's career. General Chanoine took advantage of his passage through the rue St.-Dominique to decorate his twenty-eight-year-old son with the *Legion d'honneur* and promote him to the rank of captain for his "excellent" performance with his friend Voulet on the Mossi expedition. This did not make young Chanoine particularly popular in the army. On the contrary, the dandified airs and the *manières mondaines* of this ex-St.-Cyrian and cavalryman could hardly camouflage the fact that he was a thoroughly unpleasant character. But his connections and polished drawing-room manners offered a welcome complement to the less assured Voulet as the two men laid siege to the various ministries in an attempt to scrape up support for their proposed Central African Mission. When, in May 1898, they finally received permission to proceed, Voulet was furious. Ministerial dithering meant that they must start out in the dry season.

However, there was one compensation—their orders were so vague as to be nonexistent. They were told to reconnoiter the territory between the Niger and Lake Chad and to bring the territory east of Chad under French protection: "I will neither pretend to indicate to you which route you must follow, nor the way to conduct yourself with the native chiefs and the native populations," read his instructions from the colonial ministry. How extraordinary! How could Paris complain that they lost control of their soldiers when they issued them with orders so imprecise as to be virtually an open invitation to incinerate the countryside? If one wished to look for the roots of military indiscipline in the Sudan, one need look no further than the bureaucracy, red tape and sheer incompetence of the Third Republic.

In any case, it is obvious that any plan was absent in these instructions from the colonial ministry. There is no mention of the other missions under Foureau and Lamy, and Emile Gentil, nor even a hint that they might wish to coordinate their movements. That the three expeditions eventually met at Lake Chad was the result of luck and the fact that, separate, each was isolated and, ultimately, desperate. Originally, they were very much individual initiatives, approved separately. The officers who took part were extremely jealous of their authority, and the career opportunities that these expeditions offered. The "race for Lake Chad" was run against the other officers in the French army as much as against the English or Germans. Unless this is understood, much of what occurred during the Central African Mission becomes incomprehensible.

In the absence of a coordinated Chad strategy, the two captains concocted their own—to defeat Rabih. Anyone who has read Kipling's *The Man Who Would Be King* will realize how intensely, until the twentieth century, the vast and mysterious expanses of the unexplored world stimulated the fantasies of Europe. Africa and Asia seemed to be places where men might realize their dreams of wealth and power. And such dreams, indeed, were not completely fanciful. Several men had carved out vast empires in Africa. Samori, the black chief who for years had defied the French in Senegal and Mali, was one. Rabih Zubair was another. Rabih was a Sudanese of Arab origin who became the slave of the powerful merchant Zobeir Pasha, governor in the name of Egypt of Bahr Al-Ghazal and Darfur. His administrative and military abilities brought him to the attention of his master, who named him to command his army, a post which he retained under Zobeir Pasha's son and successor, Suliman. Unlike his father, who had been content to serve Cairo, Suliman entertained ambitions of his own—he revolted against Egypt, only to be defeated and deposed by the English in 1878. Rabih collected the remnants of his army and moved west. For over a decade, he existed in the arid regions between the Nile basin and Chad until, suddenly and inexplicably, in 1892, he again moved west into the territory of the Bagarmi.

The blacks of Bagarmi were no match for Rabih's army, which was organized on the European model, and he rapidly extended his influence over the lands to the southeast of Lake Chad. In 1893, having ravaged Bagarmi, he shifted his army to the west of the lake into Bornu. By 1895, he had conquered Bornu, killed its sultan and declared himself king of his Chadian empire. He even built a new capital at Dikwa, seventy-five miles south of the lake. The ever-suspicious French saw Rabih as the cat's-paw of the English who had been sent by London to block their access to the Nile and turn the caravan trade away from the Sahara and toward Nigeria. But Rabih was strictly free-lance.

In the summer of 1898, Voulet and Chanoine assembled an expedition which they hoped would smash Rabih and ensure the unity of the French empire. The officers included Lieutenant Paul Joalland, a native of Guadaloupe and the same age as Chanoine, who had enlisted in the naval artillery at the age of nineteen. After serving in Tonkin, he had met Voulet in the Sudan and, it was said, became devoted to him. Voulet gave Joalland the job of commanding his artillery. The escort was to be the responsibility of Lieutenant Marc Pallier, a twenty-eight-year-old ex-St.-Cyrian who had joined the marines. Unlike the other officers, Lieutenant Louis Peteau had not volunteered for the mission but had been assigned to it by the colonial ministry. A Parisian, Peteau had enlisted in the marines in 1886 at the age of eighteen and had quickly climbed the ladder to lieutenant by 1894. He seemed to possess a firmer character than the other officers and, perhaps more important, was the only one among them who was not personally attached to Voulet or Chanoine. The last officer was Dr. Henric, whose weak constitution complemented an even weaker character. Henric had served with the two officers during the Mossi campaigns. Despite what he knew of their brutal methods, he nevertheless volunteered for the mission to Chad. Three French NCOs brought the total number of whites in the Central African Mission to nine. To this was added fifty regular Senegalese tirailleurs and twenty spahis *soudanais,* together with thirty interpreters and "political agents."

The bulk of the fighting, however, would be handled by some 400 "auxiliary" troops, far more than the 200 allowed by the colonial ministry. The recruitment of these auxiliaries was one of the most controversial features of campaigning in the Sudan and in many respects accounted for its notorious brutality. The French army prided itself on its ability to "go native." In the Sudan, they went native with a vengeance, passing among the "submitted" tribes to offer a bounty of fifteen francs a month, plus food and free rights of plunder, to any man who would sign up.

By catering to the piratical instincts of the African tribes, the French could claim that they had not conquered foreign lands, but had simply intervened in tribal rivalries, so that with French support one tribe defeated its enemies—in the name of France! As in many conflicts, it was not the actual belligerents who profited, but the French, who initially stood aloof, who emerged as the masters. As a method of colonial expansion, however, this had its drawbacks—especially from an African point of view. What the auxiliaries actually did was to devastate vast areas of land, murder as many men as possible, take what animals and money they could and return home. The French would then lay claim to the "submitted" territory. But they were seldom able to administer it effectively, at least in the initial instance. At best, they might plant a small post in the center of essentially unpacified country. This was not so much conquest as systematic devastation. But it provided two principal advantages: First, it allowed officers to campaign with relatively few regular troops, to write their own battle reports, and to propose their own promotions and decorations. Secondly, it usually discouraged resistance to subsequent penetration by eliminating the principal tribal leaders (and a fair percentage of their followers) and reducing the survivors to starvation.

The supplies that Voulet and Chanoine gathered for their little army were considerable and included 450 magazine-fed Lebel rifles, each fifty-one inches long and weighing nine and a quarter pounds, 50 bolt-action carbines, 180,000 rounds of ammunition, an 80-millimeter cannon with a hundred shells, boxes of sabers, 134 cases of tinned rations, 2,000 pounds of flour, sugar and coffee, 180 bottles of alcohol, 60 bottles of Bordeaux and 10 cases of champagne and liqueurs. As if this were not enough, they also packed "French works translated into Arabic . . . concerned with subjects which show the glory of our country," as well as baubles and cloth for trade.

What had been left out of these numerous stores was money to pay porters. This oversight—if, indeed, that is what it was—was to have tragic consequences. The absence of porters had been one of the major objections to the mission put by officials in the Sudan. But the ministries in Paris were far too concerned with diplomatic and territorial issues to trouble themselves with questions of logistics. Like soldiers of later generations, they simply assumed that *l'intendance suivra*. Voulet and Chanoine probably calculated that it would be a waste to spend their limited funds on blacks who could simply be dragooned into service. They fell back on the usual marine expedient for finding porters—they conscripted them. Eight hundred of them!

In early November, 1898, the Central African Mission set out from Koulikoro, 400 miles up the Niger from Timbuktu. Chanoine led the porters and the majority of tirailleurs, auxiliaries and their women overland across the 600 miles of the Niger bend, while Voulet followed the wide curve of the river, his force divided into pirogues and a marching column which met every two or three days to exchange men.

At Timbuktu, Voulet stopped several days with the commander, Lieutenant Colonel Jean François Klobb. An artilleryman and graduate of the Ecole polytechnique, the forty-one-year-old Klobb looked far more like an aging student than an officer of marines. His small, almost delicate features were accentuated by an outsized solar topee which spread over his narrow shoulders like a canopied mushroom at the end of a stalk. A large Gallic moustache drooped from his face, and a pair of pince-nez balanced on his nose screened a pair of soft, myopic eyes. Klobb was a very straightforward, dutiful man, conscientious almost to a fault—and, as well, a pious Catholic, quite rare in an army which, the accusations of its left-wing critics to the contrary, was largely indifferent to religion. Voulet's visit passed cordially. Klobb even loaned the captain seventy tirailleurs and twenty spahis from the Timbuktu garrison, and then floated with him as far as Ansongo, 250 miles downriver. Here, the two men parted on amicable terms, but Klobb noted in his diary: "I am anxious. Voulet seems to be heading off without knowing what he is doing."

Southeast of Timbuktu, the Niger becomes wider and more shallow. Voulet's flotilla nosed between the sandbanks, past large, relatively prosperous villages which were often sited on islands. On January 2, Voulet met Chanoine at Sansan-Hausa. Chanoine's march across the Niger bend had been far less trouble-free than Voulet's leisurely paddle down the river. Without adequate provisions for his porters, tirailleurs and their women, he was forced to requisition food from the villages through which they passed. Like a plague of locusts, Chanoine's column had exhausted the resources of a region which could barely support its own population. Even then, rations were inadequate. Dysentery quickly spread among his porters, who were without sufficient clothing, and at night suffered dreadfully from the cold. One-hundred-forty-eight of them had perished. Chanoine shot those who attempted to escape as an example to the others.

In January 1899, the combined columns set out from Say with 1,800 people and 800 animals. Neither captain had experience of commanding in dry regions. While the land of bush and scrub which they were entering was not exactly the Sahara, in the dry season both water and food were at a premium. The days were hot and the nights cold. The direction of the mission was soon dictated less by the "race for Chad" than by the need to feed 1,800 mouths and provide them with forty tons of water per day. They marched up and down in the sandy plateau covered with dwarf palms east of Say for most of January. Finally, on January 29, Lieutenant Peteau had had enough. Voulet sent him home via Say "for indiscipline and incompetence."

Voulet should never have let Peteau leave the expedition, for he reported to officials on the coast that things were not all that they should be with the Central African Mission. This in itself might have made little difference. By now, French functionaries in the Sudan must have been beyond being shocked by mere atrocities against blacks, and relatively expert at hushing up scandal. Voulet helped to limit that damage by dismissing his ex-subordinate as "undisciplined, very pessimistic; he had little enthusiasm." But Peteau went further. On February 5, 1899, he wrote a thirteen-page letter to his fiancée in Paris, Mademoiselle Lydia de Corvin, in which he laid bare some of the sickening details.

According to Peteau, Chanoine's atrocities had begun during the overland march across the Niger bend. The porters had been criminally mistreated. Chanoine had refused to allow Dr. Henric to examine them after the epidemic of dysentery had broken out. Twelve had been shot for attempting to escape, and the rest had been tied together by the neck in groups of five. Those unable to continue were decapitated on the spot. Voulet and Chanoine terrorized Sansan-Hausa, a "submitted" village, to get supplies and porters. Voulet ordered twenty women and children to be bayoneted and stabbed to death. Kourtey, the chief of Sansan-Hausa, put the total number of dead far higher: "Why did the whites who came to Sansan-Hausa massacre my people and ruin my large town?" he later asked investigating officers. "I had done nothing to them. I gave them everything they asked for. They told me to provide them with six horses and thirty cattle in three days. I did it, and they killed everyone they could: 101 men, women and children were massacred."

Apparently infuriated that French "control" had not been extended beyond the town of Sansan-Hausa itself, and desperately in need of porters, the two captains sent out raiding parties commanded by black NCOs who surrounded villages at dawn and shot anyone who attempted to flee. The tirailleurs brought back heads to prove that they had carried out their orders. Voulet had the heads displayed on pikes. "The few inhabitants who managed to escape the massacre in the villages which were not burned, fled with all speed at the mere sight of the tricolored flag," read the official report. While the tirailleurs were allowed to pillage freely, Voulet and Chanoine were very harsh with them: One tirailleur who shot a defaulting porter rather than bayonet him was summarily executed without benefit of a court-martial, while another suffered an identical fate for losing 124 bullets. Two tirailleurs were shot for abandoning a wounded spahi during a raid. And quite a few others felt the bite of the lash for minor infractions.

Although Peteau was hardly the outraged innocent he pretended to be (subsequent investigation revealed that he had shot one of his guides out of hand and personally ordered two villages burned), his letter was to have far-reaching consequences. Mademoiselle de Corvin, horrified by what she read, handed it to Merlou, the deputy for the Yonne, who in turn passed it on to the colonial minister in April. On April 16, the minister wired the governor general of the Sudan, Colonel Charles-Henri Vimard, at Kayes: "Understand villages being attacked for porters. Those who resist massacred." On April 20, 1899, the letter was tabled for discussion by the French cabinet.

What the ministers thought of this latest revelation of colonial army atrocities is not difficult to imagine. The political balance of the Third Republic was at this time extremely delicate. For almost thirty years, the moderate center had held power in Paris, fending off repeated challenges from radical Republicans and, increasingly, from the socialists under their charismatic leader, Jean Jaurès. They were able to do this only because they were supported by the traditional Catholic right—"If we do not share the same paradise," the saying went, "at least we share the same hell." One of the cornerstones of this political alliance was the army: The right had declared it sacred. Moderate Republicans had voted funds for the army, and in general had allowed the soldiers to run their own show. This worked well enough until 1894, when a court-martial had convicted Captain Alfred Dreyfus of treason on the basis of extremely flimsy evidence and sentenced him to life imprisonment on Devil's Island. The Republican left, and especially the fiery Georges Clemenceau, realized that this miscarriage of justice offered an excellent opportunity to split the right-center alliance which had for so long denied his radicals a share of political power.

In 1896 Clemenceau had begun his campaign for a retrial, at first quietly, and then in increasingly strident tones. The general staff, out of bureaucratic inertia and in an attempt to cover up their own negligence and incompetence, resisted this fiercely, arguing that the army should be left to discipline its own. The right, regarding the army as inviolate, naturally supported the generals. The moderate Republicans were embarrassed, and became even more so as Clemenceau and others convinced a growing collection of people, intellectuals like Emile Zola prominent among them, that Dreyfus was innocent. The moderates tried to nudge and cajole the generals and their right-wing political allies toward a compromise. But it was no use; they refused to budge.

A delighted Clemenceau continued to hammer away in the knowledge that the government would be forced eventually to intervene in an internal military matter. When this happened, the right-center alliance would crumble. By 1899, anyone but a blind man must have realized that this was in the cards. But, like a gaggle of ostriches, the government buried their heads in the sand, hoping that the Dreyfus affair would run out of steam, be forgotten, simply vanish. And now, yet another military atrocity had occurred in the Sudan. It was really too much: the soldiers were their own worst enemies, and were about to scuttle a political combination favorable to them. The minister of the colonies asked Merlou to keep quiet about Peteau's letter until an investigation could be completed.

In mid-April 1899, Lieutenant Colonel Klobb was on his way to the coast, there to catch a boat for a well-earned furlough in France. However, in Kayes he was intercepted by Colonel Vimard, who told him of the rumors circulating about the Central African Mission (probably Klobb was already well aware of them). Vimard dispatched the lieutenant colonel in pursuit of Voulet and Chanoine. Klobb set off across the Niger bend with twenty-five-year-old Lieutenant Octave Meynier, a graduate of St.-Cyr who had joined the spahis *soudanais,* and a small detachment of forty-nine tirailleurs. By early July, they had arrived at Say, where Klobb reorganized his column. Voulet and Chanoine had a head start of several months. To catch them, he had to travel quickly. He took only thirty-six tirailleurs and a handful of spahis, "auxiliary" cavalry, guides and only thirteen porters.

The trail of the Central African Mission was not difficult to follow. After dismissing Peteau, Voulet and Chanoine had marched up and down in the territory east of Say in search of food and water for their enormous column. In early February they had marched south without seeing a single village. They then turned east across the plateau of the Sahel. This vast plain covered with brambles and dwarf palms yielded little except people to butcher. What was more, they committed many of their atrocities around Sokoto, on territory which had been ceded to Britain in what is today northwestern Nigeria. By April, the food situation was desperate, as were the French officers, most of whom were ill with fever and dysentery. Perhaps this desperation clouded Chanoine's judgment, for he began to write long screeds blaming the food shortage on a "plot" by the government to sabotage the mission. Voulet agreed, and decided to "break with the government" by refusing to send couriers.

They took out their frustration on the guides: "We would hang them and most of them, hanged very close to the ground, had their legs devoured by the hyenas, while the rest were left for the vultures," Lieutenant Joalland later testified. Anyone who could not keep up was shot. Voulet's tirailleurs continued to raid for livestock and, especially, for women. On July 13, Voulet ordered 150 women and children captured in a raid on a village to be slaughtered as a reprisal for the deaths of two of his tirailleurs suffered in the assault. Klobb hurried along in a vicious heat, following this trail marked by charred villages and corpses. The remains of slaughtered guides decorated many crossroads. He found the bodies of thirteen women hanging from the trees around the ashes of the village of Tibiri a hundred miles west of Zinder. At Koran-Kaljo, the bodies of two children had been strung up. Klobb displayed no emotion. He said nothing. He simply pushed on.

On July 10, 1899, Klobb arrived at the small village of Damangara, about seventy-six miles west of Kano, where he learned that Voulet was only a few hours' march away. He dispatched Sergeant Mahmadou Kamara and three other tirailleurs with a letter for the captain informing him that he was relieved of his command. The four men found Voulet by evening. Voulet questioned Klobb's tirailleurs about the strength of their force. He then told his men to see to it that Mahmadou was not allowed to make contact with the other officers. Voulet and Chanoine held a hasty consultation. They considered flight, but concluded that their column, weighed down by sick porters and women, could never elude Klobb. They decided to disperse the other Europeans with the regular tirailleurs in various directions to raid or locate wells. The following day, Voulet handed Mahmadou a letter for Klobb and sent him back: "Tell the colonel that there is no water here, that I am going to the next village where there is water," Voulet told the sergeant.

Klobb must have been stunned when he opened Voulet's letter: "I am resolved to sacrifice my life rather than to submit to the humiliation which you have been ordered to impose upon me," the lieutenant colonel read. "But also, I prefer to gamble everything and above all not to abandon my place to an intriguer of your ilk by a stupid suicide." He continued that he had 600 rifles and would treat Klobb as an enemy if he approached.

A man less devoted to duty than Klobb might have been intimidated into renouncing his pursuit. But he forged ahead.

As a final irony, the confrontation between the two men would occur on Bastille Day 1899. On the evening of July 13, as Klobb's column drew closer, Voulet dispatched another messenger: "Tell the colonel that if he tries to catch up with my column, I will attack." Whether or not Klobb ever received this message was disputed. In any case, it appears that Voulet had little faith in its effect, for he formed up his NCOs and told them that the lieutenant colonel had come to make them give up all of their slaves and captives, "whom, he, the Captain, had given the tirailleurs." He asked them whom they would obey, him or the colonel, and they all agreed to obey the captain.

On the morning of July 14, a tirailleur in the rear guard of Voulet's column spotted their pursuers coming through the bush. Voulet drew up his men into a firing line, and sent a final message to Klobb: "My Colonel, I am here with all of my men," it read. "If you come one step closer, I will fire. I will fight to the death." Klobb called up Lieutenant Meynier. Voulet, he concluded, was quite mad. Klobb was confident that neither the seventy tirailleurs who had been under his command at Timbuktu and whom he had loaned to Voulet in December, nor the other

Europeans would fire on a senior officer. What he could not know was that Voulet and Chanoine had carefully dispersed their force, so that no member of Klobb's old command nor any other Europeans were present. Klobb gave Meynier strict orders that they were not to open fire under any circumstances. He then drew up his tirailleurs in a line, unfurled the French tricolor, and together with Meynier and an interpreter, "resolutely" approached Voulet and his men, who were standing 150 yards away. Voulet shouted at Klobb to halt, but the lieutenant colonel walked slowly toward him. The captain then ordered his tirailleurs to fire a volley into the air. Then a second one. Klobb began to harangue the tirailleurs, calling them to do their duty and obey orders. Voulet grew furious. He cursed Klobb, then drawing his revolver, he aimed it at his own tirailleurs and ordered them to fire. A bullet from the first volley caught Klobb in the side. He shouted to Meynier not to retaliate. A second volley rang out. Klobb was killed this time with a shot to the head, as were four of his tirailleurs and a spahi. Meynier was wounded in the leg. When Voulet ordered his men to fix bayonets, Klobb's tirailleurs broke and ran. (On August 1, while on patrol, Lieutenant Cornu, commander of the French post at Dosso, discovered the remnants of Klobb's column dragging seven wounded. He alerted the government.)

Voulet sent his tirailleurs forward to make sure that Klobb was dead. He came up to Meynier, and while he dressed his wound, indulged in an invective against Klobb "who had stolen his goods, his mission, which he had prepared for so many months." For the next few hours, Meynier was forced to listen to "diatribes against France, against the government, against the Colonel, at times broken by a little remorse and then a return to rage, an unsettling madness." Voulet gradually calmed down, but Meynier was convinced that he saw "a real glow of madness" in Voulet's eyes.

On the evening of July 14, Voulet broke the news of the skirmish to his officers. "Now I am an outlaw, I renounce my family, my country, I am no longer a Frenchman, I am a black chief," he told the stunned Europeans. "We are going to create a strong empire, impregnable, which I shall surround with an enormous bush without water. To take me, it will require 10,000 men and 20 million [francs]. . . . If I were in Paris, I would be master of France. History is full of a thousand such examples: Did not Henri III assassinate the Duc de Guise?" He then took his black NCOs aside and harangued them in a similar vein: "Now I am no longer a captain. I am a chief of sofas [warriors] like Samori. You see, I no longer wear my bars [of rank]. Never again will I see France. My country is over there in the east [pointing toward Chad]; we are going to conquer it. You are no longer sergeants. You are great black chiefs!"

However much one may sympathize with the plight of the French officers who witnessed this little scene, their conduct was far from courageous. Voulet told them that they might come with him or return to Say. But, if they returned to the coast, they were forbidden to take any "deserters" with them on pain of being attacked. They asked for time to reflect on Voulet's offer. In fact, they were extremely uneasy. All realized Voulet had gone too far. But they were unsure of their men. The last vestiges of military discipline had broken down during the weeks of pillaging. The chain of command was nonexistent. Only terror and a desire for spoils kept the mission together. They were also extremely disadvantaged by their inability to speak the language of the tirailleurs, forced to rely on the pidgin French of the NCOs or that of the interpreters to make themselves understood. This made communication very risky. Voulet, with his black mistress, who was in effect the "queen" of his little empire, and his loyal interpreter, had a far more direct influence on the men. The other Europeans felt "isolated in the midst of these bandits."

Their hesitation did have an effect, however, for the tirailleurs realized that the other Europeans did not support the two mutineers. Voulet and Chanoine left the whites behind, and marched away with the blacks. On the night of July 15–16, they camped at May Jirgui, a village of mud houses with conical straw roofs. Voulet, tipped off no doubt that there were murmurs of discontent among the men, called them together and threatened to shoot anyone who attempted to desert. In the volatile atmosphere of the moment, after the two captains themselves had already set the precedent for revolt, it was an imprudent threat to make. The sergeants met and decided that the bugle call for lunch would serve as the signal for mutiny. Voulet was warned by an interpreter, and, according to Meynier, shot the man for not informing him sooner. This brutality provided the spark which detonated the mutiny prematurely. Voulet mounted his horse and, with Chanoine, rode in front of the tirailleurs and began to fire at them. Quite naturally, they fired back. Chanoine was killed outright. Voulet fled with a half-dozen faithful, who soon drifted away, leaving him alone with his interpreter and a Targui woman.

When, late in the afternoon of July 16, some women brought the news to the Europeans that the tirailleurs had mutinied, they immediately prepared to defend themselves, realizing that if Voulet and Chanoine successfully suppressed it, then they would surely blame the whites for intriguing against them. A while later, however, a sergeant came in to ask for orders. Bouthel was dispatched to take charge. It was just as well that he was, for Voulet had not yet given up. He sent his interpreter to make contact with the sergeants, apparently with some success, for several of the mutinous NCOs were shot when they attempted to rejoin Voulet in the bush. The next morning Voulet came to the camp himself. The sentry refused to let him pass without Bouthel's permission. There was an exchange of shots, and Voulet fell dead with a bullet in his brain.

Lieutenant Pallier now took command. It is certain that the Europeans were badly shaken by events. While they had had no hand in the killing of Klobb, they realized that word of the mission's atrocities had reached Paris and that they could not be sure of the reception that awaited them on their return. The best course of action, they concluded, was to pick up the threads of the mission, restore order, and march toward Chad in the hope that by covering themselves with glory, the crimes might be quietly forgotten. They gathered what was left of the badly pillaged baggage train and marched toward Zinder, where they hoped to make contact with Lamy. Zinder was taken. But discipline in the Central African Mission remained fragile. A second mutiny was put down only after forty-five tirailleurs were killed. Exhausted and discouraged, Pallier handed command to Joalland and left for the coast.

In Paris, the story of Klobb's murder broke on August 23, 1899. It could not have come at a worse time for the center-right forces. Already they had bowed to pressure for a retrial of Captain Dreyfus, who at that very moment was having his case reviewed at Rennes. But everyone knew it was in reality the army that was on trial. The radical press used the reports of the Voulet-Chanoine drama to reinforce their antimilitarist campaign. Even the moderate *Temps* declared that the events "make us blush" and put paid to the propaganda about France's "civilizing mission" in Africa. The right-wing press at first refused to believe the reports —the *Echo de Paris* wrote that they were bald lies, the result of "native duplicity." When Pallier died on his way back to France, the conspiracy-conscious right accused the colonial ministry of having assassinated him to prevent him from telling the truth. But soon the reports had been confirmed by too many sources to be able to deny. So they fell back on another excuse—madness, brought on by *la soudanite.*

The *soudanite,* or its Saharian variant, *le cafard,* provided a handy excuse for the excesses committed by soldiers in Africa: "The Cafard, that legendary disease . . . seemed to chase all volatile Frenchmen wherever they went," wrote an English soldier. It was encouraged by the belief, widespread in the years before the Great War, that Africa unsettled Europeans to the point even of madness: "The sun, the atrocious sun of the bush which calcinates the brain and boils the blood in stiffened arteries," declared one deputy with more imagination than scientific knowledge. General Laperrine described the cafard as if it were an illness: "One is nervous, one becomes irritable without knowing why, the slightest joke is taken the wrong way, one becomes simply unbearable." When subordinates noticed their superiors in a foul mood (Laperrine regularly hurled his electric fan across the room when in a bad humor), they would say: "There is a scirocco blowing."

Everyone, of course, has his bad days. The heat, the solitude and the sheer boredom of many colonial stations could have done little to improve the dispositions of officers. A general staff report of 1896 recommended that officers be stationed only two years in Saharian Africa because of "the excessive bleakness of a tour of duty in the Saharian regions and the difficulties of isolation."

However, the *soudanite,* or cafard, while real enough, was also a myth carefully cultivated by colonial soldiers. It might drive them to drink, but it seldom drove them mad. It simply offered a plausible way to pass off their excesses of behavior as aberrations brought on by the African climate. "The irreparable act was committed in one of those moments of mental aberration which the strenuous life of torrid Africa seems to encourage," *Le Temps* opined on September 21, 1899. The official inquiry clutched at this straw, and laid the blame entirely on the "madness" of Voulet. General Chanoine lobbied furiously to clear his son's name, although he was considered by all who testified as Voulet's gray eminence. The crimes of the others were ignored, as was their pusillanimous behavior in the face of the mutiny. The war minister, General Louis André, wrote to the colonial minister on November 7, 1902, that the inquiry had trodden lightly because "it was necessary to avoid drawing attention once again to the unfortunate events which affected the Central African Mission."

The left let the matter drop. With the formation in 1899 of the Waldeck-Rousseau ministry, the first in the Third Republic that looked to the left, rather than to the right, for its parliamentary majority, Clemenceau had achieved his goal. The balance of French politics had now shifted in his favor.

But the verdict could have been little different. For if madness there was, it was the psychosis of a system which encouraged excessive rivalry and competition among young men to such a degree that their moral code became the first fatality. The desire for promotion, to secure "my mission" and protect it from poachers, the race to conquer territory and win fame elbowed out the most elementary notions of humanity in too many of them. French soldiers in Africa became brutalized, not by the climate, but by the excessive rivalry among themselves. Paris encouraged their misdemeanors by failing to issue explicit orders or to send older, more experienced men to offer firm supervision.

The barbarity of the Central African Mission was less of an aberration than Frenchmen cared to admit. There was little that was civil about France's "civilizing mission" in the Sudan. While it would be sentimental nonsense to portray precolonial Africa as a tropical Eden upon which the white man burst with savage fury, the simple fact was that, in the period of conquest, the French marines in the Sudan adopted methods as brutal as those of the African potentates whom they fought. (To be fair to the French, Germans, Belgians and Boers often behaved no better.) So much so, in fact, that friend was barely distinguishable from foe, a French column became the mirror image of those of Samori or Rabih: The *sofas* of both armies were dressed in colorful robes and turbans with belts of bullets lashed across their shoulders and chests, both were followed by troops of singing women and by long lines of suffering porters lashed together by the neck. Both used terror as their principal weapon. The crimes of Voulet and Chanoine were aberrations only in the grandeur of their scale. But how could one put a system on trial?

XIII

THE
CONQUEST OF LAKE CHAD

This story, or at least Bouthel's version of it, was what Lamy heard at Zinder. He led a party south to Dankori, disinterred Klobb's remains, and brought them to Zinder where he and Foureau erected a suitable tomb for the unfortunate lieutenant colonel. Lamy and Foureau then amassed a sizable caravan of horses and camels, bade adieu to Charles Dorian, who "wished to be useful to the mission in Parliament," and struck out westward in pursuit of Lieutenant Joalland and the remnants of the Central African Mission.

Winter is the dry season in the Sudan. Most of the small pools which dot the plain in summer dry up, and the ground is often scorched and blackened by brushfires, many intentionally set to burn off the bush and renew the pasture which grows up beneath the blackened trunks of the larger trees. To those who had marched through the Sahara, the country appeared pleasant enough—reasonably well watered, and filled with villages peopled by long-limbed blacks who lived almost exclusively on millet. But it was the very devil to march through. Small spiny plants tore at clothes and tormented the flesh. Many of the Algerians had been infected by the guinea worm. The column raised a fair quantity of fine, white dust, so that soon most of the men looked as if they had been dropped into a sack of flour. Gradually, however, the land was transformed—small lakes began to appear surrounded by palm trees. Fields of millet replaced the monotonous bush: "Cattle, tame ostriches, sheep in the fields, people who circulate everywhere," Foureau wrote. "One feels a normal, active life, and no more the immobility and eternal sleep of the silent and mournful steppe." With the improvement in the countryside came an improvement in diet. Dried fish and ostrich eggs came to supplement the eternal porridge of millet. This was brought by grateful blacks who, according to Foureau, wanted the Frenchmen to remove the yoke of the dreadful Rabih. More likely, they feared that the French would destroy their villages and were attempting to dissuade them.

By January 13, 1900, the French had reached the Komadougou River, which flows eastward into Lake Chad "between two great curtains of these gracious trees . . . weighted down with bird's nests suspended at the extremities of tree branches." Monkeys chattered and the snout of a caiman occasionally broke the dark surface of the water. After the Sahara, this was an Eden. But it was an ominous one: "Everywhere, but especially near the villages, human bones cover the ground," Foureau wrote. "Skulls lie everywhere. . . . It is not without reason that the blacks of this country speak of Rabih with a trembling and give all the signs of an unspeakable terror. The campsite, especially that of January 18, 1900, which before was a village of Gashagar, is a veritable ossuary." On January 21, they passed the charred remains of the village of Yao, and then at last, they saw Lake Chad.

Or at least they thought that it might be Lake Chad. For they were about to discover that this body of water—imprinted on their maps and in their imaginations as a sparkling sea set in silver sands—was so elusive that some began to wonder if it existed at all. Captain Reibell called the real thing "a depressing swamp" in which the water seemed eager to hide behind the foliage. When Barth had asked to see Lake Chad a half-century earlier, he was taken to "a drowned prairie . . . An endless grassy plain, without a single tree, extended to the farthest horizon." Yet, when he attempted to cross it, his feet sank into the mud and he was forced to retrace his steps. The eastern and southern shores were broken up by small islands "encompassed with papyrus and tall reeds, of between ten to fourteen feet in height. The thicket was interwoven with climbing plants with yellow flowers . . . while on the surface of the water were floating plants." The water contained more than plants: Crocodiles and hippos were in evidence, as were pirates who nosed around the islands in flat-bottomed pirogues to prey upon the surrounding villages. Although Lake Chad forms an enticing blue spot 160 miles long and 40 miles wide in the center of a khaki continent, in fact, it is a shallow pan which expands and contracts with the seasons but seldom attains a depth of more than twenty-two feet. However, Foureau, eager to keep the illusions of colonial riches alive for the home audience, recorded his impressions in vivid, if not strictly accurate, terms: "It is really it, this long hoped for lake, this goal of our efforts for these long months, this goal of my dreams for more than twenty years! Before us, a scintillating expanse of water stretched to the horizon, which we saw through the spaces between the numerous islands of reeds which grew near the edge."

Lamy and Foureau decided to circumvent the lake by the north shore to avoid entering territory ceded to Britain. They also had no idea of the whereabouts of the other two missions under Joalland and Gentil. Couriers dispatched with letters for the other Frenchmen were turned back by Rabih and returned with the most contradictory reports. The land to the north of the lake was far less rich than that which they had encountered to the west. Like most French expeditions in Africa, Lamy had acquired a fair number of "auxiliaries"—men who tagged along for the prospect of pillage, women who served as cooks and bedmates and did menial duties, and other hangers-on. This inevitably created logistical problems. Everyone suffered from hunger. This extended column threaded its way across the swamps and coves of the north shore, through swarms of mosquitoes and glutinous, stinking mud. The horses began to die. Some of the stragglers fell victim to bands of Tuareg who shadowed the lumbering column. On February 18, 1900, Joalland, having heard of Lamy's march, came to meet him. Foureau, no doubt in an attempt to rehabilitate Joalland and his mission, described the lieutenant as "a charming and gay companion." Together, Joalland and Lamy marched down the eastern shore of the lake to Joalland's base camp on the Chari River, which enters Lake Chad from the south. Meynier saw them approach across the flood plain, the Algerians mounted on camels and horses, followed by a turbulent escort of auxiliaries commanded by Sheik Omar Scinda, who hoped to reclaim Bornu from Rabih.

Joalland's camp had been established on the right bank of the Chari. Two hundred yards across the broad river stood the town of Goulfey. In 1900, Goulfey was little more than an overgrown village—a picturesque collection of round and square mud shapes with rounded straw roofs like something that might have been imagined by Picasso in his cubist phase. The town was encompassed by a low mud wall and garrisoned by Rabih's troops. Rabih had not proved particularly welcoming—the French emissary sent to make contact with him was hanged in the marketplace of his capital at Dikwa on a beam normally used for displaying butcher's meat.

When Foureau walked out to take a picture of Goulfey, he was shot at from the walls. Lamy trained his 80-millimeter gun on the town and fired five shells into the fragile masonry walls. This provoked the beating of drums and other warlike sounds from within. Soon, a steady rain of lead began to splatter into the French camp as Rabih's *sofas* fired for several hours from across the river. This annoyed Lamy to the point that he ordered an attack prepared for dawn on the following morning. However, at sunrise on February 25, several blacks came in to tell Lamy that Goulfey had been abandoned during the night.

The presence of two small armies camped for several weeks around Goulfey had exhausted the region's resources. Lamy ordered his force south, through the marshes which border the Chari and then across the river to the town of Mara. The attrition rate in horses, camels and cattle had been high in the wetlands. However, Mara made it all seem worth the effort. After several months of living in the open, the mud houses of Mara, mean as they were, seemed like the last word in luxury to the Algerians and Senegalese. The abandoned town also concealed a large and welcome number of grain silos. But Mara was also infested with typhus-carrying lice. Once again, Lamy ordered his men to march south. On the evening of March 2, they sighted the town of Kousseri.

Kousseri stands on the left, or western, bank of the Logone River at its confluence with the Chari. In 1900, it was a large town surrounded by high walls on three sides and the Logone on the fourth. Most of the inhabitants were fishermen. At first view, Kousseri appeared an imposing obstacle. But it was obviously ill-prepared for defense. The bush grew right up to the foot of the fortifications, mud walls which could easily be breached by Lamy's guns. Lamy would have preferred to await the arrival of Gentil before launching his attack. However, he decided that the *sofas* might interpret this delay as a sign of fear or weakness. Lamy resolved to attack on the following morning.

The battle of Kousseri proved to be a massacre. Lamy lined up his guns and blew a gaping hole in the wall. The bugle sounded, and several hundred Algerians, Senegalese and black auxiliaries ran screaming toward the town. Those who could not crowd through the breach climbed the walls by jamming their bayonets into the brittle masonry. The sight was too much for Rabih's *sofas*. They abandoned the walls and ran through the town toward the river, where they fought with the rest of the fleeing population for pirogues which would ferry them to the safety of the far bank, or simply plunged into the water and started to swim.

Sergeant Guilleux arrived to find the town bank lined with tirailleurs firing at the canoes full of men, women and children and at the heads bobbing in the water. "What a sickening carnage," he recorded. "The pirogues were brimming with blood which bathed groups of wounded, their eyes haggard and their mouths twisted in pain." The river quite literally had turned red. When they tired of this, the soldiers ordered the women that were left to bring them water. They then began to rifle the houses with their bayonets to find rice, pots of millet and honey. "Already, several women are following us to carry our spoils." Guilleux acquired a "wife" whom he found hiding in the dark corner of a house. Lamy had lost one tirailleur and had one wounded in the fight.

Life at Kousseri for the soldiers was far from unpleasant. Most had acquired wives, some even had several. They lounged about watching the women slip out of their robes and bathe in the river "without modesty." The tirailleurs fought a few skirmishes, most of them successful, in the bush with bands of Rabih's *sofas*. The great problem was the number of people driven into Kousseri by the fighting in the countryside. Foureau put their numbers at 12,000 "without exaggeration," and more arrived daily. Lamy ordered food to be rationed. On April 2, 1900, Foureau left the expedition and headed for the coast, leaving Lamy in sole command.

In Kousseri, things were building up for a climactic confrontation. Lamy held the town, but Rabih controlled the countryside. Furthermore, Rabih had moved his force a few miles north of Kousseri and established a fortified camp—a square earthwork which was a marvel of Crimean War architecture. There he sat, content to conduct a distant siege rather than attack in force. Audacious raids caused panic among the refugees crowded into Kousseri and kept everyone's nerves on edge, but otherwise caused little damage. It might have occurred to Lamy that his predicament was not unlike that of Gordon at Khartoum. He was becoming desperate for the arrival of Gentil, who was struggling up from the south, wrestling with the same problem which plagued all French expeditions in Africa—lack of transport. Until Gentil arrived, Lamy would not have enough troops to break out of Kousseri. He could only ration his food and pray that Gentil would arrive before it was too late.

The Gentil mission offered a lesson in the value of perseverance. A young naval ensign stationed at Libreville in the Congo, Emile Gentil had resigned his commission to take up the profession of exploration. In 1897, after almost two years of planning and fund-raising in Paris, he sailed up the Congo and Ubangui rivers to Fort de Possel, and then crossed overland to Fort Crampel, which stands on the Gribingui River some miles above its confluent with the Chari in the present-day Central African Republic. Here, Gentil reassembled the steamer *Léon Blot* and sailed into the headwaters of the Chari and, thus, into Rabih's very backyard. However, Rabih's command of the shore stalled his advance.

Gentil lost a number of his Senegalese in vain attempts to make his way downriver to Lake Chad. In 1898, he had returned to Paris with two black chiefs to drum up more support for a concerted campaign against Rabih. He returned to the Congo with reinforcements in February 1899. But while sailing up the Congo River, he learned that Rabih had destroyed his advance base at Kouno, about 300 miles up river from Kousseri. Gentil assembled his new force at Tounia (renamed Fort Archambault), eighty miles south of Kouno. In November, he sailed down the Chari with 344 men to mount a combined land-river attack on Rabih at his camp near Kouno. The attack failed, and cost Gentil 46 men killed and 106 wounded. Gentil had again returned to the Congo to fetch more reinforcements, when the arrival of Lamy in the north forced Rabih to shift his forces to meet this new threat. Gentil's path now lay open for a rendezvous with the other two French columns.

On April 20th, the Gentil mission marched into Kousseri. If this was the extra muscle for which Lamy had been waiting, he must have been disappointed: "What a strange procession," Guilleux observed. "There are blacks of all races, men and women, all hideous, without a stitch of clothing to cover their bodies. From time to time a soldier walks by looking exhausted. They also suffered to get here!" The Gentil mission might not have looked like much, but they had brought champagne and rifles. Lamy could now count on 700 men.

Rabih obviously had not been idle during the years when he had served the English. His camp was intelligently sited on a bend in the Chari, a high-walled fort of earth and logs pierced only by a few narrow gateways. The *sofas* had cleared the brush from all the main approaches to create for themselves "a magnificent rifle range." Squatting on his haunches, his kepi pushed back on his head and his tangled beard accentuating the movements of his mouth, Lamy explained to his officers how it was to be taken, illustrating his strategy with tracings in the sand. Lamy's plan was not particularly imaginative. After all, there were only two ways of capturing a fortress—starvation or storm. Each of the missions would form a column and invest one of the three sides of the fortress. The fourth wall, which faced the Chari, would offer to the *sofas* their only line of retreat.

At six o'clock on the morning of April 22, 1900, Lamy's force of French, Algerians, Senegalese, auxiliary tirailleurs and a contingent of black cavalry courtesy of the sultan of Bagarmi set out through the bush. One hour later, the first men arrived in view of the fortress. By eight o'clock, most of the French forces were deployed on the edge of the large clearing. Nine hundred yards away stood the squat mass of the fort, obscured in places by small huts of the *sofas* which had been constructed outside the walls. At a signal, the French-directed forces began to advance, but very slowly, one section at a time, across a blackened field completely denuded of cover. The tirailleurs lay on their stomachs with their officers and French NCOs standing behind. Lamy's plan was to advance slowly over the space of two hours to draw the noose of tirailleurs closer to the walls and presumably to exhaust the *sofas'* ammunition before the final charge.

He must have calculated that the poor marksmanship of the *sofas,* combined with a general softening up of Rabih's men by his three 80-millimeter cannon and one 44, together with his own rifle fire, would mean lighter casualties for him than if he ordered an immediate and precipitous assault on the walls. Nevertheless, Sergeant Guilleux found that lying for two hours in the middle of a burned-over field, under a torrid sun, bullets kicking up dust all around and occasionally even hitting someone, was uncomfortable to say the least. Ammunition was brought up to them on camelback, as was water, but it was too little to quench their burning thirst. Perhaps Lamy noticed that the fire of his own men was slackening, for around ten o'clock he ordered the bugles to blow the charge. The lines of tirailleurs rose and ran shouting toward the fortress. However, at the foot of the walls, the charge was momentarily arrested. Without siege ladders, the only way into the fort was through a few small doors which were barely a yard wide. Most of the *sofas* had deserted the wall, but here and there a few of the braver ones shot down into the milling tirailleurs. The doors soon gave way, and the tirailleurs streamed in. "We entered the fortress," Guilleux remembered.

> Bodies were everywhere; the wounded got up to shoot their last bullet at us. Disemboweled horses lay across the streets. The straw huts were on fire and grilled our flesh. The *sofas*

threw themselves at us, sabers in hand: we ran them through
with our bayonets. Everywhere men were fighting hand to
hand. We bellowed, we fought, we tore into them like furious
lions. Nothing stopped us. We pushed the enemy back to the
other end of the camp.

The final moments of Rabih's *sofas* were remembered most vividly
by Captain Reibell. He had pushed his way through a confusion of
corpses, panicked horses and terrified black women squatting on their
haunches begging to be spared. A line of Rabih's prisoners chained
together by the neck were being led toward the gates. In the far corner
of the camp, 200 *sofas* who had been cornered were attempting to scale
the wall and escape: "We shot them down at point-blank range," Reibell
recounted.

It was a terrible atrocity which I will never forget. This mass
which swarmed and jostled, the men stepping over the bodies,
climbed over each other to grasp the top of the rampart, where
a bullet would bring them tumbling back down. Faces upon
which was painted the anguish of death turned toward us, a
few in desperation firing their last shot at us which would hit
someone. The horse of a chief reared up and added to the
disorder. This is the vision of horror which I still have before
my eyes. Not one of them escaped and a mound of cadavers
gradually piled up from which rose a sickening and insipid
stench of hot blood. I turned away to be sick, and walked
toward a gate which led to the Chari.

Guilleux, too, was there, and excused the butchery by the single
fact that "the tirailleurs were thirsty for vengeance, they set upon them.
For every black that we shot, ten fell with him, quickly suffocated in the
mass of their comrades who trampled them." Soon there was "a human
pyramid, three or four high."
Reibell stumbled toward the river, stepping over the bodies of dead
sofas.

I was making my way through the cadavers when next to me a
tirailleur, noticing that one of the bodies was still moving, stuck
in his bayonet to the hilt. The blood spurted out all over me.

We were now at the camp exit. Before us, small groups and individual *sofas* were fleeing in all directions. I arrived at the river with the troops of the Saharian mission. Several blacks were swimming across. We fired on them. The water grew red with blood.

Reibell gathered together a few soldiers and pursued the deserters, who were fleeing southward. In the confusion, he found it difficult to distinguish friend from foe. Everyone was black, and dressed more or less alike. Furthermore, the auxiliaries furnished by the sultan of Baguirmy were far more interested in pillage than in defeating Rabih (and proved reluctant to risk their lives). They busied themselves with stripping the bodies, even those of dead Frenchmen and tirailleurs, and reaching for horses. Reibell's sword was stolen, and he even had to reclaim his horse from a young Baguirmian who had taken it as spoils of war. There was little but isolated groups to pursue. The tirailleurs spent their time finishing off wounded *sofas* whom they found hiding in the bush. Reibell was about two miles from Rabih's camp when he heard the crash of a cannon and a lively firefight to his rear.

Rabih had been wounded and driven from his camp. But he was not yet finished. He gathered what he could of his army and counterattacked just at a point where Lamy stood with several of his officers. The major fell, mortally wounded. Captain Emile Cointet and four spahis were also killed, and Lieutenant Clément de Chambrun wounded in the arm. The attack was driven off by cannon fire followed by a fierce charge by the Senegalese. The tirailleurs pursued the fleeing *sofas* through the bush. The wounded Rabih was carried by some of his men until abandoned in the heat of the chase. One of the Senegalese found him stretched on the ground and shot him in the head.

When the tirailleur returned to camp, he discovered that Emile Gentil had put a bounty on Rabih's head. He went back to the body, cut off the head and one hand, and took them to the dying Lamy, who had been laid out on a low bed in the tent of Rabih. "His jacket had been removed," wrote Reibell, "his shirt was stained with blood. His broken left arm was bandaged up. The bullet which had pierced his chest could not be removed." He asked for the number of casualties. Twenty-eight tirailleurs dead and seventy-five wounded. He was told that Rabih was dead. "Is it true?" he asked. The head was brought in and identified by several people.

Rabih's body was then dragged into Kousseri, where "men, women and children, everyone trampled on it shouting their wild cries, so that tomorrow morning nothing will remain but a shapeless jelly." Lamy, too, died, and was buried at Kousseri. The French established a permanent garrison across the river and baptized it Fort Lamy. (Today it is called Njadmena.)

The French took another year to subdue the remnants of Rabih's army, which was now commanded by one of his lieutenants, Fadalallah. Reibell led a column to raze Rabih's capital at Dikwa, on territory ceded to Britain, and scattered Fadalallah's remaining forces. The rebel chief was finally run to ground and killed at Goudjba on August 23, 1901. The Algerians of the Saharian mission paddled down the Congo River and were transported to Bordeaux, where the Right laid on their traditional rhapsodic reception reserved for returning colonial heroes.

The conquest of Chad virtually completed the conquest of the Sudan. The desert had now been encircled. Foureau and Lamy had proved that the Sahara could be crossed. They had not proved that it could be conquered. This would provide a more difficult task, one which would require tactical imagination and which could only be accomplished by stages. And the first stage was to close off the last "port" open to the desert pirates—the Tuat.

XIV

THE
TUAT

Temassinin was not especially scenic—a few date palms which straggled down a narrow ravine between bare, gray hills. Nevertheless, in the several months which he had lived there, Lieutenant Théodore Pein had become rather attached to the place. He had assumed, quite naively, as he now readily admitted, that its occupation as a revictualing station for the Foureau-Lamy mission was simply the first step in transforming it into a permanent base, a springboard for the conquest of the Ahaggar. Now he had been ordered back to Ouargla. What then, he asked in an exasperated letter to his friend Captain Ferdinand Levé, military secretary to the governor general of Algeria, had been the purpose of the Foureau-Lamy expedition? "The mission has just traversed the Sahara like a ship on the sea, leaving behind nothing but a wake which closes immediately," he wrote. (The metaphor had been lifted from General Bugeaud, but Pein nurtured no literary pretensions.) "No treaty, no claims, no vigorous act showing that we are the masters. Pass through, pass through quickly, that seems to be the goal."

Pein's exasperation was perfectly justified. Although he had served in the Sahara long enough to realize that the Third Republic was incapable of formulating a coherent colonial policy, he supposed that the Foureau-Lamy expedition would at least have created an irreversible momentum for the conquest of the Sahara. Now he was ordered to abandon a perfectly good outpost and march back to Ouargla. He simply wanted to know what had been the point of it all.

People outside the Armée d'Afrique might have found it difficult to take Pein seriously. Although he was almost thirty-two years old in 1899, his slim frame, short-cropped brown hair, sensible moustache and large brown eyes made him appear only recently emerged from adolescence. When he spoke, he had the habit of inclining his head forward and shifting his weight onto his right leg, as if mental concentration required a great physical effort. Pein was no genius. But he was intelligent enough, and angry enough, to realize that he was well placed to give the government the Sahara policy which it so grievously lacked. Théodore Pein was to become the true midwife of the French conquest of the Sahara.

There could be no doubt that Pein was a soldier. Even when not parading about Ouargla in his splendid white uniform with gold braid (it impressed the Arabs!) or dispensing justice at the town gate in the manner of a caid, he exuded the erect, almost aggressive confidence of a military man. He came to it naturally. His father had been an *Africain* during what was referred to in the Armée d'Afrique as the great period of Algerian conquest. A sailor who had participated in the invasion of Algiers in 1830, Théodore Pein, Senior, had been seduced by North Africa from the moment he had first spied it over the gunwales of the frigate *Calypso*. As soon as his ship touched base in Toulon, he had enlisted as a private in the nineteenth infantry regiment, which was bound for Algiers. For the next thirty years, he had fought in the campaigns that gradually were to carve out France's greatest colony in the Maghreb. A childhood fed on stories of battles fought with Bugeaud, Cavaignac, Lamouricière, Changarnier and other heroes of the Algerian conquest could hardly have failed to fire the imagination of the young Pein. He had, however, been forced to wait almost five years following his graduation from St.-Cyr for a vacancy to occur in the Arab Bureau at Touggourt.

It is difficult to penetrate the character of Théodore Pein. Europeans who met him invariably described him as quiet and modest. This may have been part of the hagiography of procolonialist writers. But he probably felt uncomfortable, perhaps even slightly intimidated, in the company of Europeans. It is obvious from his letters that Pein was a man with strong views, which he could neither hide nor even nuance. Among his Chaamba, Pein was a lord—they called him M'soupa, pidgin French for Monsieur Pein.

In the years after 1892, Pein served in most of the Saharian outposts of southern Algeria, where he perfected his skills as a leader of *goumiers,* or Chaamba irregulars. It had proved extremely valuable experience, in at least two respects. First, he had gained a reputation as a man who dared test the elasticity of his superiors' toleration by authorizing raids by his Chaamba into the Fezzan and Tripolitania. On one of these raids, he hid for a week in an abandoned shrine on the outskirts of Ghadames, while his Arabs carried out a razzia against the Ajjer Tuareg in Turkish territory. Another party dispatched by Pein had captured the murderers of the Marquis de Morès, much to the embarrassment of the Tunisian authorities. In the useful art of blurring that fine line between initiative and insubordination, Pein had achieved the status of a master craftsman.

Second, Pein's experience of mobile desert raiding had served to convince him that the French army in southern Algeria must be radically transformed before it could hope to invade the Sahara successfully. The French policed the oases with infantry—tirailleurs—and spahis mounted on horseback, troops recruited for the most part in the Tell. They hated the desert. They could neither adapt to life there nor successfully counter Arab raiders who bolted out of the wastes, seized what they wanted and made off again into the dunes. The long supply lines required to feed them were costly to maintain, and difficult to defend. Furthermore, they stretched the meager resources of the oases, and especially water, to the breaking point, as an official report noted in July 1900: "I do not hesitate to say that this is the most serious complaint which the population can and do make against us," it read. "The presence of blacks in our ranks has caused far less friction than our exaggerated consumption of water."

This reference to blacks serving in the French ranks can also be traced to Pein's experiments with the Saharian tirailleurs and spahis, recruited in part among free blacks and the despised Haratin. These men, Pein reckoned, would adapt better to desert life than men recruited in the Tell, the highlands near the Mediterranean coast, could survive on the meager diet of the oases (and therefore would not need to be supplied from the north), and last, would serve the French faithfully because they occupied the lowest rungs on the Sahara's social ladder. It was rather crude Marxist logic, and, as will be seen, it did not work well, either as a social or as a military experiment. But a detachment of Pein's Saharian tirailleurs had accompanied Foureau and Lamy to the Sudan.

It was precisely that mission which had enraged Pein. Despite all the crowing in the press about the two explorers having "united Algeria with the Sudan," Pein knew that they had proved only that "when you carry with you your own supplies, munitions and a hundred faithful men, you can thumb your nose at the Ajjers and Hoggars." But this cannot form the basis of a conquest: "We should not stumble on blindly," he told Levé. "We should simply continue with the Tuareg the same policy which has always served us well with the Arabs: Support those who seek our alliance, make them, thanks to our aid, stronger than their enemies." Foureau had made a "mistake" by simply barging through the desert; he had not laid the groundwork for a conquest. But, Pein added, "perhaps we could remedy the bad effects if you would like to help me."

This letter, written on March 14, 1899, at the oasis of Gassi Touil while Pein was still puce with rage over being ordered out of Temassinin, was to change the history of the Sahara. Colonial conquest was a business that required political as well as military skills. Those who represent it as the product of soldiers "slipping the leash" tell only half of the story, for the soldiers in the field invariably had accomplices in high places. In this way, colonial conquest, while often unsanctioned, was what a writer of crime fiction might call an inside job. Pein could not have found a more willing partner in crime than Levé. The captain was as passionate an advocate of Saharian conquest as was his friend Pein, and had vowed publicly that he would give his boss, Julien Laferrière, no peace until the Tuat was occupied. Now, Levé and Pein conspired to do just that.

That colonialists had set their sights on the Tuat was the final irony of the Foureau-Lamy mission. Planned as a major stepping-stone in the history of the French conquest of the Sahara, that mission was exposed as an irrelevance. By the time that Rabih's *sofas* had finally extinguished Lamy's life, talk about transforming Chad into a "French India" had virtually died out in colonialist circles. For decades it had been only too apparent to those who took the trouble to study such questions that the Sudan was hardly an El Dorado. Now that Frenchmen had actually tramped the length and breadth of their new colony, there could be no doubt about this fact, even among those blessed with fertile imaginations. But it made no difference, for colonialists now shifted their emphasis from economics to strategy.

The Fashoda crisis of 1898 had helped to concentrate the minds of French colonialists, who now realized how vulnerable their colonies were to British forces who could be given global mobility and local superiority by the Royal Navy. Therefore, Frenchmen began to look for ways in which they might bring pressure to bear on the British in the event of a war.

Nigeria seemed to be the most vulnerable of the major British colonies. The problem for the French was how to concentrate and supply an army for a campaign against Nigeria. What else but the old Transsaharian railway, which in consequence received yet another kiss of life, with long-filed plans dusted off and moribund committees revivified for yet more deliberations. While the economic advantages of building a railroad across the desert to Chad had been proven to be nonexistent, the strategic arguments for building one to Timbuktu were now, as far as the colonialists were concerned, irrefutable. With the Transsaharian, troops could be transported from France to the very borders of Nigeria in only a matter of days.

The shift in argument from economic to strategic, and the shift in the proposed direction of the railway from southeast to southwest, placed the Tuat directly in the path of French ambitions. Any Transsaharian to Timbuktu must run through In Salah, the chief settlement of the Tuat. Unfortunately for the French, the Tuat was claimed by the sultan of Morocco. On the face of it, this was a minor problem, for the sultan could neither garrison the Tuat nor collect taxes there. The French argued that the allegiance proffered by the people of the Tuat to the sultan of Morocco was merely a tactic to stall a French takeover. But in fact, it was more than that. Islamic notions of polity differed radically from European ones. Moslems drew no distinctions between spiritual and temporal power—as far as they were concerned, the two were inseparable. As a descendant of the Prophet, the sultan was regarded as a holy personage. They sent him gifts of fealty and mentioned him in their Friday prayers. For the Tuatans, there was no contradiction in acknowledging the sultan as lord and then refusing to pay his taxes. The important thing was to be included in the Dar al Islam—the House of Islam—of which, in the northwest corner of Africa, he was head.

The French might have been excused if they chose to ignore what was, for them, a notion of sovereignty so arcane as to be virtually incomprehensible. The difficulty lay with the fact that several European nations, and especially Great Britain, supported the sultan's claim to Tuat. Fearing that the seizure of these oases would provoke a diplomatic incident, Paris restrained the Algerian soldiers. In 1899, however, the situation altered drastically. Great Britain became embroiled in a war with the Boer Republics of South Africa. What London first thought would provide their army with no more than training exercise was soon transformed into a grueling war of attrition which was to last for about four years. With the British army fully occupied in tracking down the elusive Boer, colonialists decided that the moment to incorporate Tuat into Algeria had arrived.

Tuat is the name commonly given to an oasis complex which, in fact, includes three oases which curl around the Hammada of Tademaït.

Together, they appear like a *U* lying on its side, the bowl opening to the east. The top bar is the Gourara and the bottom the Tidikelt. They are joined by the Tuat. The Gourara oasis to the north, with its 800,000 palm trees and its Berber-speaking population, is by far the largest and richest of the three. The Gourara is a low, elongated basin opening out to the west. Because this is the lowest point between the Saharian Atlas and the Hammada of Tademaït, the water which runs off the mountains and disappears under the Grand Erg Occidental—a vast expanse of dunes running 400 miles from east to west, and 100 miles across—reappears in the *sebkha,* or water pans, of the Gourara. The largest of these *sebkha* is that of Timimoun, the principal fortified *ksar* of the oasis.

The Tuat oasis is a long, relatively narrow strip of palm trees and fortified villages running between the western slopes of Tademaït and the vast Erg Chech which sweeps southwest into what is today the northern tip of Mali. The Tuat forms part of the "palm road" which strings along the Wadi Saoura, the only true river in the Sahara, as it flows for 120 miles from Beni Abbès in the north until it gradually spreads out and disappears south of the *ksar* of Adrar. The Tuat's 450,000 date palms are cultivated by a mainly Arabic-speaking population.

The last oasis of the Tuat group is the Tidikelt, which folds beneath the Tademaït. The Tidikelt is the least well watered of the three, depending almost exclusively on the water that runs down from the hammada along the north-south folds of rock. It also differs geographically from the oases to the north. While the oases of Gourara and Tuat are continuous from end to end, the Tidikelt consists of a series of parallel oases, each with its own characteristics and source of water. In 1899, water was extracted principally from *foggaras,* an ingenious system of galleries which run into the limestone, sometimes for a distance of ten miles, to draw off moisture from the subsoil. The French estimated that there were 2,000 miles of foggaras in the Tidikelt. At regular points along the foggara, ventilation shafts were cut to provide air and light for the slaves who maintained them.

Before the French conquest, the Tidikelt also differed from the other oases in its social structure. As the last green patch between Algeria and the Niger, it was very much a frontier between Arab and Tuareg. The Ahaggar Tuareg came to the Tidikelt, and its principal town, In Salah, to trade. They dominated the political life of the oasis, because they depended on it for their survival. Therefore, for those Frenchmen interested in conquering the Sahara, as well as those interested in the Transsaharian railway to Timbuktu, the Tidikelt was a military target of prime importance.

In 1899, the British had their hands full in South Africa. The sultan of Morocco could not prevent the French from walking in. Still, a sudden invasion of the Tuat would raise eyebrows in Paris. The government was not convinced of the need to occupy Tuat. If the colonialists wanted to seize it, they needed a plausible pretext which could be sold to Parliament and the council of ministers. Captain Levé and Théophile Delcassé, the French foreign minister and an ardent colonialist, concocted a plan. The man whom they selected to carry it out was Théodore Pein.

The formula was a simple one, essentially the same as that used with the Foureau-Lamy expedition. Pein's orders even made reference to that expedition: He was to take charge of the military escort of a scientific mission under the command of Monsieur Flamand, a teacher of geology in the Ecole des hautes études scientifiques at Algiers, "in the same way as that of the Foureau-Lamy mission and in the same conditions." Some historians have attempted to present Pein's subsequent capture of In Salah as the result of a set of fortuitous circumstances. But such conclusions are quite simply naïve. The Foureau-Lamy mission was itself an expedition of conquest under the thinnest trappings of scientific research. It is also certain that Foreign Minister Delcassé had approved the plan and told Levé to execute it. Even Flamand, who later attempted to portray himself as used by Pein to pursue his own ambitions, could have had no doubt that an armed group of men under French command which attempted to penetrate the Tidikelt would be resisted.

On November 28, the group of ninety cameleers, fifteen horsemen and forty goumiers left Ouargla for the south. It took them almost a month to cross the Tademaït. On December 27, 1899, the expedition came down the southern slopes of the hammada and camped at the small oasis of Foggaret ould Badjouda. There they learned that the French were unwelcome—couriers sent out by Pein returned with reports that the Tidikelt was massing against them. If Flamand was really concerned with avoiding a conflict, now was the time to retreat. But he did not, and on the following morning, the column broke camp at eight o'clock and marched east, preceded by a screen of goumiers. As they approached the palm grove of Igosten, they saw about a mile ahead a group of around 300 ksourians—sedentary inhabitants of the oases—milling about, shouting, obviously stoking themselves up for a fight. Pein halted, and it was just as well that he did, for several hundred more men, realizing that the French would not be drawn into their ambush, came out from behind the dunes and—singing, chanting, clapping, throwing their muskets into the air—moved in a line toward the expedition.

Flamand, understandably intimidated by the great number of adversaries (1,000 according to the French), wanted to retire. Pein, disappointed that the geologist had lost his nerve at the critical moment, refused. The two men began to argue as the line of ksourians shuffled closer. Pein's goumiers rode backwards and forwards on their horses, nervously awaiting the order to fire. The discussion between Pein and Flamand grew more heated. Flamand probably calculated that with odds of almost ten to one, their position was hopeless. Pein, more experienced in these matters, assured him that victory was as good as theirs. He knew that his men were far better armed than the undisciplined mob in front, which would probably break and run at the first volley. Nor was aid far away: Flamand's expedition was being shadowed by a contingent of Saharian spahis. (Whether Flamand was aware of this is unclear, but it could not easily have been kept secret.) The firing of a red rocket was the prearranged signal that would bring them galloping to the rescue. A retreat in these conditions would almost certainly be costly, as it would bring the ksourians howling on their heels. Besides, and more to the point, Pein had not come this far simply to withdraw. He had been sent to the Tidikelt to provoke an incident, and Flamand was not going to deprive him of his chance.

The two men were still debating when shots rang out in front of the goumiers on the left. The French later claimed that the ksourians had fired just as Pein agreed to withdraw. But it is impossible to know. The ksourians were barely a hundred yards away when Pein ordered his men to fire. Their line broke with the first volley and the goumiers, shouting, yelling, shooting, pursued them through the trees and houses of the oases. By ten o'clock in the morning, the Battle of Igosten was over. Pein was not sure of the casualties: Fifty-six bodies lay on the ground. "As for the wounded, their number is over fifty, but it is difficult to calculate, because each family tries to hide them," he reported. The ksourians had been so confident of victory that they had brought a substantial number of camels to carry off the booty. These were now the property of Pein, as were 500 weapons "of every description."

That afternoon, Captain Germain and his spahis arrived, alerted by the rocket. He found that he had stepped into a minefield. The Battle of Igosten had not settled matters between Pein and Flamand. On the contrary, Flamand still urged a retreat, while Pein wanted to seize the initiative and march on In Salah before the Tidikelt had time to mobilize. According to Pein, Flamand attempted to enlist Germain's support. But logistics, rather than politics, settled the argument: Germain had exhausted his supplies, both of dates for his men and of forage for his horses. There could be no question of retracing his steps over the barren Tademaït. They must push on to In Salah. Still, Pein handed Germain a letter absolving him of all responsibility: "As I find myself, due to circumstances over which I have no control [sic!], in a situation in which the slightest retrograde movement could prove critical, not only for me, but also for the honor of France, I have the honor to ask you to support me," his letter of December 30, 1899, read. "I also accept the entire responsibility for what has taken place and for what might happen in the future."

Flamand may have been frightened, and Germain overly cautious. However, it is also possible that the two men may have been unsettled by the intensity with which Pein now pursued the conquest of the Tidikelt, and the lengths to which he was prepared to go to capture In Salah. In fact, In Salah surrendered without a fight on December 29. The ksourians probably had no wish to try a test of arms so soon after being so badly blooded at Igosten. But the fact that Pein scooped up hostages and presumably was prepared to execute them may have gone some way toward deciding the elders of In Salah to open their gates. Pein raised the tricolor over the casbah of Badjouda, the principal casbah of In Salah, and imposed a 10,000-franc fine on the town. But even in this moment of triumph, his spahis brought news that a large *harka* was forming at In Rhar, thirty-five miles west of In Salah. This news did nothing to calm the feud between Flamand and Pein. As the notables of In Salah came to ask for the *aman,* or pardon, from the two officers, Flamand grabbed Germain by the shoulder and shoved him aside to take his place. "I had to step back to avoid contact with Monsieur Flamand," Pein wrote, and pulled Germain away saying: "Let's go or I am going to slap him!" This only postponed the final confrontation. Flamand and Pein went to visit a son of the caid of Touggourt who had been wounded in the stomach in the battle and was dying by inches. As they came away, Pein could not resist reminding the civilian, "that would not have happened if we had fired several minutes earlier." Flamand replied that he had followed the dictates of his conscience. "A strange conscience which lets you kill those who serve you." This provocative remark was enough to bring Flamand to the boil. He advanced toward Pein and said: "Captain, do you pretend to dictate my conscience!" Pein slapped him, and a duel between the two men was now inevitable.

For the moment, however, that must be postponed while Pein dealt with a far more serious problem. On January 3, 1900, goumiers came in to announce that the *harka* had left In Rhar marching east. On the 4th they arrived at the small oasis of El Barka, three miles from In Salah across a dry salt lake, and sent word to the French that they must leave the Tidikelt or be attacked. Pein, of course, did not budge. On the morning of January 5, Pein's *chouafs,* or lookouts, brought word that the *harka,* over 1,000 strong, was advancing on In Salah.

In Salah in 1900 was not a town. Rather, it was made up of a string of honey-colored *ksours,* or fortified villages, running north to south behind a screen of date palms. Pein had spent a week strengthening the defenses of the *ksar* of Badjouda, which stood roughly in the center of the line and dominated the track running east to El Barka and In Rhar. It is probably for this reason that the *harka* turned off the track and swung south, hoping to roll up the French position from the bottom of the oasis rather than to collide with it head on. But a *harka* is a slow-moving animal. By the time it had turned the corner around the palm groves and begun to move north, Pein had stationed his spahis in the dunes and the goumiers in the *ksar* of Deghamcha, the most southerly link in the In Salah chain. The attackers found themselves caught in a crossfire. As most were on foot, many sought refuge behind the mounds of earth around the ventilation shafts of the foggaras. They attempted to crawl to the *ksar,* but without success. The goumiers and spahis kept the level ground well swept with fire. When Pein ordered the spahis to attack the *harka's* convoy, the attackers broke and fled, leaving behind 150 bodies. Pein lost one spahi, and two had been wounded.

Flamand, who had listened to the battle from the safety of Bad-jouda, two miles away from Deghamcha, was now in a state of extreme anxiety. The fighting had unsettled him to the point where he began to send a stream of panicked letters to Major Maurice-Eugène Baumgarten, the commander of El Goléa, urgently requesting munitions and reinforcements to head off what he saw as imminent disaster: "I fear one thing," he wrote to Baumgarten on January 15, "the forced march of the people of Tuat and their arrival before yours. Come quickly and deliver us." He did. Baumgarten rode into In Salah on January 18, 1900, at the head of a company of Saharian tirailleurs. A relieved Flamand recrossed the Tademaït for home.

That, however, was not the end of the Flamand-Pein saga. The Algiers press, most of it of the gutter variety, got wind of their dispute. In the Algeria of 1900, soldiers were only slightly more popular than the Jews. Few people had been taken in by the story of the innocent mission being attacked by the wicked Arabs. Delcassé managed to convince the cabinet not to recall the troops. But the prime minister, René Waldeck-Rousseau, found it difficult to lie convincingly. Most people suspected, quite rightly, that the affair had been staged. Flamand's side of the story in his dispute with Pein was given prominent treatment. On his first leave, an enraged Pein took the train to Algiers and demanded satisfaction from Flamand. The two men named their seconds, and met early one morning beneath the umbrella pines outside Algiers. They contrived to fire two shots without hitting each other, and parted unreconciled.

Nor was the Tuat affair finished, politically or militarily. Waldeck-Rousseau had agreed to allow the French to remain in In Salah. He hoped that a symbolic garrison of a few troops who followed a live-and-let-live policy with their neighbors, would satisfy the colonialists without committing France to the expense, and the adverse international publicity, of a new campaign of conquest. However, the prime minister had not counted on the tenacity of his officers. Hardly had Major Baumgarten arrived at In Salah than he was writing directly to Julien Laferrière (bypassing in this way the chain of command which led through the commander of the Nineteenth Army Corps, to the war minister and the cabinet), complaining that there was not enough forage for his camels at In Salah. This, Baumgarten told the governor general, could only be found at In Rhar, thirty-five miles away. Laferrière, no doubt harassed by Levé, told him to go find his pasture.

In Rhar is a series of square mud cubicles which spill out of an expanse of deep green date palms. In 1900, this village was protected by two large casbahs, or fortresses—thick-walled blocks of mud capped by square, crenellated towers. To Baumgarten, arriving across the dunes which separated In Rhar from In Salah, on January 24, they looked like toy forts. A few skirmishes challenged the French, but the majority of the ksourians simply took refuge behind their wall. All day and much of the next, Baumgarten's goumiers dashed about in an attempt to draw the defenders into the open. This they wisely declined to do. Without artillery, Baumgarten was helpless, and on January 26, he returned to In Salah.

This had been the first French setback. The prime minister would have been just as happy to leave things as they were. But he was doomed to torment by the colonialists and the soldiers. "Leave such a small garrison isolated and undefended at In Salah? . . . The very idea! . . . The Pashas of Timmi and Timimoun are plotting to raise a *harka* of 4,000 men . . . must send reinforcements." Waldeck-Rousseau, with more important things on his mind than a skirmish in the desert (police reports had informed him that some generals and their right-wing supporters were planning a *coup d'état*) heaved a sigh and gave his permission for a relief column to be organized.

The Armée d'Afrique did not do things by halves. At El Goléa, Lieutenant Colonel Clément d'Eu, the commander of the "relief column," massed two companies of Algerian tirailleurs, a company of *"Bats d'Af"*—a collection of heavily tattooed French criminals serving in the desert in lieu of penal servitude—a half-squadron of spahis, a few 80-millimeter guns, a section of sappers, 1,579 camels, 200 cattle and 2,424 sheep. On February 24, 1900, he set out across the Tademaït in three squares formed by the infantry, with the animals in the middle and spahis on the flanks. The march was not an easy one, and a large number of animals perished. On March 14, d'Eu arrived at In Salah, and by the 18th he was camped within sight of In Rhar.

D'Eu knew almost nothing of his adversary. In the absence of intelligence, Pein volunteered to do an extraordinary thing—dressed in a burnous and accompanied by two of his Chaamba, he walked about In Rhar noting the defensive dispositions of the ksourians, counting heads, lingering beside their campfires to listen to their gossip. The night, the numbers of Arabs milling about who were strangers to each other, and Pein's dark complexion made even darker by nearly a decade spent in the Sahara, served as a successful disguise. Pein returned to the French lines to inform d'Eu that he faced a force of 3,000 poorly armed men.

At five o'clock on the morning of March 19, 1900, only days after, unknown to the Algerians, Lamy had taken Kousseri, d'Eu formed his men into a square and marched on In Rhar, whose two towers were barely visible in the dawn light. Pein's goumiers and Germain's spahis who screened the force fought a running skirmish for an hour before they cleared the dunes and pushed the ksourians back into the palm grove. D'Eu deployed his infantry along the crest of the dunes, while his artillery sent shells over the tops of the trees to burst on the khaki fortresses beyond. Hardly had they fired more than a few shells, however, when a violent sandstorm reduced visibility to one hundred yards. D'Eu's troops clambered off the dunes and dragged the artillery through the palm groves to within point-blank range of the walls.

On the right, the artillery had a clear field of fire. However, on the left, the more southerly of the two casbahs was obscured by a mosque. Shortly after ten o'clock, d'Eu judged the breach in the wall of the north casbah practicable. The Algerian tirailleurs and the *joyeux* of the Bats d'Af came through the wall to find themselves confronted with a series of terraces. The sappers blew holes in the floor and the infantrymen dropped down to clear the casbah level by level, beginning at the top.

The southern bastion proved far more difficult to storm. The mosque in front of it had first to be cleared of defenders, who proved surprisingly tenacious. At 11:30 they finally fell back into the casbah for a last stand. D'Eu ordered his Saharian tirailleurs through a small breach in the wall, but they were repulsed by the defenders. The sappers attempted to collapse a section of wall by dynamiting a corner, but the solidity of the fortress defied their best efforts. An artillery piece was placed on the wall of the north casbah, and for an hour pounded the ksourian Alamo.

Finally, a small man with a white beard emerged to ask for terms. It was the pasha of Timmi. At three o'clock in the afternoon, the French walked into the casbah, where they discovered bodies and pieces of bodies lying half buried in the rubble. The wounded, many of them women and children, moaned in anguish. Wives searched for their husbands, children for their mothers. Beyond, the desert stretched away empty and silent. That evening, the sun went down in a blood-red glow.

The defense of In Rhar, courageous as it was, broke the resistance of the Tidikelt. D'Eu divided his men up into detachments which circulated through the oasis encountering no opposition. On April 22, 1900, d'Eu marched back to El Goléa, leaving a garrison of Algerians, *joyeux* and artillery at In Salah. In May, a second large column of 1,000 legionnaires, *joyeux* and tirailleurs occupied Timimoun in the Gourara without firing a shot. In May also, General Armand Servière, commander of the Algiers division, personally led a force of 230 spahis and tirailleurs through the Tuat. He reported back to Paris that the Tuat, Tidikelt and Gourara were pacified. Delcassé, Pein and the colonialists had got their oases, and pretty cheaply at that.

XV

RESISTANCE

The colonialists were cock-a-hoop in the early summer of 1900. After the ignominious climb-down over Fashoda two years earlier, they had won the "race for Chad" and ended what Delcassé called the "humiliating" independence of the Tuat. The Transsaharian, and with it the "unity of the French Empire from the Mediterranean to the Congo," had been brought one step closer to realization.

Yet for those who cared to look, the Tuat expedition had created problems, both political and military. Politically, Waldeck-Rousseau's claim that the occupation of the Tuat had been the result of a chain of fortuitous circumstances came in for a good deal of public derision, and lowered the credibility of his government both abroad and at home. Even the *Bulletin du comité de l'Afrique française,* the official newspaper of the colonial party, waxed sarcastic: "The truly statesmanlike explanation advanced by M. Waldeck-Rousseau," it wrote in August 1900,

> has been that the whole affair resulted from the excursion of a peaceable geologist, M. Flamand, who had been breaking stones with his little geologist's hammer a little too close to In Salah, and had been attacked by its wicked inhabitants. The government was forced to protect M. Flamand, then Captain Pein, then Colonel d'Eu—in other words, occupy in succession all the Tidikelt, the Gourara and Igli, in order to protect detachments which had gone to each other's assistance after the first detachment had gone to assist the original geologist. Thus, the whole policy of our country in the Sahara would appear to have been nothing but a rescue operation in several stages. "Occupation was inescapable," M. Waldeck-Rousseau humbly tells the Chamber, invoking, as it were, *force majeure.* Like a child before its elders, he swears he did not do it on purpose.

One need not look far for an explanation as to why Waldeck-Rousseau allowed himself to be dragged along on yet another mad colonialist adventure. The Dreyfus Affair had reached its climax. Tempers were running high and there was even talk of a possible coup d'état, talk which the prime minister could not afford to ignore. He needed the support of Etienne's colonial party, which counted 102 deputies at the turn of the century. He fell back, therefore, on the tactic so often adopted by French governments in the Third Republic: He offered the colonialists a free hand in Africa in return for support on domestic issues at home.

From the politician's point of view, this was a sound tactic. Frenchmen were largely indifferent to what went on beyond the shores of France. Ninety-nine percent of the country did not know where the Tuat was and cared less. In a real sense, Etienne and his colonial party became the power brokers of French politics around the turn of the century. This also helps to explain the spasmodic nature of French colonial expansion, and why there appears to have been so little rationale behind it.

But the invasion of the Tuat had also brought the military problems of campaigning in the Sahara into focus, problems which were to worsen over the next year. French colonial campaigns tended to follow a monotonously regular pattern. The initial invasion succeeded in breaking the back of local opposition. The invasion force then withdrew, leaving behind a few garrisons. As soon as the bulk of the French troops had disappeared, the inhabitants recovered their courage and revolted, requiring a second invasion. This is what had happened time and again in Algeria, Tunisia, Tonkin and Madagascar.

History was about to repeat itself in the Tuat. The initial and relatively easy success of Lieutenant Colonel d'Eu and General Servière had lulled the army into a false sense of security. They should have realized that their opponents required time to organize. The various tribes and factions, living hundreds of miles apart, speaking different languages, with different and often diametrically opposed economic interests to defend, with centuries of hatred and bad blood between them, could not form an effective coalition overnight. They needed time to talk, negotiate, time for a man of sufficient presence and with the prerequisite pedigree of holy lineage to emerge and weld them into a fighting coalition.

Given this pattern of experience, why did these revolts so often take French officers by surprise? The answer is to be found in part in the general perspective of the French army. Their primary mission was to defend their northeastern frontier against Germany. Ninety percent of the army was stationed in France, and this was the task for which it prepared. Colonial conquests remained very much a sideshow. The history and methods of colonial conquest were not studied in the French war college. No equivalent of the Indian army staff college existed for the French colonial army. Therefore, French colonial soldiers must learn their trade in the field, and no reservoir of knowledge based on the experience of other generations could be passed on to new men.

A second reason why these colonial rebellions so often forced the French into such frantic displays of improvisation had very much to do with the fact that the initial invasion had been prepared by stealth. Because French colonial officers knew that conquests would meet political opposition, they conspired with colonialists in Paris to find a pretext for new advances. The Flamand-Pein expedition was only one example of their methods. There had been, and there were to be, many others. The territory would be seized, provoking the inevitable political storm. The colonial soldiers would then be forced to lie low while the politicians and propagandists in Paris praised the benefits and minimized the costs of the new conquest. As territory once seized could never be relinquished without a loss of diplomatic face, the opposition, after initial protests aimed at embarrassing the government in the short term rather than at rolling back colonialism, would then forget the matter.

But what is not often realized is that opposition to the conquest of new territory came not only from politicians. Many soldiers, too, complained about the headstrong officers who set out on their own initiative to bring new territory under the flag. Officers in France, as one might expect, objected that people like Pein diverted the army from its primary European mission and spread France's military resources too thin. They also resented the decorations and promotions that colonial men might earn, while they themselves were forced to endure the tedium of garrison life at home. Even more surprising, Pein discovered that some of his colleagues in the Armée d'Afrique, and not the least powerful among them, argued that he had jumped the gun in the Tuat: they had no desire to commit men and money to defend worthless territory. Pein and his fellow conspirators, therefore, had to pretend that the initial occupation had been successful, that the newly acquired territory could be held with a minimal garrison—and to pray that they were right.

August 1900 brought the first indications that they were no more successful in the Tuat than their predecessors had been elsewhere in the French empire: The new Arab Bureau chief at Timimoun, Captain Léon Falconnetti, had hoped to nip rebellion in the bud by arresting a number of notables in the Gourara. But his action simply provoked a coalition against the French which had its center at Metarfa. On August 28, Falconnetti arrived at Metarfa with a detachment of spahis. The ksourians resisted. He called for reinforcements, which arrived on the 30th in the form of Captain Pein and his goumiers. For most of the day, the two sides skirmished in the dunes around Metarfa without result. Falconnetti called in still more troops from Timimoun. At dawn on the morning of September 5, the goumiers and spahis, reinforced by sixty tirailleurs and an 80-millimeter cannon, reappeared before Metarfa. The ksourians had abandoned the village for the security of the dunes, where the French artillery would prove less lethal.

As the French-led troops filed into position for the attack, they heard a low murmur from the dunes which grew stronger as the ksourians' prayers and incantations reached a crescendo. Pein believed that he detected a faltering of morale in his goumiers, who recognized not only that they were employed on the side of the roumi against good Moslems, but also that their friends and relations were fighting with the resistance. After years of leading goumiers, Pein had become especially sensitive to such subtle shifts of morale. The cannon fired the signal for attack. Pein had wanted to take the village, which was undefended. But Falconnetti directed his men against the insurgents in the dunes. All morning, in a torrid heat, the two sides engaged in a series of formless skirmishes in the sand. At one o'clock in the afternoon, Falconnetti called off the attack after one of his officers and several men had been killed.

They remained at Metarfa until the 8th, when he ordered a retreat to Timimoun. Pein was furious. He reported that Metarfa could easily have been taken (although what that might have achieved is not clear). He was also disappointed by his goumiers' lackluster performance, which he put down to "the prayer which they heard from the enemy camps; the presence of some of their relations whom they heard and saw against them stopped their élan." But there was another, extremely important factor which helped to explain the poor battle performance of Pein's Chaamba—they had not been paid. Pein had been as enterprising as a *condottiere:* he had imposed a fine on In Salah to keep them in the field;

when that proved insufficient, he had borrowed 3,000 francs from a Mzabite. The rate of interest must have been catastrophic, however, for Levé had to send him 14,000 francs to pay it off. At Timimoun, Falconnetti learned that he had lost a lieutenant and seven spahis to Berber raiders out of the Tafilalet in Morocco on September 30. He dispatched a courier to El Goléa requesting urgent reinforcements.

Major René Reibell commanded an unhappy garrison. Captain Claude Quisard, for one, complained that he had spent almost a decade in Africa and he had never heard a shot fired in anger. But that was the army. It was so much a question of luck. Men who longed to test their courage, who dreamed of distinguishing themselves in battle, were condemned, so it seemed, to be in the wrong place at the wrong time. February 1901 was no exception. General Servière had just led an enormous column out of Timimoun to show the flag in the Tuat. A few restive spirits would no doubt try their luck with him. Meanwhile, Reibell, Quisard, eleven other officers and 180 *joyeux,* tirailleurs and an assortment of male nurses, supply clerks, sappers, Arab Bureau personnel and malingerers remained behind in Timimoun. It was rotten luck.

Approached from the northeast across a bleak rock plain which seemed to stretch to the horizon, Timimoun was invisible. About a mile and a half from the oasis, the ground suddenly dropped away. The track led down the steep side of the hammada, past the outlines of foggaras, into the sandy pan of the sebkha of Timimoun, where two large casbahs stood guard over a deep green carpet of date palms which stretched away to the west until they ended at a line of sand hills.

The French had occupied the principal oasis of the Gourara for less than a year, and already the place had been transformed beyond recognition. In April 1900, Timimoun had been a labyrinth of narrow, covered streets which ran among a confusion of low, mud houses built behind a high wall anchored against the two casbahs. It was not defensible. It was not even livable. Much of the town had been ripped out "to facilitate communications" between the two casbahs. The northernmost casbah, a rambling, dilapidated structure, had been designated as a magazine. The soldiers were quartered in the second fortress which consisted of a square walled enclosure one hundred yards on each face. The walls were of dried mud, seven to nine feet high, and supported at each corner by a square, crenellated tower. A small gate opened toward the magazine, and to the east, a larger gate measuring three yards across allowed loaded camels into the central courtyard. Reibell also noticed a substantial breach in the south wall. He made a mental note to have it repaired.

The northern casbah of Timimoun was simply too small to contain a garrison of 180 men. The hospital, the ovens and kitchen, and storage areas had been arranged around the walls. Near the breach on the south wall, sacks of barley had been stacked in a neat row. But the garrison had spilled out of the narrow confines of the casbah to take over some of the houses. Along the southern wall, beyond the breach, the animal park had been established, in the middle of which was a hut for the Arab watchmen.

Life in the casbah of Timimoun was tedious. There was nothing to do but drink absinthe and sleep. With General Servière nearby, the ksourians would attempt nothing, or so Servière thought, for he had taken all of the artillery with him. On February 17, the Arab Bureau officers had left with the spahis and goumiers to visit the oasis of Oulad Said, twenty-three miles to the north. Reibell was now deprived of his outriders. But this did not worry him: Timimoun was as safe from attack as the war ministry in Paris.

On February 16, 1901, Captain Pein was operating on the fringes of Servière's column in the region of Adrar in the Tuat, about a hundred miles south of Timimoun, when his Chaamba brought a black to him who, they said, had some interesting information. According to this man, a *harka* of Berbers out of Morocco was massing at Tabelbala, in the extreme northwest corner of the Tuat at the foot of the Hammada of the Guir, the plateau which separates the Tafilalet of southern Morocco from the Tuat. Pein passed this information on to the native affairs officer of Servière's column. Perhaps this officer did not believe the story; perhaps he calculated that, as Tabelbala is 250 miles from Timimoun, Reibell's garrison was in no immediate danger. In any case, instead of dispatching a courier to warn Timimoun of a possible attack, he wrote a note and placed it among the ordinary dispatches. Reibell received it on February 23. By that time the message was about as interesting as last week's newspaper.

When Pein had learned that a *harka* was massing at Tabelbala, it was in fact at Charouine, thirty miles southwest of Timimoun. It was remarkable that 1,500 Berbers accompanied by twice as many camels could come under the very walls of Timimoun and catch the garrison asleep in their beds. But that is precisely what happened on the morning of February 18, 1901. By moving at night, avoiding villages and keeping their camels tightly together, these Moroccans had succeeded in traversing hundreds of miles without being detected. At one o'clock in the morning, they stopped in the palm trees about a mile from the casbahs of Timimoun. There they left their camels. Mouley el-Madhi, a Moroccan merchant who had traded with the French in Timimoun and knew their dispositions, led the attackers silently to a cemetery at the foot of the walls.

The sentry later testified that he had heard noises, but that he had hesitated lest he raise a false alert. He must have been virtually deaf or asleep, for 1,500 men shuffling through the night, their rifles hitting against trees and stones barely a few yards away, must cause a fair hubbub. While the sentry was trying to make up his mind whether it was an attack or simply a herd of camels, thirty men who inevitably took the collective name of "the thirty thieves," slipped into the animal park against the south wall, cut the throat of one of the watchmen and crawled through the breach to hide away among the sacks of barley inside the central courtyard. When the *muezzin* climbed the minaret to call out the morning prayers, the Moroccans and their ksourian allies leaped out of hiding and rushed the south wall.

The confusion within the French fort was extreme. Men rushed into the courtyard in various stages of undress, clutching a Lebel rifle in one hand and holding up their trousers with the other. Bullets kicked up the dust at their feet and nicked the masonry close to their ears. But in the pitch blackness, it was difficult to locate the direction of these shots. Officers gathered their men and led them across the courtyard through the hail of shots toward the south wall. The initial secrecy and audacity of the attack had now given away to a rather formless series of charges against the wall by the Moroccans, chanting prayers and directing shots from their Remingtons and antique muzzle-loaders at the dim outline of the fort. Lieutenant Georges Maurice briefly attempted an outside sortie to turn the flank of the attack, but was driven back by superior numbers.

The tirailleurs and *joyeux* were relatively safe. The only casualties they were taking were *inside* the fort. As the outline of objects became clearer in the dawn light, they realized why—the "thirty thieves" were shooting at them from the sacks of barley. Not a man among the thieves escaped alive, but it took an hour and a half to clean them out.

The strength of the Moroccan attack began to slacken soon after seven o'clock. Already, groups could be seen falling back to the palm oasis of Bou Noua, about a mile away. Now was the moment to counterattack.

Two platoons of tirailleurs crept out along the east wall and, with a shout, began to roll up the Moroccan flank with a charge that brushed along the face of the south wall. Initially, the attack worked well. Discouraged, already abandoned by many of their friends, the Moroccans were taken completely by surprise and competed with each other to escape the tirailleurs. In fact, the attack succeeded a trifle too well, for it cut off two groups who were unable to flee fast enough. One group held a crumbling house at the far end of the oasis. The dispersed tirailleurs attempted to flush them out, but gave up after two of their officers were wounded. A second clutch of thirteen men had sought refuge from the charging tirailleurs in the watchmen's hut which stood in front of the south wall in what had been the animal park. The soldiers on the south wall riddled the hut with rifle fire, but the defenders were relatively safe behind the mud walls of the enclosure.

Reibell called up Sergeant Vialis, who commanded the sapper detachment. Standing on the south wall, Vialis lit a stick of dynamite with his cigarette, and hurled it at the hut. There was a terrific explosion. The hut disappeared in a cloud of dust and smoke, and everyone assumed that the Moroccans had been eliminated—until the cloud began to dissipate and the crackle of rifle fire again picked up. Vialis hurled a second stick. Again there was a terrific explosion, and again the Berbers loosed a few shots to demonstrate that they were far from finished. In all, Vialis threw eight sticks of dynamite before Reibell called a halt. He then brought up the caid of Timimoun. The Arab was frightened. He was only too aware that the French suspected his complicity in the surprise attack, and feared that they might take his life at any moment. When Reibell ordered him out to the hut to persuade the defenders to throw down their arms, the caid's nerve gave way. Reibell realized that this blubbering piece of jelly was useless to him: the hut must be taken by storm. The tirailleurs had done their bit. Now it was the turn of the *joyeux*.

The *joyeux* were not popular in the Armée d'Afrique. They served reluctantly, were quarrelsome and at times even mutinous, hence their nickname. They possessed most of the disadvantages of the Foreign Legion without the saving grace of its romantic panache. But at their best—when confronted with a particularly difficult piece of fighting—they could be magnificent. That was why Reibell selected them for this job.

The atmosphere preceding this final attack must have been a strange one. The French and tirailleurs ranged along the wall had an excellent view of the hut directly in front of them. To their right, ten *joyeux* led by a sergeant, crouched behind the barrier which had formed the edge of the animal park, their kepis pushed back on their heads and the sleeves of their white shirts rolled up to reveal forearms covered with imaginative tattoos. The short, triangular bayonets fixed to their Lebels appeared over the top of the barrier like spikes on a particularly lethal picket fence. It must have been like watching a gladiatorial event in a Roman theater.

The plan was to have Vialis hurl yet another piece of dynamite at the hut and, while the ears of the entrapped Moroccans were still ringing, to send the *joyeux* surging through the smoke to skewer them on the ends of their bayonets. But the Frenchmen must have been nervous, or have misunderstood the plan, for they broke screaming across the fifty yards of open ground before Vialis had time to light his cigarette. The Moroccans shot the sergeant and a private before they reached the hut. Then the *joyeux* put the defenders to the knife. It was nine o'clock in the morning. Reibell collected 153 Moroccan bodies. His own garrison had 9 dead and 21 wounded. Captain Quisard's body was found in the courtyard. He had, at last, witnessed a battle.

General Servière was at the village of Tamentit the afternoon of February 20, 1901, when a courier brought him news of the attack on Timimoun. Captain Pein and his goumiers were dispatched immediately to harass the retreating Moroccans. At ten o'clock on the morning of February 21, Pein came in sight of the oasis of Charouine. He led his men into a depression filled with palm trees which formed one of the southwestern arms of the oasis, and up the slope on the far side. As they climbed onto the plateau, they spied a swarm of men pouring out of Charouine and headed in their direction. Pein plunged back down the hill, crossed the wadi at the gallop, and hurried to tell Servière that he had located the *harka*.

Servière's column was composed mainly of infantry and followed by a heavy convoy. As a consequence, it took him rather a long time to reach

Charouine—a week, in fact. With so many animals which had to be watered in turn at wells that could hardly support a human population, progress was necessarily slow. Finally, he abandoned his convoy and force-marched his infantry through much of the night of February 27. The advanced elements of tirailleurs crested the dunes overlooking Charouine around three o'clock in the afternoon of February 28, but it was five o'clock before Servière could bring the *joyeux* and artillery into line. For an hour he fired his guns into the oasis. But imminent darkness caused him to postpone army action until the following morning.

On March 1, his guns occupied a commanding position on the dunes. Beneath him a crowd of badly armed Moroccans and ksourians huddled in the bowl of the oasis. Now was the time to attack. But he did not. Perhaps he wanted to await the arrival of his convoy, for he spent the next two days maneuvering his troops so that he dominated the plateau on three sides of Charouine.

On March 2, the Moroccans streamed out of the oasis toward the Saoura to the northwest. Servière sent Pein with his goumiers, spahis and a contingent of Saharian tirailleurs to pursue. They set out at eleven o'clock on the evening of March 2. The route was difficult to follow at night. At two o'clock in the morning Pein called a halt. At sunrise, he again marched, following a trail which led into some dunes. They had walked hardly more than an hour, when the scout spotted the Moroccans massed in a deep depression in the dunes. By the time Pein could concentrate his troops, the Moroccans had streamed away into the dunes. Pein ordered his men to pursue. They had gone into the depression and were climbing up a large dune on the opposite side when the Moroccans appeared on the crest above them and began to fire. The goumiers, afraid for their horses, rode back down the hill. The tirailleurs tried to hold, but the fire was intense. Their captain fell dead. Pein ordered them to retreat, and they too tumbled back down the dune. Pein rallied his men and blew the charge, and they surged back across the depression and up the sand hill. "Perhaps, if we had had more troops, we could have climbed the dune and reclaimed our dead," Pein reported. "But we had to seek shelter behind some clumps of tamarisk and fight there until help came."

But help did not come. After two hours of sitting under the fire of the Moroccans, Pein ordered a slow withdrawal. They disengaged man by man, and were pursued back into the oasis. Pein had been badly mauled: twenty-five men and two officers dead, forty-one men wounded. But what was worse, a number of his men, particularly (but not exclusively) his goumiers, had simply run away. It had proved a discouraging display of discipline and an inconclusive pursuit. The Moroccans returned toward the Tafilalet. Servière took a few more badly defended oases, left garrisons in several strategic casbahs, and marched back up the Saoura for home.

XVI

DARK SIDE
OF BEAU GESTE

French colonialism at the turn of the century was like an airplane with no place to land. Each time its pilot selected an airstrip and began his approach, the patch seemed to recede into a haze before him. The Foureau-Lamy expedition seized Lake Chad at the very moment that colonialists in Paris had switched their focus to the strategic advantages offered by a railway to Timbuktu. The conquest of the Tuat had been contrived as the first step of a plan to bring pressure to bear on the British in Nigeria.

However, one of the unlooked-for consequences of the Kitchener-Marchand confrontation on that desolate Nile sandbank in 1898 was, paradoxically, a steady improvement in Anglo-French relations. The British, isolated and friendless in the last months of the Boer War, hankered for a European ally. "Splendid Isolation" and "Imperial Destiny" were all well and good as long as Britain felt strong. But Admiral Von Tirpitz's two naval laws of 1898 and 1900 had laid down a challenge to Britain's mastery of the seas. France's criticism of Britain's "aggression" against the Boer Republics was mild in comparison with the blustering and barely veiled threats to intervene on the Boer side that poured out of Berlin. The idea began to percolate through the political milieus on both sides of the Channel that, diplomatically speaking, France and Britain might share many common interests. The colonies, which for a decade had been a source of conflict between the two countries, might serve as the basis for an agreement, an "entente."

Once French colonialists realized that they could count on no international support to ease the British out of Egypt, they turned their attentions to Morocco. The only thing that prevented France from stealing Morocco outright was the fact that Britain stood as the traditional guarantor of Moroccan independence. Now, if Britain could be persuaded to drop her support of the sultan in return for a renunciation by the French of their "historic claims" in Egypt, then all major sources of conflict in Africa would be settled between those two countries. It was an interesting idea, and one which began to assume a definite shape in the first years of the new century. It would be realized in the Entente Cordiale of 1904.

The shift of direction of French colonial and foreign policy from south to west, away from the Sahara toward Morocco, left the Saharians in the Tuat quite literally high and dry. This might have proved just another disappointment to the men in the field who, like Pein, had spent most of their careers watching French colonial policy lurch from one objective to another. This time, however, things were far more serious. The prime minister was decidedly angry. He had risked the credibility of his government, endured the heckling in the red plush amphitheater of the Palais Bourbon and the sarcastic editorials in the press. Not only had the objective, as it now became clear, been largely irrelevant, but, more important, the army had also bungled the Tuat campaign. The conquest of the Tuat had proven so costly that, for the first time in the history of French colonial conquest, there was a serious possibility that the government might order the French army to withdraw from a conquered piece of Africa.

Why it should have taken a modern European army two years to subdue a handful of undernourished desert people, armed mainly with weapons which had been obsolete in Europe when the Bastille fell in 1789, baffled Waldeck-Rousseau. By foolishly attacking the French behind the walls of Timimoun, the Moroccans had handed them a victory which they did not deserve. The Moroccans later confessed that it was not their normal style to attack a casbah, but that they had expected to find a much weaker garrison. A potentially brilliant coup had failed because of poor intelligence and execution. They had learned quickly, however. Once the Moroccans shifted their campaign to the dunes, the French were drawn into ambushes and suffered losses. Servière's infantry, followed by his rapidly dying camels, were unable to keep up with their foe, who had slipped away with little difficulty. The commander of the nineteenth military division, General Paul Adolphe Grizot, complained to the war minister that Servière had lost 116 men, one-fifth of his force, in fifteen days: "These battles have certainly not provided the successes that we need to impose our domination and lower the prestige of our adversaries by inflicting hard lessons on them," he wrote.

What had really staggered Paris, however, was the sheer cost. In 1900 alone, the army had spent almost 20 million francs on the Tuat campaign. The following year, the government handed Parliament a request for 33 million to indemnify the owners of camels requisitioned for the military convoys in the Tuat. On March 25, 1902, the government came in for some very severe criticism in the Senate from those who questioned the wisdom, not to mention the sanity, of a government willing to spend so much to conquer a region whose total annual trade did not equal that of "a grocery store in a large town." But what upset public opinion in France was not so much the cost as the reports in the press about the routes of march lined with dead and dying camels.

A modern army needed a large supply train. In 1900, the railway ran as far as Biskra. Heavy, two-wheeled araba wagons, squeaking like squadrons of protesting gulls, transported supplies between Biskra and Ouargla. But south of Ouargla and El Goléa, the French were dependent exclusively on the camel for transportation. Grizot complained that of 9,090 camels which had been requisitioned (some from as far away as Constantine) for General Servière's promenade in the Tuat, 3,538—or almost 40 percent—had died even *before* Servière had left El Goléa. Most of the rest had died en route, which helps to explain Servière's slow progress around the oases and why the more mobile and camel-wise Moroccans were able to elude and ambush him so successfully. In all, the French had requisitioned 35,000 camels in Algeria to feed the Tuat expeditions of 1900 and 1901. Of these, 25,000 had perished from thirst or from clumsy and inexpert handling by the novice French cameleers. The routes of march of the French columns were well signposted by the bleached bones and mummified remains of these animals. "I do not think that there has been a massacre comparable to that of 1901," the Sahara expert E. F. Gautier wrote. "The jackals and the vultures along the way were overwhelmed with the immensity of their task."

To be sure, the furor raised in Paris over the Tuat expedition had its origins in domestic politics rather than in any real concern with colonial issues *per se.* Delcassé, a political moderate in a left-leaning government, was not popular among his colleagues and their supporters in Parliament. His policy of seizing the Tuat by stealth had failed owing to a lack of imagination among his Algerian officers and, also, to the absence of units specialized in desert operations. The Left in Paris was happy to exploit the cost and cruelty of this wastage of camels to embarrass Delcassé and the Algerian army. What they did not realize was the ruinous effect the Tuat campaign had had on the economy of southern Algeria. General Grizot, who had opposed the Tuat expedition, but whose chain of command had been deliberately bypassed by officers communicating directly with Captain Levé and the governor general, argued that

> the requisitioning [of camels] is ruinous for the State, which must pay indemnities greater than the value of the animal and which again reimburses the price when the animal dies. It exasperates the natives, who are deprived of their camels to work, and ends by reducing them to misery, because all the money which we give them—and it does not come quickly—disappears before they can replace their lost camels. Ruined, the native is ready to follow the worst impulses.

There was obviously little love lost between Grizot and Servière, and the senior general, probably upset with his subordinate for having ridden roughshod over his authority, might be accused of bias. But on this score, Grizot knew exactly what he was talking about. This was the dark side of *Beau Geste.* Grizot led a chorus of officers who argued that the Tuat should not be occupied because it was unoccupiable: "According to General Servière, the Tidikelt, the Gourara, the Tuat have been much maligned. They are richer regions than people are prepared to admit." But this was simply fantasy:

> This country will never feed, together with its inhabitants, the soldiers whom we wish to station there. I personally believe that General Servière has allowed himself to be carried away by his natural affinity for desert regions, and believes them to have resources which they do not possess. . . . In the present state of affairs, a few more native troops, even the most frugal ones, cannot live off the country.

Until a railway was built to the Tuat to supply a French garrison there, all talk of occupying these regions was a "utopia."

Grizot's argument was a circular one: The Tuat could not be occupied until there was a railroad; but a railroad could not be built until the Tuat was occupied. Nevertheless, Grizot realized what the avidly Sahar-

ian officers—blinded by their nationalist idealism, competitive spirit and
desire for promotion and decorations—refused publicly to admit, and
that was that the French conquest and occupation had upset the fragile
economy of the oases, and of all of southern Algeria. Harding-King, who
was traveling to Ouargla at the time of the Tuat invasion, recorded the
great fear which the mere mention of a campaign produced among
camel-owning Arabs:

> [I told my guide], Aissa, that I could not see that, even if war
> between France and Morocco did occur, that it would have
> much effect upon us. But that was not his difficulty. The
> French, it seemed, were requisitioning through the *Kaids* an
> enormous number of camels for the purpose of carrying stores
> to Tuat, and he had left three camels at Biskra which he was
> terribly afraid would be taken. "What am I to do?" he asked.
> "There is only my wife. She cannot arrange anything. I am away
> and the *Kaid* is sure to take them. He has orders to send five
> thousand. If I were there, I would take them and hide them in
> the desert. But I am not, and as I am away, they are sure to be
> taken. Then, if they are killed, the camel drivers will not trouble
> to bring back their ears, and so I shall get no government
> compensation; and even if they are not killed, they will be so
> badly treated that they will be good for nothing afterwards.
> Oh! I wish I had stayed at Biskra. If my camels are taken, my
> wife will not be able to sleep for crying." Aissa was in a terrible
> state of perplexity. His three camels represented a very large
> proportion of his worldly goods, and if they were taken the loss
> would be a very serious one to him.

Aissa went to a letter-writer in a café who, assisted by a good percentage
of the male population of Touggourt, composed a letter with instructions
to his wife. As he did not trust the French post to handle such delicate
information, he confided it to a camel driver going north.

Whether this letter had any effect is not recorded. But it is certain
that French operations in the Tuat, and subsequently in Morocco, reduced a large number of families in southern Algeria to poverty. For the
young and virile, there was only one alternative form of employment:
banditry. Lawlessness increased in southern Algeria at the time of the

Tuat campaign. To a certain extent this was inevitable, as the garrisons had been denuded of troops. But because the men no longer had their camels, or were unable to use them openly in lawful commerce lest they be requisitioned, some took to the desert and a life of raiding.

While the effect on the economy of southern Algeria of the Tuat expedition had been severe, the arrival of the French in the Tuat brought the oases to the verge of economic collapse. On July 19, 1900, Captain Jules Jacques, a member of the Tuat expedition, wrote, prematurely as it happened, that the ksourians had greeted the French invasion "with indifference. They were only bothered, it seemed to me, by our enormous consumption of water and perhaps a little by the disturbance to their morals and habits caused by our large numbers." To increase the water supply in the desert, the French sank artesian wells. When Lamy took over as commander of El Goléa in 1891, he found that he had to dig extra wells for his garrison of 230 men. Once the bedrock was pierced, the water came rushing out—fifty gallons a minute, Lamy claimed, "from our first attempt."

For the French conquerors, artesian wells seemed at first to solve several problems. The first was that of labor. When the French first arrived in the oases, they declared the slaves to be free. Even later, when this was not the case, many blacks and Haratin simply assumed that the arrival of the French ended all their obligations to their old masters; they now refused to perform their traditional menial tasks, "for they knew that one no longer had the right to apply the necessary stimulant of several blows of a whip, and they took it easy." The Arabs would not replace them. The French put this down to laziness. But the refusal to work sprang from a social system which allocated menial tasks to the lower social orders. So the economies of the oases threatened to collapse, and the Arabs began to dream again of the manly life of a desert raider.

The old water systems, whether wells which operated on the bucket system or foggaras as in the Tuat, required hours of slave labor to empty the water into the *seguias* or channels which fed the gardens, and to clean and maintain them. Foggaras especially became choked with sand, rock and other debris and had constantly to be cleaned out and shored up. To Lamy and other French soldiers serving in the Sahara, the artesian wells seemed to be the answer to these problems, because they provided more water to irrigate more gardens and removed, at least in part, the need to depend on black or Haratin labor for the general duties of maintaining the water supply: "The old gardens of the Mouadhi were almost all condemned to die of thirst simply because we took over El Goléa," Lamy wrote. "I consider the artesian wells as a means of retaining the Mouadhi. When the nomads possess lovely palm trees, fruit trees and vegetables, they will think twice before abandoning all of that to go into dissidence."

But the artesian wells were a mixed blessing. As the oases occupied the depressions in the desert, the water had no place to run, so it collected in stagnant pools. The oases which had once had too little water now had too much. Malarial mosquitoes bred in the stagnant, fetid pools, as did other diseases, like typhoid. Ouargla, El Goléa and other settlements, which had once been havens for nomads in the summer months, were, within a few years of the French occupation, deserted by people fleeing disease. At the same time, the artesian wells lowered the water table and dried out the oases while flooding them. The military engineers, or *génie militaire,* charged with digging the wells, became known as the *génie malfaisant* or "evil genie." "Is this not the history of El Goléa?" concluded Captain Jacques. It was also the story of every other oasis that the French had occupied.

To the lack of water can be added the absence of sufficient food. Major Pierron reported that the inhabitants of the Tuat were so famished that they walked behind the French horses to collect "the grains of barley which [the horses] passed." Major Charles Charlet, who came to the Sahara in 1911, found the Tuat beautiful but poverty-stricken: "If one saw only the color, our troops in this green setting—its palm trees, beautiful dunes sprinkled with houses of red earth—would make a splendid picture," he wrote to his wife. "But alas! one must see the misery of the population. These poor souls, emaciated, degenerate, in rags, who live on dried dates and a little grain! We can expect nothing from these people, and even less from the country, which is drying up more and more." This, of course, was the effect of more than a decade of sinking artesian wells. The government reached the same conclusion in 1901: "The government decided that this conquest has until now cost us dearly in men, money and camels to conquer a country which is unhealthy, miserable, hardly able to nourish its inhabitants, producing only dates, uninhabitable for European troops, in a word, not worth the sacrifices made," a March 29, 1901, report read.

In the climate of the Dreyfus years, when the army had already been the object of much bad publicity over the conviction of Captain Dreyfus by irregular, not to say fraudulent, methods, the Tuat expedition hardly won the soldiers many friends, as some officers were only too well aware. To the reputation for dishonesty was added one for incompetence: "The army, which for several years has been the object of criticism, now hears itself reproached for dragging the nation into adventures which only profit the army, for wasting millions and for having perverted the reality of things," Major Deleuze, the interim commander of the Tuat, concluded in 1901. Parliament agreed. Deputies spoke of the "Algerian scandal" and the "abuse of power" of the Algerian generals whose "prodigalities threaten to ruin the treasury." They exaggerated, of course, but Pein and Levé had handed the Dreyfusard left yet another issue with which they could berate the army and undermine the confidence of Frenchmen in the honesty and competence of their military leaders.

In 1902, Parliament passed a law making the "southern territories" of Algeria the direct responsibility of the governor general, rather than the commander of the nineteenth military division, in order to strengthen the control of the government over these military adventurers. Typically, the deputies had picked up the wrong end of the stick, for it was the governor general, not Grizot, who had contrived the occupation of the Tuat. But no matter, they had to make a gesture.

Even the most avid partisans of linking Algeria with the Sudan were forced to admit that the Tuat expedition had set back their cause. Desperate for a pretext to extend the conquest beyond the Tuat—indeed, just to hold on to the Tuat—they even considered sending Pein into the Ahaggar at the head of a geological expedition to discover if there were any exploitable minerals there: "The mission which we propose that you lead is not, despite appearances to the contrary, a mission to provoke an affair," Le Châtelier, a veteran of the first Flatters expedition, wrote to Pein on March 11, 1900. "It is uniquely a mission charged with the scientific study of a limited question: Does the Sahara have mineral deposits or does it not? Are these mineral deposits valuable enough to permit the construction of the Transsaharian if we do not take it to the Sudan, upon which it seems we should not count?" But it must have occurred to the colonialists that the mere suggestion of placing Pein at the head of another "peaceful" geological expedition was likely to provoke a volcanic reaction in France, and the idea was quietly abandoned.

Nor could colonialists play to the volatile nationalism of Frenchmen by evoking colonial competition with England or Germany: "No power desires to beat us to the Sahara and interpose themselves between our two domains [Algeria and the Sudan]," the right-wing deputy Henri de Castries admitted sadly. Nor had the Algerian soldiers proved that they were capable of anything but leading heavy columns into areas which could not support them. Despite all the crowing by colonialists about the Foureau-Lamy expedition, the simple fact was that it had come within a whisker of extinction. And what had it proved? "Monsieur Foureau has linked Algeria with Lake Chad," Deleuze wrote in 1901. "So what? What's the use? It is just as difficult to go from Ouargla to Lake Chad today as it was yesterday."

The difficulty of the Saharian soldiers for the moment was not to conquer the desert, but to hold on to the Tuat. If they could not reduce the expenses of occupation, then they risked pushing the tolerance of the government beyond the limit and finding themselves ordered to withdraw. Late in 1900, Waldeck-Rousseau told the governor general to cut the umbilical cord—if the oases were to be occupied, it would be by native troops. The long supply lines, the enormous expenses must stop. This, then, was the problem the soldiers must solve. And their solution was the Saharians.

French colonial soldiers were fond of presenting their military innovations as responses to the new conditions of warfare which they met abroad. Proposals for light, mobile units of locally recruited troops, able to move rapidly and live off the land, joined the "hearts and minds" theories of Gallieni and Lyautey as examples of the natural response of imaginative and innovative soldiers to the challenges of warfare outside of Europe. In certain respects, this was true. In another, very real way, however, French colonial soldiers proved amazingly rigid and hidebound, wedded to the heavy column which intimidated the enemy by its force and ground him down by its firepower. Attrition, not persuasion or small-unit tactics based on light, mobile forces, was their favored method of conquest. The simple truth was that many military innovations instigated by French soldiers in the colonies were products of pressure brought to bear upon them from home. Lyautey's "hearts and minds" never worked as a tactic to persuade Moroccans to lay down their arms and join the French "in their own interests." It did, however, persuade Frenchmen that Lyautey was employing peaceful methods of conquest that ultimately benefited the conquered. The development of the Saharians was also the result of pressure applied from home. French soldiers had long recognized that the column was an unsatisfactory method of operating in the desert. But only when Paris informed them that it was no longer willing to finance their costly campaigns did they look for other solutions. The Saharians, therefore, owed their inception more to Europe than Africa.

The traditional method by which the French assured the security of Algeria south of the Tell was through the *goum*. French writers sometimes compared the goum to a militia, but it was far more like a posse. Goumiers, mounted on horses or camels, could range widely, sometimes for hundreds of miles, far beyond the capabilities of European troops, or Europeanized native troops like tirailleurs or spahis. However, the goum had several disadvantages. In the first place, it was not a force in being, but one assembled more or less hastily in response to a crime committed or a conquest sought. When, for instance, the Arab Bureau officer in an oasis like Ouargla learned that a group of dissident Chaamba from the Tuat, or Ajjer Tuareg had raided the douars or the camels in pasture of a tribe or *ksar* which had submitted to the French, he had to ask permission from Algiers to organize a pursuit. If permission was given (which was not always the case), he called in one or two of the more prominent caids and notables and asked them to furnish men to track down the culprits. The willingness of the Arabs to cooperate was affected by the personal relations between the caid and the officer, whether or not the government had cut his stipend or the taxes he was allowed to collect —any one of a number of personal or political factors.

The nature of the crime or the identity of the criminals might also play a part. But this was usually easy enough to ascertain: So well did the Chaamba understand the politics and personalities of the Sahara, so well could they read the peculiarities of camel tracks, that they were often able to identify the guilty parties to the Arab Bureau officer simply by studying the ground. Captain Robert Hérison was astonished when one of his trackers announced: "It is the *rezzou* [raiding party] of Moussa, without a doubt. I recognize the footprints of my father's camel." The goum set out in pursuit.

In the hands of an aggressive commander like Pein, who simply ignored inconvenient orders and procedures, the goums might have a fair measure of success. But as a method of policing, the goums left much to be desired. They could not prevent crime, only retaliate for damage done. By the time a goum was assembled, the raiders might have an unbeatable head start. Goums, especially large ones, might also be very fragile coalitions of different groups or families, opposing *sofs,* ksourians and Chaamba nomads. Their cohesion often crumbled once they had ventured too far from home. When commanded by a French officer, they might better obey orders. But it was something of a cliché in the Arab Bureau that "an officer at the head of a goum destroys its élan, prevents it from acting." Therefore, they were often commanded by a caid, or by one of the caid's sons, whose authority might be called into question by the independent men of the desert.

The prospect of an easy target might lure the goum away from an arduous pursuit. Most of the men who joined a goum did so for the prospect of pillage, and an isolated douar or herd of camels in pasture often offered a target too tempting to pass up—why run risks by venturing too far from home? The goumiers would begin to quarrel among themselves, divide into *sofs,* and split up. At other times, the caid, "a little frightened," would turn for home, often stealing a few camels so as not to endure the humiliation of returning empty-handed. Very rarely did they punish the raiders, content usually to press them closely enough to make them abandon their stolen camels "without inflicting losses on the enemy." Officers also complained that goums were expensive because the men had to be paid and armed and reimbursed for lost camels or horses, as well as the caid given a little something for his trouble. One or two operations of this sort were probably enough to deplete the budgets of most Arab Bureaus.

If goumiers were inadequate as police, they were next to useless as conquerors. Part of the mythology of the French conquest was that the French did not conquer Africa themselves but used other Africans to do it for them, in this way cleverly turning the traditional hostility between tribes to their own advantage. This, as will be seen, was true only up to a point. First, the threat of a French invasion often caused tribes to suspend long-standing feuds and hatreds to unite against the French. Secondly, when goumiers were used, their instincts (as already noted) were simply to pillage, not conquer. They were useful, when they were useful, only as adjuncts to columns of regular soldiers as scouts, outriders and skirmishers. Last, as the Tuat expedition demonstrated all too well, when fighting against their own people, they often proved reluctant combatants.

Pein discovered that when his goumiers were fighting their own relatives, they became lukewarm soldiers. Their resolve faltered, they aimed their shots high and refused to press home their attacks. Some families deliberately hedged their bets by placing sons and cousins in both camps. Therefore, the French claims to have harnessed the traditional rivalries and hatreds of tribal warfare to their own colonial juggernaut are, in great part, mythical.

What, then, were the alternatives to the goumiers? Originally, the French had attempted to hold the southern oases with Algerian tirailleurs and mounted spahis recruited from the Tell. It had not worked well, and worked even less once the French expanded south of El Goléa to forts MacMahon and Miribel in 1893. A general staff report of that year said that Kabyles sent south so hated it that they refused to reenlist once their term of service was completed. The suggested solution was to recruit the numerous blacks in the oases into new companies of Saharian tirailleurs. First, the report claimed, they would make excellent soldiers: "The black above all seems well adapted to serve in the new infantry units. He is vigorous, healthy, resistant to fever and heat stroke. He becomes, with education, training and discipline, a good soldier, submissive, courageous, faithful. What is more, in the regions where we shall be called upon to make use of him, he has no family ties which can undermine his loyalty to us. It is, therefore, the black whom we must recruit."

It is an interesting commentary on the mentality of French colonial officers, and of how little they understood the societies which they sought to conquer by "divide and rule" methods, that they also appeared to believe that the recruitment of blacks would facilitate their conquest of the oases—by appealing to this downtrodden and helot class of blacks and Haratin, the French could fragment resistance in the Tuat:

> The number of [blacks] which we can recruit will increase greatly as we approach the Gourara, the Tuat and the Tidikelt. . . . There exist in these regions three to four thousand black slaves, mistreated, living in terrible misery, who will rally to us as soon as they are aware of the situation offered to their congenerics and when our posts will be close enough so they can reach them without fear of being retaken.

Blacks in the oases were employed mainly as agricultural laborers. Few possessed skills as horsemen or cameleers. They might serve as infantry to garrison the oases and advanced posts, but the French needed men who could dominate the dunes beyond. For this, they turned to the "great nomads of the south," the Chaamba. They needed no training, as they already knew how to ride and shoot. It was the Chaamba who were recruited into the Saharian spahis.

The Saharian tirailleurs and spahis were an interesting and not altogether unsuccessful experiment. Detachments of each had accompanied the Foureau-Lamy mission and, according to Pein, had fought well during the invasion of the Tuat, at least better than the goumiers. But, on balance, these units had proved disappointing, both in their military performance and as part of a divide and rule method of conquest. The cadre provided for the Saharian tirailleurs appears to have been mediocre in the extreme. The Algerian tirailleurs used the creation of the Saharian tirailleurs to pass on the worst elements among their lieutenants: "The native officers are complete strangers to their men, because of their diverse origins, no previous shared experience, no common customs," read an 1896 report. "They do not even have a superior education because they are usually completely illiterate. The result is that their men despise them and it is often difficult to keep them from showing it openly." The NCOs were no better, and considered "hardly up to the standards of the other corps." "Inertia, complete lack of interest in their jobs, that is the salient point of their character." Attempts to stiffen the Saharians with French NCOs had failed because most had been seconded from desk jobs or supply depots and were too young or unable to endure the climate: "Some volunteered out of curiosity, most never expected their requests to be taken seriously," a July 1900 report concluded, noting, however, that if conditions of pay and service were improved, if, for instance, they were given accommodation other than the slum-like casbahs abandoned by the ksourians, then they might attract better cadres.

The soldiers reflected the poor quality of their cadres. Originally intended to be recruited among black slaves from the oases, the Saharian tirailleurs became a ragbag of Algerian tirailleurs—"not the flower of the volunteers"—"adventurers" from Laghouat or Kabyles "brought in by chance. . . . While in general very bad people, they can make good soldiers. Frugality, it is true, is not their dominant quality. They adapt better to another sort of regime, even to daily rations of wine or Pernod than to the Saharian regime of cakes and dates." Few, they concluded, would reenlist. Most of the blacks who joined were not ex-slaves from the oases, but rather from the Tell: "They possess only the sobriety born of laziness and fatigue or of the poverty of the country."

This jaundiced view of the Saharian tirailleurs may not have been completely disinterested. Most French officers probably felt uncomfortable policing the oases with a collection of vagabonds and blacks—it tarnished their prestige as white chiefs. No doubt, more than one caid told his Arab Bureau officer that the Saharian tirailleurs were a social *faux pas:* "The other reproach against the black *is the bad impression which his presence in our ranks produces on the local populations,*" Captain Jacques underlined in a 1900 report.

A heterogeneous and not altogether respectable collection of men, indifferently led, the Saharian tirailleurs had no real military function. They had virtually nothing to do but sit around the oases and fritter away their pay: "He has made the brothel his home." The Tuat invasion apart, the tirailleurs had proved to be more of a liability than an asset. One of General Lyautey's favorite dictums was that, "In Africa, one defends oneself by moving." The tirailleurs provided small defense against mobile Arab raiders. On the contrary, their presence at Miribel and MacMahon provided the Chaamba with an easy target.

The nomads lived very well by pillaging the convoys which linked these two outposts to the north. The French created the mounted Saharian spahis to deal with these raiders, but they proved to be less than useless: "For the moment, the [Saharian] spahis have neither killed a dissident nor recaptured a stolen camel," read a report of March 5, 1897. The Saharian spahis suffered from many of the same problems which afflicted the infantry, the tirailleurs: "The better class of the populations, with rare exceptions, never volunteer for military service." The French forces were simply not as effective as the men whom they were sent to fight. "The expenses required are therefore out of proportion with the services rendered."

If the Saharians failed as a military experiment, they also failed as part of a divide and rule method of military conquest. French visions of turning blacks against their Arab masters in the oases proved to be a mirage. When the French invaded the Tuat, the expected social revolution caused by blacks rushing to join their ranks simply did not occur. On the contrary, the blacks fought beside their Arab masters to resist the French. Europeans imbued with crude Marxist notions of social layering and class conflict were surprised again and again when the desert populations responded to traditional hierarchy and a vertical, rather than horizontal, social structure. Forts Miribel and MacMahon had certainly not become the way stations on an underground railway to the north and freedom. Only three blacks attempted to enlist in the Saharians in the Tuat, and they were rejected on medical grounds.

The French officers in the Sahara were in a dilemma. The goums offered limited advantages as ad hoc police, but as a force of conquest they were not to be relied upon. Attempts to replace them with locally recruited regular units had met with only limited success. Some officers complained that the Saharian tirailleurs and spahis had been used unimaginatively as garrison troops and convoy escorts. But the simple truth was that they were good for little else. Of course the French could hold the oases indefinitely with these troops. But they would thereby be condemning themselves to be ambushed, raided and robbed, a humiliating and intolerable existence.

That seemed precisely the existence which the government expected them to endure, however. The prime minister had made a great scene, telling the army to reduce their expenses drastically or withdraw from the Tuat. It is unlikely that he meant to abandon the oases—that would have caused ructions. He simply did not want them to spill out of the Tuat and conquer the Ahaggar. In November 1901, the war minister, General Louis André, announced that the commander of the Saharian oases would be given enough troops to police the Tuat and no more. In this way, he hoped to keep his headstrong officers on the leash. "As for the Commander of the Saharian Oases, he must adopt a purely passive role of local defense, from which the government had decided that he must not deviate, and for which the Saharian companies were specially created," he repeated in July 1902.

As might be expected, the Algerian officers had other ideas.

XVII

THE
SAHARIANS

It is hardly surprising that soldiers and politicians so often disagree, for their temperaments are so divergent. And so they should be, for the requirements of the two professions are radically different. For men who spend their lives preparing to meet death on the battlefield, a personal code that includes courage, character and honor becomes inseparable from their professionalism and technical proficiency. Without this rigorous personal code, their profession becomes impractical. Consequently, soldiers are brought up to view issues in black-and-white terms. Negotiation is equated with weakness, compromise with capitulation.

Politics, as is well known, is the art of the possible. It is also the art of survival. Unless the politician is willing to compromise, to haggle and trade in the political *souk,* to depend less on principle and more on practicality, then he will not long survive as a politician. Most soldiers do not appreciate this. They believe that politics should be a debate about principles, which is one reason why generals who trade their military success for political office seldom succeed. The very personal qualities which helped to make them good soldiers become their undoing as politicians.

The differences in style, mentality and method between the politicians and the Saharian officers now began to emerge following the conquest of the Tuat. Of course, we cannot know what words passed between Waldeck-Rousseau and the colonialist politicians in the anterooms of the Palais Bourbon or over cognac and cigars at the Hôtel Matignon. But in all likelihood, the prime minister offered them a perfectly honorable compromise—the Tuat would remain occupied, but with a number of Saharian tirailleurs too small to allow for further conquests. It is unlikely that he needed to stress that they had to keep their soldiers in line, or hint at the consequences if they did not. Already General André was employing Freemasons in garrison towns to send reports on the political beliefs and religious practices of officers—and of their wives!—which were catalogued in the rue St.-Dominique and consulted for purposes of promotion.

So far, the colonialists had managed to protect colonial officers from political retribution. But how long would immunity last if officers in the colonies continued "to take Timbuctus without orders?" The debate over the new organization of the southern Algerian territories occupied much parliamentary time in 1902. New examples of military indiscipline there would hardly produce a good effect. Pein, especially, was warned: "In the interests of Algeria, calm things down."

But officers in the Sahara, and least of all Pein, had no intention of calming things down. "In my four years in Ouargla, I have received nothing but criticism," he wrote to Captain Gaston Cauvet, the commander of In Salah, "which has never stopped me from doing what I thought was my duty." It was no use appealing to Pein's sense of *intérêt général*. He did not possess one. He charged through life as if it were a foot race, unaware of what was to the left or right, only that there was a finish line ahead which he must cross. With such a man, the government's wisest step would have been to transfer him to an infantry regiment at Lille or Belfort, somewhere wet and windy, and let him cool off. But Paris had probably never heard of Pein, or if they had, he must have seemed like a small fish in a very large pond. They were unaware of the waves he made.

Algiers was certainly aware of Pein's presence. Together with Cauvet, Pein worked to create a sense of panic among his distant commanders. Pein even invented a "Mahdi" who, with Turkish support, might lead an Islamic *jihad* which could threaten France's hold over North Africa. Despite his petulance and immaturity, Pein was an extremely astute man. He knew how to play to the insecurity of Algiers, to the feeling that, just beyond the gleaming white cubes of *la ville blanche,* a sullen, resentful and fanatical mass of Moslems awaited the word to rise and throw the French into the sea. The *pieds noirs* were like the Protestants in Ireland, dominant but insecure, a garrison state living in perpetual fear of rebellion.

The role of Pein and Cauvet in the conquest of the Sahara was far from finished. But it was obvious to the colonialists that, in the delicate political situation in which they found themselves in the Tuat, another sort of military commander was needed: A discreet man prepared to transform the Saharian tirailleurs quietly into a mobile force capable of operating effectively in the desert. The man must also have a firm grasp of desert politics. The French army possessed just such a man in Henri Laperrine.

Laperrine did not appear the soldierly type. He was a rather small man with delicate hands and feet, a thin, pale face hidden behind a full beard, and brown, expressionless eyes. In an army that took great care to appear well turned out to impress the Arabs, Laperrine inevitably wore a cloth kepi tilted over the left ear and a dark blue tunic buttoned up to the neck even in the most desperate heat, which made him appear more like a post-office clerk than a cavalryman with panache and a diplomat with flair. He struck people who met him as a timid person. In Algeria, where he had spent a great deal of his career, he was remembered for his detestation of both the obligatory receptions and the long evenings spent conversing about nothing in particular in the officers' mess, which characterized regimental life in the Tell. He had fled the *chasseurs d'Afrique* to serve in the spahis *soudanais* and had joined Joffre in the occupation of Timbuktu. (Indeed, many whispered that he had forced Joffre into it.) He then returned north to serve for two years in the bleak wastes of Fort MacMahon, and there helped to organize the Saharian spahis. Therefore, he understood the desert and the shortcomings of French tactics based on fixed garrisons and immobile troops.

Like so many of the men who served in the Sahara, Laperrine seemed perfectly content in his own company. At MacMahon, he would sit for hours in his whitewashed room simply staring at the wall. He never took a mistress in the oases, which most Saharian officers considered one of the more pleasant perquisites of their job, indeed, virtually their only diversion. His frail appearance belied a resilience which permitted him to spend ten hours on camelback in 120-degree heat and show fewer signs of fatigue than many of his men. He had a morbid habit of allowing scorpions and horned vipers to run and twist over his arms and shoulders. This impressed the Chaamba, but left Frenchmen a trifle apprehensive for his safety, and his sanity.

And yet, despite his laconic manner and spartan tastes, Laperrine was hardly antisocial. A native of Castelnaudary in the Midi, he had inherited the southern Frenchman's love of storytelling, and excelled as a raconteur. His father, also an *Africain,* had frittered away a large inheritance to pay for his gambling debts and poor business deals. Henri, however, accepted the plunge in the family fortunes with equanimity. One of his favorite stories concerned the visit of Marshal MacMahon to St.-Cyr. When the venerable soldier was presented with the young cadet, his eyebrows knitted together and he said: "Laperrine? Don't I know your father?" When Henri replied yes, MacMahon scowled and said: "Tell him I've never forgiven him." When telling these stories around a makeshift mess table, his eyes took on a mischievous look and he became extremely animated. But his apparent good humor could erupt in violent flashes of temper, when he was liable to hurl the first thing that came to hand at the object of his discontent. Although he spoke Arabic fluently, he retained a strong southern French accent with its rolled *r*'s rather than the guttural sounds of the Arabs, and his Chaamba often could not understand him. Whenever this happened, he became agitated, then angry, increased the cadence of his speech and became even less comprehensible than before. His men simply stared at him, their eyes growing larger and their expressions more perplexed, until Laperrine finally exploded with rage. He never allowed his good humor to impinge upon his relations with the Arabs. Like many Saharians, he believed that it never paid to become too familiar with them. Relationships with Arabs were always a contest of wills which an officer could not afford to lose.

Historians have perhaps given Laperrine credit for too much originality. He did not, after all, fight a long battle against skeptics for his Saharians. The shortcomings of the old military system, of which he had been a principal architect, were obvious. "If we want a real fighting unit, it must be a mobile one," Major Victor Pierron of the Saharian tirailleurs wrote in March 1900. "It is only in these conditions that we can recruit the Arab nomads. Only in this way will it have any value in the Sahara." General Auguste-Constant Cauchemez agreed that: "It would be extremely easy to occupy and rule the Saharian oases if we were dealing only with ksourians. But we must take account of the nomadic tribes."

It was easy enough to identify the problem. Pierron offered a solution:

> I believe that the Saharian troops should be neither spahis nor tirailleurs, but a troop which combines the two, trained to fight as infantry, but transported on camels without which soldiers in the Sahara are unable to move and are useless. But there is no gainsaying that such an organization is difficult to realize and will be worth as much as the commander in charge.

The emphasis of French strategy in the desert must shift from sedentary infantry to mobile, camel-mounted troops, that much was clear. It would not be an easy reform to realize. For one thing, it depended for its success on the incorporation of the notoriously independent Chaamba into some sort of formal military unit. This would require great ingenuity, flexibility and tact on the part of the men who would engineer it. Secondly, such a mobile unit was expressly against the wishes of the government. For this reason, Paris had strictly limited the number of troops allowed in the Sahara. Far from bothering Laperrine, this actually aided his task: "Those people do not realize how easy it is to move with 150 camels and how difficult with 1,200," he wrote to Pein.

When Laperrine arrived from France in June 1901, to occupy the newly established post of commander of the oases, his role was set out for him. He carried orders allowing him to create three companies of Saharians, one each for the Gourara, the Tuat and the Tidikelt, each with 300 "natives" and 42 Frenchmen, 6 of whom were officers. Of the 300 "natives," 230 were to be infantry and the remaining 70 to compose the *faction mobile.* The intention of the decree creating these "new" Saharian units was clear—to restrict them to a purely defensive role in the Tuat. This, Laperrine needed no one to tell him, would be disastrous. Furthermore, and more important, this force could never seize and police the Ahaggar. Laperrine was interested in conquest, not defense.

From almost the first moment that Laperrine took up his new post in the Tuat, he began to bombard Algiers with complaints about "the insufficiency of the mobile contingent." In fact, the entire contingent was "insufficient." In November 1903, fully two years after Laperrine's arrival, only 58 of the 300 Saharians had been recruited in the Tidikelt, so that the Gourara company had to be amalgamated with the other two to bring them closer to full strength. Even as late as November 1906, he was complaining that his soldiers were not mobile enough. Of course, this did not stop him from going on long promenades in the desert. But he had to rely on a very heterogeneous force of Saharian spahis, mounted Saharians from the *faction mobile* at In Salah, and any goumiers who might be enticed along. The Saharians as he dreamed of them were not yet a force in being, and would not be until he could enlist the Chaamba in strength.

The recruitment of the Chaamba offered at least two advantages. Most important, they were the only inhabitants of the desert able to match—well, almost match—the mobile and camel-wise Tuareg. General Joseph-Louis-Albert Caze, who had replaced Grizot as commander of the nineteenth corps, argued that "the incorporation in our ranks of several nomads of these tribes will furnish the best means to prepare the way for our expansion into the Central Sahara." The precedent most frequently cited by French officers was the use made by the Russians of the Cossacks, who were transported thousands of miles with their families to police the distant frontiers of their empire. A second, and very important, advantage of recruiting Chaamba is that it would take them from the dissidence and put them on the French payroll. What better way of solving the problems of poachers than to make them all into gamekeepers? Therefore, the Saharians were seen as a way to buy off the bandits and to bring them under the iron thumb of French army discipline.

This was all well in theory, but how would it work in practice? For years, the Chaamba had opposed and raided the French. Under Pein's influence, some of the Chaamba of Ouargla had served in goums. But pillage, not a desire to serve the French conquest, had been their primary motivation. When used in the Tuat, they had proved a disappointment. French officers admitted that it seemed a contradiction to forge a force from men known to be "sober, independent, supporting neither the yoke of a master, nor even the yoke of property." But they had little choice. The ksourians made mediocre soldiers. Frenchmen could not handle camels as well as Arabs, even with expert instruction. They were forced to appeal to the Chaamba who had traditionally opposed them.

The force which Laperrine sought to create lay between the goum and the more formally organized Saharian tirailleurs and spahis. Laperrine sought to retain the natural mobility of the Chaamba goums, but at the same time stiffen their discipline with a hand-picked cadre of French officers and NCOs. In short, it was a brilliant compromise between two methods of military organization, one African, the other from Europe.

The Saharians were to become one of the most exotic units in the French colonial army, which seemed to be in the business of manufacturing colorful regiments. Few visitors to Biskra, which became a popular tourist resort, especially with the English, before World War I, could resist sending home postcards featuring these turbaned and robed Saharians, their red belts crossed on their chests, armed to the teeth, in postures of prayer or guiding their camels along the sharp ridge of a dune. These "Sharks of the Desert" became part of the decor, and of the romantic imagery, of the Sahara. In the process, however, a number of myths settled on the Saharians, myths encouraged by the memoirs of a few fanatically devoted Saharian officers who helped to propagate the concept of a tough but benign group of men imposing the *Pax Gallica* in the desert more by their very presence than by brute force.

By harnessing the natural antipathy of Chaamba for Tuareg to the juggernaut of French expansion, Laperrine was able to accentuate the divisions among his enemies and conquer the Sahara with a minimum of French blood and money. In dealing with the notoriously independent Chaamba, Laperrine and his Saharian officers used flexibility and imagination rather than force and coercion. Saharians liked to refer to themselves as a tribe, of which the captain was the caid.

But to see the Saharians simply as the military expression of the Chaamba Arabs is an exaggeration. The force which Laperrine commanded in the early years of the twentieth century was a heterogeneous one of *mokhaznis* (native police), spahis, blacks, tirailleurs and Chaamba. Laperrine discovered that these different elements often meshed badly together, and settled on the Chaamba of Ouargla as the most versatile soldiers.

The French found it relatively easy to recruit Moslems to serve in the ranks. But what sort of men came forward? Time and again in Algeria, the French had entertained visions of drawing an elite of Arabs into their units, especially the mounted ones. Time and again, they were destined to be disappointed. The Saharians were to prove no exception. As with the spahis, the Arab notables "of the great tents" declined to serve. In 1909, when he joined the Saharians at In Salah, Hérison found them to be recruited from the sweepings of the oases. Some had enlisted after committing a crime. The fact that many of the Chaamba were related gave the Saharians a certain cohesion, but "if a native of the country comes to serve us," Hérison wrote, "they treat him as a pagan and refuse to accept him as an in-law." Even the adolescent "wives" whom the French took at In Salah were not given by fathers eager to acquire the good opinion of their conquerors. On the contrary, these girls were considered simple prostitutes: "None of these women gives the illusion of a home. Most of them are nothing but pretty, luxurious little animals, devoid of morality." The children of such unions were shunned. *La politique des races* allowed the ignoble and the debased to improve their power, but not their social position. The French, and their Chaamba, remained very much an alien force, the scalawags of the Sahara, imposed upon desert and oasis alike, and not, as they claimed, integrated into it.

The knowledge that they were mercenaries in their own land and despised because of it made the Chaamba especially sensitive to any slight on their honor. Saharian officers, therefore, needed tact in large measure, and could not fall back exclusively on the sometimes harsh discipline of the European barrack square to make themselves obeyed. One had to be alert to the superstitions and sensibilities of the men: When on patrol in the Ahaggar, Dervil awoke one morning to find the ground covered with a light sprinkling of snow. Short of water, he ordered his Chaamba to fill the *guerbas* with snow before it melted. However, the men remained huddled together and refused to budge—never having seen snow, they were frightened. An Arab corporal, claiming descent from the Prophet and thus the status of a marabout, reinforced their reluctance to act by declaring the snow to be "damned." As it would have been foolish to attempt to force the men to carry out the order, Dervil called the corporal into his tent "and in terms as diplomatic as menacing, asked him to change his mind. He stroked his beard for an instant, and went out to pray toward the East, so that Allah would inspire him."

Hérison found that different social customs could lead to misunderstandings which could cause great offense. After picking the meat from a bone, he threw it to his dog. His Chaamba were insulted: "With us, a dish passes from hand to hand, from one group to another," they told him. "It is normal to eat from a dish after others have touched it. The meharists have seen that you prefer the dog to them. It was for them, the lowest-ranking among them, to throw the bone to the dog."

However, Saharian officers could not be accused of coddling their men. Discipline in the Saharians was not as brutal as in, say, the Foreign Legion; but it was far more coercive than many officers were prepared, in public, to admit: Deserters were sometimes tied by their hands to the tails of their camels, and the men had on occasion to be beaten to force them to march in difficult conditions.

While it is true that the Saharians imposed their conquest with far less ferocity than the marines and Senegalese who campaigned south of the Sahara, policing the desert could hardly be described as a *Boy's Own* outing. "I am profoundly grateful for the way they, the Arabs, sworn enemies of the Tuareg, have supported me in my pacific campaign of conquest," Laperrine reported in 1904. "In our daily contact with the camps, there was not a discordant note, not a brutal act or a theft. Even better, often they did not hesitate to share their meager rations with the Tuareg who came into my camp." This was written more with an eye on public relations than as an accurate description of the Saharians' methods of police. The earlier expeditions led by Pein and Lieutenant René Guillo-Lohan—who led a raid into the Ahaggar, ostensibly to punish camel thieves—practiced a policy of systematic intimidation. Laperrine was more benign, and attempted, without great success, to win the confidence of the Tuareg. It is also certain that the Saharians indulged in a certain amount of extracurricular harassment of their old enemies.

French military practice in the colonies relied upon harnessing the traditional pillaging instincts of blacks and Arabs to the work of war. By recruiting the Saharians mostly from among the criminal classes, the French solved at a stroke the problem of lawlessness in the desert: "The job of gendarme has become more advantageous than that of bandit." The prospect of loot, the power that a Lebel rifle and tight discipline gave one man over his neighbors, provided a strong incentive for enlistment. French colonial officers did not attempt to suppress these instincts —to have done so would have taken the hearts out of their regiments. They merely directed them toward their own ends. That records of abuses, even of brutalities, do not exist is hardly surprising. It would be surprising, however, if they had not occurred, given the nature of the beasts, French and Arab, and the centuries of bad blood between Arab and Tuareg.

This, however, was in the future. For the moment, what is important to note, what has been obscured in the praise of Laperrine's genius, is that the Saharians as Laperrine conceived them never conquered the Ahaggar. This would be done with old-style goums and Saharian spahis.

The Saharians, as important as they were to become later in solidifying the conquest of the Sahara, were still in a state of transition during this final phase of the conquest. Laperrine's major contribution to the conquest of the Sahara was less as an architect of an exotic colonial regiment than as an able desert politician and daring and energetic commander. What Laperrine realized and Paris did not, was that the Tuat could not be treated separately from the rest of the desert.

"The submission of the Ahaggar is an economic consequence of the occupation of In Salah," Laperrine's lieutenant at In Salah, Captain

F. A. Métois, wrote in 1904. "It must inevitably follow." The desert and the oases formed two halves of an integrated economic and social structure. The Ahaggar Tuareg came to the Tuat, mainly in the hot summer months when they had little pasture and water for their sheep and camels, to trade for dates. It was a modest commerce, but it kept everyone alive. When the French seized the Tuat, the Tuareg ceased to frequent it. "Like the ksourians, we need them. This is the most important question for the Tidikelt," Major Pierron wrote.

> All our efforts in local politics must attempt to reactivate trade and secure their annual return. One must realize that if we do not obtain friendly relations through persuasion, then we shall be obliged to secure them at great cost through force. . . . We must look to avoid hostilities immediately which will make us irreconcilable.

The French had at last realized that they must piece together the economic life of the desert which their conquest had shattered. The Tuareg had to be brought back to the Tidikelt, by force if necessary. This fact alone did not motivate the final French push into the Sahara. There were far deeper pressures which drew them toward the Ahaggar. But the realization among French officers who firmly believed (against the evidence) that colonialism should benefit the conquered, that, once again, they had helped to increase the impoverishment of yet another oasis lent a special urgency to the conquest of the Sahara.

The difficulty was that the Tuareg were unlikely to return voluntarily to the Tuat. They needed the oases. But as an extremely independent and proud people, they would rather starve than give up without a fight. Laperrine knew that there were elements among the Tuareg of the Ahaggar favorable to a reconciliation with the French—a few members of the drum groups of the Taitok and Kel Ahnet had asked for the *aman,* or pardon, at In Salah. However, they would not be able to win the confidence of enough of the drum groups until the Tuareg had been defeated in battle. On the face of it, this was an easy enough task: "The Tuareg are even less well armed [than the ksourians] and they can hardly unite in large numbers," Major Pierron reasoned. "Except in cases of surprise, their attacks seem to offer little to fear, unless, without attacking us directly, they simply operate against our communications." The difficulty was how to dig them out of the immensity of the Ahaggar. This was the problem that Laperrine must face.

The politics of the Sahara, always complicated, had been rendered virtually incomprehensible by the invasion of the Tuat in 1899 and the death in the following year of the chief of the Ahaggar Tuareg, Aitarel. The question of succession among the Tuareg entered its usual twists and turns as each candidate tried to convince enough followers that he possessed the necessary lineage through the female line as well as the required personal qualities—courage and reputation as a redoubtable warrior and raider, combined with the wisdom required to navigate the treacherous waters of Tuareg politics, a wisdom that would have taxed Solomon's ingenuity. Given the tradition of independence and the frag- mentation of Tuareg society, this meant an astute man with a sense of the limitations of his power, rather than a forceful leader. The process of selecting an amenoukal was complicated by the fact that there was no authority among the Tuareg which traditionally decided such questions. The Arabs could turn to the *ulama,* or groups of religious doctors in the major cities to arbitrate their disputes. But among the Tuareg, the leader simply emerged after long meetings and arguments among the leaders of the drum groups. Even in normal times this could sometimes take years. In 1900, it was further complicated by the encroachment of the French into the desert, and by changes in Tuareg society.

The society which the French confronted at the beginning of the twentieth century was in the process of a complicated social evolution. The Ahaggar Tuareg were divided into three principal drum groups— the Kel Rela, by far the most numerous and powerful, the Taitok and the Teghe-Mellet. Relations among these three drum groups were always difficult, especially because the Taitok chafed under the dominance of the Kel Rela. However, power was traditionally concentrated in the hands of the chiefs and their principal nobility, and it was relations within this relatively small group of men that determined the direction of Tuareg politics. Furthermore, the nobles controlled the camels and had the exclusive right to wear the *takouba,* or double-edged sword. Their vassals kept the herds of sheep within the territory allotted to each drum group, while the nobles handled the fighting and the politics. However, in the nineteenth century, nobles began to arm their vassals, a process which was accelerated by the war of 1875–78 between the Ajjer and Ahaggar Tuareg and by subsequent French encroachments. The vassals acquired a taste for raiding and fighting and, by 1900, were "warriors in their own right." As the traditional social divisions began to break down, the vassals showed disobedience and claimed a voice in the election of the amenoukal. Indeed, it is possible that it was the vassals— in absolute terms eight times more numerous than the nobles—who actually decided the election of the new amenoukal at the turn of the century.

Three candidates offered themselves in the leadership contest. The first, Mohammed ag Ourzig, was considered too old and lacking sufficient authority. The second, Attici ag Chikkat, represented those who bitterly opposed the French. His credentials were impeccable: His mother was the sister of Aitarel, and his father had been the *amar,* or chief, of the Teghe-Mellet faction of the Ahaggar Tuareg. He had also connived actively to draw Flatters into the ambush which took his life and, according to French sources, "prepared with his own hands the poisoned dates which, at Amguid, were to be so fatal to those who escaped the massacre." For the French, Attici was a dark and sinister figure. His attitudes to them were on record: "If you come to the Ahaggar, I will destroy you by force or by ruse," read the declaration of war which he sent to In Salah. "If you prevent my caravans from resupplying in the markets of the Tidikelt, I will come and cut down the palm trees."

The third candidate was the one favored by the French. In 1900, Moussa ag Amastane was still relatively young. Major Charlet—who met Moussa just before the Great War, when, well supplied by the French, he had lost his spare Targui look—described him as "fat and heavy" but with "a dignified bearing, (and) a pleasant friendly face." However, it was Moussa's attitudes, rather than his bulk, that interested Laperrine: "He seems to be perfectly aware of the futility of resistance and the advantages which one can draw from our friendship," he wrote. Perhaps it is for this reason that he found Moussa on their first meeting in 1905 to be "intelligent and straightforward," but nevertheless his own man.

> Very simple in appearance and very confident, he does not hesitate when one asks him to speak his mind frankly even when his views do not conform to ours. He is very deferential, specifying that he only speaks his mind because we ask and not to oppose us. Now, if he is a Targui very superior to the immense majority, he remains a Targui and as such is on the one

hand very greedy for money and honors and on the other amuses himself like a child as soon as he feels at home. For the legend of the majestic and impassible Tuareg receives a knock as soon as one makes these nomads relax.

Moussa was the peace candidate in the Ahaggar, and for this reason the French favored him. Laperrine was even to take him on a visit to France in 1910 (and, judging by the restaurant bills conserved in the war archives, they dined extremely well), a trip that Moussa frequently discussed with visitors: "Imagine, not one camel in that country." After this, he could never understand why the French had come to Ahaggar, and suspected that they were criminals who had been sentenced to transportation: "What did you do, then, to be sent to our country, when yours is so beautiful?" Charles de Foucauld distrusted him, believing that he would desert the French if things began to go badly for them in the Sahara. Nevertheless, even this severe man found Moussa to be an "interesting . . . mixture of natural gifts and profound ignorance, [a] man who on one hand is a savage, and on the other merits esteem and respect; for his justice, his courage, his high position and generosity have made for him a peerless situation, from the Tuat and Ghat to the Niger."

Laperrine's political goal was clear: make Moussa amenoukal of the Ahaggar, and "from the moment that he is my servant, I will see that his influence is as great as possible," by giving the traditionally independent Tuareg "a sort of apprenticeship of discipline." Before he could do that, however, he must discredit Attici, and that meant an invasion of the Ahaggar.

Laperrine had no intention of waiting until his Saharians were battle-ready before he began to launch patrols into the desert. He planned to demonstrate to the Tuareg that nowhere were they safe, not even in the deepest recesses of the Ahaggar. It is unlikely that he sought a climactic battle with the Tuareg—he probably thought that he could not bring them to fight. What he needed was simply to keep them off balance, to demonstrate their vulnerability in small raids and in what the French euphemistically called "administrative tours." In this way he might prove the futility of resistance and gradually strip away support for Attici and his war party.

Laperrine needed no excuse to launch his campaign, but it was just as well to present his invasion of the Sahara as retaliation for violence done. The immediate *casus belli* was, in effect, a case of petty theft against Mohammed ben M'sis and his sister, a noble Targui named Fatma, both citizens of In Rhar and thus "submitted" to French authority. According to Captain Cauvet, Fatma walked into his office at In Salah in March 1902 to claim that she had been robbed of her camels in the Mouydir, a bleak plateau studded with hills which runs west from the Ahaggar, by a Targui of the Kel Rela, Baba ag Tamahlat. "Baba came towards me while his blacks took my camels," Fatma told Cauvet.

> "It is Allah who put me on your path," he told me. "You have betrayed your brothers and prostituted yourself to the French. I will punish you as you deserve." Then he ordered his slaves to beat me with sticks. Then they left me and made off with my caravan. You know, Captain, that I am a noble woman and this outrage demands to be avenged. I have come to ask your aid to obtain just reparation and to make them return the goods which they have stolen.

It was certainly no way to treat a lady. What is more, it was an "insult to France."

Laperrine is often given credit for launching the reprisal raid that was to alter the complexion of the power game in the Ahaggar. In fact, he knew nothing about it until it was well on its way. Captain Cauvet was not afraid that Laperrine would disapprove, simply that he might have orders forbidding such expeditions: "I had no orders," Cauvet later confessed. "There were none at In Salah. I even avoided asking Laperrine who might have received some or who would have felt obliged to ask for some. Therefore I did not overstep my orders. The distinction is perhaps a trifle subtle, for I know exactly what the reply would have been if I had proposed to send my people on a tour of the Hoggar. But it exists nevertheless." Cauvet argued that his "certain premeditation not to receive orders" was especially successful because Algiers was "so surprised that they forgot to give me any afterwards." This allowed him to send out other expeditions, so that "the Saharians were definitely emancipated and had, from that moment, complete liberty to march."

This was not quite true. Algiers did attempt to recall Cauvet's expedition—when eventually they learned of it! But by that time, Lieutenant Gaston Cottenest and his goum were well beyond reach. Standing

orders in the Sahara required all officers to consult Algiers before ordering an operation. But it was the willingness to bend, or simply ignore,
orders from superiors that had gained for France an empire.

After the return of Cottenest, there was much praise in procolonialist circles, praise that historians have echoed, for "our valiant
troops." In fact, the 130-man expedition counted only five soldiers, only
one of whom—Cottenest—was French. The rest of the goum was made
up of Chaamba and ksourians from around In Salah. It was such a
heterogeneous collection of men from different groups and factions that
it almost failed to march. Usually, in such circumstances, the goum might
simply march back and forth along the "borders" of their territory in a
threatening display of muscle flexing, as if to say, "Don't do that again!"
This time, however, Cauvet and Cottenest had resolved to aim the goum
directly at the Koudia, the central mountain massif which was the heart
of the Ahaggar. Not surprisingly, some of the volunteers had second
thoughts when they discovered the destination of the raid. But in the
end, 130 pointed their camels southward on March 23, 1902.

A native of the greener lands around Dunkirk, Cottenest was a tall,
thin man. His angular face together with his beard, which followed the
line of his jaw, reminded his fellow officers of Henri IV. It is certain that
Cauvet and Cottenest had embarked on this mission à la légère. Neither
was aware of the real risks involved. Cauvet wrote to his friend Pein in
Ouargla that he hoped the patrol would yield "some happy results, even
if only from a geographical point of view . . . I think that the Hoggars
will avoid him, but it will be a good result if we can promenade in the
heart of their country." Even Cottenest subsequently reported that "personally, I did not want to engage in combat unless it was the only way to
save ourselves." To distract and confuse the Tuareg, Laperrine sent a
force of sixty Saharian spahis and twenty tirailleurs into the Mouydir,
while Pein took some of his Chaamba into Ajjer territory and landed
himself in hot water when the Turks complained to the Quai d'Orsay
that he had killed 10 Ajjer Tuareg, stolen 10 black slaves, 120 camels and
50 donkeys near Ghat. Pein also confessed to having "eaten 500 sheep.
In sum, the raid was more or less a failure."

Cottenest's goum marched down the broad bed of the Wadi Rharis
to the wells of Asekseme. During a night march, Cottenest and several
of his goumiers tumbled into a ravine, injuring themselves badly enough
to require several days' rest at Asekseme. Cottenest threw out small

raiding parties which returned with 510 sheep and 53 donkeys, as well as a number of women and children. The men had fled at the approach of the goumiers. Desert etiquette required that the women be treated with respect, so he left them enough to eat "according to the Targui practice in such cases." The sheep he sent back to In Salah.

While at Asekseme, several emissaries of the Dag-Rali came in to tell the lieutenant that they disapproved of Baba's theft, that they only wanted peace and that the culprit was to be found to the south. Cottenest seems to have ignored the fact that this might be a ploy to draw him further into the desert, where he might be more easily ambushed. On April 25, he arrived at Ideles, at the very foot of the Ahaggar. Ideles was not a particularly scenic village—seven or eight red clay houses, a scattering of *zeribas* built of brush inhabited by Haratin, and thirty palm trees. In one of the houses, the goumiers discovered several carbines which Cottenest concluded must have come from the Flatters expedition. He ordered the house to be razed, and a monument erected out of dried brick, surmounted by a Targui shield, which read: "Mission Flatters, 18 fevrier 1881—25 avril 1902." The Haratin informed Cottenest that he was being shadowed by the Dag-Rali. As soon as they could draw together enough men, they would attack.

Ideles stands at the northern edge of the Ahaggar massif. From here, the members of the expedition could gaze out to the broad dome of rock which forms the Ahaggar. What they saw could hardly have steadied their nerves. Here was the Tuareg heartland, and to the Chaamba it appeared as dark and forbidding as the enemy they pursued.

The Ahaggar is a land of jagged peaks and necks of rock, trenched and broken by volcanic erruptions of past geological epochs. From a distance, it appears as desolate as a desecrated graveyard: The dark towers of rock are stripped of vegetation and the valleys filled with the slag of petrified flows of lava. The Ahaggar offers a tableau of frozen violence, a vision of Hell or, at the very least, of a land which has incurred the wrath of God, an appropriate home for devils and spirits and, in Chaamba eyes, for the black-clad men who served them. In the setting sun, the vision becomes even less real, when the black needles of rock are transformed into a wilderness of lilac forms.

Yet the Ahaggar is far from uninhabitable. Eagles and other birds of prey nest in the high crags. Water is fairly plentiful—in the summer, when clouds on occasion drift northward from the Sudan, rain can fall in torrents, so that the Tuareg are careful to pitch their camps on the hillsides or beneath some overhanging rock, rather than in the valley floor. After such a rainfall, the valleys are covered by a green carpet of annual plants. Permanent or semipermanent streams flow in the higher altitudes, while, lower down, water collects in small lakes or pools in the crystalline rocks of the valleys and hillsides. In the nineteenth century, a few Haratin were able to coax small gardens out of the broader valleys, like that of Tamanrasset. However, the soil is too ungenerous to allow the Tuareg to become anything but a pastoral people. Consequently, the men raid, while the women follow their flocks of sheep from valley to valley, their haunting cries echoing between the black folds of rock.

The remoteness and uninviting appearance of the Ahaggar made it especially attractive to the Tuareg. It offered them a base of operations from which they could raid and plunder between Ouargla and the Sudan. Its inaccessibility transformed it into a sanctuary, a citadel which insured against attack or reprisal raids. Within its dark canyons, the Tuareg pursued their way of life in the virtual certainty that they were beyond the reach of their enemies. For them, the Ahaggar offered a haven of peace, a bleak and brooding Shangri-la. That is why, when Cottenest appeared at Ideles, the Tuareg could not allow his audacity to go unpunished. If their enemies once realized that they could come unchallenged into the Ahaggar, then the floodgates of invasion would be opened. If the French had reflected upon this, it would have become obvious that Cottenest would have to fight his way home. He, however, seems to have seen this expedition as merely a flag-waving exercise on a slightly more ambitious scale.

Cottenest left Ideles in late April, marching due east. His plan was to circumvent the entire Ahaggar, before turning north and home. It was a daring march, almost a foolhardy one. It was an open invitation to the Tuareg to attack him. Even Flatters and Lamy had not taken such risks, and they were far more strongly armed and organized than was Cottenest. The first indication that the Tuareg might not be content simply to allow him free passage came on May 3, when his camp was attacked by a small raiding party. A patrol was sent in pursuit and tracked the Tuareg for fifty miles before they returned empty-handed. Cottenest reported that they had found a conical tent which, he claimed, had once belonged to the Marquis de Morès. This was probably just an embellishment added to convince people in France that he was on the trail of vicious criminals.

On May 4, two scouting parties were attacked. Cottenest now began to feel that the Tuareg were closing in for the kill. On May 4, he broke camp at Tarhaouaout, the most southerly point of their march, and began to ride west and north along the western edge of the Ahaggar. Two days later, they reached Tamanrasset.

Tamanrasset in 1902 was not a place which made one want to linger. A few Haratin living in straw huts called *zeribas* attempted to cultivate millet along a sandy wadi. At five o'clock on the morning of May 7, 1902, the Arabs broke camp as the first rays of the sun shone on the somber chimneys of the Koudia to the north. The day grew progressively hotter, and it was with some relief that they spied the *zeribas* of the village of Tit around 3:30 in the afternoon. Tit did not look like a promising rest stop —low hills of sand and large boulders lay scattered over a sandy plain. There was not even a tamarisk to offer a hint of shade. But Tit in the Tamahak tongue means "spring," and the prospect of water was welcomed, even if the scenery was disappointing.

Cottenest was a good soldier. For some days he had been alert to the possibility of attack and did not intend to settle into his campsite without first having a good scout around. His force had marched in three sections. The first he sent through the village to establish a defensive position on the far side. The second he divided into two, and sent them out to scout the *gour* to the east and west. The third group guarding the convoy of camels waited, the men squatting beside their animals, brushing away flies and saying little.

At four o'clock some of the goumiers who had been sent to reconnoiter suddenly burst out of the rocks screaming that 300 Tuareg were camped in a wadi to the east. Hardly had they got the words out of their mouths than a swarm of black-clad men mounted on camels emerged from behind the embankment about 800 yards away. Cottenest was in serious trouble: The Tuareg had caught him with his force divided. His advance and flank guards were out of sight, leaving him with 70 men and the convoy. The goumiers grabbed their rifles and took up positions among some rocks which lay between the convoy and the advancing Tuareg. By now, the Tuareg were only 600 yards away, advancing toward them in a packed rank, but so slowly that "they left me a second of hope that their intentions were not hostile," Cottenest wrote. For this reason, and perhaps also because he realized that they would only waste precious ammunition at that distance, he ordered his goumiers to hold their fire.

Goumiers, of course, are not soldiers, so it was only with great difficulty that he made himself obeyed. Every instinct of the Arabs told them to fire as quickly and as rapidly as possible, hoping that the noise would frighten off the Tuareg, even if the bullets caused few casualties. The wait seemed impossibly long. The Tuareg came on slowly, not firing, simply sweeping forward in a long, black rank. Cottenest was surprised, and not a little disappointed, to note that almost all of them held rifles, in addition to the traditional Targui lance and shield. When only twenty yards away, the Tuareg suddenly hurled their lances, then slipped off their camels to the ground holding their rifles in their left hands and their swords in their right, and advanced, hacking at the French line: "They were large men, with an imposing walk, who marched straight at us with a real disdain of danger," Cottenest remembered. "Before this human wave which continued to advance without stopping and without firing, we withdrew little by little behind our convoy. We were out-flanked and they were going to surround us completely, when I ordered my men to rally at the top of the *gara*."

Outnumbered by more than three to one, ill-equipped for the hand-to-hand combat at which the Tuareg were expert, the goumiers broke with the advancing Tuareg, abandoned their animals, and scrambled up a low hill, half of boulders, half of sand, to take positions as best they could on the exposed summit. Cottenest's situation was not quite hope-less, but it had all the ingredients of another massacre in the making. He must keep the Tuareg at a distance with his rifle fire, for close in, they would hack his goumiers to pieces with their long swords. The Tuareg had rifles, but they probably had little ammunition, which is why they delayed firing for so long. Cottenest's ammunition was relatively plenti-ful. But Arabs were notoriously bad shots, very excitable in battle and liable to use up their cartridges very rapidly.

The Tuareg occupied the rocks which had been abandoned by the goumiers and began to sweep the summit with rifle fire while creeping among the rocks to get as close as they could—some to within twenty-five yards—to the Arab positions. Cottenest was impressed by the skill and discipline of the attackers: "We would see behind the rocks which protected them a head, a puff of smoke and then everything disap-peared." The goumiers, on the other hand, were blasting away as if there were no tomorrow, as there certainly would not be unless they became more frugal with their ammunition: "The goumiers were firing like madmen," and although the Tuareg were not particularly good shots, the exposed position of the Arabs on top of the *gara* meant that some of their bullets were finding a target. Cottenest was standing next to his interpreter when the poor man dropped without uttering a sound, a bullet in the forehead. A second goumier dropped. The Tuareg were gradually moving closer, and the goumiers had already exhausted half of their ammunition in wild firing. At 4:45 a Targui got to within twenty-five yards of the lieutenant and raised up to fire on him while he was loading. One of the goumiers threw himself in front of Cottenest to shoot the Targui but was instead brought down by a bullet which pierced his hand and ricocheted off his sword to enter Cottenest's shoulder. The wounded goumier continued to pass his ammunition to Cottenest. Another goumier fell, his spinal column shattered by a bullet.

It looked as if Tit might prove to be Cottenest's Little Big Horn. The circle of Tuareg was drawing tighter around the Arabs, whose ammunition was close to exhaustion. A sandstorm had blown up which might prevent the outlying patrols from hearing the noise of battle. Then the Tuareg did a foolish, though altogether predictable, thing. Several allowed their pillaging instincts to get the better of them and broke cover to seize the camels of the French convoy which stood at the foot of the *gara*. The goumiers opened a murderous fire, dropping most of them. Unfortunately they also killed many of the camels. Only three of these Tuareg escaped, one on Cottenest's camel. The lieutenant looked on helplessly as his camel with all of his notes and photographic equipment disappeared down the wadi.

The firefight had lasted almost an hour, when two of the Arab patrols suddenly reappeared. One attacked the Tuareg positions while the other threw themselves across the line of retreat. Surprised, the fire of the Tuareg momentarily slackened. Cottenest's Arabs charged down the hill. Cottenest described the ensuing melée as a "violent hand-to-hand fight, the butts of the rifles broke over skulls, etc." The Tuareg began to run. The Arabs pursued, on foot or on camels if they could catch one. Any man found lying wounded behind a bush or rock was dispatched—twenty-two in all. Seventy-one other bodies were found lying among the rocks. Cottenest buried his three dead, packed his ten wounded on the surviving camels, and began the 600-mile trek back to In Salah. Laperrine rode out to meet him with a contingent of spahis.

The last shot in the Battle of Tit had yet to be fired, however.

Europe's attention concentrated on Pein's diversionary raid toward the Fezzan which had raised the protests of the Turks. Cottenest's victory was ignored by virtually every newspaper except the *Bulletin du comité de l'Afrique française.* So secret had Cottenest's departure been, that he had not even had time to inform his wife in Algiers. The first Madame Cottenest heard about her husband's adventure was when she met an officer from 19th Corps headquarters on the street: he ungallantly informed her that her husband was as good as dead. Cottenest, after receiving a brief, almost routine, word of congratulation in the order of the day of the 19th Army Corps, was transferred back to France. But the axe fell on Cauvet, who was sent into retirement.

Laperrine, however, had been spared, and from Paris' point of view, this proved to be a mistake. The lieutenant colonel realized that the victory at Tit must be followed up if it was to produce a lasting effect. The Ahaggar Tuareg were still stealing camels to the south of the Tidikelt, thefts which the French put down to the malevolence of Attici, but which were more likely the product of their traditional raiding instincts which had sustained them for centuries. Laperrine dispatched Lieutenant Guillo-Lohan at the head of seventy-one Saharian tirailleurs, thirty-five spahis and sixty goumiers to punish the raiders, but at the same time to prove that those who cooperated with the French would be treated fairly. This was part of a deliberate policy to win friends for Moussa and to demonstrate that the French yoke would be a light one. "So as not to deprive Moussa of his influence, one must probably begin with great moderation in the protection which we accord him," wrote Captain Métois, Cauvet's successor at Tidikelt.

Departing on October 1, 1902, Guillo-Lohan followed Cottenest's general route of march, but at a more leisurely pace and with frequent detours to capture douars and explore the deeper recesses of the Koudia. On October 19, he captured three Tuareg "extremely frightened to be our prisoners, they are persuaded that their last hours have arrived." At Ideles, they reerected the monument to Flatters constructed by Cottenest which the Tuareg had destroyed. At the end of October, three Tuareg were killed when, cornered, they tried to fight. Their camels and donkeys were taken as prizes. The Tuareg were especially impressed by the range of the French rifles "and above all by their accuracy." At the end of November, Guillo-Lohan released a number of Tuareg women whom he had captured with their camels: "They will tell the tribes that the French are people who keep their word and respect women." On November 25, they came upon the battlefield of Tit,

> which resembles a real charnel house. The ground is littered with the bodies of camels and horses, above all in the depression where the convoy was located. The Tuareg have not buried their dead: they have left them where they fell, almost all on the rock itself, and have only raised small pyramids of stones. Through the chinks of these primitive tombs, one can clearly distinguish the Tuareg stretched out completely clothed, just as they were on the day of the combat. Decomposition has done its work, and the corpses are literally spread out on the ground. It has been six months since the battle, but this cemetery still reeks of an insupportable stench. . . . We learned that two days after the combat, the Tuareg returned to Tit in great numbers. . . . They paid their last respects to their brothers, and several fanatics disinterred the corpses of our men. . . . Since this day, all of the Tuareg of the Hoggar have come on pilgrimage to Tit: all are now convinced of the reality of their defeat, which wounds their pride more deeply than their hearts.

At this point, the order recalling Guillo-Lohan back to In Salah, dispatched as soon as news of his patrol reached Algiers, arrived. He ambled slowly home, to be greeted by an ecstatic Laperrine. Both men were aware of the significance of Guillo-Lohan's march. Tuareg resistance had been broken at Tit. The French had proved that they could penetrate into the very heart of the Ahaggar. This could only swell the ranks of those who supported Moussa ag Amastane and further diminish the prestige of Attici. Cottenest had broken the myth of Tuareg power: "Our *séjour* in their territory has demonstrated that they recognize themselves to be powerless in the face of a small, well-organized detachment."

Guillo-Lohan's march had forced Attici to flee toward Ghat. Pein raised a goum to march along the borders of Ajjer territory to encourage Attici to remain in the Fezzan: "I asked for 100, and 250 came along on the appointed day," Pein wrote to his cousin. "I selected those I wanted, armed 150 of them and set out. I had to use my crop to chase off those who were rejected." Pein marched them around the Tassili for much of

July, but encountered no resistance, which was just as well, for discipline in his goum was fragile. "After a month of marching, we discovered some abandoned campsites. We took 400 camels and 100 donkeys, and we returned leisurely." But it was no picnic herding these animals "in a country without water, or pasture, in a temperature of 100° to 110°, when one cannot even enjoy the shade of a telegraph pole. But I pulled them through to the great joy of my Chaamba, with whom I shared the prizes." On his return, a request for promotion was rejected because there had been no *faites d'armes*. Poor Pein: censured when he got into a scrap, but unable to win the praise of Algiers even when he succeeded in an effective piece of preventative raiding.

The French now well and truly had their tails up, and so they should, for the ability to cross a land virtually at will which for centuries had been the inviolate territory of the Tuareg was no mean achievement. The struggle for control of the desert now ceased to be one between French and Tuareg and became one between Algeria and the Sudan. It was the old story of competition between soldiers of different colonies, as Laperrine discovered in 1904 when he led a patrol of seventy-six Chaamba Saharians across the desert toward Timbuktu. It was to be the first French expedition to cross to the Niger bend, realizing at long last the link-up between Algiers and Timbuktu. However, when Laperrine arrived in the Adrar, he was met by a contingent of Sudanese spahis under the command of Captain Jean-Baptiste Theveniault. The Captain carried a letter from the commander of Timbuktu forbidding Laperrine to cross into the Sudan. The two men held a long discussion, but Theveniault was adamant. Laperrine was justifiably enraged, and had Père de Foucauld not been along as chaperon, the two French contingents might well have come to blows. This was an extreme, but all too typical, example of empire-building, and one which should have been understood by the Algerian soldiers, who had effectively reduced the Tunisian slice of the Saharian cake, and who were about to begin seriously to nibble away at Morocco. But to those on the outside, it appeared to make a mockery of claims to unite the French empire from the Mediterranean to the Congo. After a dinner between officers of the two contingents, which, despite the heat, passed off in a glacial atmosphere, the two columns broke camp and returned in their opposite directions.

These expeditions, and others, had the effect of chasing Attici from the Ahaggar. But Moussa remained elusive. On more than one occasion, he agreed to meet Laperrine at some isolated spot, only to fail to keep the appointment. The French sent one of their caids, El Hadj Ahmed Bilou, to treat with Moussa, but he refused to come to In Salah: "They fear that he will be poisoned and killed because of the death of the colonel [Flatters]," Bilou reported. He added, however, that if Moussa chose to come to In Salah, no one in the Ahaggar would oppose him, an indication that Moussa had the support of the drum groups and was simply waiting for the right moment to submit. But Moussa's problem lay with the Ajjer, who had gathered in all of the refugees of Attici's war party.

Moussa traveled east to meet In Gueddassen, the amenoukal of the Ajjer Tuareg, in a futile attempt to win him over to a reconciliation with the French. In Gueddassen refused to be persuaded. After all, he had the best of both worlds: His territory was claimed by Turkey, a power too weak to control the Fezzan but influential enough to keep the French out of it. It was on his return from this unsuccessful interview that the greater part of Moussa's wardrobe was pillaged by Amma ag Doua, an Ahaggar Tuareg who opposed reconciliation with the French. As it would have been unthinkable for Moussa to appear at In Salah without a full array of fine robes, the visit had to be postponed until his stock of clothes could be replenished.

In January 1904, Moussa finally came into In Salah in the company of a small number of Tuareg nobles for preliminary discussions with Captain Métois. The talks did not go well. Moussa asked that several French posts be set up in the Ahaggar so that "a negress carrying gold on her head can go everywhere in safety." Métois knew that his government had forbidden the creation of new posts south of the Tidikelt, so he replied tactlessly that these could not be established because France had no faith in Moussa's word. The amenoukal stalked out, and rode back to the Ahaggar. The French must have realized that in a society like that of the Tuareg, in which anarchy had been raised to the level of a political system, no amenoukal could hope to reign effectively as a "king" unless the French were prepared to back him strongly. Otherwise, his position would become untenable.

Although for the moment, Paris forbade Laperrine to establish posts south of the Tidikelt, his "administrative tours" continued. One by one, the various drum groups to the west of the Ahaggar made their separate peace with the French—the Taitok, the Kel Ahnet and the Kel Iforas all came into In Salah to ask for the *aman*. Métois was replaced at In Salah by Captain Jean Dinaux, who attempted to reopen negotiations with Moussa. The amenoukal replied to Dinaux's invitations by moving his tents further south, so the Captain wrote to him in strong terms: "We have reopened our markets to your people and we welcome them with kindness," the letter read.

> . . . The Tuareg are now the subjects of the French government. And you, Moussa ag Amastane, who are among the wisest and most influential, it is absolutely necessary that you understand this and that you make your people understand it. And it is also necessary, that in your own interests, you follow our advice and that you act as the hand of the government. Can you understand my advice and follow it with enthusiasm?

In the summer of 1905, Laperrine led a clutch of Saharians to Tamanrasset, there to meet with Moussa and around sixty delegates of the various drum groups of the Ahaggar Tuareg. The heat was intense, and no one seemed to be in any particular hurry to enter into serious discussions. They talked, they slept, they listened to the women play music and sing. The noble Tuareg "walked at a slow pace, made even slower by their large, flat leather soles, rhythmically striking the ground with their lances," Dinaux wrote. "Others, wearing brightly-colored clothes, uncovered a part of their faces and amused themselves by arriving shouting and galloping at great speed on their camels. The first group gave the impression of dignity, impassiveness, inarticulate hostility; the second of curiosity, happiness, exuberance and confidence." Finally, on August 25, 1905, a "treaty of peace" between France and the Ahaggar Tuareg was signed. Laperrine dropped a red burnous with gold border over the shoulders of Moussa, the symbol that his authority as amenoukal had been bestowed upon him by France. Moussa was given fifteen rifles and placed on a salary. The Sahara was, at last, conquered. Perhaps it would have been churlish to ask if it had been worth the effort. In any case, the time for such questions had long since passed.

XVIII

"ADMINISTRATIVE TOUR"

It was not enough to accept Moussa's "submission" and to declare him "king" of the Ahaggar. The French must make their presence concrete in the desert. This much was obvious to the new commander of the oases, Captain Dinaux. As he had been forbidden to establish permanent posts south of In Salah, he concluded that the only way to make French force a reality in the Sahara was through long-range patrols—"administrative tours," he euphemistically called them—like the one he had now ordered.

Lieutenant Guy Dervil was new to the Saharians, but not as new as Dinaux. The captain had dispatched him with a detachment of Chaamba to establish a revictualing camp for the bulk of the patrol which was to follow. Alerted by the sentry, Dervil saw Dinaux approaching and, judging by the size of the blur on the horizon, with a substantial force. The Saharians busied themselves in the hour which remained before Dinaux's camels would lope into camp by changing into clean gandouras and turbans. Soon, Dervil's small camp would be transformed into a sizable square, the tents of the Europeans in the middle, the Chaamba chatting like magpies around campfires on the periphery, and the camels sprinkled over the plain.

The Chaamba thought Dinaux mad to order an "administrative tour," the largest yet undertaken by the French, in the middle of summer. Any sane man would be dozing away in his room at In Salah, a small boy pulling at the rope that kept the fan swishing backward and forward on the ceiling, going out only at night to squat or lie in the cool sand and talk. But Dinaux wished to prove that he and his French officers and NCOs were tough, tougher even than the Arabs whom they commanded. He felt such a demonstration important if the French were to establish their authority in this new unit, and not allow it to be led from below. The Chaamba had no choice but to obey. They were no longer in a goum, although many had ridden often enough with Pein at Ouargla. If they had still been goumiers, then they might simply have refused to ride.

273

But Laperrine had changed all that. They were soldiers now, French soldiers, even though this fact might not be readily accepted by military men of a more traditional stamp. The Chaamba enlisted only for four months at a stretch and brought their own camels with them; the government provided the rifle and a small—very small—amount of food. Brief enlistments allowed Laperrine to get rid of "bad elements." The Chaamba were good fighting men, about that there could be no doubt. But they were independent, with a prickly sense of honor. They did not always bend well to military discipline. Better to make an open-ended contract that left each side with an escape clause.

Many had also thought Dervil mad to volunteer for the Saharians. Since 1903, when General Hubert Lyautey had taken over as commander of the South Oranais, the military region which covered the frontier between Algeria and Morocco, things had certainly become more interesting along the Zousfana River. Lyautey had breathed fire into the lethargic units which had for years allowed themselves to be plundered by Moroccan raiders. There was action to be had at Beni Abbès, Taghit and Béchar. Even Pein had left Ouargla to fight under Lyautey in the northwest.

But Dervil had been bored by it all. Ain Sefra, the district headquarters of the South Oranais, was a dreadful place, more dreadful than most of the dreadful towns which the French constructed in Algeria; a central square flanked by a few clipped, skeletal trees imported from France which obviously did not thrive in the desert climate, the post-office *style Troisième République,* the inevitable "Hôtel de la Gare" (it was only a narrow-gauge railway), and one or two other buildings of mud and corrugated iron, all sad, dusty and overheated. Why did the French abroad always attempt to recreate, badly, the world which they had left behind? Perhaps it was not nostalgia but simply lack of imagination.

Ain Sefra did possess a cosmopolitan atmosphere of sorts. The two cafés which faced each other across the dusty square—Madame Julia and the more imaginatively named Le Môme Qui Pue, or "The Stinking Kid" —heaved with drunken legionnaires bellowing German songs and picking fights with Zouaves or *joyeux* foolish enough to wander into what they had staked out as their territory. Madame Julia had set aside a room for officers. It was more peaceful, though hardly more elegant, than the saloon bar next door—a few chairs, a worn settee, last year's calendar, and an out-of-tune piano comprised the furnishings. There the officers could talk among themselves, compare careers or indulge in spirited arguments about regiments, tactics or their controversial commander, General Lyautey. Sometimes Lyautey's friend Isabelle Eberhardt would wander in to sing songs from her native Russia while accompanying herself on the piano. It might have seemed incongruous to have this Jewish writer who called herself Si Mahmoud, dressed as an Arab man and who, as far as Dervil could make out, was employed principally in sleeping her way through the Armée d'Afrique, sing Russian songs on the fringes of the Sahara. But the atmosphere of Ain Sefra was already surreal—French, Arabs, Berbers, Moroccans, Algerians, legionnaires of every conceivable nationality, an array of uniforms which the Austrian and Italian armies combined would have been hard-pressed to match for color and variety, a real Tower of Babel. One Russian Jewish writer more or less made little difference.

When Dervil was transferred to the spahi detachment at Beni Abbès 250 miles to the south, he had been marginally more content. The French influence there, at least architecturally, was more discreet. Beni Abbès had a garrison, but it was not, like Ain Sefra, a garrison town. The crenellated walls and square bastions of her white fortress dominated a palm oasis which followed the Saoura as it cut a path between a black hammada stretching away westward toward Morocco and, to the east, the Grand Erg, which looked like a sea whose swells had been frozen in mid-gale. As in most Saharian oases, the inhabitants seemed to exist on the very margins of survival. The "inevitable Jewish merchant" manufactured chemical wine for sale to the garrison, and a *maison de joie* contained three or four unattractive Algerian women who, after having prowled the towns in the north, had followed the conquest to the end of the road "to sell their vanishing charms at bargain prices."

Although it hardly seemed possible, Beni Abbès turned out to be even less exciting than Ain Sefra: "Life flows monotonously by," Dervil recorded in his diary. "Hour follows hour, sometimes broken by the alert of a *rezzou* always pursued in vain, or the periodic arrival of a supply convoy." One could not even ride out alone for fear of ambush by nomads. South of Ben Abbès, the Sahara ran, bleak and mysterious, to the horizon:

> Each day, a little before sunset, I go to stretch out on the sand
> at the end of the wall and, inevitably, I look toward the south
> until it is too dark to see. My relatively inactive life bores me.

A passionate wish tortures me; to go over there, beyond the
horizon, further always further. I dream of long patrols, of
razzias, of pursuing Tuareg, the "Men of the Veil," and, in my
mind, I turn over one thousand plans to escape from this
prison. . . .

Dervil was feeling what drew many men to the Sahara—a curiosity, an
ache, a need to go further than the last French post.

When Dervil had spied his first Saharian at Beni Abbès, he had
been staggered. The man standing before him had the dark skin of an
Arab, a shaved head, a tangled beard, a turban, a filthy gandoura, a
dagger stuck in his belt and no shoes. Nevertheless he insisted, in perfect
French, that he was Corporal Cotte-Bouteillat of the Saharian company
at In Salah who had come to pick up the month's pay for his unit.
Dervil's captain took some convincing before he would relinquish the
cash: "Are you sure that you're a corporal? Odd chaps, these Saharians."
With a sigh suggesting that he didn't know what this man's army was
coming to, he signed the receipt. Dervil foolishly offered to count the
money. It took him two and one-half hours.

I did not realize what I had volunteered for! The total sum was
four thousand and a few francs . . . a weight of almost seventy-
five pounds! There are coins there of every caliber, of every
epoch, from every country, of every value: Maria-Theresa dollars (Bou Tyr), dublons, duros, four-franc pieces (Bou Medva,
with crossed cannons), three-franc pieces, two-franc fifty, two-
francs, one-franc twenty-five, one franc; 18, 14, 10, 8, 5, 4, 2
and one sou: some of the coins were cut in half "to make
change!"

Dervil had had a glimpse of what he desired above all else. He
requested a transfer to the Saharians. He waited, he badgered, he pes-
tered and, finally, one day in 1904, he caught Laperrine on his way
through Beni Abbès:
"You speak Arabic?"
"Fluently, Major."
He chewed his pen and then, brusquely: "You had many charges
against you?"
"Quite a few, Major."

"What sort?"

"AWOL, women, drunkenness. . . ."

Laperrine laughed: "All right, then. I'll take you. There is a vacancy in the Tidikelt. . . . You won't get up to much mischief there." Dervil had rushed out of Laperrine's bureau down to the *souk,* where he bought a "superb" white camel.

The Chaamba greeted each other like old friends. Already they had begun to settle into their *sofs.* Dinaux introduced the roumis—military slang for civilians—in the expedition to Dervil. There were five of them, and a strange collection they were. Professor Chudeau stook awkwardly, his rock hammer in one hand and a box for collecting insect specimens in the other. A small, thin man, he looked overwhelmed by his situation, his eyes wide behind a pair of wire-rimmed spectacles. His trousers were rolled up over the knees, revealing a pair of thin but surprisingly hairy calves. Judging by the dents in his solar topee, he had yet fully to master the art of camel-riding. Hardly had he spoken than he began to prowl around the camp, his nose a few inches from the ground, looking for specimens to collect.

Chudeau's frail appearance contrasted sharply with that of his colleague from the University of Algiers, Professor E. F. Gautier. A barrel-chested man with a full beard and a head of gray hair, he spoke French of a purity seldom heard outside of the Comédie française. He already possessed a profound academic knowledge of the Sahara. Now, he had come to meet her face to face. Beside these academics stood two functionaries from the Administration des Postes et Télégraphes. The senior of the two, a Monsieur Etiennot, was detestable on sight. Self-important, verbose, shaped like a drum, Etiennot treated his assistant—a junior civil servant who had volunteered for this mission in the hope of advancement—like his skivvy. Etiennot had been sent by Algiers to survey a route for a Transsaharian telegraph. But as he was incapable of drawing a topographical map, he was forever borrowing those made by French NCOs "to compare them." He then ordered his assistant to trace them, before signing his own name.

The last man was the strangest of all.

He is on the small side. A short, graying beard frames a face upon which the prominent cheekbones accentuate the thinness.

He is mostly bald in front. In deep sockets, beneath thick eyebrows, his dark eyes wear a curious expression, a mixture of modesty and authority, of intelligence and self-effacement. I judge them to be capable of firmness, even of harshness.

Dervil had met Charles de Foucauld before at Beni Abbès. The lieutenant was not a religious man, but he had attended mass in the chapel which Foucauld had constructed a few yards across an expanse of sand from the fort. The chapel would not have been a building worthy of note had it not spoken an entire sermon about the priest who inhabited it: a small rectangle of crumbling mud walls covered by a roof of branches and a scrap of tarpaulin. Twelve men formed a capacity congregation. On that Sunday, Dervil had joined other French officers and NCOs who stood about outside, heads uncovered, listening to the mass or contemplating the crude wooden cross that hung above the chapel door. A few yards away an even cruder building, hardly more than a mound of rocks surmounted by a cross, served Foucauld as a rectory. It was as if the priest had deliberately made his parish church appear miserable, impoverished, uncomfortable. Then Dervil had watched him walk away, a cadaverous silhouette dressed in a filthy, ill-fitting gandoura drawn together at the waist by a leather belt, a pair of sandals and a cross of red cloth stitched to his breast. This was obviously a man who had raised the Christian virtue of self-abnegation to the level of an obsession.

Yet, it had not always been so. Dervil could hardly credit that this poorly dressed, skeletal figure had once been "a brilliant cavalryman," a renowned explorer and more than a bit of a roué. Foucauld was a modern-day Saint Augustine, a man who had exchanged a life of what he saw as extreme sin (in fact, it had been nothing more than healthy boyish insouciance), for one of extreme, one might even say unnatural, piety. Laperrine like to joke about his old St.-Cyr classmate: "The only thing Foucauld liked about the mass was the wine." In fact, Foucauld was no laughing matter. He was not an easy man to live with. His obsession with his religion seemed to have drained him of every ounce of that once-abundant stock of youthful humor. He carried his vow of poverty to the very brink of starvation. One might accept the first invitation to dine with Père Foucauld; one never accepted a second. His "meals" were so miserable that by comparison the Tuareg dined in great style.

Foucauld's importance to the history of the desert has perhaps been exaggerated by historians, and by some Christians eager to see his life, and his eventual martyrdom, as a lesson in Christian sacrifice. Foucauld's biographer brackets him and Laperrine together as "the tutelary geniuses of France in the Hoggar and in the desert. We must cultivate their memory." In fact, Foucauld was to fail, both as a colonialist and as a missionary. That he was an extraordinary character, there can be no doubt. His importance to the men around him was that, to them, he symbolized the emotional complexity of their, and of France's, relationship with the desert. All officers who volunteered for duty in the Sahara automatically placed themselves in one of the outer circles of the military profession. All were obliged to confront the solitude and loneliness of the desert, if only that of being separated from their own kind. Foucauld did not greatly aid the mission of the Saharians; to the contrary, as will be seen, he imperiled it in many ways. What he did offer them, however, was a distilled version of the solitude of their own lives. For this reason, like the youngest and weakest member of an adolescent gang who is protected by his fellows, Foucauld became a kind of mascot, to be cocooned, humored and protected. Despite appearances, he was one of them, a Frenchman in a very strange place.

Charles de Foucauld had been born in Strasbourg in 1858, the son of a subinspector of forests. His father's rather modest position in the middle echelons of the French civil service must not be taken as an indication of the family's social status, for the de Foucaulds were definitely *vieille France*. Charles' ancestors had fought in the Crusades with Saint Louis, stood beside Jeanne d'Arc at the coronation at Reims, served Henri IV and any number of other kings as soldiers and churchmen. And they had suffered for it in the Revolution. The major contribution of the Foucaulds throughout the history of France was to demonstrate how to die well.

Yet, by the high standards of the Foucauld clan, Charles had seemed unpromising material. Perhaps this was the result of his unhappy childhood. Orphaned in 1864 at the age of six, Charles and his only sibling, Marie, were cared for by their maternal grandfather, a retired colonel of engineers and already a man of advanced years. Charles was pampered and indulged by the old man, and allowed to escape with mediocre marks in school. The outbreak of the Franco-Prussian War in 1870 and the subsequent siege of Strasbourg by German troops drove them to Berne in Switzerland. With Bismarck's annexation of Alsace in 1871, Charles,

Marie and their grandfather returned to live in Nancy, in unoccupied Lorraine. There, Charles continued his undistinguished school career.

In later life, he blamed his poor performance as a student on the lack of Christian principles and religious inspiration in his teachers: "Youth needs to be taught, not by neutral men, but by believing and saintly souls." But the conclusion is inescapable that Charles was not a man to be left to work out his own solutions, to find his own way. He craved guidance. He needed to be shown a path, *the* path, to follow. Perhaps this was the result of the lack of a father. But in the absence of a firm hand, Charles was rudderless. He remembered this adolescent "liberty" as next to intolerable. He had no real interest in anything. His grandfather pushed him toward the École polytechnique. But that required three grueling years of preparation. Charles took the easier path which led to St.-Cyr.

The normal course for a young man preparing for the entrance examinations for one of France's *grandes écoles* was to attend a preparatory school upon graduation from *lycée,* the most famous being the Jesuit-run École de Sainte-Geneviève in Paris' rue des Postes. Ordinarily, one year in the hands of the Jesuits sufficed to pull even the dullest lad through the St.-Cyr examinations. Charles took two, and even then just scraped through among the last candidates in 1876. "That's all right," he told his disappointed grandfather, "it will allow me to move up more quickly in the class rankings." But Foucauld moved nowhere. At St.-Cyr, he made a virtue of indolence. While many of his contemporaries, such as Laperrine, avidly studied the military theories which they believed would soon prove useful in the imminent return match with Prussia, Foucauld ostentatiously read Greek and Latin authors, wrote, or simply lolled.

In 1878, Foucauld had left St.-Cyr to follow a year-long course at the cavalry school at Saumur. His roommate there was another young aristocrat who would add an important footnote to the history of the Sahara—Antoine de Vallombrosa, the Marquis de Morès. For the moment, however, the desert was the last place in the world which occupied the thoughts of these two young men. On the surface, they seemed to have little in common. Morès was tall, elegant, an energetic sportsman, an accomplished rider. Foucauld, by contrast, was fat (he had almost been refused admission to St.-Cyr for "precocious obesity"), listless and composed. Soon, however, they discovered a common taste for dinner parties, fine cigars and marathon card games, which made their room the school's main social center. This ceaseless social activity was in great part a product of necessity: hardly a week went by when at least one of the two sub-lieutenants was not confined to quarters for some infraction of the rules; they had to find some way to pass the time. One night while confined to barracks, Foucauld dressed in civilian clothes (strictly against the rules), put on a false moustache, climbed the school wall and walked into Saumur, where he entered the town's best restaurant and ordered a meal. Hardly had the first course arrived, however, when his moustache fell off and into his soup. The waiter, believing Foucauld to be an escaped convict, called the police, who delivered him to the sergeant of the guard.

In 1879, Foucauld had been assigned to the Fourth Hussars, garrisoned in the dreary town of Pont-à-Mousson in eastern France. There, he continued to make a reputation as a high-living, frivolous young man, running up debts and regularly being expelled from his lodgings for late-night parties. It was probably just as well that, in 1880, the Fourth Hussars were transferred to Algeria, for Foucauld's reputation had either exhausted the patience, or served as a warning, to virtually every landlord in Pont-à-Mousson. When the regiment, now rechristened the Fourth Chasseurs d'Afrique, unpacked their bags in Sétif, a small town one hundred miles west of Constantine, Foucauld's baggage was found not to conform to army regulations—the object in question was a mistress, a woman who had followed him from France. The colonel disapproved, and had a quiet word with one of Foucauld's fellow lieutenants, who suggested tactfully to his comrade that perhaps his friend should return to France. Charles ignored him—he disdained this sort of bourgeois prudishness. It simply served to demonstrate how desperately middle-class the French army had become when even a regiment of hussars worried about the moral welfare of its officers. In Austria or Prussia, keeping a mistress would not only be tolerated, it would be de rigueur among subalterns. Foucauld dug in his heels.

The colonel sent him on maneuvers for a few weeks, but on his return, he again took up with his lady. More subtle methods having failed, the colonel finally called his subordinate on the carpet. The two men had words, and Foucauld was given a simple choice: Either the woman went, or he would. This was not a question of passion for Foucauld, nor even one of principle. It was simply one of will, stubborn, brutal will, which until this moment Foucauld had successfully dissembled behind a mask of frivolity. It also gave the first hint of a strain of unreasonableness noticed by many who subsequently met him. He requested an extended leave and retired to Evian-les-Bains, the beautiful spa town on Lake Léman, presumably with his mistress in tow.

His premature retirement lasted only a few months. In 1881, French troops in Algeria invaded neighboring Tunisia. With the French occupied in the east, the tribes on the western borderlands of Algeria rebelled under the leadership of Bou Amama. Foucauld must have grown tired of Evian, or of his mistress, or both. He requested a return to active duty, and a hard-pressed war minister gratefully obliged. Those who knew Foucauld well traced the beginning of a change in his character from the Bou Amama insurrection, a change that would eventually lead him to abandon the sword for the altar. As yet, however, these changes were subtle.

The campaign was not a highly dangerous one. After experiencing some desperate moments in the initial uprising, the French found Bou Amama's *harkas* to be elusive. There is no record that Foucauld ever saw action—just a season of marching and countermarching beneath a dusty sun, constantly short of food, tormented by thirst, and always alert for an Arab ambush. But this did test Foucauld's mettle and offer him a challenge. By all accounts, he acquitted himself well, and by providing rum for his men to disguise the taste of fetid water, he even earned the esteem of the grizzled veterans of Napoleon III's Mexican campaigns: "Of the Foucauld of Saumur and Pont-à-Mousson, there remained only a small edition of Aristophanes, which he always carried with him, and the slightest trace of his old snobbism, which caused him to give up smoking the day he could no longer procure his favorite brand of cigars," Laperrine remembered.

More important, Foucauld had been entranced by North Africa. The overwhelming emptiness of the desert, its desolate beauty and, above all, its inhabitants intrigued him. Foucauld the debauched, dissolute subaltern became Foucauld the explorer and ethnographer. At least, that is what he wanted to become; but the war ministry denied his request to explore the South Oranais. And so, at age twenty-four, Foucauld resigned from the army and moved to Algiers to begin preparations for what was to become the most celebrated adventure of his young life—the exploration of Morocco.

Morocco in the 1880s was virtually a closed book for Europeans. This was part of deliberate policy on the part of the sultan, who feared, with reason, that European powers and especially France nurtured designs of conquest. Tangier had a fairly large population of Spaniards, and it was possible, with the sultan's permission, to visit several of the larger cities of the west, like Fez and Marrakech. However, most of the country, and especially the mountainous regions of the Atlas and the Rif, remained impenetrable and therefore unknown to the outside world. European maps of Morocco were virtually blank. This was a situation that Foucauld, at great personal risk, set out to correct.

In Algiers, Foucauld busied himself with the study of Arabic. He consulted Oscar MacCarthy, considered the greatest North African expert of his time, in his small library on the rue d'Etat Major. The two men spent hours in the central courtyard of the library, consulting the works of ancient geographers, and discussing under what guise Foucauld should travel. To go openly as a Christian would at best invite failure; at worst, it would be suicidal. His Arabic was not proficient enough to allow him to pass as a Moor. MacCarthy offered a third alternative: He could travel through Morocco disguised as a Russian rabbi.

Had Foucauld realized the vexations which his Jewish disguise would invite, he might have selected another flag under which to sail. However, MacCarthy convinced him that traveling as an apostate Christian as had Caillié, Rohlfs and Lentz would only arouse suspicion. Traveling as a Jew, Foucauld

> would pass unnoticed . . . no one would pay attention, no one would bother to speak to a poor Jew who, meanwhile, consulted his compass, watch, barometer, and noted the path that he followed. Also, everywhere I would obtain from my cousins, as the Jews of Morocco refer to themselves, true and detailed information about the country. Finally, I would excite no suspicion. My bad accent could give me away, but are there not Jews in all countries?

"Rabbi Joseph Aleman"—driven from Moscow by religious persecution and now, after a visit to Jerusalem, embarked on a journey across North Africa—left Algiers in June 1883. He was accompanied by a real rabbi, Mardochée Abi Serour, from whom Foucauld had received instruction in Jewish customs and manners, and who had agreed to act as his guide in Morocco. Even before he left Algiers, Foucauld realized that the new disguise he had adopted would require a new attitude of mind: Everyone, even the meanest servant, addressed him with the familiar *tu*. The proud Foucauld had to accustom himself to the fact that, for the moment, he no longer belonged to one of the grand families of France, but was a despised and lonely Jew. The final proof of this occurred in Tlemcen, the last large town in northwestern Algeria before the Moroccan frontier: "We arrived in Tlemcen at nine o'clock in the morning," Foucauld wrote. "Tired, we bought some bread and olives, and we began to eat, sitting on the ground in the square. While we were there, a group of officers of the Chasseurs d'Afrique came out of the mess and walked by, not two feet from me. I knew almost all of them. They looked at me without suspecting who I was." On the contrary, one even remarked that the Jew eating the olives looked like a monkey. It was probably the most satisfying humiliation Foucauld ever received, for at least he knew that his disguise was as near-perfect as he could make it.

Reconnaissance au Maroc, the record of Foucauld's travels in Morocco in 1883–84, makes disappointing reading today. This is not surprising, since Foucauld's main purpose was to describe the land in such detail that cartographers might be able to draw maps from his descriptions. *Reconnaissance* imparts little of the drama that one finds in other travelogues, like that of René Caillié, for instance. But one must also remember that, in his day, Caillié was considered to have contributed little to the advancement of the geographical knowledge of Africa. Foucauld's record is more coldly scientific, though not exclusively so. He does give a full account of an incident in which a band of Arabs plotted openly to kill the two Jews, as well as other vignettes of his travels.

By 1887, when *Reconnaissance* was published to enormous acclaim, Foucauld was well on his way to a new sort of existence, although this was hardly apparent at the time. Since his return from Morocco, he had been restless, even aimless. After a few months in Algiers spent organizing his notes for publication, he had hired a few camels and toured the oases of southern Algeria. He then returned to France, finally settling into an apartment in Paris' rue de Miromesnil, which he decorated *à l'arabe* with cushions and carpets. He would receive guests dressed in gandoura and slippers. He began to read pagan philosophy again. For some, it looked as if Foucauld might be slipping back into his old ways.

Far from it. Charles de Foucauld, seemingly at the height of his success—he had received the coveted gold medal of the Geographical Society of Paris—was a troubled man. All meaning seemed to have gone out of his life. He confessed that he had even flirted with the idea of converting to Islam, but after a few hours of instruction rejected that religion as too "materialist." In 1886, he had been introduced to Abbé Huvelin, a graduate of France's elite teacher-training college, the Ecole normale supérieure, who had abandoned a teaching career to become a parish priest in Paris. The two men met frequently. Finally, in October 1886, Foucauld entered the confessional and then took his "second first communion." The first step taken, Foucauld, in keeping with his character, followed his decision to what he saw as its natural conclusion: In 1889, after a voyage of several weeks in the Holy Land, he entered the Trappist monastery of Nôtre-Dame-des-Neiges in southern France.

From that time on, Foucauld gained a reputation in the French Church as a man prepared to test the limits of self-denial. The once-corpulent figure melted away, the youthful face became lined and prematurely old. He wore rags and ate so little that his family and his superiors had constantly to remind him that dead priests could not carry out the work of God. Foucauld, with characteristic stubbornness, declined to take heed. He admitted that he wanted to die a martyr to his faith. It appeared that only the fierce desire to remain in this world until the murderous infidel could dispatch him to the next kept him from starvation. He spent several years in the Holy Land, studied theology in Rome, and, finally, in 1901, after taking orders, asked to be sent to the Sahara.

When Dervil had first come to In Salah, he had thought that the primary quality of a Saharian was a strong stomach. The first meal he had eaten with his new commander—sardines, lamb, rancid butter out of a tin and wine gone sour in the heat—had seemed an ordeal at the time. Now he suspected that it was better to have no stomach at all. For weeks his daily menu had been composed of a few dates, a cake made of millet mixed with water and then thrown on the fire, supplemented from time to time by a scrap of gazelle meat which had had only the briefest encounter with a flame. The men even put pepper in the coffee to disguise the taste of sulfur. He would give almost anything for a meal of crushed locusts and peppers which his "wife" Khatty prepared for him at home in In Salah.

Foucauld seemed little troubled by the poor diet. Even at Beni Abbès when Laperrine offered him extra rations to improve his meals, he simply gave them away to the blacks and Haratin who came each night to his hermitage. Nor did the heat appear to affect him: He walked for hours at the head of his camel in the blistering sun. Some might see Foucauld as a saint. Dervil thought him simply inhuman.

The attitude of the Saharian officers toward Foucauld was one of ambivalence. They admired him, certainly. In a strange way they even liked him—after all, he had chosen to share their hardships. On this trip the simplicity and dignity of the man were shown to great advantage against the odious functionary from the Algiers Postes et Télégraphes. Monsieur Etiennot, a good servant of the Republic and as such an enemy of priests and soldiers, called Foucauld Brother Charles. (The officers, therefore, made a point of addressing their colleague as Father.) "Well, Brother Charles, you don't say much, do you?" Etiennot, bored, wandering about the campsite with his ubiquitous bottle of Pernod, which he offered to share with no one, made one of his rare attempts to be charming. Foucauld looked up from his sewing: "That's because I have a horror of garrulous people, Monsieur." The officers chuckled to themselves.

The trouble with Foucauld was that he was hardly more charming with them. "He's not an easy character," they agreed. Some went even further: His self-abnegation was only disguised egotism. He seldom had time for them. They quickly learned not to disturb Foucauld when he was in prayer, meditating or working on his dictionary of Tamahak—which was most of the time. He would only pop up at inconvenient moments to lecture them against sin. Of course, one job of the priest is to rattle the consciences of his flock. But Foucauld's advice was usually unsolicited and always unwanted.

Foucauld and the Saharians disagreed on virtually every subject, not the least on the life-style that French officers and NCOs had created for themselves in the Tuat. The widely held view in the Armée d'Afrique was that "one only finds madmen to serve in the south." This was not an altogether unfair assessment. Certainly the Saharians made a virtue of nonconformity: "The style of the Saharian is not to be a roumi," wrote Robert Hérison, who joined the Saharians as a military doctor in 1909.

"It is to appear to hold none of the prejudices of the *petite bourgeoisie provinciale* and above all to be shocked by nothing. . . . To declare banal and unimportant that which would scandalize the priest."

Foucauld was indeed scandalized. The Saharians had transformed In Salah into a *belle époque* Club Med, where they spent their days playing tennis, walking about barefoot dressed only in gandouras, taking ten cold showers a day and sleeping. What Foucauld especially objected to was the fact that virtually all of the Frenchmen had taken young girls, many of them only twelve or thirteen, as mistresses. Dervil had paid what he considered to be a high "dowry" for his thirteen-year-old wife: "a piece of blue cloth, two haiks (one for the mother, the other for the girl), one ring and two silver bracelets, several glass necklaces, a silk scarf, 12 pounds of Arab butter, sugar, tea and flour! For an enormous sum of 300 francs!" Which, he might have added, was the amount one paid for a moderately priced camel. Dervil rationalized his menage: His "wife," who was half-Arab, half-Tuareg, would teach him Tamahak. Besides, this type of arrangement avoided the spread of disease or "disagreeable errors" which might otherwise occur. Nor did the girls do badly, as upon departure, most of the Frenchmen left them a few goats, chickens and date palms, which made them substantial women of property and therefore highly sought as brides. But Foucauld had not been convinced: "I have only one piece of advice to give you," he told Dervil. "Avoid having children. When their father leaves this country to return to France, they become pariahs, the objects of derision and disdain of everyone . . . the poor things."

The differences between Foucauld and the Saharians went beyond quibbles over morality, however. To them, Foucauld seemed obsessed, even blinded, by his religion, to the point that he argued that France's entire policy in North Africa should be based on the conversion of the Arabs to Christianity: "We Catholics meet systematic opposition from the authorities," Foucauld complained, "who support and encourage the Moslem religion! By doing this, they are committing a sort of suicide, for, I must say it, Islam is our enemy: We will always be the despised roumis." On the face of it, Foucauld's view made sense. He saw perhaps more clearly than many that Islam could, and did, serve as a rallying point for opposition to France in North Africa. He also realized that the French conquest had facilitated the spread of Islam and of Arabic, the language of the Koran, in those Berber regions where before both had been kept at arm's length. That is why he was so keen to preserve Tamahak, the language of the Tuareg, to insulate the Tuareg against Arab influence and possibly win them to Christianity. But, as Foucauld feared, the conquest of the Tuareg by Chaamba under French command (the Tuareg always referred to the Saharians as the Arabs) strengthened the hold of Islam on the desert.

Most Saharians were unconvinced by Foucauld's arguments. In the first place, they found questions of religion, quite frankly, boring. Secondly, they were dangerous: As their task was to lead men whose religion they did not share, it was hardly in the interests of discipline to point up the ecclesiastical differences between French and Arab Saharians. On the contrary, their position was that religion was a matter of indifference. To attempt to proselytize among the Chaamba Saharians would have been disastrous. When Hérison asked one of his Chaamba what he thought of Christianity, the man replied diplomatically that he respected that religion, "but," he added, "it pleases me to think that our lord Mohammed was a warrior and that he was of our race." This policy of tolerance was reflected on the official level: France was a large and tolerant empire which encompassed men of all faiths. There was no contradiction in serving both France and Islam.

Another, infinitely sadder, refutation of Foucauld's arguments was his own admission that during the years he had spent in the Sahara (and which he was to spend there), he had made only one conversion, "an old black woman at Beni Abbès. I also baptized a small baby who was in danger of dying, who had the joy of leaving this earth almost immediately for heaven. Lastly, I baptized a thirteen-year-old boy, but it was not I who converted him. He was brought to me by a French sergeant who had taught him his catechism and prepared him to receive the sacraments. You see, my dear brother, I am really a useless servant."

In many respects, Foucauld had only himself to blame for his lack of success. Although it is unlikely that any Christian missionary would have counted many conversions in North Africa, Foucauld burdened himself with almost insurmountable handicaps. His association with French soldiers, while inescapable and desired by him, hardly encouraged confidence in a people so recently conquered, although he did on occasion attempt to arbitrate their grievances with the garrison. But more, Arab and Tuareg alike were confused by his life of Christian self-renunciation. In North Africa, holy men lived well. If they did not live well, then they had no *baraka,* or the gift from God, and therefore were not favored by Him. How could a man who wandered about in a robe which was too short for him, cut his own hair (without a mirror) and ate hardly enough to keep a two-year-old child alive, claim to be holy?

Perhaps, as Foucauld insisted, a vast gulf existed between the "materialism" of Islam and the spirituality of Christianity. To the inhabitants of the Sahara, the Christian idea of fasting on Fridays or during Lent seemed a joke, because they had to go without meat all of their lives. Conversion to Christianity offered no advantages on earth. On the contrary, the *m'tourni* (as Moslems converted to Christianity were called) were outcasts in their own communities. Vague promises about spiritual riches in heaven did not tempt them. Islam also offered a path to heaven, and by all accounts it was a jolly nice place, no angels flitting about from cloud to cloud, but a paradise of green grass and trees, rivers of milk and honey, and women! That was something worth being virtuous for.

Foucauld's impossible personality and life-style not only helped deprive him of converts, but deprived him as well of his most cherished dream—the founding of a monastery. For the simple truth was that no one could be found who was able to endure his regime. A young Frenchman called Father Michel briefly joined Foucauld at Beni Abbès, but went home after three months, unable to survive the "fearful mortification" of his would-be superior. Foucauld was thus condemned by his own nature, and by the severity of his life, to live alone. One can hardly escape the conclusion that, despite his claims to the contrary, he preferred it that way. Foucauld did not really expect to convert the Sahara to Christianity. Rather, the desert seemed to ensure his own salvation.

"I Allah! Noudou!" "Everyone up!" The men rose slowly. It was still dark. In their burnouses, they looked like phantoms rising out of the earth. Several fires were lit. The light reflecting off the bronzed faces made the scene appear even more ghostly. Some of the men held their stiff, cold fingers toward the flames. Others pulled down the tents or lashed the triangular saddles onto the backs of the protesting camels.

The Saharians moved out into the night in silence, every man walking at the head of his camel. Gradually, the horizon began to light up. The mist made the distant peaks appear as if they were hovering in midair. The dunes grew pink. A herd of startled gazelles fled with great bounds. The transition from dark to light was swift—the black of the night sky gave way to the molten copper of day with almost indecent haste. The low, black peaks dropped away to the north. Before them stretched the level, overheated plain of the Ahnet.

The men walked or rode toward an horizon that obstinately refused to come any closer. Somewhere, further on, were the wells of In-Ziza. Dinaux asked the guide when they would arrive. He replied simply *"grib"*—"soon." That could mean anything from four hours to four days. But in four days, the Dinaux expedition would be a collection of bleached bones if they did not reach water soon. Camel Number 23 was the first to falter. He no longer chewed his cud. Suddenly, he stopped and went down on his knees. It was useless to prod him forward. He was obviously finished. The men unsaddled him. His long neck curved behind him, and his head rested on his thigh. The men walked on. Before they were out of sight, the crows were fluttering around the dying camel. One alighted on his forehead and pecked out his eyes.

Like most *Africains,* Dinaux held an instinctive distrust of guides. They seldom told the truth. The officer must attempt to divine their ulterior motive: "There is no water on that route; you will die of thirst; the path is difficult; it is too hot for you; the country is dangerous; etc. . . . The principal reason is that they do not want to tear away the veil and show us things," Lamy had written. "Once the paths and wells are known to us, they are at our mercy . . . I must be careful of everything without showing it, and I always take the greatest precautions." It took time to learn the country well enough to strike out without a guide. Until then, they were an unfortunate necessity. Laperrine had issued advice about dealing with guides: Remember that they are "sons and grandsons of brigands" who might want to lead the French toward a vulnerable flock or herd, or away from danger. Sometimes, they "lost their way" because they wanted to sleep, in which case they might be made to walk for a week at the head of their camel. Dervil discovered that one of his guides who had "lost his way" recovered his sense of direction instantly when given a little tea and sugar. But in this case, Dinaux had no choice but to trudge along behind his guide and hope for the best.

The camels, their stomachs flat and their flanks caved in like deflated *guerbas,* bleated in a sinister way. Even the men were showing signs of thirst: sunken eyes and cheeks and an empty stare. Dinaux called a halt. The Arabs threw themselves on the ground and pulled their gandouras over their heads in an attempt to escape the merciless sun. They were beyond commanding now. The French officers and NCOs had to unsaddle the camels. Two of the Chaamba tried to wander off, no one, not even they, knew where. Dinaux ordered the sentinels to shoot anyone who attempted to flee. "How far is In-Ziza?" Dinaux insisted. *"Grib"* was the only reply he received from the guide. Dinaux selected six of the strongest men and camels and sent them forward with the bone-dry *guerbas.* The camels' instincts, it was hoped, would lead them to water. Then, he settled down to wait.

Not surprisingly, Etiennot was the first to crack, perhaps because he had been deprived of his daily ration of Pernod. "Posterity will learn of this!" the feckless civil servant, considerably slimmer after a few weeks in the desert, shouted at Dinaux. "If we escape death, I will tell everyone that it was your fault that we all almost died. . . ."

Dervil fought down an almost uncontrollable urge to throttle him. "Monsieur Etiennot, be quiet!" Dinaux's voice was calm but forceful. "There's only one person in command here, and that's myself!"

Etiennot walked away through the torpid camp. Foucauld offered the last of his water to him. It stank horribly of tar, but Etiennot gulped it down avidly. "God! It's awful!" was all that Foucauld received in the way of thanks. The interpreter, a Jew from Algiers, sobbed and called on his mother and wife. *"Cheheda"*—"delirious"—the Chaamba next to Dervil muttered. Dervil's throat felt like the inside of a brick kiln. He tried to suck a stone, but he had no saliva. He felt as if his tongue were in shreds. Tomorrow, we shall be dead, he thought, before he fell into an exhausted sleep.

At two o'clock in the morning, someone shook him awake. It was his turn to mount guard. What was the use? A flock of sheep could have stormed the camp and no one would have had the energy to resist. The night was calm, not a breath of air stirred across the dark *tanezrouft.* Next to him, a Saharian lay completely naked, his ribs so prominent that he looked like a skeleton. Dervil sat down on a case of cartridges. His head was spinning. A few yards away, he could distinguish the captain sitting in a camp chair. Dervil moved closer to the sentinel on the western edge of the camp, so they might help each other to remain awake. Another hour passed.

Suddenly, his Chaambi straightened up. He peered out into the blackness, then threw himself down on his stomach and pressed his ear to the ground. "They're back!" he shouted. Instantly, the sleeping camp came alive with one cry: *"El ma! El ma!"*—"Water! Water!" The six volunteers, their camels laden with sweating *guerbas,* bounced into the camp. This was enough to touch off a riot. Hardly had one man begun to drink than he was thrown to the ground and the *guerba* wrestled from his grasp. The French NCOs waded in with their camel whips and restored order. Everyone patiently waited his turn. The officers drank last. Dervil, his turn come round at last, took up the *guerba* and began to drink the tepid water in long, deep gulps. It came straight up. He began again, more slowly this time. *"Que la vie est belle!"*

The following morning at ten o'clock they reached In-Ziza, a filthy pool stagnating between rocky hills. Men and camels alike plunged their faces into the greenish liquid, ignoring the camel turds that floated on the surface, and began to drink. The animals were allowed to browse among the tamarisks. The officers were furious with Etiennot: He had been the only Frenchman to lose face. Otherwise, they, comparative novices in the desert, had to a man proved more resistant than the Chaamba. They were not a little proud of that fact. It was a good beginning.

The Dinaux mission marched southwest toward the Adrar of the Iforas. Dervil continued to marvel at the stamina of Foucauld. He rose fifteen minutes before reveille to say mass, walked all day and spent several hours each night writing and arranging his notes. When they encountered a Targui, Dinaux, after the ritual salutations, sent him to Foucauld, who interrogated him on his tribe and his family, then asked him to recite the legends and poetry of his people, all of which he would write down.

At the edge of the Adrar of the Iforas, they halted. To the south lay territory claimed by the Sudan. To avoid difficulties of the sort encountered by Laperrine the year before, the expedition would turn northeast and follow the Wadi Tamanrasset through Silet and Abêlessa to Tamanrasset, 7,000 feet high in the Ahaggar. Everyone, that is, but the civilians —the professors would continue south to Timbuktu, while Etiennot would retrace his steps back to In Salah. Before his departure, Etiennot's unfortunate subordinate, who for weeks had endured his boss's abuse and boorish behavior, asked the officers to sign a letter attesting to his unfair treatment. In this way, the poor man might be forearmed against the unfavorable report which he was bound to receive on his return to Algiers. The officers signed without hesitation. They watched the corpulent Etiennot, swaying on his camel, ride north without a word of goodbye.

The Ahaggar loomed up before them. Sometimes during the day it lay obscured by a haze of heat. But in the evening, at sunset, the brooding plugs of rock reflected a multitude of colors. The Ahaggar inspired awe. It also inspired fear. At night, when the Chaamba sat around the camp-fires smoking tobacco, if they had any (otherwise they fabricated ciga-rettes out of gazelle dung), their stories turned away from confident boasts about *razzias* against the Ajjer Tuareg to the legends and myths of this "land of fear." Of course, to them, they were not legends and myths. They were history.

One of the Chaamba outriders spotting a gazelle, slipped gently to the ground and crawled along on all fours "becoming a gazelle," until he arrived behind a rock. There he removed the rags which protected the mechanism of his Lebel from sand, took aim and fired. With a whoop, he leaped toward the wounded animal, grabbed its head, turned it in the direction of Mecca and slit its throat. He then threw it over his shoulder and walked back to his camel.

The atmosphere in the camp that night was heavy with expectation. Everyone had seen the gazelle killed and waited for it to be deposited in front of the captain's tent. The captain, as the caid, had the first choice of meat. His cook would cut off a leg, and then the Chaambi could reclaim his carcass which, customarily, he would share with his compan-ions. However, today the Arab had decided that this was *his* kill, which he would not share with the roumi. Everyone waited. The captain bided his time. Finally, after several hours, the Chaambi was summoned before the commander. "You are obviously unhappy with us," he was told. "I do not want to keep you against your will. You may leave. Take the two camels which you brought with you on enlistment. Take as much food and water as you need for your trip to In Salah. However, the rifle belongs to the government. That must be left with me." The Arab's eyes grew wide with disbelief, then with panic. Unarmed and alone in the land of his people's traditional enemies, his chances of survival were slim, and he knew it. He began to apologize. Soon, the gazelle lay outside the captain's tent.

Tamanrasset in 1905 was an unprepossessing place—fifteen miser-able *zeribas* inhabited by Haratin who tried to coax a crop of millet out of the impoverished soil. However, the air was clear and fresh even in mid-summer. The poverty and remoteness of the place at once attracted Foucauld, who announced that he intended to remain. "It does not seem to me that there will ever be a garrison here, a telegraph, Europeans," he wrote in his diary. "I choose this forgotten place and I remain." The men threw up a small *zeriba* of branches for him, and then constructed a mud hermitage twenty feet long and four feet wide with a thatched roof. A simple curtain separated the chapel from his living quarters.

The Saharians remained for the next few weeks at Tamanrasset, occasionally launching reconnaissance parties along the goat tracks which traversed the Koudia. One patrol even penetrated as far as Iferouane in the Air, which, after the deprivations endured in the Ahaggar, was a comparative paradise: "People bring us jars of honey, butter, and—what a marvel!—vegetables and fruit: enormous pumpkins and watermelons; and divine fare of which we have been deprived for months—onions!" On the return journey to Tamanrasset, the officers passed the time by debating what would be their first meal when they reached France—filet of sole Mornay, lobster *à l'américaine,* a thick piece of roast beef with *sauce béarnaise.* . . . Dinaux told them to shut up. His stomach ulcer condemned him to a diet of rice and noodles.

The order to return to In Salah was greeted with regret by Dervil. "France, Paris and her pleasures, seemed far away, unimportant," he thought. "It is curious to realize how quickly a civilized man reverts to a primitive one without needs." The expedition filed through the gorges of Tahount-Aarak. The dark rocks towered above them. The men were decidedly nervous: Here, they said, "live the most powerful *djenouns* in an underground palace full of gold and diamonds . . . only a pure woman can enter it. . . . My father Bika knew one. . . . She was beautiful and virtuous. . . . The king of the *djenouns* with a gesture moved the rock and took her inside the enchanted palace. Happy, laden with all the gifts, she will never know old age, nor death. At night, one can hear her clear voice singing in the silence to charm the genies!" Dervil listened for a long time before he finally drifted off to sleep: "The beautiful one did not want to sing for me that night."

Soon, the dunes of farewell came into sight. A line of camels appeared on the horizon. The men began to sing and beat on saucepans. The tricolor floated over the gate of the casbah of In Salah. As the camels filed into the courtyard, a phonograph blared out the *Marseillaise,* loudly but indistinctly. Dervil went to the mess to celebrate. Unused to the food, and especially the wine, he became ill and spent the next two days in bed.

EPILOGUE

"It is easier to cross the Sahara from one end to the other than the outer
—or even the central—boulevards of Paris," Major Paul Duclos wrote
to his wife from In Salah in 1911. "The security there is unique in the
world." Given the attrition rate of pedestrians on the Paris boulevards,
the statement was probably not excessive. That this was so was due to
expeditions like that which had been led by Dinaux. These received little
publicity at the time: "Two lines in small print will appear on page 50 of
a newspaper. That is enough!" Dervil wrote. However, this expedition,
like other similar ones which constantly crisscrossed the central Sahara
were important. In this way, the French were able to demonstrate beyond
doubt that the Ahaggar was no longer an inaccessible fortress. This
divided the Tuareg of the Ahaggar, strengthened the peace party, drove
those who opposed them to Ghat and Ghadames in Turkish territory,
and consolidated their hold on the Ahaggar under their chosen amenoukal, Moussa ag Amastane. Thus, the history of the conquest of the
Sahara, which reads like a series of small detonations, ended with something more like a whimper than an ear-splitting explosion.

The French conquest of the Sahara at the turn of the century has
quite rightly been hailed as a significant military achievement. The problem was never one of resistance—the Tuareg were neither numerous nor
well-armed. Rather, it was one of accessibility. The French were pushed
to find some rather imaginative solutions to campaigning in such a vast
and inhospitable land. That they did so is certainly a credit to the determination, physical resistance and intelligence of the French officers and
NCOs who pioneered and later served in the Saharians, a group who by
their own (probably correct) estimation formed an elite within the
French army. However, it must not be forgotten in the general praise
heaped upon the Saharians that it was the goum of Lieutenant Cottenest
which broke Tuareg resistance at Tit. The Saharians became the police-
men of the desert, the cops who enforced the conquest.

While the French were able to police the Ahaggar effectively, incursions by "dissidents" from east and west were a constant source of annoyance. In 1911, Italy invaded Libya and began a conflict there which was to last for the better part of twenty years. The French profited from that war by occupying Djanet, opposite Ghat, which had been claimed by Turkey. This gave them a base of operations in the east from which they could patrol the Ajjer country more effectively.

The real problem for the Saharians came out of the west. Raiders from the Moroccan oasis of the Tafilalet proved a constant head-ache, and one which they controlled with only intermittent success. While these were small-scale snatches of camels and women, they could on occasion prove bloody affairs indeed. For instance, in 1903, a Saharian patrol ambushed at the wells of Hassi Rezel lost twenty-one men. One of their number sent for help rode the eighty miles back to In Salah in twenty-four hours and collapsed on the steps of the offi-cers' mess.

The most epic chase occurred in 1912, when a "light group" of fifty Saharians under Major Charlet set off in pursuit of Berbers from the Tafilalet. These Berbers had carried out a series of successful raids in the Sudan which included the annihilation of a patrol of eleven Senegalese tirailleurs and their French officer. Able to move faster than the *rezzou* (raiding party) laden with its booty of captured camels and blacks, Char-let made good progress. Then a violent sandstorm forced him to halt for a day and, incidentally, wiped out the tracks of the Berbers. By guessing correctly that the *rezzou* would make for the wells of Zmila, 400 miles southwest of In Salah, Charlet was able to inflict a nasty surprise on them: "We had to move quickly," wrote Charlet. "Our animals were exhausted. Several stopped altogether. The others, energetically stimu-lated, got up a little speed." The victory was complete:

The enemy left nineteen dead today. He abandoned to us 5 prisoners, 66 captive black men, women and children; 67 re-peating rifles 1874 model, 21 sabers, 32 saddles, 621 camels . . . and spoils enough to encourage our men the next time. . . . Only 20 men without water or food escaped from Zmila and they will not get far on their harassed camels. There must be a few to take to the Tafilalet, and to Mauritania for that matter, the holy terror of the "Red Belts" of the Tidikelt. We should have some peace for a while.

Charlet's peace had yet to begin, however, for he had to transport his prizes back to In Salah. Fortunately, he came upon a caravan from which he was able to buy provisions at "exorbitant prices." Otherwise, much of his time was taken up baby-sitting for his "black nursery" of twenty-eight children, the oldest of whom was only four. They were carried in leather *guerbas,* captured from the *rezzou,* suspended from the saddles of the camels: "As several contained butter, the kids emerged shining, until the wind dusted them with sand and gave them masks."

As for the prisoners, "I let them live and allow them to follow us, but I do not feed them. They can live off the carcasses of the camels which are killed when they can no longer walk." This was a major concession. Prisoners were not infrequently killed, especially if badly wounded, which was perhaps not a bad thing. Dervil's Saharian corporal killed a captured bandit who insulted him: "God damn you, son of a Chaamba prostitute who has sold himself to the roumi!" The corporal shot him in the head, and then filled his mouth with sand. Charlet wrote that what his prisoners feared most was being abandoned in the desert.

Charlet's *contre-rezzou* was extremely successful, by his own admission unexpectedly so. However, the cost had been extremely high: 2 officers, 3 caids, and 40 Senegalese tirailleurs killed and 200 others "dead of thirst . . . and more than 1,500 camels, not to mention 80 to 100 blacks." Most pursuits fell far short of success, merely striking into thin air. The Berbers of the Tafilalet and the Blue Men of Mauritania (so called because the indigo dye used in their clothing colors their skins blue) were able to scurry back to the sanctuary of Morocco or lose themselves in the desert wastes before they could be run to ground. This is not to disparage the Saharians. They worked under enormous handicaps, not the least of which was the vast area which they policed. There were seldom more than 200 Saharians on patrol at any one time, and this was for an area twice the size of France. Raiders enjoyed the advantage of surprise and often a superior knowledge of the terrain. Also, try as they might, the French were never able to match the raiders in speed and mobility. The raiders would travel through a relatively populated area, mix their tracks with those of caravans or herds of camels, and then disperse in different directions. The astonishing thing is not that so many raiders escaped, but that a few were actually caught.

The effectiveness of the Saharians also declined with the approach of the Great War. This was due in part to the fact that many of the most energetic and pioneering officers were siphoned off to participate in the conquest of Morocco and subsequently to fight, and die, on the Western Front. This was the fate of Pein. This *enfant terrible* of the Sahara who in many respects deserves more credit than Laperrine for its conquest, was called to serve on the Moroccan frontier, where General Lyautey was nibbling away at the sultan's territory in mouthfuls so small that Paris would not notice. One of those mouthfuls was Ras-el-Ain, a hundred miles into Morocco, which Lyautey "diplomatically" rebaptized Berguent in the hope that his indiscipline might pass unnoticed.

Pein was put in charge of the goum at Berguent, and behaved with typical impetuosity. He could not be made to understand that this insistence on pursuing raiders into the Rif provoked howls of protest from the Sultan, protests echoed by Berlin and Madrid, which threatened Lyautey's prudent, piecemeal absorption of Morocco. In 1908, enraged by what he saw as Lyautey's hesitation in achieving the Moroccan conquest, Pein requested and received a transfer to Algiers, and there began to plan the project which many saw as proof positive of his dementia— the crossing of the Sahara from Algiers to Timbuktu *on a motorcycle!*

In fact, Pein's plan was less insane than it first appears. He saw it as the first experiment in the use of motorized transport in the desert and as a way for the Saharians eventually to gain an unbeatable advantage over their enemies. Also he believed that a road between Algiers and Timbuktu offered a cheap and practical alternative to the elusive Transsaharian railway. Pein left Algiers in April 1909 with his batman and reached Ouargla a few days later without serious difficulty. However, between Ouargla and El Goléa he became hopelessly stuck in the dunes. He tried to force a passage, and in doing so exhausted his reserve stocks of petrol and his rations. Fortunately, Pein had taken the precaution of having several of his Chaamba follow on their camels. But when they finally caught up with him twenty-four hours later, the two Frenchmen were almost dead from thirst.

Many, including Lyautey, had hoped that Pein would succeed Laperrine as commander of the oases. But in 1909, he was promoted to lieutenant colonel and named to command the Forty-sixth infantry regiment in Paris. In 1912, he was transferred to Morocco, which the French had invaded in earnest, to serve on the staff of General Henri Gouraud, commander of the Fez region. On the outbreak of war, he was sent to the Western Front, there to command the first brigade of the Moroccan

Division, composed of tirailleurs and foreign legionnaires. This was to become the French army's most decorated division in the Great War. And no wonder, with officers like Pein leading from the front.

On May 9, 1915, his brigade was ordered to attack Hill 140 on the Artoise front near Givenchy. After a preliminary bombardment lasting four hours, the men rushed from the trenches toward the German positions. The result was a massacre; the shrapnel shells had hardly dented the German trenches. Pein could not contain himself: He leaped out of his command post and joined the second attack wave. Incredibly, his men managed to seize Hill 140, but at colossal cost. As the survivors arranged themselves in the trenches to await the inevitable counterattack, Pein went forward personally to reconnoiter the ground to his front. A sniper brought him down with a bullet that entered his side and penetrated his chest. He crawled into a shell hole, where two legionnaires found him. Pein was transported to the rear, but died soon after. He was buried in the cemetery of the small village of Acq, just behind the lines, his head appropriately pointing toward the enemy lines. That afternoon, a German counterattack drove Pein's brigade from Hill 140.

Many Saharians were to die in the Great War, but no death attracted as much attention as that of Charles de Foucauld.

The war could not fail to upset the stability of the Sahara. In October 1912, Turkey had relinquished control of Libya to Italy. The Arabs and Bedouins of the Fezzan and Tripolitania did not wait for Rome to declare war on Constantinople before they began to harass their new colonial masters. By December 1914, many of the Italian garrisons in the Fezzan had fled to the sanctuary of Southern Algeria and Tunisia. In March 1915, Rome ordered a counteroffensive. Four thousand Italian troops and 3,500 Libyan auxiliaries marched south from Tripoli. The campaign was a disaster. Encouraged by their coreligionists, the auxiliaries turned on the Italians, only a handful of whom managed to regain the coast. In the process, they abandoned 5,000 rifles and ammunition by the cratefuls. For the first time in their history, the desert tribes were extremely well armed.

The French Sahara soon reaped the whirlwind of the Italian debacle. On March 16, a *harka* of several hundred men led by Turkish officers laid siege to Djanet, which was held by a minuscule garrison of forty-three Saharians and goumiers from Ouargla under the command of two French corporals. After withstanding a siege of nine days, the garrison escaped on the night of March 25, to begin an exhausting march across the Tassili, only to be captured two days later after having been betrayed by two deserters.

The fall of Djanet was followed by the siege of Agadez in the Air. The Ahaggar was now open to raiders from the south and east. Moussa had adopted an equivocal posture now that the French were hard-pressed. Rumors ran like wildfire through the Ahaggar of an imminent French collapse. Despite this, Foucauld refused to move to the safety of Fort Motylinski, fifty miles southeast of Tamanrasset. His only conces-sion was to agree to the construction of a small fortress at Tamanrasset —a mud square eighteen yards long on each side, with no exterior openings save a thick wooden door, reinforced at each angle by crenel-lated towers and surrounded by a ditch eighteen feet deep: "There is nothing new under the sun," he wrote to a friend in France. "When I see my walls, I think of the fortified churches and convents of the tenth century. How old things come back, and how that which we think gone forever reappears. They have given me six cases of cartridges and thirty Gras carbines which remind me of our youth."

At sunset on December 1, 1916, Foucauld was working inside his fortress behind a bolted door when a group of twenty Ajjer, and an equal number of Ahaggar Tuareg and Haratin who had joined them, ap-proached silently. One of their number, a Haratin named El Madani who knew Foucauld, knocked on the door and called out that he was "the courier from Motylinski." Foucauld opened the door and held out his hand to receive his post. Madani grabbed it and held tight while the others jumped from their hiding places and forced their way into the small fortress. Some began to question Foucauld about the garrison at Motylinski, while others helped themselves to the rifles. Suddenly, from outside came the cry: "The Arabs! The Arabs!" Two Saharians ap-proached on camels. All the Tuareg with the exception of three rushed out, and a lively firefight began. The two Saharians were killed, but the Targui guarding Foucauld, a young man named Serni ag Thera, panicked and shot the priest in the head, killing him instantly. His body was stripped and thrown into the ditch that surrounded the fortress.

The French were understandably indignant over Foucauld's death, although in all probability he had been murdered by accident. The raiders probably had wanted to abduct him and use him as a political bargaining card. And yet, Foucauld was not simply an innocent priest basely murdered. He sent reports on the state of Tuareg opinion and politics in the Ahaggar to In Salah, and, above all, was a symbol of French presence in the desert. He was a legitimate target. Still, his murder could not be left unavenged. Captain La Roche, in command of Fort Motylinski, killed several of the raiders as they fled toward Ghat. Laperrine circulated a list of thirty men who had taken part in the raid. In February 1917, a detachment of Saharians surprised a camp in the Tassili, killing seven men. Among their effects were discovered several articles which had belonged to Foucauld. In 1922, Serni ag Thera, the Targui who had fired the fatal shot, was captured and summarily executed. El Madani, the Haratin who had betrayed Foucauld, fled to Libya and was only arrested by the French in 1944. An old man and very senile, he was released.

Foucauld was buried at Tamanrasset beneath a large monument paid for by the governor general of Algeria. (Later, the body was moved to El Goléa within the confines of a mission established by the White Fathers.) In 1920, another body was put beside Foucauld—that of his friend Laperrine. In 1917, Laperrine had been recalled to the Sahara from the Western Front to put the French back onto the offensive there. The old aggressiveness which had made the reputation of the Saharians in his day had given way to a policy of holding permanent posts, many of which had been abandoned because of the difficulty of supplying them. Laperrine reinstituted his old policy of vigorous patrolling. Moussa, who had been dithering on the fringes of the fight in the Adrar, was brought back to the Ahaggar virtually at gunpoint, as a clear indication that he supported France. A column sent from Zinder broke the siege of Agadez. This took the heart out of the rebellion. By January 1918, the central Sahara was again secure. The Chaamba wanted to punish the Tuareg for their equivocal attitude, and Laperrine restrained them only with difficulty.

In 1920, Laperrine became a passenger in a squadron of five planes which were to cross the Sahara from north to south. His plane disappeared south of Tamanrasset on February 18, 1920. When the wreckage was found nine days later, the pilot and mechanic were still alive. Laperrine, who had sustained a broken collar bone in the crash, had perished. His body was wrapped in airplane cloth and transported on the back of a camel to Tamanrasset.

Laperrine is often seen as the architect of the French conquest of the Sahara. He was certainly an energetic and, as far as the evidence suggests, a humane conqueror. However, he was far less original than his admirers like to claim. The victory at Tit owed little to Laperrine. He perfected the Saharians, eliminated undisciplined elements, transformed them from a heterogeneous force into one which was composed almost exclusively of Chaamba Arabs. However, he did not invent the Saharians, not did he bring about the situation which allowed the conquest to proceed. Laperrine inherited a situation ripe for the conquest, and which had been brought about by a number of officers: Bonnier, Lamy, Cottenest and, above all, Théodore Pein. It was Pein who avenged the Marquis de Morès and cut Tunisia out of the race for the Sahara. It was Pein who forced the occupation of the Tuat. The part-time bandits who manned Pein's goum at Ouargla eventually furnished the hard core of Laperrine's Saharians. Pein (and Cottenest) had done most of the spadework. Laperrine reaped the benefits. The best which could be said of Laperrine was that he policed the desert, more or less efficiently, at remarkably small cost to France.

The coming of the French accelerated changes in the life of the Tuareg. For one thing, it opened the Ahaggar to settlement by Arabs and blacks. With the Arabs came stricter observance of Islam, a trend that Foucauld had resisted in vain. Many Tuareg have abandoned the nomadic life to drift to the Tuat or to Tamanrasset. In the Arabized atmosphere of these new towns, old customs are gradually eroded. Women are increasingly confined, take the veil, and the informality of relationships between men and women which once ruled in the desert is lost. These oases also support the new populations with difficulty. More wells are sunk, the water table drops further, and the vital date palms are threatened. In Salah, which Pein found a collection of honey-colored *ksars* set in a deep green drift of date palms, is now a forest of oil rigs.

At the same time, the life of the desert has diminished to the point of extinction. The great caravans that once marched between the Sudan and the Mediterranean with their cargos of gold, ivory and slaves have vanished. In their place, an occasional truck, army vehicle or tourist car races through a bleak and empty landscape. But the Sahara is no longer one of the world's crossroads. Deprived of its actors, it retains only a shadow of its former glory and mystery. It is like an empty theater, its vast plains, abrupt cliffs and green oases so many stages set for human dramas now long past. But if one climbs to Foucauld's hermitage in the mountains above Tamanrasset and looks out over the dark chimneys of rock, the grandeur, the silence, the sense of sheer infinity is powerful. One then understands why the Tuareg resisted for so long, and why a very few Frenchmen wanted this land for themselves.

NOTES

INTRODUCTION

page ix in central Africa. E. W. Bovill, *The Golden Trade of the Moors.*

I THE MIRAGE

5 originally set himself. G. Moorhouse, *The Fearful Void.*
6 "Nothing but sand . . ." F. Bernard, *Les Deux Missions du Colonel Flatters,* 88.
  "very monotonous." W. J. Harding-King, *A Search for the Masked Tawareks,* 112.
  covered by ocean. E. W. Bovill, *Missions to the Niger,* vol. I, 357.
8 "contrived by man." Moorhouse, *Void,* 274.
  "an interior fire." L. Lehuraux, *Au Sahara avec le Commandant Charlet,* 48.
  in taxes annually. E. F. Gautier, *La Conquête du Sahara,* 218–19.
9 south to In Salah. H. Schirmer, *Le Sahara,* 270.
  "a value in itself." Gautier, *La Conquête,* 235.
  "shall pour millions." Archives historiques de guerre (henceforth AHG).
       IH1032.
10 the French people. *Ibid.*
  per palm tree. Harding-King, *A Search,* 46.
11 stage of nationalism. M. Andrew and A. S. Kanya-Forstner, *France Overseas.*

II THE SHORES OF TRIPOLI

13 "in Mecca or Egypt." L. C. Briggs, *The Tribes of the Sahara,* 49.
14 of the Niger. R. Hallett, *The Penetration of Africa,* 129–31, 156–59.
15 saw it in 1825. E. W. Bovill, *Missions to the Niger,* vol. I, 344.
  to collapse. S. Dearden, *Letters Written During Ten Years' Residence at the
       Court of Tripoli,* p. 14.
  take the place. Bovill, *Missions,* vol. I. 344.
16 "in this manner." Dearden, *Letters,* 36–38.
  "they have obtained." G. F. Lyon, *A Narrative of Travels in Northern Africa in
       the Years 1818–19 and 1820,* 14.
19 for the Marine Hymn. Alan R. Millett, *Semper Fidelis: A History of the U.S.
       Marine Corps,* 43–45.
  this spectacle unseen. Dearden, *Letters,* 39–42.
  according to Laing. Bovill, *Missions,* 345.
20 a staple industry. Lyon, *A Narrative,* 13.
  "of this world." *Ibid.,* 42.
  "at all events silly." W. J. Harding-King, *A Search for the Masked Tawareks,*
       131.

page 20 sun and flies. Dearden, *Letters*, 16.
   21 way of life. A. Chouraqui, *Between East and West: A History of the Jews in North Africa*, 53-55.
      "and fainted." Dearden, *Letters*, 194.
   22 infected person. *Ibid.*, 112–19, 123.
   23 "walked together." *Ibid.*, 157.
      "in cold water." *Ibid.*, 85.
   24 "cost them their lives." *Ibid.*, 162.
   25 "somber melodramas." *Ibid.*, 21.
   26 prove untrustworthy. Bovill, *Missions*, vol. I, 306.

   III   THE DESERT

   27 "find them too true." E. W. Bovill, *Missions to the Niger*, vol. I, 242, 269.
   28 "as low as 62°!" *Ibid.*, 246.
      "still missing." F. Bernard, *Les Deux Missions du Colonel Flatters*, 86, 89.
      Harding-King remarked. W. J. Harding-King, *A Search for the Masked Tawareks*, 156.
      "during this fever." R. Caillié, *Travels through Central Africa, Timbuctoo and across the Great Desert, to Morocco: Performed in the Years 1824–1828*, vol. II, 110.
      of water daily. H. Schirmer, *Le Sahara*, 246.
      unable to swallow it. L. Lehuraux, *Au Sahara avec le Commandant Charlet*, 9.
   29 "by fresh thirst." Caillié, *Travels*, vol. II, 15.
      "love of God." *Ibid.*
      their own urine. *Ibid.*, vol. I, 7.
      "for our camels." Lehuraux, *Charlet*, 62.
   30 "he was saved!" G. Dervil, *Trois grands Africains*, 69.
      "in the Sahara." C. Guilleux, *Journal de route d'un caporal de tirailleurs de la mission saharienne*, 30.
      "Dantesque vision." Lehuraux, *Sur les pistes du désert*, 155.
   31 the camels to drink. Caillié, *Travels*, vol. II, 118.
      "snows of December." Bovill, *Missions*, vol. I, 175.
      beside these oases. Bernard, *Flatters*, 60–61.
      kidney failure. L. C. Briggs, *The Tribes of the Sahara*, 30.
      "sewer-like water." J. Richardson, *Travels in the Great Desert of the Sahara in the Years of 1845 and 1846*, vol. I, 38.
      "an Arab meal." G. F. Lyon, *A Narrative of Travels in Northern Africa in the Years 1818–19 and 1820*, 27.
      "It's depressing." F. Lamy, "Lettres d'El Goléa," *Revue de Paris*, 1903, 285.
      preserved in oil. H. Duveryier, *Les Touareg du nord*, 411.
   32 "greatest delight." Caillié, *Travels*, vol. II, 111.
      "steaming soup." Guilleux, *Journal de route*, 29.
      "his usual food." H. Barth, *Travels and Discoveries in North and Central Africa, 1849–1855*, vol. II, 192.
      from too little. G. Moorhouse, *The Fearful Void*, 69.
      "the courage to eat." Caillié, *Travels*, vol. I, 6–7.
   33 strike out again. Moorhouse, *Void*, 174.

page 33 *"enlivening scenes."* Bovill, *Missions,* vol. I, 365.
(unbeliever). Richardson, *Travels,* vol. I, 150, 194.
Caillié recounted. Caillié, *Travels,* vol. II, 79.
33–4 *to the coast.* E. E. Evans-Prichard, *The Sanusi of Cyrenaica,* 83.
34 *he was courting.* M. Benhazera, *Six Mois chez les Touareg du Ahaggar,* 8.
"motivates this conduct." Duveryier, *Les Touareg,* 273.
"for animals to graze." Richardson, *Travels,* vol. I, 54.
35 *Lyon recounted.* Lyon, *A Narrative,* 54, 59, 90–91.
"the sun did not set." Richardson, *Travels,* vol. I, 150, 163.
36 *"crossing the desert."* Caillié, *Travels,* vol. II, 79.
37 *with the gun cloth.* Harding-King, *A Search,* 8–9.
letters of introduction. Bovill, *Missions,* vol. I, 195.
38 *"pay for everything."* Schirmer, *Le Sahara,* 279.
their meager meal. Moorhouse, *Void,* 103.
"he has offered." Schirmer, *Le Sahara,* 280.
"within closed doors." Lyon, *A Narrative,* 283.
Schirmer concluded. Schirmer, *Le Sahara,* 280.
39 *"the party broke up."* Harding-King, *A Search,* 60–61.
"of my belongings." *Ibid.,* 7.
40 *inconsequential errand.* Moorhouse, *Void,* 178–79.
"tea and sugar." *Ibid.,* 108.
41 *"and discontent."* Bovill, *Missions,* vol. I, 361.
on his stomach. Caillié, *Travels,* vol. I, 75.
"for the complaint." Lyon, *A Narrative,* 117, 210–11.
42 *"literally choaked."* S. Dearden, *Letters Written During a Ten Years' Residence at the Court of Tripoli,* 119.
"to bear children!" Bovill, *Missions,* vol. I, 363.
"to their temperance." Caillié, *Travels,* vol. I, 72.
of the Arabs. R. Hérison, *Avec le Père Foucauld et le Général Laperrine,* 222.
insalubrious posting. Duveryier, *Les Touareg,* 282.
43 *"in the desert."* Harding-King, *A Search,* 220.
"disease is madness." E. F. Gautier, *La Conquête du Sahara,* 30.
"in a steam vessel." Bovill, *Missions,* vol. I, 808.
43–4 *[chart of expenses]* *Ibid.,* 199.
45 *"of his superiority."* Bernard, *Flatters,* 16.
runs an Arab proverb. G. Gester, *Le Sahara,* 4.
nauseating liquid. *Ibid.,* 5–6.
to recuperate. Lamy, *"Lettres d'El Goléa,"* *Revue de Paris,* 1903, 283.
"the bandstand at Cannes." *Ibid.,* 285.
enough water. Bernard, *Flatters,* 81.
46 *hunter was close enough.* Harding-King, *A Search,* 173–74.
well be imagined. Hérison, *Père Foucauld,* 122.
"expression of love." J. P. Dorian, *Quinze nuits au pays de la peur: Souvenirs inédits du grand Amenokal, Chef des Touareg,* 12.
came the answer. Harding-King, *A Search,* 103.
"with a grunt." *Ibid.,* 13.
47 *"are impressive."* Hérison, *Père Foucauld,* 55.
always swearing. F. R. Rodd, *People of the Veil,* 255.

page 47 *"But there is none."* Lehuraux, *Lettres d'un saharien, Commandant Paul Duclos,* 110.

"some banisters." *Ibid.*

school at Saumur. *Ibid.,* 111.

unless doped. G. Gester, *Le Sahara,* 3.

48 *crossing from France.* Gautier, *La Conquête,* 81.

"serpentine movement." Lehuraux, *Lettres,* 110.

"the lord of creation." Moorhouse, *Void,* 209.

IV   THE OASIS

50 *had snatched them.* R. Caillié, *Travels through Central Africa, Timbuctoo and across the Great Desert, to Morocco: Performed in the Years 1824–1828,* vol. II, 106–7.

conjectures were formed. E. W. Bovill, *Missions to the Niger,* vol. I, 347.

"the loads arranged." *Ibid.,* 349.

"of doing business." J. Richardson, *Travels in the Great Desert of the Sahara in the Years of 1845 and 1846,* vol. I, 68.

"haste from Satan." C. Trumelet, *Les Français dans le désert,* 4.

51 *among themselves.* W. J. Harding-King, *A Search for the Masked Tawareks,* 12, 90.

"musical language." *Ibid.,* 9.

"tumultuous array." Richardson, *Travels,* vol. I, 37.

52 *"are bare-headed."* *Ibid.,* 32.

wrote Laing. Bovill, *Missions,* vol. I, 353.

"nearly suffocated." Richardson, *Travels,* vol. I, 49.

53 *of grazing camels.* Harding-King, *A Search,* 121.

celestial navigation. H. Duveyrier, *Les Touareg du nord,* 423.

the tracks of the camels. Caillié, *Travels,* vol. II, 91.

he concluded. G. Dervil, *Trois grands Africains,* 51.

54 *the deal was concluded.* Harding-King, *A Search,* 18.

the guardian angel. Trumelet, *Les Français,* 11.

each other up. G. Moorhouse, *The Fearful Void,* 108.

on their faces. Harding-King, *A Search,* 36.

55 *are unnecessary.* *Ibid.,* 119.

"of the horizon." Richardson, *Travels,* vol. I, 88.

Laing reported. Bovill, *Missions,* vol. I, 374.

a tropical garden. Harding-King, *A Search,* 70.

56 *"closely built town."* Bovill, *Missions,* vol. I, 376.

of dead animals. Harding-King, *A Search,* 57.

of skye light. Bovill, *Missions,* vol. I, 376–77.

bring out in droves. G. F. Lyon, *A Narrative of Travels in Northern Africa in the Years 1818–19 and 1820,* 187.

57 *commercial falsehoods.* *Ibid.,* 283–84.

"or his mind?" Trumelet, *Les Français,* 3.

58 *not at all revengeful.* Lyon, *A Narrative,* 283.

"it goes to the head." R. Hérison, *Avec le Père Foucauld et le Général Laperrine,* 150.

page 58 *"good humoured drunkards."* Lyon, *A Narrative,* 283, 292.
from the Sudan to Tripoli. Bovill, *Caravans of the Old Sahara,* 253.
59 *to roam freely. Ibid.,* 257.
by the slavers. Caillié, *Travels,* vol. II, 115.
"for feigning sickness." Lyon, *A Narrative,* 79, 331.
"their native melody." H. Barth, *Travels and Discoveries in North and Central Africa, 1849–1855, vol. I,* 308.
"a few weeks before." Lyon, *A Narrative,* 326.
"sitting on the sand." Ibid., 263.
60 *sufficiently docile.* R. Maugham, *The Slaves of Timbuktu,* 169.
higher prices than men. Lyon, *A Narrative,* 154.
found no buyer. Bovill, *Caravans,* 259.
"season of pleasure." Bovill, *Missions,* I, 384–5.
"as mere slaves." Riley, *The Loss of the American Brig Commerce,* 400.
lost face. J. Keenan, *The Tuareg, People of the Ahaggar,* 98.
61 *a moment of anger.* Maugham, *Slaves,* 168.
"feel myself a slave." Ibid., 171.
the traffic in slaves. Lehuraux, *Lettres d'un saharienne, Commandant Paul Duclos,* 119.
bought slaves themselves. M. Baroli, *La Vie quotidienne des français en Algérie, 1830–1914,* 154.
over economic interests. Briggs, *The Tribes of the Sahara,* 789.
62 *Turkish and Tuareg parties.* H. Schirmer, *Le Sahara,* 300.
of the "Gharba" (westerners). L. C. Briggs, *Tribes,* 196.
"the rival sof." Richardson, *Travels,* 191–192, 203.
Schirmer concluded. H. Schirmer, *Le Sahara,* 300.
"All the people govern." Richardson, *Travels,* 142.
63 *by artesian wells.* Schirmer, *Le Sahara,* 288.
to other gardens. Harding-King, *A Search,* 54–5.
64 *"war around a well."* Schirmer, *Le Sahara,* 301.

V   THE PEOPLE OF THE VEIL

65 *"the arms of treachery."* H. Duveyrier, *Les Touareg du nord,* 283.
"the Christians of the desert." E. W. Bovill, *The Golden Trade of the Moors,* 49.
"were fond of saying." J. Richardson, *Travels in the Great Desert of the Sahara in the Years of 1845 and 1846, vol. I,* 172.
"not understand you." H. Schirmer, *Le Sahara,* 274–76.
66 *of grain and seeds.* G. Dervil, *Trois grands Africains,* 60.
anthropologist F. R. Rodd. F. R. Rodd, *The People of the Veil,* 157.
Dervil wrote. Dervil, *Africains,* 88.
67 *that of another.* H. Lhote, *Les Touareg du Hoggar,* 315.
68 *"of the desert."* Richardson, *Travels,* 135.
"captain of a ship." L. C. Briggs, *The Tribes of the Sahara,* 202–3.
cannot prevent it. Richardson, *Travels,* 34.
between Murzuk and Bornu. Rodd, *People,* 192–93.
70 *obtain their object.* H. Barth, *Travels and Discoveries in North and Central Africa, 1849–1855, vol. I,* 239.

page 71 as best they could. Bovill, *Missions to the Niger*, vol. I, 299–300.

"after much washing." G. F. Lyon, *A Narrative of Travels in Northern Africa in the Years 1818–19 and 1820*, 111.

required by Islam. M. Benhazera, *Six Mois chez les Touareg du Ahaggar*, 33.

of blacks. R. Maugham, *The Slaves of Timbuktu*, 177.

72 "of European manufacture." W. J. Harding-King, *A Search for the Masked Tawareks*, 303.

"to other people." Rodd, *People*, 163.

"he is an amrid [serf]." Benhazera, *Six Mois*, 47.

"of Arab women." Duveyrier, *Les Touareg*, 383.

72–3 "strong robust, tireless." *Ibid.*, 382.

73 saying his prayers. R. Hérison, *Avec le Père Foucauld et le Général Laperrine*, 125.

basketball coach. L. C. Briggs, *Tribes*, 124.

were too small. F. Bernard, *Les Deux Missions du Colonel Flatters*, 45.

inexhaustible. Duveyier, *Les Touareg*, 383–85.

74 "a rascally lot." L. C. Briggs, *Tribes*, 155.

"I have ever seen." Harding-King, *A Search*, 220.

"over the shoulders." Hérison, *Père Foucauld*, 212.

its silk lining. Benhazera, *Six Mois*, 35–37.

75 to undertake talks. Lhote, *Les Touareg*, 352.

they announced confidently. Hérison, *Père Foucauld*, 220–21.

"coveted possessions." Rodd, *People*, 194.

extremely tedious. Hérison, *Père Foucauld*, 195.

"give me." *Ibid.*, 192–94.

76 "would be naked." Dervil, *Africains*, 60.

than to give. *Ibid.*, 61–62.

driven to shifting camp. Benhazera, *Six Mois*, 54.

"on a still night." Harding-King, *A Search*, 43.

upside down. J. Keenan, *The Tuareg, People of the Ahaggar*, 151.

77 on to destruction. Harding-King, *A Search*, 71.

within a year. Hérison, *Père Foucauld*, 154.

"an evil way." Dervil, *Africains*, 208–9.

78 faithful lieutenant. *Ibid.*, 67.

made them go. R. Bazin, *Charles de Foucauld*, 327.

"in the singer." L. Lehuraux, *Au Sahara avec le Commandant Charlet*, 88.

"credulous." Bazin, *Foucauld*, 327.

"openness." Schirmer, *Le Sahara*, 279.

not subsistence. Keenan, *The Tuareg*, 34.

79 their ugliness. *Ibid.*, 129–35.

"two assistants." Caillié, *Travels through Central Africa, Timbuctoo and across the Great Desert, to Morocco: Performed in the Years 1824–1828*, vol. II, 66.

could wear. Harding-King, *A Search*, 314.

"a sculptor." C. Guilleux, *Journal de route d'un caporal de tirailleurs de la mission Saharienne, 1898–1900*, 59.

"of their breeding." Rodd, *People*, 172–73.

slightest pretext. Lhote, *Les Touareg*, 294.

page 79   *the Tuareg said.* Dervil, *Africains,* 63.
    wrote Dervil. Ibid., 62.
    "their own way." Rodd, *People,* 165.
  80 *western battlefields.* AHG, 1 H 1036.
    Briggs writes. L. C. Briggs, *Tribes,* 132.
    no word for "virgin." Lhote, *Les Touareg,* 289.
    all had syphilis. Hérison, *Père Foucauld,* 222.
    "surpass all others." R. Kipling, *Plain Tales from the Hills,* 86.
  81 *"sign of perversion."* Lhote, *Les Touareg,* 289.
    light-hearted reply. Dervil, *Africains,* 61.
    "take no notice." Ibid.
    "it is unknown." Ibid.
    "have us believe." Briggs, *Tribes,* 130–31.
  82 *"sort of customs?"* Benhazera, *Six Mois,* 9.
    outlaw the abal. Bazin, *Foucauld,* 376–77.
    to have their child. Lhote, *Les Touareg,* 290.
    throughout the Sudan. Briggs, *Tribes,* 250.
    to their parents. Benhazera, *Six Mois,* 19.

VI   THE TRANSSAHARIAN

  86 *"to its yoke."* Duponchel, *Le chemin de fer transsaharien,* 338.
    social undesirables. Ibid., 227, 243–245, 338.
  92 *"listen to this nonsense."* Lamy, "Lettres d'El Goléa," *Revue de Paris,* 1903,
      296–98.
  93 *"start to wrangle." Ibid.*
  95 *"the interior of Africa."* R. Pottier, *Flatters,* 51.
    "with these oases." Ibid., 52.
    "considered definitely lost." Ibid., 53.
  96 *"to carry out." Ibid.,* 52–53.

VII   THE FIRST EXPEDITION

  97 *"assassinated peacefully?"* R. Pottier, *Flatters,* 78.
  98 *"preparations for departure." Ibid.*
  99 *"the rest in Barbary."* M. Baroli, *La Vie quotidienne des français en Algérie,*
      1830–1914, 93.
 100 *take care of them. Ibid.,* 76.
    "inextinguishable volcano." V. G. Kiernan, *From Conquest to Collapse:*
      European Empires from 1815 to 1960, 75.
 101 *"a detestable cesspool."* Pottier, *Flatters,* 83.
    small mounds of mud and sticks. W. J. Harding-King, *A Search for the Masked*
      Tawareks, 121.
    "kitchen refuse which may be handy." Ibid., 27.
    "polished by continual use." Ibid., 73.
 102 *"he trotted through them." Ibid.,* 73–75.
    "speech of the men." Ibid., 75.
 103 *"we shall buy nothing."* Pottier, *Flatters,* 84.
    "a pair of boots." F. Bernard, *Les Deux Missions du Colonel Flatters,* 25.
    "which flow freely." Ibid., 29.

page 103 forehead of one of them. Harding-King, *A Search*, 79–81.
"smoking their kef." Bernard, *Flatters*, 278.

104 rift in the expedition. *Ibid.*, 35.
"immense forest." *Ibid.*, 40.
over the rooftops. *Ibid.*, 40–41.
"even morals." H. Duveryier, *Les Touareg du nord*, 289.

105 sampling fingers. Harding-King, 36.
"individual in existence." *Ibid.*, 20–21.
in two days. Bernard, *Flatters*, 45.

106 force of Arabs. Pottier, *Flatters*, 87–8.
"the first Tuareg attack." Bernard, *Flatters*, 49.

107 of his command. *Ibid.*, 67.

108 will die immediately. J. Mélia, *Le Drame de la mission Flatters*, 66.
spy out the expedition. Bernard, *Flatters*, 96–98.

109 of his subordinates. *Ibid.*, 102–3.
"a fantastic dimension." *Ibid.*, 105.
"a fantastic price." *Ibid.*, 108.
"which was unbelievable." *Ibid.*, 125.

110 "can get away." R. Pottier, *Flatters*, 100.
"against his better judgment." Bernard, *Flatters*, 133.
"the price of things." Pottier, *Flatters*, 102.

VIII   THE MASSACRE

111 "Algerian Chaamba and Tuareg." R. Pottier, *Flatters*, 105.

112 "guaranteeing better security." *Ibid.*, 111.

113 "we will not open it." H. Schirmer, "*Pourquoi Flatters et ses compagnons sont morts*," 565.

114 "walking on sand." Ministère des travaux publiques, *Documents relatifs à la mission dirigée au sud d'Algérie par le Lieutenant colonel Flatters*, 432.
he wrote to his wife. R. Pottier, *Flatters*, 115.
"water man and beast." *Ibid.*, 118.

115 "in their undertaking." *Ibid.*, 120.
who "know nothing." *Ibid.*, 122.

116 who opposed him. F. Bernard, *Les Deux Missions du Colonel Flatters*, 205.
"a desert of rock and sand." R. Pottier, *Flatters*, 124.
"bring us bad luck?" *Ibid.*, 125.
"and will guide you." *Ibid.*, 126.

117 "over his shoulder." F. Patorni, *Récits faits par trois survivants de la mission Flatters*, 20.
as quickly as possible. Ministère des travaux publiques, *Documents*, 337.
via Ghat. Pottier, *Flatters*, 128–30.

118 to the wells. Bernard, *Flatters*, 233–4.

120 allowed the tirailleurs to escape. Patorni, *Récits*, 26.

122 "his legs paralyzed." *Ibid.*, 29.

123 eaten raw by the men. Pottier, *Flatters*, 145.

124 "perfidiousness and ferocity." *Ibid.*, 148–9.
"an extraordinary competence." *Ibid.*, 150–1.

IX   THE SOUTHERN APPROACHES

page 127 *"scratch it as he pleases."* S. Howe, *Les Héros du Sahara*, 48.
128 *"spring up from the soil."* Ibid., 51.
"tenacity of old errors." H. Schirmer, *Le Sahara*, 407–9.
he proclaimed. S. Howe, *Les Héros*, 48.
128–9 *Miribel and MacMahon.* Ibid., 51.
129 *Schirmer declared.* Schirmer, *Le Sahara*, 420.
130 *"but a reality."* A. S. Kanya-Forstner, *The Conquest of the Western Sudan*, 162–3.
of military expansion. V. G. Kiernan, *From Conquest to Collapse: European Empires from 1815 to 1960*, 165.
132 *"to excite admiration."* R. Caillié, *Travels through Central Africa, Timbuctoo and Across the Great Desert, to Morocco: Performed in the Years 1824–1828*, vol. II, 49.
"market is a desert." Ibid., vol. II, 51.
"a sort of closet." Barth, *Travels and Discoveries in North and Central Africa, 1849–1855*, vol. III, 303.
"and his followers." Caillié, *Travels*, vol. II, 47, 49–50, 56, 64.
133 *killed in action.* P. Chalmin, *L'Officier français de 1815 à 1870*, 29.
135 *published in 1911.* R. Girardet, *L'Idée coloniale en France*, 77.
their immediate superiors. W. B. Cohen, *"French Colonial Service"*, 492.
from Chez Maxim's. Kanya-Forstner, *Conquest*, 209–14.
136 *"use your own judgment."* E. Bonnier, *L'Occupation de Tombouctou*, 33.
141 *"extremely trying."* J. J. Joffre, *Opérations de la colonne Joffre avant et après l'occupation de Tombouctou*, Paris, 1895.
142 *Jewish financiers.* La Libre Parole, February 11, 1894.
"the French public." Kanya-Forstner, *Conquest*, 223.
"in the Sudan." S. Howe, *Les Héros du Sahara*, 84.
of the government. Kanya-Forstner, *Conquest*, 228.
"beat them to it." C. Andrew, *Théophile Delcassé and the Making of the Entente Cordiale*, 36.
144 *in the field.* See Andrew and Kanya-Forstner, *France Overseas*.
brought to book. M. Mathieu, *La Mission Afrique Centrale*, 14.
145 *"who can blame them?"* Andrew, *Delcassé*, 39.

X   THE MORÈS AFFAIR

151 *"only by swimming."* R. Pottier, *Mission Foureau-Lamy*, 76.
153 *referring to Flatters.* Ibid., 85.
154 *"republican and socialist."* The quotations in the following pages are taken from A. Martel, *Les Confins Sahara—Tripolitains de la Tunisie, 1881–1911*, vol. I, pp. 680–725. For Morès, see also: M. Barrès, *Une vengeance dans le désert*; J. Delahaye, *Les Assassins et les vengeurs de Morès*; F. Pascal, *L'assassinat de Morès, un crime d'état*.
160 *man to benefit.* Martel, *Ibid.*
162 *not all "ogres."* Pottier, *Mission*, 95.
163 *"brève mais touchante."* Ibid., 96–8.

XI   THE FOUREAU-LAMY MISSION

page *164* the Saharian cake. A. Martel, *Les Confins Sahara—Tripolitains de la Tunisie,
1881–1911,* vol. I, 800. See also K. J. Perkins, *Quaids, Captains and
Colons, French Military Administration in the Colonial Maghreb, 1844–
1934,* 154, 215–16.

166 "thousands of stars." R. Pottier, *Mission Foureau-Lamy,* 103.
"mark on the neck." C. Guilleux, *Journal de route d'un caporal de tirailleurs de
la mission saharienne, 1898–1900,* 21–22.

167 "seduce the natives." R. Pottier, *Mission,* 109.
"on our coattails." *Ibid.,* 110.
"very lucky." C. Guilleux, *Journal,* 22.

168 "Reibell wondered." R. Pottier, *Mission,* 112.
"into the pot." C. Guilleux, *Journal,* 24–25.
"search for water." *Ibid.,* 29.

169 "of heavy oppression." R. Pottier, *Mission Foureau-Lamy,* 121.
in the bottle. *Ibid.,* 122.
stomachs in agony. Guilleux, *Journal,* 31.
Lamy wrote. R. Pottier, *Mission,* 127.

171 "their inflated stomachs." Guilleux, *Journal,* 38.
one French soldier. R. Hérison, *Avec le Père Foucauld et le Général Laperrine,
1909–1911,* 252–53.
through the Sahara. Guilleux, *Journal,* 36.
above their heads. *Ibid.,* 40.

172 Guilleux wrote. *Ibid.,* 40–41.
men in tears. *Ibid.,* 41–42.

173 in situ. *Ibid.,* 47.
"such a pillage." *Ibid.,* 54.

174 "nor death." *Ibid.,* 68.
"getting better." *Ibid.,* 73.

175 "this damned country." *Ibid.,* 74.
of dead camels. E. W. Bovill, *Caravans of the Old Sahara,* 251.

176 because of the Tuareg. H. Barth, *Travels and Discoveries in North and Central
Africa, 1849–1855,* vol. I, 319, 329.
"any kind of offal." *Ibid.,* vol. I, 310, 323–24.

177 in the background. Guilleux, *Journal,* 98–99.
"so that we suffer." *Ibid.,* 145.

178 of them to bathe. *Ibid.,* 149.

179 in his diary R. Pottier, *Mission,* 144.
"never seen them." Guilleux, *Journal,* 201.

180 hangs over everything. *Ibid.,* 203.

XII   THE MEN WHO WOULD BE KINGS

181 Ministry of War. O. Meynier, *Les Conquérants du Tchad.*

182 "an intolerable situation." M. Mathieu, *La Mission Afrique Centrale.* 39.
Much of this chapter is drawn from the material in this excellent
thesis.
"out of pleasure." *Ibid.,* 41.

page 182 his black mistress. *Ibid.,* 40.
 183–4 from the colonial ministry. *Ibid.,* 60.
 185 was strictly free-lance. Martel, *Les Confins Sahara-Tripolitains de la Tunisie, 1881–1911,* vol. I, 677.
 186 cloth for trade. Mathieu, *La Mission,* 52.
 187 "what he is doing." *Ibid.,* 79.
 188 on the spot. *Journal officiel—Députés,* November 23, 1900, 2272.
 189 "were massacred." Mathieu, *La Mission,* 102.
    the official report. *Ibid.,* 97.
 191 to send couriers. *Ibid.,* 132.
    Joalland later testified. *Ibid.,* 138.
 192 told the sergeant. *Le Temps,* 20 September, 1899.
    "I will attack." *Ibid.*
    obey the captain. *Ibid.*
    "to the death." Mathieu, *La Mission,* 148.
 193 "so many months." *Ibid.,* 150.
    in Voulet's eyes. *Ibid.*
    "the Duc de Guise?" *Ibid.,* 151.
 194 "of these bandits." *Ibid.,* 156.
 195 "civilizing mission" in Africa. *Le Temps,* 23 August, 1899.
    "native duplicity." *Echo de Paris,* August 23, 1899.
 196 an English soldier. V. G. Kiernan, *From Conquest to Collapse: European Empires from 1815 to 1960,* 130.
    scientific knowledge. Mathieu, *La Mission,* 192.
    "a scirocco blowing." S. Howe, *Les Héros du Sahara,* 80.
    "difficulties of isolation." AHG, 1 H 1016.
    "the Central African Mission." Mathieu, *La Mission,* 185.

XIII   THE CONQUEST OF LAKE CHAD

 198 "the mission in Parliament." R. Pottier, *Mission Foureau-Lamy,* 147.
    "silent and mournful steppe." *Ibid.,* 151.
 199 "a veritable ossuary." *Ibid.,* 154.
    behind the foliage. E. Reibell, *Carnet de route de la mission saharienne, Foureau-Lamy,* 262–63.
    floating plants. Barth, *Travels and Discoveries in North and Central Africa, 1849 to 1855,* vol. II, 62–63.
 200 "near the edge." R. Pottier, *Mission,* 155.
    Bornu from Rabih. O. Meynier, *Les Conquérants du Tchad,* 268.
 202 of a house. Guilleux, *Journal de route d'un caporal de tirailleurs de la mission saharienne, 1898–1900,* 292–93.
    "without modesty." *Ibid.,* 295.
    more arrived daily. R. Pottier, *Mission,* 164.
 203 "to get here!" Guilleux, *Journal,* 323.
    "magnificent rifle range." *Ibid.,* 328.
 205 of the camp. *Ibid.,* 329.
    "to the Chari." E. Reibell, *Carnet de route,* 328.
    "three or four high." Guilleux, *Journal,* 330.

page 206 *"red with blood."* Reibell, *Carnet,* 328.
207 *"a shapeless jelly."* Guilleux, *Journal,* 330.

XIV   THE TUAT

210 *"consumption of water."* AHG, 1 H 1032, July 19, 1900, 9.
211 *"to help me."* L. Lehuraux, *Le Conquérant des oasis, Colonel Théodore Pein,* 34-36.
the Tuat was occupied. *Le Figaro,* January 9, 1900.
213 in the Tidikelt. G. Gester, *Le Sahara,* 73.
214 *"in the same conditions."* L. Lehuraux, *Le Conquérant,* 52.
to execute it. C. Andrew, *Théophile Delcassé and the Making of the Entente Cordiale,* 154.
215 *"of every description."* L. Lehuraux, *Le Conquérant,* 54.
216 *"in the future."* Ibid., 57.
to open their gates. L. Voinot, *Opérations dans les oasis sahariennes,* 7.
217 *"dictate my conscience!"* L. Lehuraux, *Le Conquérant,* 60–61.
218 *"and deliver us."* Ibid., 59.
find his pasture. Tillion, *La Conquête des oasis sahariennes,* 25.
219 3,000 poorly armed men. Lehuraux, *Le Conquérant,* 74–75.

XV   THE RESISTANCE

222 *"do it on purpose."* quoted in C. Andrew, *Théophile Delcassé and the Making of the Entente Cordiale,* 153–4.
226 pay it off. Lehuraux, *Le Conquérant des oasis,* 80–81.
urgent reinforcements. Voinot, *Opérations dans les oasis Sahariennes,* 19–21.
230 witnessed a battle. *Revue de Paris,* "L'Attaque de Timimoun," July 15, 1903, 361–72.
231 *"until help came."* Lehuraux, *Le Conquérant,* 88.

XVI   THE DARK SIDE OF BEAU GESTE

234 *"hard lessons on them."* AHG, 1 H 1032, March 12, 1901.
235 the Tuat campaign. Ibid., 1 H 1017.
of these animals. Tillion, *La Conquête des oasis,* 57.
"immensity of their task." Lehuraux, *Les Français au Sahara,* 102.
236 *"the worst impulses."* AHG, 1 H 1032, February 2, 1901.
was a *"utopia."* Ibid.
237 driver going north. Harding-King, *A Search for the Masked Tawareks,* 75–7, 90.
238 denuded of troops. Ibid., 102.
"our large numbers." AHG, 1 H 1032, July 19, 1900, 13.
"from our first attempt." F. Lamy, "Lettres d'El Goléa," *Revue de Paris,* 1903, 277.
"they took it easy." Ibid., 295.
239 *"go into dissidence."* Ibid.
"evil genie." F. Bernard, *Les deux missions du Colonel Flatters,* 14.

page 239 *concluded Captain Jacques.* AHG, 1 H 1032, July 19, 1900, 10.
  which [*the horses*] *passed. Ibid.,* February 11, 1901.
  "more and more." Lehuraux, *Au Sahara avec le Commandant Charlet,* 13, 25.
  a March 29, 1901, report read. AHG, 1 H 1032. March 29, 1901, 6.

240 *concluded in 1901.* AHG, 1 H 1032, Deleuze report, no date, 7.
  "we should not count?" Lehuraux, *Le Conquérant des oasis, Colonel Théodore
    Pein,* 70.

241 *Castries admitted sadly.* Lehuraux, *Les Français au Sahara,* 115.
  "as it was yesterday." AHG, 1 H 1032, Deleuze report, n.d., 8.
  expenses must stop. Ibid., letter, December 22, 1900.

242 *"my father's camel."* R. Hérison, *Avec le Père Foucauld et le Général Laperrine,
    1909–1911,* 224.

243 *would turn for home.* Lehuraux, *Le Conquérant,* 117.
  "on the enemy." AHG, 1 H 1016, March 5, 1897 report.
  most Arab Bureaus. AHG, 1 H 1016, February 1899 Report.

244 *"whom we must recruit." Ibid.* 1893 general staff report.
  "fear of being retaken." Ibid.

245 *"showing it openly." Ibid.,* 1896 report.
  attract better cadres. AHG 1 H 1032, July 19, 1900, 35–37.

246 *"the poverty of the country." Ibid.,* 21–22, 19.
  in a 1900 report. Ibid., 24.
  "the brothel his home." Ibid., January 27, 1901, report.
  report of March 5, 1897. AHG, 1 H 1016.
  "the services rendered." Ibid., February 1899 report.

247 *on medical grounds.* AHG, 1 H 1032, July 19, 1900 report, 19.
  in July 1902. Ibid., November 19, 1901, and July 4, 1902, reports.

XVII THE SAHARIANS

249 *"take Timbuctus without orders."* L. Lehuraux, *Le Conquérant des oasis,
    Colonel Théodore Pein,* 111.
  "calm things down." Ibid., 113.
  over North Africa. Ibid.

251 *"never forgiven him."* R. Pottier, *Laperrine,* 21.
  exploded with rage. Hérison, *Avec le Père Foucauld et le Général Laperrine,*
    247.
  "in the Sahara." AHG, 1 H 1032, July 19, 1900.
  "the nomadic tribes." P. Denis, *L'évolution des troupes sahariennes françaises
    de Bonaparte à nos jours,* 140.
  "commander in charge." AHG, 1 H 1032, February 11, 1901 report.

252 *he wrote to Pein.* Lehuraux, *Le conquérant,* 142.
  "the mobile contingent." P. Denis, *Evolution des troupes sahariennes
    françaises,* 153.
  to full strength, AHG, 1 H 1016.
  not mobile enough. AHG, 1 H 1086, November 17, 1906.

253 *"the Central Sahara."* AHG, 1 H 1010, June 25, 1902.
  French army discipline. Ibid.
  "the yoke of property." AHG, 1 H 1032, July 19, 1900, 17.

page 254 tirailleurs and Chaamba. Laperrine, "Une Tournée dans le sud de l'annexe de Tidikelt, 1904," *Bulletin du comité de l'Afrique Française*, supplément 1905, 46.

unions were shunned. Hérison, *Père Foucauld*, 43–44, 194, 185.

255 *"Allah would inspire him."* G. Dervil, *Trois grands Africains*, 68.

"bone to the dog." Hérison, *Père Foucauld*, 216.

in difficult conditions. Lehuraux, *Lettres d'un saharien, commandant Paul Duclos*, 130, 132.

256 *"into my camp."* Laperrine, "Une Tournée." 46.

systematic intimidation. "Un Contre-rezzou au Hoggar." *Bulletin du comité de l'Afrique française*, supplément, 1903, 205, 239, 257.

"than that of bandit." E. F. Gautier, *Le Sahara*, 121.

257 *"must inevitably follow."* AHG, 1 H 1036, February 10, 1904.

"make us irreconcilable." AHG, 1 H 1032, February 11, 1901.

at In Salah. H. Lhote, *Les Touareg du Hoggar*, 347.

"against our communications." AHG, 1 H 1032, February 11, 1901.

259 *"warriors in their own right."* J. Keenan, *The Tuareg, People of the Ahaggar*, 54–55.

at the turn of the century. J. Nicolaisen, *Ecology and Culture of the Pastoral Tuareg*, 398.

"escaped the massacre." Lhote, *Les Touareg*, 346.

"the palm trees." P. Denis, *L'Evolution des troupes sahariennes françaises de Bonaparte à nos jours*, 170.

260 *"these nomads relax."* AHG, 1 H 1086.

"yours is so beautiful." Lehuraux, *Au Sahara avec le commandant Charlet*, 144, 52, 98–99.

"Ghat to the Niger." R. Bazin, *Charles de Foucauld*, 321–22.

"apprenticeship of discipline." AHG, 1 H 1086, July 9, 1906.

261 *"they have stolen."* Lehuraux, *Le Conquérant*, 100–110.

"liberty to march." Ibid., 112.

262 *"our valiant troops."* Lhote, *Les Touareg*, 350.

heart of their country. Lehuraux, *Le Conquérant*, 102, 104.

"to save ourselves." AHG, H 1036.

"more or less a failure." Lehuraux, *Le Conquérant*, 126.

263 back to In Salah. AHG, 1 H 1036, Cottenest's report.

267 a contingent of spahis. Ibid. See also *Bulletin du comité de l'Afrique française*, 1902, 307, 317.

268 wrote Captain Métois. AHG, 1 H 1036, February 10, 1904 report.

"last hours have arrived." Renseignements coloniaux, *Bulletin du comité de l'Afrique française*, supplément, August 1903, 212.

269 *"well-organized detachment."* Ibid., 242, 264, 267.

270 *"I shared the prizes."* Lehuraux, *Le Conquérant*, 138–39.

faites d'armes. AHG, 1 H 1036.

271 would oppose him. Pottier, *Laperrine*, 126.

in Moussa's word. Ibid., 129–30.

272 *"follow it with enthusiasm?"* Ibid., 145.

"exuberance and confidence." Captain Dinaux, "Une Tournée du chef de l'annexe d'In Salah," *Bulletin du comité de l'Afrique française*, 1905.

XVIII AN "ADMINISTRATIVE TOUR"

page 275 *"a supply convoy."* G. Dervil, *Trois grands Africains*, 15.
  276 *"from this prison."* *Ibid.*, 16.
    " 'to make change!' " Ibid., 29, 31.
  277 *a "superb" white camel. Ibid.*, 31, 25–26.
    signing his own name. Ibid., 40–41.
  278 *"even of harshness." Ibid.*, 14.
    "was the wine." Ibid., 93.
  279 *"cultivate their memory."* R. Bazin, *Charles de Foucauld*, 445.
  280 *"believing and saintly souls." Ibid.*, 6.
    "precocious obesity." Ibid., 10.
  282 *Laperrine remembered. Ibid.*, 14.
  283 *"Jews in all countries?"* C. de Foucauld, *Reconnaissance au Maroc*, avant-propos.
  284 *looked like a monkey.* R. Bazin, *Charles de Foucauld*, 23.
  285 *too "materialist." Ibid.*, 86.
  286 *chuckled to themselves.* Dervil, *Africains*, 48–49.
    "to serve in the south." L. Lehuraux, *Le Conquérant des oasis, Colonel Théodore Pein*, 113.
  287 *"scandalize the priest."* R. Hérison, *Avec le Père Foucauld et le Général Laperrine, 1909–1911*, 30–31.
    "sum of 300 francs." Dervil, *Africains*, 33.
    "the poor things." Ibid., 31, 34.
    "the despised roumis." Ibid., 56.
  288 *"of our race."* R. Hérison, *Père Foucauld*, 217.
    "a useless servant." Bazin, *Foucauld*, 339–40.
  289 *all of their lives.* Hérison, *Père Foucauld*, 217.
    his would-be superior. Bazin, *Foucauld*, 338.
  290 *"the greatest precautions."* F. Lamy, "Lettres d'El Goléa," *Revue de Paris*, 1903, 282–283.
    away from danger. AHG, 1 H 1086, February 29, 1908.
    tea and sugar. Dervil, *Africains*, 52.
  292 *a good beginning. Ibid.*, 52.
  293 *the captain's tent.* Hérison, *Père Foucauld*, 52–53, 114. This incident did not actually occur during the Dinaux expedition. However, I have included it to illustrate a widely used method of enforcing discipline among the Saharians.
  294 *"and I remain."* Bazin, *Foucauld*, 310.
    "for months—onions!" Dervil, *Africains*, 52.
    "one without needs." Ibid., 64.
    "for me that night." Ibid., 65.

EPILOGUE

  295 *"unique in the world."* L. Lehuraux, *Lettres d'un saharien, commandant Paul Duclos*, 120.
    Dervil wrote. G. Dervil, *Trois grands Africains*, 66.

page *296* *the officers' mess.* E. F. Gautier, *La Conquête du Sahara*, 50.

297 *"peace for a while."* L. Lehuraux, *Au Sahara avec le Commandant Charlet*, 132.

"no longer walk." Ibid., 133–34.

his mouth with sand. Dervil, *Africains*, 79–81, 92.

"80 to 100 blacks." L. Lehuraux, *Au Sahara avec le Commandant Charlet*, 119–35.

twice the size of France. E. F. Gautier, *La Conquête du Sahara*, 118.

speed and mobility. L. Lehuraux, *Le conquérant des oasis, Colonel Théodore Pein*, 225.

300 *"remind me of our youth."* R. Bazin, *Charles de Foucauld*, 445.

301 *only with difficulty.* Lehuraux, *Sur les pistes du désert*, 145–46.

302 *observance of Islam.* Keenan, *The Tuareg, People of the Ahaggar*, 149.

date palms are threatened. G. Gester, *The Sahara*, 78.

SELECTED BIBLIOGRAPHY

NEWSPAPERS:

Bulletin du comité de l'Afrique française
Dépêche Tunisienne
Echo de Paris
L'Evénement
Le Figaro
La Libre parole
La Patrie
Le Petit journal
Le Temps
The *Times* of London

OFFICIAL PUBLICATIONS:

Journal officiel
Archives historiques de guerre, Château de Vincennes, série H.

Andrew, C., *Théophile Delcassé and the Making of the Entente Cordiale,* London, 1968.
———, and Kanya-Forstner, A. S., *France Overseas,* London, 1981.
Anon. "L'Attaque de Timimoun par les Marocains, 18 février 1901," *Revue de Paris,* 15 July 1903; pp. 361–72.
Arnaud, Captain E., and Cortier, Lieutenant M., *Nos Confins sahariens,* Paris, 1908.
Baroli, M., *La Vie quotidienne des français en Algérie, 1830–1914,* Paris, 1967.
Barrès, M., *Une Vengeance dans le désert,* Paris, 1902.
Barth, Heinrich, *Travels and Discoveries in North and Central Africa, 1849–1855,* 3 vols., London, 1865.
Bazin, R., *Charles de Foucauld,* Paris, 1921.
Bell, Mrs. Arthur, *Among the Women of the Sahara,* London, 1900.
Benhazera, M., *Six Mois chez les Touareg du Ahaggar,* Algiers, 1908.
Bernard, A., and Lacroix, N., *La Pénétration saharienne, 1830–1906,* Algiers, 1906.
Bernard, F., *Les deux missions du Colonel Flatters,* Paris, 1884.
Bissuel, Captain H., *Les Touareg de l'ouest,* Algiers, 1888.
Blaudin du Thé, C. *Historique des compagnies méharistes, 1902–1952,* Algiers, 1955.
Bonnier, General E., *L'Occupation de Tombouctou,* Paris, 1926.
Bovill, E. W., *Caravans of the Old Sahara,* London, 1933.
———, *The Golden Trade of the Moors,* London, 1968.
———, *Missions to the Niger,* vol. I, Cambridge, 1964.
Briggs, L. C., *The Tribes of the Sahara,* Cambridge, Mass., 1960.

Brosselard, H., *Voyage de la mission Flatters*, Paris, 1883.

Caillié, R., *Travels through Central Africa, Timbuctoo and Across the Great Desert, to Morocco: Performed in the Years 1824–1828, 2 vols.*, London, 1968.

Chalmin, P.,L'Officier français de 1815 à 1870, Paris, 1957.

Chouraqui, A., *Between East and West: A History of the Jews of North Africa*, Philadelphia, 1969.

Cohen, W. B., "French Colonial Service," in *France and Britain in Africa*, edited by P. Gifford and W. Louis, New Haven, 1970.

Cooke, J. J., *The New French Imperialism, 1880–1910*, Newton Abbot, 1973.

Curtin, P. D., *The Image of Africa, British Ideals and Action, 1780–1850*, Madison, Wisconsin, 1964.

Deardon, S., *Letters Written During a Ten Years' Residence at the Court of Tripoli*, London, 1957.

Delahaye, J., *Les Assassins et les vengeurs de Morès*, 3 vols., Paris, 1905–7.

Denis, P., *L'Évolution des troupes sahariennes françaises de Bonaparte à nos jours*, thèse de 3ᵉ cycle, University of Rennes, 1963.

Dervil, G., *Trois grands Africains*, Paris, 1945.

Dinaux, Captain, "Une Tournée du chef de l'annex d'In Salah," *Bulletin du comité de l'Afrique française*, 1905.

Dorian, J.-P., *Quinze Nuits au pays de la peur: Souvenirs inédits du grand Amenokal, Chef des Touareg*, Paris, 1936.

Duponchel, A., *Le Chemin de fer transsaharien*, Montpellier, 1878.

Duveyrier, H., *Les Touareg du nord*, Paris, 1864.

Duveyrier, H., *Journal de route*, Paris, 1905.

Eberhardt, I., *Mes Journaliers*, Paris, 1923.

Evans-Prichard, E. E., *The Sanusi of Cyrenaica*, Oxford, 1954.

Faye, S., and Germain, J., *Le Général Laperrine, grand saharien*, Paris, 1936.

Foucauld, C., *Reconnaissance au Maroc*, Paris, 1887.

Foureau, F., *D'Alger au Congo par le Tchad*, Paris, 1902.

Gautier, E. F., *La Conquête de Sahara*, Paris, 1910.

Geographical Handbook Series, *Algeria*, vol. I, Naval Intelligence Division, London, 1943.

Gerster, G., *The Sahara*, London, 1960.

Guillo-Lohan, Lt., "Un Contre-rezzou au Hoggar," *Bulletin du comité de l'Afrique française*, supplément 1903.

Girardet, R., *L'Idée coloniale*, Paris, 1972.

Gouverneur Général d'Algérie, *Deuxième Mission Flatters: Historique et rapport rédigés au service central des affaires indigènes*, Algiers, 1882.

Guilleux, Sergeant C., *Journal de route d'un caporal de tirailleurs de la mission saharienne, 1898–1900*, Belfort, 1904.

Hallett, R., *The Penetration of Africa*, London, 1965.

Harding-King, W. J., *A Search for the Masked Tawareks*, London, 1903.

Hérison, R., *Avec le Père Foucauld et le Général Laperrine, 1909–1911*, Paris, 1937.

Howe, S., *Les Héros du Sahara*, Paris, 1931.

Huré, R., *L'Armée d'Afrique*, Paris, 1977.

Joffre, J., *My March to Timbuctu*, Paris, 1915.

Kanya-Forstner, A. S., *The Conquest of the Western Sudan*, Cambridge, 1969.

Keenan, J., *The Tuareg, People of the Ahaggar,* London, 1977.

Kiernan, V. G., *From Conquest to Collapse: European Empires from 1815 to 1960,* New York, 1982.

Kipling, R., *Plain Tales from the Hills,* New York, 1913.

Lamy, Major F., "Lettres d'El Goléa," *Revue de Paris,* 1903.

Laperrine, H., "Une Tournée dans le sud de l'annexe de Tidikelt, 1904," *Bulletin du comité de l'Afrique française,* supplément 1905.

Leclerc, R., *World Without Mercy,* London, 1954.

Lehuraux, L., *Alger,* Algiers, n.d.

――――, *Au Sahara avec le Commandant Charlet,* Paris, 1932.

――――, *Le Conquérant des oasis, Colonel Théodore Pein,* Paris, 1935.

――――, *Laperrine,* Paris, 1947.

――――, *Les Français au Sahara,* Algiers, n.d.

――――, *Lettres d'un saharien, Commandant Paul Duclos,* Algiers, 1933.

――――, *Sur les pistes du désert,* Paris, 1928.

Lenz, O., *Timbuctou,* Paris, 1886.

Lepetit, C., *Plus loin sur la piste de Charles de Foucauld,* Paris, 1981.

Lhote, H., *Les Touareg du Hoggar,* Paris, 1944.

Lyon, G. F., *A Narrative of Travels in Northern Africa in the Years 1818–19 and 1820,* London, 1966.

Martel, A., *Les Confins Sahara—Tripolitains de la Tunisie, 1881–1911,* 2 vols., Paris, 1965.

Mathieu, M., *La Mission Afrique Centrale,* thèse du 3ᵉ cycle, University of Toulouse-Mirail, 1975.

Maugham, R., *The Slaves of Timbuktu,* London, 1961.

Mélia, J., *Le Drame de la mission Flatters,* Paris, 1942.

Meynier, O., *Les Conquérants du Tchad,* Paris, 1923.

Millett, Alan R., *Semper Fidelis: A History of the U. S. Marine Corps,* New York and London, 1980.

Ministère des travaux publiques, *Documents rélatifs à la mission dirigée au sud d'Algérie par le Lieutenant colonel Flatters,* Paris, 1884.

Moorhouse, G., *The Fearful Void,* London, 1974.

Nicolaisen, J., *Ecology and Culture of the Pastoral Tuareg,* Copenhagen, 1963.

Pascal, F., *L'Assassinat de Morès, un crime d'état,* Paris, 1902.

Patorni, F., *Récits faits pax trois survivants de la mission Flatters,* Paris, 1884.

Perkins, Kenneth J., *Quaids, Captains, and Colons, French Military Administration in the Colonial Maghrib, 1844–1934,* New York, 1981.

Porch, D., *The March to the Marne, The French Army 1871–1914,* Cambridge, 1981.

――――, *The Conquest of Morocco,* New York, 1983.

Pottier, R., *Flatters,* Paris, 1948.

――――, *Laperrine,* Paris, 1943.

――――, *Mission Foureau-Lamy,* Paris, 1951.

Reibell, E., *Carnet de Route,* Paris, 1931.

Richardson, J., *Travels in the Great Desert of the Sahara in the Years of 1845 and 1846,* 2 vols., London, 1848.

Riley, J., *The Loss of the American Brig Commerce,* London, 1817.

Rodd, F. R., *People of the Veil,* London, 1926.

Schirmer, H., *Le Sahara,* Paris, 1893.

Schirmer, H., "Pourquoi Flatters et ses compagnons sont morts," *Bulletin de la Société de géographie de Lyon*, 1896.

Tillion, Captain, *La Conquête des oasis sahariennes*, Paris, 1903.

Trumelet, Colonel C., *Les Français dans le désert*, Paris, 1885.

Voinot, L., *Opérations dans les oasis sahariennes*, Paris, 1903.

Wellard, James, *The Great Sahara*, New York, 1965.

INDEX

A NOTE ABOUT THE AUTHOR

Douglas Porch was born in Tallahassee, Florida, in 1944. He was educated at the University of the South and at Cambridge University in England, where he received his doctorate in 1971. Until 1983 he taught modern European history at the University College of Wales in Aberystwyth, where he was a senior lecturer. Currently, he is Mark W. Clark Professor of History at The Citadel in Charleston, South Carolina. He is the author of four other books, the most recent being *The Conquest of Morocco.*

A NOTE ON THE TYPE

The text of this book was set in a type face known as Garamond. The design is based on letter forms originally created by Claude Garamond (c. 1480–1561). Garamond was a pupil of Geoffrey Tory and may have patterned his letter forms on Venetian models.

Composed by Dix Type Inc.,
Syracuse, New York.
Printed and bound by
The Maple-Vail Book Manufacturing Group,
York, Pennsylvania.
Designed by David Connolly.

28 DAYS
DATE DUE

		WITHDRAWN	
			PRINTED IN U.S.A.